SPANISH
VOCABULARY

FOR ENGLISH SPEAKERS

ENGLISH-SPANISH

The most useful words
To expand your lexicon and sharpen
your language skills

9000 words

Spanish vocabulary for English speakers - 9000 words

By Andrey Taranov

T&P Books vocabularies are intended for helping you learn, memorize and review foreign words. The dictionary is divided into themes, covering all major spheres of everyday activities, business, science, culture, etc.

The process of learning words using T&P Books' theme-based dictionaries gives you the following advantages:

- Correctly grouped source information predetermines success at subsequent stages of word memorization
- Availability of words derived from the same root allowing memorization of word units (rather than separate words)
- Small units of words facilitate the process of establishing associative links needed for consolidation of vocabulary
- Level of language knowledge can be estimated by the number of learned words

Copyright © 2014 T&P Books Publishing

T&P Books Publishing
www.tpbooks.com

ISBN: 978-1-78071-293-2

This book is also available in E-book formats.
Please visit www.tpbooks.com or the major online bookstores.

SPANISH VOCABULARY
for English speakers

T&P Books vocabularies are intended to help you learn, memorize, and review foreign words. The vocabulary contains over 9000 commonly used words arranged thematically.

- Vocabulary contains the most commonly used words
- Recommended as an addition to any language course
- Meets the needs of beginners and advanced learners of foreign languages
- Convenient for daily use, revision sessions, and self-testing activities
- Allows you to assess your vocabulary

Special features of the vocabulary

- Words are organized according to their meaning, not alphabetically
- Words are presented in three columns to facilitate the reviewing and self-testing processes
- Words in groups are divided into small blocks to facilitate the learning process
- The vocabulary offers a convenient and simple transcription of each foreign word

The vocabulary has 256 topics including:

Basic Concepts, Numbers, Colors, Months, Seasons, Units of Measurement, Clothing & Accessories, Food & Nutrition, Restaurant, Family Members, Relatives, Character, Feelings, Emotions, Diseases, City, Town, Sightseeing, Shopping, Money, House, Home, Office, Working in the Office, Import & Export, Marketing, Job Search, Sports, Education, Computer, Internet, Tools, Nature, Countries, Nationalities and more ...

T&P BOOKS' THEME-BASED DICTIONARIES

The Correct System for Memorizing Foreign Words

Acquiring vocabulary is one of the most important elements of learning a foreign language, because words allow us to express our thoughts, ask questions, and provide answers. An inadequate vocabulary can impede communication with a foreigner and make it difficult to understand a book or movie well.

The pace of activity in all spheres of modern life, including the learning of modern languages, has increased. Today, we need to memorize large amounts of information (grammar rules, foreign words, etc.) within a short period. However, this does not need to be difficult. All you need to do is to choose the right training materials, learn a few special techniques, and develop your individual training system.

Having a system is critical to the process of language learning. Many people fail to succeed in this regard; they cannot master a foreign language because they fail to follow a system comprised of selecting materials, organizing lessons, arranging new words to be learned, and so on. The lack of a system causes confusion and eventually, lowers self-confidence.

T&P Books' theme-based dictionaries can be included in the list of elements needed for creating an effective system for learning foreign words. These dictionaries were specially developed for learning purposes and are meant to help students effectively memorize words and expand their vocabulary.

Generally speaking, the process of learning words consists of three main elements:

- Reception (creation or acquisition) of a training material, such as a word list
- Work aimed at memorizing new words
- Work aimed at reviewing the learned words, such as self-testing

All three elements are equally important since they determine the quality of work and the final result. All three processes require certain skills and a well-thought-out approach.

New words are often encountered quite randomly when learning a foreign language and it may be difficult to include them all in a unified list. As a result, these words remain written on scraps of paper, in book margins, textbooks, and so on. In order to systematize such words, we have to create and continually update a "book of new words." A paper notebook, a netbook, or a tablet PC can be used for these purposes.

This "book of new words" will be your personal, unique list of words. However, it will only contain the words that you came across during the learning process. For example, you might have written down the words "Sunday," "Tuesday," and "Friday." However, there are additional words for days of the week, for example, "Saturday," that are missing, and your list of words would be incomplete. Using a theme dictionary, in addition to the "book of new words," is a reasonable solution to this problem.

The theme-based dictionary may serve as the basis for expanding your vocabulary.

It will be your big "book of new words" containing the most frequently used words of a foreign language already included. There are quite a few theme-based dictionaries available, and you should ensure that you make the right choice in order to get the maximum benefit from your purchase.

Therefore, we suggest using theme-based dictionaries from T&P Books Publishing as an aid to learning foreign words. Our books are specially developed for effective use in the sphere of vocabulary systematization, expansion and review.

Theme-based dictionaries are not a magical solution to learning new words. However, they can serve as your main database to aid foreign-language acquisition. Apart from theme dictionaries, you can have copybooks for writing down new words, flash cards, glossaries for various texts, as well as other resources; however, a good theme dictionary will always remain your primary collection of words.

T&P Books' theme-based dictionaries are specialty books that contain the most frequently used words in a language.

The main characteristic of such dictionaries is the division of words into themes. For example, the *City* theme contains the words "street," "crossroads," "square," "fountain," and so on. The *Talking* theme might contain words like "to talk," "to ask," "question," and "answer".

All the words in a theme are divided into smaller units, each comprising 3–5 words. Such an arrangement improves the perception of words and makes the learning process less tiresome. Each unit contains a selection of words with similar meanings or identical roots. This allows you to learn words in small groups and establish other associative links that have a positive effect on memorization.

The words on each page are placed in three columns: a word in your native language, its translation, and its transcription. Such positioning allows for the use of techniques for effective memorization. After closing the translation column, you can flip through and review foreign words, and vice versa. "This is an easy and convenient method of review – one that we recommend you do often."

Our theme-based dictionaries contain transcriptions for all the foreign words. Unfortunately, none of the existing transcriptions are able to convey the exact nuances of foreign pronunciation. That is why we recommend using the transcriptions only as a supplementary learning aid. Correct pronunciation can only be acquired with the help of sound. Therefore our collection includes audio theme-based dictionaries.

The process of learning words using T&P Books' theme-based dictionaries gives you the following advantages:

- You have correctly grouped source information, which predetermines your success at subsequent stages of word memorization
- Availability of words derived from the same root (lazy, lazily, lazybones), allowing you to memorize word units instead of separate words
- Small units of words facilitate the process of establishing associative links needed for consolidation of vocabulary
- You can estimate the number of learned words and hence your level of language knowledge
- The dictionary allows for the creation of an effective and high-quality revision process
- You can revise certain themes several times, modifying the revision methods and techniques
- Audio versions of the dictionaries help you to work out the pronunciation of words and develop your skills of auditory word perception

The T&P Books' theme-based dictionaries are offered in several variants differing in the number of words: 1.500, 3.000, 5.000, 7.000, and 9.000 words. There are also dictionaries containing 15,000 words for some language combinations. Your choice of dictionary will depend on your knowledge level and goals.

We sincerely believe that our dictionaries will become your trusty assistant in learning foreign languages and will allow you to easily acquire the necessary vocabulary.

TABLE OF CONTENTS

MISCELLANEOUS

MAIN 500 VERBS

PRONUNCIATION GUIDE

Letter	Spanish example	T&P phonetic alphabet	English example

Vowels

a	agua	[a]	shorter than in ask
e	escuela	[ɛ]	man, bad
i	idilio	[i]	shorter than in feet
o	ropa	[o], [ɔ]	drop, baught
u	uva	[u]	book
y [1]	yo	[j]	yes, New York
y [2]	comen y beben	[i]	shorter than in feet
ai, ay	paisaje, hay	[aj]	time, white
au	autor	[aʊ]	now, down
ei, ey	aceite, rey	[eɪ]	age, today
eu	Europa	[eu]	boat, stroll
oi, oy	boina, joyas	[ɔɪ]	oil, boy, point
ou	boutique	[au]	loud, powder

Consonants

b [3]	bolígrafo	[b]	baby, book
b [4]	hombre	[b]	baby, book
b [5]	Isabel	[β]	between b and v
c [6]	cine	[θ]	month, tooth
c [7]	cobre	[k]	clock, kiss
ch	chófer	[ʧ]	church, French
d	domingo	[d]	day, doctor
f	fecha	[f]	face, food
g [8]	gato	[g]	game, gold
g [9]	general	[h]	huge, hat
gu [10]	guerra	[ɣ]	between [g] and [h]
h	hijo	[h]	silent [h]
j	juego	[h]	huge, hat

Letter	Spanish example	T&P phonetic alphabet	English example
k	kilogramo	[k]	clock, kiss
l	ley	[l]	lace, people
ll	calle	[ʎ], [j]	million, yes
m	madre	[m]	magic, milk
n	nariz	[n]	name, normal
n	cinco	[ŋ]	English, ring
ñ	año	[ɲ]	canyon, new
p	puerto	[p]	pencil, private
q	queso	[k]	clock, kiss
qu [11]	cheque	[k]	clock, kiss
r	rosa	[r]	rice, radio
s	sal	[s]	city, boss
t	tienda	[t]	tourist, trip
v [12]	vaso	[b]	baby, book
v [13]	invitar	[b]	baby, book
v [14]	la vista	[β]	between b and v
x [15]	texto	[ks]	box, taxi
x [16]	experimento	[s]	city, boss
x [17]	México	[h]	huge, humor
z	zumo	[ð]	weather, together

Comments

[1] with vowels
[2] between consonants
[3] at the beginning of a word
[4] after n and m
[5] usually between vowels
[6] before e, i
[7] before a, o, u
[8] before a, o, u
[9] before e, i
[10] before e, i
[11] before e, i
[12] at the beginning of a word
[13] after n and m
[14] usually between vowels
[15] between vowels
[16] before a consonant
[17] in México

ABBREVIATIONS
used in the vocabulary

ab.	-	about
adj	-	adjective
adv	-	adverb
anim.	-	animate
as adj	-	attributive noun used as adjective
e.g.	-	for example
etc.	-	et cetera
fam.	-	familiar
fem.	-	feminine
form.	-	formal
inanim.	-	inanimate
masc.	-	masculine
math	-	mathematics
mil.	-	military
n	-	noun
pl	-	plural
pron.	-	pronoun
sb	-	somebody
sing.	-	singular
sth	-	something
v aux	-	auxiliary verb
vi	-	intransitive verb
vi, vt	-	intransitive, transitive verb
vt	-	transitive verb
m	-	masculine noun
f	-	feminine noun
m pl	-	masculine plural
f pl	-	feminine plural
m, f	-	masculine, feminine
vr	-	reflexive verb

BASIC CONCEPTS

Basic concepts. Part 1

1. Pronouns

I, me	yo	[jo]
you	tú	[tu]
he	él	[εʎ]
she	ella	['εja]
we (masc.)	nosotros	[no'sotros]
we (fem.)	nosotras	[no'sotras]
you (masc.)	vosotros	[bo'sotros]
you (fem.)	vosotras	[bo'sotras]
you (polite, sing.)	Usted	[us'tεd]
you (polite, pl)	Ustedes	[us'tεdεs]
they (masc.)	ellos	['εjos]
they (fem.)	ellas	['εjas]

2. Greetings. Salutations. Farewells

Hello! (fam.)	¡Hola!	['ɔʎa]
Hello! (form.)	¡Hola!	['ɔʎa]
Good morning!	¡Buenos días!	['buεnos 'dias]
Good afternoon!	¡Buenas tardes!	['buεnas 'tardεs]
Good evening!	¡Buenas noches!	['buεnas 'notʃəs]
to say hello	decir hola	[dε'θir 'ɔʎa]
Hi! (hello)	¡Hola!	['ɔʎa]
greeting (n)	saludo (m)	[sa'lydɔ]
to greet (vt)	saludar (vt)	[saly'dar]
How are you?	¿Cómo estás?	['kɔmɔ εs'tas]
What's new?	¿Qué hay de nuevo?	[ke aj dε nu'εβɔ]
Goodbye! (form.)	¡Adiós!	[a'dʲɔs]
Bye! (fam.)	¡Hasta la vista! (fam.)	['asta ʎa 'βista]
See you soon!	¡Hasta pronto!	['asta 'prontɔ]
Farewell!	¡Adiós!	[a'dʲɔs]
to say goodbye	despedirse (vr)	[dεspε'dirsε]
So long!	¡Hasta luego!	['asta lu'εgɔ]
Thank you!	¡Gracias!	['graθjas]

Thank you very much!	¡Muchas gracias!	['muʧas 'graθjas]
You're welcome	De nada	[dɛ 'nada]
Don't mention it!	No hay de qué	[nɔ aj dɛ 'ke]
It was nothing	De nada	[dɛ 'nada]
Excuse me! (fam.)	¡Perdóname!	[pɛr'dɔnamɛ]
Excuse me! (form.)	¡Perdóneme!	[pɛr'dɔnɛmɛ]
to excuse (forgive)	disculpar (vt)	[diskuʎ'par]
to apologize (vi)	disculparse (vr)	[diskuʎ'parsɛ]
My apologies	Mis disculpas	[mis dis'kuʎpas]
I'm sorry!	¡Perdóneme!	[pɛr'dɔnɛmɛ]
to forgive (vt)	perdonar (vt)	[pɛrdɔ'nar]
It's okay!	¡No pasa nada!	[nɔ 'pasa 'nada]
please (adv)	por favor	[pɔr fa'βɔr]
Don't forget!	¡No se le olvide!	[nɔ sɛ le ɔl'widɛ]
Certainly!	¡Desde luego!	['dɛsdɛ lu'ɛgɔ]
Of course not!	¡Claro que no!	['kʎarɔ ke 'nɔ]
Okay! (I agree)	¡De acuerdo!	[dɛ aku'ɛrdɔ]
That's enough!	¡Basta!	['basta]

3. How to address

mister, sir	señor	[sɛ'ɲɔr]
ma'am	señora	[sɛ'ɲɔra]
miss	señorita	[sɛɲɔ'rita]
young man	joven	['hɔβən]
young man (little boy)	niño	['niɲɔ]
miss (little girl)	niña	['niɲja]

4. Cardinal numbers. Part 1

0 zero	cero	['θærɔ]
1 one	uno	['unɔ]
2 two	dos	[dɔs]
3 three	tres	[trɛs]
4 four	cuatro	[ku'atrɔ]
5 five	cinco	['θiŋkɔ]
6 six	seis	['sɛjs]
7 seven	siete	['sʰete]
8 eight	ocho	['ɔʧɔ]
9 nine	nueve	[nu'ɛβə]
10 ten	diez	[djeθ]
11 eleven	once	['ɔnθæ]
12 twelve	doce	['dɔθæ]
13 thirteen	trece	['trɛθæ]
14 fourteen	catorce	[ka'tɔrθæ]

15 fifteen	quince	['kinθæ]
16 sixteen	dieciséis	['djesis 'ɛjs]
17 seventeen	diecisiete	['djesi 'sʰetɛ]
18 eighteen	dieciocho	['djesi 'ɔtʃɔ]
19 nineteen	diecinueve	['djesi nu'ɛβə]
20 twenty	veinte	['bɛjntɛ]
21 twenty-one	veintiuno	['bɛjntɛ i 'unɔ]
22 twenty-two	veintidós	['bɛjntɛ i 'dɔs]
23 twenty-three	veintitrés	['bɛjntɛ i 'trɛs]
30 thirty	treinta	['trɛjnta]
31 thirty-one	treinta y uno	['trɛjnta i 'unɔ]
32 thirty-two	treinta y dos	['trɛjnta i 'dɔs]
33 thirty-three	treinta y tres	['trɛjnta i 'trɛs]
40 forty	cuarenta	[kua'rɛnta]
41 forty-one	cuarenta y uno	[kua'rɛnta i 'unɔ]
42 forty-two	cuarenta y dos	[kua'rɛnta i 'dɔs]
43 forty-three	cuarenta y tres	[kua'rɛnta i 'trɛs]
50 fifty	cincuenta	[θiŋku'ənta]
51 fifty-one	cincuenta y uno	[θiŋku'ənta i 'unɔ]
52 fifty-two	cincuenta y dos	[θiŋku'ənta i 'dɔs]
53 fifty-three	cincuenta y tres	[θiŋku'ənta i 'trɛs]
60 sixty	sesenta	[sɛ'sɛnta]
61 sixty-one	sesenta y uno	[sɛ'sɛnta i 'unɔ]
62 sixty-two	sesenta y dos	[sɛ'sɛnta i 'dɔs]
63 sixty-three	sesenta y tres	[sɛ'sɛnta i 'trɛs]
70 seventy	setenta	[sɛ'tɛnta]
71 seventy-one	setenta y uno	[sɛ'tɛnta i 'unɔ]
72 seventy-two	setenta y dos	[sɛ'tɛnta i 'dɔs]
73 seventy-three	setenta y tres	[sɛ'tɛnta i 'trɛs]
80 eighty	ochenta	[ɔ'tʃenta]
81 eighty-one	ochenta y uno	[ɔ'tʃenta i 'unɔ]
82 eighty-two	ochenta y dos	[ɔ'tʃenta i 'dɔs]
83 eighty-three	ochenta y tres	[ɔ'tʃenta i 'trɛs]
90 ninety	noventa	[nɔ'βənta]
91 ninety-one	noventa y uno	[nɔ'βənta i 'unɔ]
92 ninety-two	noventa y dos	[nɔ'βənta i 'dɔs]
93 ninety-three	noventa y tres	[nɔ'βənta i 'trɛs]

5. Cardinal numbers. Part 2

| 100 one hundred | cien | [sjen] |
| 200 two hundred | doscientos | [dɔθ'sjentɔs] |

300 three hundred	**trescientos**	[trɛθ'sjentɔs]
400 four hundred	**cuatrocientos**	[kuatrɔ'θjentɔs]
500 five hundred	**quinientos**	[ki'njentɔs]
600 six hundred	**seiscientos**	[θæejθ'sjentɔs]
700 seven hundred	**setecientos**	[θætɛ'θjentɔs]
800 eight hundred	**ochocientos**	[ɔtʃɔ'θjentɔs]
900 nine hundred	**novecientos**	[nɔvɛ'θjentɔs]
1000 one thousand	**mil**	[miʎ]
2000 two thousand	**dos mil**	['dɔs 'miʎ]
3000 three thousand	**tres mil**	['trɛs 'miʎ]
10000 ten thousand	**diez mil**	['djeθ 'miʎ]
one hundred thousand	**cien mil**	['sjen 'miʎ]
million	**millón** (m)	[mi'jon]
billion	**mil millones**	[miʎ mi'jonɛs]

6. Ordinal numbers

first (adj)	**primero** (adj)	[pri'mɛrɔ]
second (adj)	**segundo** (adj)	[sɛ'gundɔ]
third (adj)	**tercero** (adj)	[tɛr'θæerɔ]
fourth (adj)	**cuarto** (adj)	[ku'artɔ]
fifth (adj)	**quinto** (adj)	['kintɔ]
sixth (adj)	**sexto** (adj)	['sɛkstɔ]
seventh (adj)	**séptimo** (adj)	['sɛptimɔ]
eighth (adj)	**octavo** (adj)	[ɔk'taβɔ]
ninth (adj)	**noveno** (adj)	[nɔ'βənɔ]
tenth (adj)	**décimo** (adj)	['dɛsimɔ]

7. Numbers. Fractions

fraction	**fracción** (f)	[frak'θᶦon]
one half	**un medio**	[un 'mɛdiɔ]
one third	**un tercio**	[un 'tɛrθiɔ]
one quarter	**un cuarto**	[un ku'artɔ]
one eighth	**un octavo**	[un ɔk'taβɔ]
one tenth	**un décimo**	[un 'dɛθimɔ]
two thirds	**dos tercios**	[dɔs 'tɛrθiɔs]
three quarters	**tres cuartos**	[trɛs ku'artɔs]

8. Numbers. Basic operations

subtraction	**sustracción** (f)	[sustrak'θᶦon]
to subtract (vi, vt)	**sustraer** (vt)	[sustra'ɛr]

division	división (f)	[diwi'θion]
to divide (vt)	dividir (vt)	[diwi'dir]
addition	adición (f)	[adi'θion]
to add up (vt)	sumar (vt)	[su'mar]
to add (vi, vt)	sumar (vt)	[su'mar]
multiplication	multiplicación (f)	[muʌtiplika'θion]
to multiply (vt)	multiplicar (vt)	[muʌtipli'kar]

9. Numbers. Miscellaneous

digit, figure	cifra (f)	['θifra]
number	número (m)	['numɛrɔ]
numeral	numeral (m)	[numɛ'raʎ]
minus sign	menos (m)	['mɛnɔs]
plus sign	más (m)	[mas]
formula	fórmula (f)	['fɔrmuʌa]
calculation	cálculo (m)	['kaʎkulɜ]
to count (vt)	contar (vt)	[kɔn'tar]
to count up	calcular (vt)	[kaʎku'ʎar]
to compare (vt)	comparar (vt)	[kɔmpa'rar]
How much?	¿cuánto?	[ku'antɔ]
sum, total	suma (f)	['suma]
result	resultado (m)	[rɛsuʎ'tadɔ]
remainder	resto (m)	['rɛstɔ]
a few …	unos pocos	['unɔs 'pɔkɔs]
few, little (adv)	poco (adv)	['pɔkɔ]
the rest	resto (m)	['rɛstɔ]
one and a half	uno y medio	['unɔ i 'mɛdiɔ]
dozen	docena (f)	[dɔ'θæna]
in half (adv)	en dos partes	[ɛn 'dɔs 'partɛs]
equally (evenly)	en partes iguales	[ɛn 'partɛs igu'ales]
half	mitad (f)	[mi'tad]
time (three ~s)	vez (f)	[bɛθ]

10. The most important verbs. Part 1

to advise (vt)	aconsejar (vt)	[akɔnsɛ'har]
to agree (say yes)	estar de acuerdo	[ɛs'tar dɛ aku'ɛrdɔ]
to answer (vi, vt)	responder (vi, vt)	[rɛspɔn'dɛr]
to arrive (vi)	llegar (vi)	[jɛ'gar]
to ask (~ oneself)	preguntar (vt)	[prɛgun'tar]
to ask (~ sb to do sth)	pedir (vt)	[pɛ'dir]
to be (~ a teacher)	ser (vi)	[sɛr]

to be (~ on a diet)	estar (vi)	[ɛs'tar]
to be afraid	tener miedo	[tɛ'nɛr 'mjedɔ]
to be hungry	tener hambre	[tɛ'nɛr 'ambrɛ]
to be interested in …	interesarse (vr)	[intɛrɛ'sarsɛ]
to be needed	ser necesario	[sɛr nɛθæ'sariɔ]
to be surprised	sorprenderse (vr)	[sɔrprɛn'dɛrsɛ]
to be thirsty	tener sed	[tɛ'nɛr 'sɛd]
to begin (vt)	comenzar (vi, vt)	[kɔmɛn'θar]
to belong to …	pertenecer a …	[pɛrtɛnɛ'sɛr a]
to boast (vi)	alabarse (vr)	[aʎa'βarsɛ]
to break (split into pieces)	romper (vt)	[rɔm'pɛr]
to call (for help)	llamar (vt)	[ʝa'mar]
can (v aux)	poder (v aux)	[pɔ'dɛr]
to catch (vt)	coger (vt)	[kɔ'hɛr]
to change (vt)	cambiar (vt)	[kam'bjar]
to choose (select)	escoger (vt)	[ɛskɔ'hɛr]
to come down	descender (vi)	[dɛθæn'dɛr]
to come in (enter)	entrar (vi)	[ɛnt'rar]
to compare (vt)	comparar (vt)	[kɔmpa'rar]
to complain (vi, vt)	quejarse (vr)	[kɛ'harsɛ]
to confuse (mix up)	confundir (vt)	[kɔnfun'dir]
to continue (vt)	continuar (vt)	[kɔntinu'ar]
to control (vt)	controlar (vt)	[kɔntrɔ'ʎar]
to cook (dinner)	preparar (vt)	[prɛpa'rar]
to cost (vt)	costar (vt)	[kɔs'tar]
to count (add up)	contar (vt)	[kɔn'tar]
to count on …	contar con …	[kɔn'tar kɔn]
to create (vt)	crear (vt)	[kre'ar]
to cry (weep)	llorar (vi)	[ʝo'rar]

11. The most important verbs. Part 2

to deceive (vi, vt)	engañar (vi, vt)	[ɛŋa'ɲjar]
to decorate (tree, street)	decorar (vt)	[dɛkɔ'rar]
to defend (a country, etc.)	defender (vt)	[dɛfɛn'dɛr]
to demand (request firmly)	exigir (vt)	[ɛksi'hir]
to dig (vt)	cavar (vt)	[ka'βar]
to discuss (vt)	discutir (vt)	[disku'tir]
to do (vt)	hacer (vt)	[a'θær]
to doubt (have doubts)	dudar (vt)	[du'dar]
to drop (let fall)	dejar caer	[dɛ'har ka'ɛr]
to excuse (forgive)	disculpar (vt)	[diskuʎ'par]
to exist (vi)	existir (vi)	[ɛksis'tir]

to expect (foresee)	**prever** (vt)	[prɛ'vɛr]
to explain (vt)	**explicar** (vt)	[ɛkspli'kar]
to fall (vi)	**caer** (vi)	[ka'ɛr]
to find (vt)	**encontrar** (vt)	[ɛŋkont'rar]
to finish (vt)	**terminar** (vt)	[tɛrmi'nar]
to fly (vi)	**volar** (vi)	[bɔ'ʎar]
to follow … (come after)	**seguir …**	[sɛ'gir]
to forget (vi, vt)	**olvidar** (vt)	[ɔʎbi'dar]
to forgive (vt)	**perdonar** (vt)	[pɛrdɔ'nar]
to give (vt)	**dar** (vt)	[dar]
to give a hint	**dar una pista**	[dar 'una 'pista]
to go (on foot)	**ir** (vi)	[ir]
to go for a swim	**bañarse** (vr)	[ba'ɲjarsɛ]
to go out (from …)	**salir** (vi)	[sa'lir]
to guess right	**adivinar** (vt)	[adiwi'nar]
to have (vt)	**tener** (vt)	[tɛ'nɛr]
to have breakfast	**desayunar** (vi)	[dɛsaju'nar]
to have dinner	**cenar** (vi)	[θæ'nar]
to have lunch	**almorzar** (vi)	[aʎmɔr'θar]
to hear (vt)	**oír** (vt)	[ɔ'ir]
to help (vt)	**ayudar** (vt)	[aju'dar]
to hide (vt)	**esconder** (vt)	[ɛskɔn'dɛr]
to hope (vi, vt)	**esperar** (vi)	[ɛspɛ'rar]
to hunt (vi, vt)	**cazar** (vi, vt)	[ka'θar]
to hurry (vi)	**darse prisa**	['darsɛ 'prisa]

12. The most important verbs. Part 3

to inform (vt)	**informar** (vt)	[infɔr'mar]
to insist (vi, vt)	**insistir** (vi)	[insis'tir]
to insult (vt)	**insultar** (vt)	[insuʎ'tar]
to invite (vt)	**invitar** (vt)	[inbi'tar]
to joke (vi)	**bromear** (vi)	[brɔmɛ'ar]
to keep (vt)	**guardar** (vt)	[guar'dar]
to keep silent	**callarse** (vr)	[ka'jarsɛ]
to kill (vt)	**matar** (vt)	[ma'tar]
to know (sb)	**conocer** (vt)	[kɔnɔ'θær]
to know (sth)	**saber** (vt)	[sa'βər]
to laugh (vi)	**reírse** (vr)	[rɛ'irsɛ]
to liberate (city, etc.)	**liberar** (vt)	[libɛ'rar]
to like (I like …)	**gustar** (vi)	[gus'tar]
to look for … (search)	**buscar** (vt)	[bus'kar]
to love (sb)	**querer** (vt)	[kɛ'rɛr]

to make a mistake	equivocarse (vr)	[ɛkivɔ'karsɛ]
to manage, to run	dirigir (vt)	[diri'hir]
to mean (signify)	significar (vt)	[signifi'kar]
to mention (talk about)	mencionar (vt)	[mɛnθio'nar]
to miss (school, etc.)	faltar a ...	[faʎ'tar a]
to notice (see)	notar (vt)	[nɔ'tar]
to object (vi, vt)	objetar (vt)	[ɔbhɛ'tar]
to observe (see)	observar (vt)	[ɔbsɛr'var]
to open (vt)	abrir (vt)	[ab'rir]
to order (meal, etc.)	pedir (vt)	[pɛ'dir]
to order (mil.)	ordenar (vt)	[ɔrdɛ'nar]
to own (possess)	poseer (vt)	[pɔsɛ'ɛr]
to participate (vi)	participar (vi)	[partisi'par]
to pay (vi, vt)	pagar (vi, vt)	[pa'gar]
to permit (vt)	permitir (vt)	[pɛrmi'tir]
to plan (vt)	planear (vt)	[pʎanɛ'ar]
to play (children)	jugar (vi)	[hu'gar]
to pray (vi, vt)	orar (vi)	[ɔ'rar]
to prefer (vt)	preferir (vt)	[prɛfɛ'rir]
to promise (vt)	prometer (vt)	[prɔmɛ'tɛr]
to pronounce (vt)	pronunciar (vt)	[prɔnun'θjar]
to propose (vt)	proponer (vt)	[prɔpɔ'nɛr]
to punish (vt)	castigar (vt)	[kasti'gar]
to read (vi, vt)	leer (vi, vt)	[le'ɛr]
to recommend (vt)	recomendar (vt)	[rɛkɔmɛn'dar]
to refuse (vi, vt)	negarse (vr)	[nɛ'garsɛ]
to regret (be sorry)	arrepentirse (vr)	[arrɛpɛn'tirsɛ]
to rent (sth from sb)	alquilar (vt)	[aʎki'ʎar]
to repeat (say again)	repetir (vt)	[rɛpɛ'tir]
to reserve, to book	reservar (vt)	[rɛsɛr'var]
to run (vi)	correr (vi)	[kɔr'rɛr]

13. The most important verbs. Part 4

to save (rescue)	salvar (vt)	[saʎ'var]
to say (~ thank you)	decir (vt)	[dɛ'θir]
to scold (vt)	regañar (vt)	[rɛga'ɲjar]
to see (vt)	ver (vt)	[bɛr]
to sell (vt)	vender (vt)	[bɛn'dɛr]
to send (vt)	enviar (vt)	[ɛmbi'jar]
to shoot (vi)	tirar (vi)	[ti'rar]
to shout (vi)	gritar (vi)	[gri'tar]
to show (vt)	mostrar (vt)	[mɔst'rar]
to sign (document)	firmar (vt)	[fir'mar]

to sit down (vi)	sentarse (vr)	[sɛn'tarsɛ]
to smile (vi)	sonreír (vi)	[sɔnrɛ'ir]
to speak (vi, vt)	hablar (vi, vt)	[ab'ʎar]
to steal (money, etc.)	robar (vt)	[rɔ'βar]
to stop (please ~ calling me)	cesar (vt)	[θæ'sar]
to stop (for pause, etc.)	pararse (vr)	[pa'rarsɛ]
to study (vt)	estudiar (vt)	[ɛstu'djar]
to swim (vi)	nadar (vi)	[na'dar]
to take (vt)	tomar (vt)	[tɔ'mar]
to think (vi, vt)	pensar (vi, vt)	[pɛn'sar]
to threaten (vt)	amenazar (vt)	[amɛna'θar]
to touch (with hands)	tocar (vt)	[tɔ'kar]
to translate (vt)	traducir (vt)	[tradu'θir]
to trust (vt)	confiar (vt)	[kɔn'fjar]
to try (attempt)	tratar de ...	[tra'tar dɛ]
to turn (~ to the left)	girar (vi)	[hi'rar]
to underestimate (vt)	subestimar (vt)	[subɛsti'mar]
to understand (vt)	comprender (vt)	[kɔmprɛn'dɛr]
to unite (vt)	unir (vt)	[u'nir]
to wait (vt)	esperar (vt)	[ɛspɛ'rar]
to want (wish, desire)	querer (vt)	[ke'rɛr]
to warn (vt)	advertir (vt)	[advɛr'tir]
to work (vi)	trabajar (vi)	[traba'har]
to write (vt)	escribir (vt)	[ɛskri'βir]
to write down	tomar nota	[tɔ'mar 'nɔta]

14. Colors

color	color (m)	[kɔ'lɔr]
shade (tint)	matiz (m)	[ma'tiθ]
hue	tono (m)	['tɔnɔ]
rainbow	arco (m) iris	['arkɔ 'iris]
white (adj)	blanco (adj)	['bʎaŋkɔ]
black (adj)	negro (adj)	['nɛgrɔ]
gray (adj)	gris (adj)	['gris]
green (adj)	verde (adj)	['bɛrdɛ]
yellow (adj)	amarillo (adj)	[ama'rijo]
red (adj)	rojo (adj)	['rɔhɔ]
blue (adj)	azul (adj)	[a'θuʎ]
light blue (adj)	azul claro (adj)	[a'θuʎ 'kʎarɔ]
pink (adj)	rosado (adj)	[rrɔ'sadɔ]
orange (adj)	anaranjado (adj)	[anaran'hadɔ]

violet (adj)	**violeta** (adj)	[bɨɔ'lɛta]
brown (adj)	**marrón** (adj)	[mar'rɔn]
golden (adj)	**dorado** (adj)	[dɔ'radɔ]
silvery (adj)	**argentado** (adj)	[arhɛn'tadɔ]
beige (adj)	**beige** (adj)	['bɛjhɛ]
cream (adj)	**crema** (adj)	['krɛma]
turquoise (adj)	**turquesa** (adj)	[tur'kesa]
cherry red (adj)	**rojo cereza** (adj)	['rohɔ se'reθa]
lilac (adj)	**lila** (adj)	['liʎa]
crimson (adj)	**carmesí** (adj)	[karmɛ'si]
light (adj)	**claro** (adj)	['kʎarɔ]
dark (adj)	**oscuro** (adj)	[ɔs'kurɔ]
bright, vivid (adj)	**vivo** (adj)	['biβɔ]
colored (pencils)	**de color** (adj)	[dɛ kɔ'lɔr]
color (e.g., ~ film)	**en colores** (adj)	[ɛn kɔ'lɔrɛs]
black-and-white (adj)	**blanco y negro** (adj)	['bʎaŋkɔ i 'nɛgrɔ]
plain (one-colored)	**unicolor** (adj)	[unikɔ'lɔr]
multicolored (adj)	**multicolor** (adj)	[muʎtikɔ'lɔr]

15. Questions

Who?	**¿Quién?**	[kjen]
What?	**¿Qué?**	[ke]
Where? (at, in)	**¿Dónde?**	['dɔndɛ]
Where (to)?	**¿A dónde?**	[a 'dɔndɛ]
From where?	**¿De dónde?**	[dɛ 'dɔndɛ]
When?	**¿Cuándo?**	[ku'andɔ]
Why? (What for?)	**¿Para qué?**	[para 'ke]
Why? (reason)	**¿Por qué?**	[pɔr 'ke]
What for?	**¿Por qué razón?**	[pɔr ke ra'θɔn]
How? (in what way)	**¿Cómo?**	['kɔmɔ]
Which?	**¿Cuál?**	[ku'aʎ]
To whom?	**¿A quién?**	[a 'kjen]
About whom?	**¿De quién?**	[dɛ 'kjen]
About what?	**¿De qué?**	[dɛ 'ke]
With whom?	**¿Con quién?**	[kɔn 'kjen]
How many? How much?	**¿Cuánto?**	[ku'antɔ]
Whose?	**¿De quién?**	[dɛ 'kjen]

16. Prepositions

with (accompanied by)	**con**	[kɔn]
without	**sin**	[sin]

to (indicating direction)	**a**	[a]
about (talking ~ ...)	**de**	[dɛ]
before (in time)	**antes de ...**	['antɛs dɛ]
in front of ...	**delante de ...**	[dɛ'ʎantɛ dɛ]
under (beneath, below)	**debajo de ...**	[dɛ'bahɔ dɛ]
above (over)	**sobre ...**	['sɔbrɛ]
on (atop)	**en, sobre**	[ɛn], ['sɔbrɛ]
from (off, out of)	**de**	[dɛ]
of (made from)	**de**	[dɛ]
in (e.g., ~ ten minutes)	**dentro de ...**	['dɛntrɔ dɛ]
over (across the top of)	**encima de ...**	[ɛn'θima dɛ]

17. Function words. Adverbs. Part 1

Where? (at, in)	**¿Dónde?**	['dɔndɛ]
here (adv)	**aquí** (adv)	[a'ki]
there (adv)	**allí** (adv)	[a'jı]
somewhere (to be)	**en alguna parte**	[ɛn aʎ'guna 'partɛ]
nowhere (not anywhere)	**en ninguna parte**	[ɛn ni'ŋuna 'partɛ]
by (near, beside)	**junto a ...**	['huntɔ a]
by the window	**junto a la ventana**	['huntɔ a ʎa bɛn'tana]
Where (to)?	**¿A dónde?**	[a 'dɔndɛ]
here (e.g., come ~!)	**aquí** (adv)	[a'ki]
there (e.g., to go ~)	**allí** (adv)	[a'jı]
from here (adv)	**de aquí** (adv)	[dɛ a'ki]
from there (adv)	**de allí** (adv)	[dɛ a'jı]
close (adv)	**cerca**	['θærka]
far (adv)	**lejos** (adv)	['lehɔs]
near (e.g., ~ Paris)	**cerca de ...**	['θærka dɛ]
nearby (adv)	**al lado (de ...)**	[aʎ 'ʎadɔ dɛ]
not far (adv)	**no lejos** (adv)	[nɔ 'lehɔs]
left (adj)	**izquierdo** (adj)	[iθ'kjerdɔ]
on the left	**a la izquierda**	[a ʎa iθ'kjerda]
to the left	**a la izquierda**	[a ʎa iθ'kjerda]
right (adj)	**derecho** (adj)	[dɛ'rɛtʃɔ]
on the right	**a la derecha**	[a ʎa dɛ'rɛtʃa]
to the right	**a la derecha**	[a ʎa dɛ'rɛtʃa]
in front (adv)	**delante**	[dɛ'ʎantɛ]
front (as adj)	**delantero** (adj)	[dɛʎan'tɛrɔ]
ahead (look ~)	**adelante**	[adɛ'ʎantɛ]

behind (adv)	detrás de ...	[dɛt'ras dɛ]
from behind	desde atrás	['dɛsdɛ at'ras]
back (towards the rear)	atrás	[at'ras]

| middle | centro (m), medio (m) | ['θæntrɔ], ['mɛdiɔ] |
| in the middle | en medio (adv) | [ɛn 'mɛdiɔ] |

at the side	de costado (adv)	[dɛ kɔs'tadɔ]
everywhere (adv)	en todas partes	[ɛn 'tɔdas 'partɛs]
around (in all directions)	alrededor (adv)	[aʎrɛdɛ'dɔr]

from inside	de dentro (adv)	[dɛ 'dɛntrɔ]
somewhere (to go)	a alguna parte	[a aʎ'guna 'partɛ]
straight (directly)	todo derecho (adv)	['tɔdɔ dɛ'rɛtʃɔ]
back (e.g., come ~)	atrás	[at'ras]

| from anywhere | de alguna parte (adv) | [dɛ aʎ'guna 'partɛ] |
| from somewhere | no se sabe de dónde | [nɔ sɛ 'saβə dɛ 'dɔndɛ] |

firstly (adv)	en primer lugar	[ɛn pri'mɛr lu'gar]
secondly (adv)	segundo (adv)	[sɛ'gundɔ]
thirdly (adv)	tercero (adv)	[tɛr'θærɔ]

suddenly (adv)	de súbito (adv)	[dɛ 'suβitɔ]
at first (adv)	al principio (adv)	[aʎ prin'sipiɔ]
for the first time	por primera vez	[pɔr pri'mɛra vɛθ]
long before ...	mucho tiempo antes ...	['mutʃɔ 'tiempɔ 'antɛs]
anew (over again)	de nuevo (adv)	[dɛ nu'ɛβɔ]
for good (adv)	para siempre (adv)	['para 'sjemprɛ]

never (adv)	jamás (adv)	[ha'mas]
again (adv)	de nuevo (adv)	[dɛ nu'ɛβɔ]
now (adv)	ahora (adv)	[a'ɔra]
often (adv)	a menudo (adv)	[a mɛ'nudɔ]
then (adv)	entonces (adv)	[ɛn'tɔnθæs]
urgently (quickly)	urgentemente	[urhɛntɛ'mɛntɛ]
usually (adv)	normalmente (adv)	[nɔrmaʎ'mentɛ]

by the way, ...	por cierto, ...	[pɔr 'θjertɔ]
possible (that is ~)	es probable	[ɛs prɔ'βable]
probably (adv)	probablemente	[prɔbable'mɛntɛ]
maybe (adv)	es posible	[ɛs pɔ'sible]
besides ...	además ...	[adɛ'mas]
that's why ...	por eso ...	[pɔr 'ɛsɔ]
in spite of ...	a pesar de ...	[a pɛ'sar dɛ]
thanks to ...	gracias a ...	['graθjas a]

what (pron.)	qué	[kɛ]
that (conj.)	que	[kɛ]
something	algo	['aʎgɔ]
anything (something)	algo	['aʎgɔ]
nothing	nada	['nada]

who (pron.)	quien	[kjen]
someone	alguien	['aʎgjen]
somebody	alguien	['aʎgjen]

nobody	nadie	['nadje]
nowhere (a voyage to ~)	a ninguna parte	[a ni'ɲuna 'partɛ]
nobody's	de nadie	[dɛ 'nadje]
somebody's	de alguien	[dɛ 'aʎgjen]

so (I'm ~ glad)	tan, tanto (adv)	[tan], ['tantɔ]
also (as well)	también	[tam'bjen]
too (as well)	también	[tam'bjen]

18. Function words. Adverbs. Part 2

Why?	¿Por qué?	[pɔr 'ke]
for some reason	no se sabe porqué	[nɔ sɛ 'saβǝ pɔr'ke]
because ...	porque ...	['pɔrke]
for some purpose	para algo (adv)	['para 'aʎgɔ]

and	y	[i]
or	o	[ɔ]
but	pero	['pɛrɔ]
for (e.g., ~ me)	para	['para]

too (~ many people)	demasiado (adv)	[dɛma'sjadɔ]
only (exclusively)	sólo (adv)	['sɔlɔ]
exactly (adv)	exactamente (adv)	[ɛksakta'mɛntɛ]
about (more or less)	unos ...	['unɔs]

approximately (adv)	aproximadamente	[aprɔksimada'mɛntɛ]
approximate (adj)	aproximado (adj)	[aprɔksi'madɔ]
almost (adv)	casi (adv)	['kasi]
the rest	resto (m)	['rɛstɔ]

each (adj)	cada (adj)	['kada]
any (no matter which)	cualquier (adj)	[kuaʎ'kjer]
many, much (a lot of)	mucho (adv)	['mutʃɔ]
many people	muchos	['mutʃɔs]
all (everyone)	todos	['tɔdɔs]

in return for ...	a cambio de ...	[a 'kambʲɔ dɛ]
in exchange (adv)	en cambio (adv)	[ɛn 'kambʲɔ]
by hand (made)	a mano	[a 'manɔ]
hardly (negative opinion)	es poco probable	[ɛs 'pɔkɔ prɔ'βable]

probably (adv)	probablemente	[prɔbable'mɛntɛ]
on purpose (adv)	a propósito (adv)	[a prɔ'pɔsitɔ]
by accident (adv)	por accidente (adv)	[pɔr akθi'dɛntɛ]
very (adv)	muy (adv)	['muj]

for example (adv)	**por ejemplo** (adv)	[pɔr ɛ'hɛmplɔ]
between	**entre**	['ɛntrɛ]
among	**entre**	['ɛntrɛ]
so much (such a lot)	**tanto**	['tantɔ]
especially (adv)	**especialmente** (adv)	[ɛspɛθjaʎ'mɛntɛ]

Basic concepts. Part 2

19. Weekdays

Monday	lunes (m)	['lynɛs]
Tuesday	martes (m)	['martɛs]
Wednesday	miércoles (m)	['mjerkɔlɛs]
Thursday	jueves (m)	[hu'ɛβəs]
Friday	viernes (m)	['bjernɛs]
Saturday	sábado (m)	['saβadɔ]
Sunday	domingo (m)	[dɔ'miŋɔ]
today (adv)	hoy (adv)	[ɔj]
tomorrow (adv)	mañana (adv)	[ma'ɲjana]
the day after tomorrow	pasado mañana	[pa'sadɔ ma'ɲjana]
yesterday (adv)	ayer (adv)	[a'jer]
the day before yesterday	anteayer (adv)	[antɛa'jer]
day	día (m)	['dia]
working day	día (m) de trabajo	['dia dɛ tra'βahɔ]
public holiday	día (m) de fiesta	['dia dɛ 'fjesta]
day off	día (m) de descanso	['dia dɛ dɛs'kansɔ]
weekend	fin (m) de semana	['fin dɛ sɛ'mana]
all day long	todo el día	['tɔdo ɛʎ 'dia]
next day (adv)	al día siguiente	[aʎ 'dia sighᵘ'entɛ]
two days ago	dos días atrás	[dɔs 'dias at'ras]
the day before	en vísperas (adv)	[ɛn 'wispɛras]
daily (adj)	diario (adj)	[di'jariɔ]
every day (adv)	cada día (adv)	['kada 'dia]
week	semana (f)	[sɛ'mana]
last week (adv)	semana (f) pasada	[sɛ'mana pa'sada]
next week (adv)	semana (f) que viene	[sɛ'mana ke 'bjenɛ]
weekly (adj)	semanal (adj)	[sɛma'naʎ]
every week (adv)	cada semana (adv)	['kada sɛ'mana]
twice a week	dos veces por semana	[dɔs 'bɛsɛs pɔr sɛ'mana]
every Tuesday	todos los martes	['tɔdɔs lɔs 'martɛs]

20. Hours. Day and night

morning	mañana (f)	[ma'ɲjana]
in the morning	por la mañana	[pɔr ʎa ma'ɲjana]
noon, midday	mediodía (m)	[mɛdⁱɔ'dia]

in the afternoon	**por la tarde**	[pɔr ʎa 'tardɛ]
evening	**tarde** (f)	['tardɛ]
in the evening	**por la noche**	[pɔr ʎa 'nɔtʃə]
night	**noche** (f)	['nɔtʃə]
at night	**por la noche**	[pɔr ʎa 'nɔtʃə]
midnight	**medianoche** (f)	[mɛdja'nɔtʃə]

second	**segundo** (m)	[sɛ'gundɔ]
minute	**minuto** (m)	[mi'nutɔ]
hour	**hora** (f)	['ɔra]
half an hour	**media hora** (f)	['mɛdja 'ɔra]
quarter of an hour	**cuarto** (m) **de hora**	[ku'artɔ dɛ 'ɔra]
fifteen minutes	**quince minutos**	['kinθæ mi'nutɔs]
24 hours	**veinticuatro horas** (f pl)	['bɛjti ku'atrɔ 'ɔras]

sunrise	**salida** (f) **del sol**	[sa'lida dɛʎ 'sɔʎ]
dawn	**amanecer** (m)	[amanɛ'θær]
early morning	**madrugada** (f)	[madru'gada]
sunset	**puesta** (f) **del sol**	[pu'ɛsta dɛʎ 'sɔʎ]

early in the morning	**por la mañana temprano**	[pɔr ʎa ma'ɲjana temp'ranɔ]
this morning	**esta mañana**	['ɛsta ma'ɲjana]
tomorrow morning	**mañana por la mañana**	[ma'ɲjana pɔr ʎa ma'ɲjana]

this afternoon	**esta tarde**	['ɛsta 'tardɛ]
in the afternoon	**por la tarde**	[pɔr ʎa 'tardɛ]
tomorrow afternoon	**mañana por la tarde**	[ma'ɲjana pɔr ʎa 'tardɛ]

| tonight (this evening) | **esta tarde, esta noche** | ['ɛsta 'tardɛ], ['ɛsta 'nɔtʃə] |
| tomorrow night | **mañana por la noche** | [ma'ɲjana pɔr ʎa 'nɔtʃə] |

at 3 o'clock sharp	**a las tres en punto**	[a ʎas 'trɛs ɛn 'puntɔ]
about 4 o'clock	**a eso de las cuatro**	[a 'ɛsɔ dɛ ʎas ku'atrɔ]
by 12 o'clock	**para las doce**	['para ʎas 'dɔsɛ]

in 20 minutes	**dentro de veinte minutos**	['dɛntrɔ dɛ 'bɛjntɛ mi'nutɔs]
in an hour	**dentro de una hora**	['dɛntrɔ dɛ 'una 'ɔra]
on time (adv)	**a tiempo** (adv)	[a 'tⁱempɔ]

a quarter of ...	**... menos cuarto**	['menɔs ku'artɔ]
within an hour	**durante una hora**	[du'rantɛ una 'ɔra]
every 15 minutes	**cada quince minutos**	['kada 'kinsɛ mi'nutɔs]
round the clock	**día y noche**	['dia i 'nɔtʃe]

21. Months. Seasons

January	**enero** (m)	[ɛ'nɛrɔ]
February	**febrero** (m)	[fɛb'rɛrɔ]
March	**marzo** (m)	['marθɔ]

April	**abril** (m)	[ab'riʎ]
May	**mayo** (m)	['majo]
June	**junio** (m)	['hunio]

July	**julio** (m)	['hulio]
August	**agosto** (m)	[a'gosto]
September	**septiembre** (m)	[sɛp't'æmbrɛ]
October	**octubre** (m)	[ɔk'tubrɛ]
November	**noviembre** (m)	[nɔ'v'æmbrɛ]
December	**diciembre** (m)	[di'sjembrɛ]

spring	**primavera** (f)	[prima'βəra]
in spring	**en primavera**	[ɛn prima'βəra]
spring (as adj)	**de primavera** (adj)	[dɛ prima'βəra]

summer	**verano** (m)	[bɛ'rano]
in summer	**en verano**	[ɛm bɛ'rano]
summer (as adj)	**de verano** (adj)	[dɛ bɛ'rano]

fall	**otoño** (m)	[ɔ'toɲo]
in fall	**en otoño**	[ɛn ɔ'toɲo]
fall (as adj)	**de otoño** (adj)	[dɛ ɔ'toɲo]

winter	**invierno** (m)	[im'bjerno]
in winter	**en invierno**	[ɛn im'bjerno]
winter (as adj)	**de invierno** (adj)	[dɛ im'bjerno]

month	**mes** (m)	[mɛs]
this month	**este mes**	['ɛstɛ 'mɛs]
next month	**al mes siguiente**	[aʎ 'mɛs si'gjentɛ]
last month	**el mes pasado**	[ɛʎ 'mɛs pa'sado]

a month ago	**hace un mes**	['asɛ un 'mɛs]
in a month	**dentro de una mes**	['dɛntrɔ dɛ 'una mɛs]
in two months	**dentro de dos meses**	['dɛntrɔ dɛ dɔs 'mɛsɛs]
the whole month	**todo el mes**	['tɔdɔ ɛʎ 'mɛs]
all month long	**todo un mes**	['tɔdɔ un 'mɛs]

monthly (~ magazine)	**mensual** (adj)	[mɛnsu'aʎ]
monthly (adv)	**mensualmente** (adv)	[mɛnsuaʎ'mɛntɛ]
every month	**cada mes**	['kada 'mɛs]
twice a month	**dos veces por mes**	[dɔs 'vɛθæs pɔr 'mɛs]

year	**año** (m)	['aɲo]
this year	**este año**	['ɛstɛ 'aɲo]
next year	**el próximo año**	[ɛʎ 'prɔksimɔ 'aɲo]
last year	**el año pasado**	[ɛʎ 'aɲo pa'sado]

a year ago	**hace un año**	['aθæ un 'aɲo]
in a year	**dentro de un año**	['dɛntrɔ dɛ un 'aɲo]
in two years	**dentro de dos años**	['dɛntrɔ dɛ dɔs 'aɲos]
the whole year	**todo el año**	['tɔdɔ ɛʎ 'aɲo]

all year long	**todo un año**	['tɔdɔ un 'aɲɔ]
every year	**cada año**	['kada 'aɲɔ]
annual (adj)	**anual** (adj)	[anu'aʎ]
annually (adv)	**anualmente** (adv)	[anuaʎ'mentɛ]
4 times a year	**cuatro veces por año**	[ku'atrɔ 'βesɛs pɔr 'aɲɔ]
date (e.g., today's ~)	**fecha** (f), **día** (m)	['fɛtʃa], ['dia]
date (e.g., ~ of birth)	**fecha** (f)	['fɛtʃa]
calendar	**calendario** (m)	[kalen'darɔ]
half a year	**medio año** (m)	['mɛdiɔ 'aɲɔ]
six months	**seis meses**	['sɛis 'mɛsɛs]
season (summer, etc.)	**temporada** (f)	[tɛmpɔ'rada]
century	**siglo** (m)	['siglɔ]

22. Time. Miscellaneous

time	**tiempo** (m)	['tⁱempɔ]
instant (n)	**instante** (m)	[ins'tantɛ]
moment	**momento** (m)	[mɔ'mentɔ]
instant (adj)	**instantáneo** (adj)	[instan'taneɔ]
lapse (of time)	**lapso** (m) **de tiempo**	['ʎapsɔ dɛ 'tⁱempɔ]
life	**vida** (f)	['bida]
eternity	**eternidad** (f)	[ɛtɛrni'dad]
epoch	**época** (f)	['ɛpɔka]
era	**era** (f)	['ɛra]
cycle	**ciclo** (m)	['siklɔ]
period	**período** (m)	[pɛ'riɔdɔ]
term (short-~)	**plazo** (m)	['pʎaθɔ]
the future	**futuro** (m)	[fu'turɔ]
future (as adj)	**que viene** (adj)	[ke bʰenɛ]
next time	**la próxima vez**	[ʎa 'prɔksima 'βeθ]
the past	**pasado** (m)	[pa'sadɔ]
past (recent)	**pasado** (adj)	[pa'sadɔ]
last time	**la última vez**	[ʎa 'uʎtima 'βeθ]
later (adv)	**más tarde** (adv)	[mas 'tardɛ]
after (prep.)	**después**	[dɛspu'ɛs]
nowadays (adv)	**actualmente** (adv)	[aktuaʎ'mentɛ]
now (adv)	**ahora** (adv)	[a'ɔra]
immediately (adv)	**inmediatamente**	[immɛdjata'mentɛ]
soon (adv)	**pronto** (adv)	['prontɔ]
in advance (beforehand)	**de antemano** (adv)	[dɛ antɛ'manɔ]
a long time ago	**hace mucho** (adv)	['asɛ 'mutʃɔ]
recently (adv)	**hace poco** (adv)	['asɛ 'pɔkɔ]
destiny	**destino** (m)	[dɛs'tinɔ]
memories (childhood ~)	**recuerdos** (m pl)	[rɛku'ɛrdɔs]

archives	archivo (m)	[arˈʧiβɔ]
during …	durante …	[duˈrantɛ]
long, a long time (adv)	mucho tiempo (adv)	[ˈmuʧɔ ˈtⁱempɔ]
not long (adv)	poco tiempo (adv)	[ˈpɔkɔ ˈtⁱempɔ]
early (in the morning)	temprano (adv)	[tɛmpˈranɔ]
late (not early)	tarde (adv)	[ˈtardɛ]
forever (for good)	para siempre (adv)	[ˈpara ˈsjemprɛ]
to start (begin)	comenzar (vt)	[kɔmɛnˈθar]
to postpone (vt)	aplazar (vt)	[apʎaˈθar]
at the same time	simultáneamente	[simuʎˈtanɛaˈmɛntɛ]
permanently (adv)	permanentemente	[pɛrmaˈnɛntaˈmɛntɛ]
constant (noise, pain)	constante (adj)	[kɔnsˈtantɛ]
temporary (adj)	temporal (adj)	[tɛmpɔˈraʎ]
sometimes (adv)	a veces (adv)	[a ˈβəsɛs]
rarely (adv)	rara vez (adv)	[ˈrara bɛθ]
often (adv)	a menudo (adv)	[a mɛˈnudɔ]

23. Opposites

rich (adj)	rico (adj)	[ˈrikɔ]
poor (adj)	pobre (adj)	[ˈpɔbrɛ]
ill, sick (adj)	enfermo (adj)	[ɛnˈfɛrmɔ]
healthy (adj)	sano (adj)	[ˈsanɔ]
big (adj)	grande (adj)	[ˈgrandɛ]
small (adj)	pequeño (adj)	[pɛˈkɛɲɔ]
quickly (adv)	rápidamente (adv)	[ˈrapidaˈmɛntɛ]
slowly (adv)	lentamente (adv)	[lentaˈmɛntɛ]
fast (adj)	rápido (adj)	[ˈrapidɔ]
slow (adj)	lento (adj)	[ˈlentɔ]
cheerful (adj)	alegre (adj)	[aˈlegrɛ]
sad (adj)	triste (adj)	[ˈtristɛ]
together (adv)	juntos (adv)	[ˈhuntɔs]
separately (adv)	separadamente	[sɛparadaˈmɛntɛ]
aloud (to read)	en voz alta	[ɛn ˈbɔθ ˈaʎta]
silently (to oneself)	en silencio	[ɛn siˈlenθiɔ]
tall (adj)	alto (adj)	[ˈaʎtɔ]
low (adj)	bajo (adj)	[ˈbahɔ]
deep (adj)	profundo (adj)	[prɔˈfundɔ]
shallow (adj)	poco profundo (adj)	[ˈpɔkɔ prɔˈfundɔ]

yes	**sí**	[si]
no	**no**	[nɔ]
distant (in space)	**lejano** (adj)	[le'hanɔ]
nearby (adj)	**cercano** (adj)	[θær'kanɔ]
far (adv)	**lejos** (adv)	['lehɔs]
nearby (adv)	**cerco** (adv)	['sɛrkɔ]
long (adj)	**largo** (adj)	['ʎargɔ]
short (adj)	**corto** (adj)	['kɔrtɔ]
good (kindhearted)	**bueno** (adj)	[bu'ɛnɔ]
evil (adj)	**malvado** (adj)	[maʎ'vadɔ]
married (adj)	**casado** (adj)	[ka'sadɔ]
single (adj)	**soltero** (adj)	[sɔʎ'tɛrɔ]
to forbid (vt)	**prohibir** (vt)	[prɔi'βɪr]
to permit (vt)	**permitir** (vt)	[pɛrmi'tir]
end	**fin** (m)	[fin]
beginning	**principio** (m)	[prin'sipiɔ]
left (adj)	**izquierdo** (adj)	[iθ'kjerdɔ]
right (adj)	**derecho** (adj)	[dɛ'rɛtʃɔ]
first (adj)	**primero** (adj)	[pri'mɛrɔ]
last (adj)	**último** (adj)	['uʎtimɔ]
crime	**crimen** (m)	['krimɛn]
punishment	**castigo** (m)	[kas'tigɔ]
to order (vt)	**ordenar** (vt)	[ɔrdɛ'nar]
to obey (vi, vt)	**obedecer** (vi, vt)	[ɔbɛdɛ'θær]
straight (adj)	**recto** (adj)	['rɛktɔ]
curved (adj)	**curvo** (adj)	['kurvɔ]
paradise	**paraíso** (m)	[para'isɔ]
hell	**infierno** (m)	[in'fjernɔ]
to be born	**nacer** (vi)	[na'θær]
to die (vi)	**morir** (vi)	[mɔ'rir]
strong (adj)	**fuerte** (adj)	[fu'ɛrtɛ]
weak (adj)	**débil** (adj)	['dɛβɪʎ]
old (adj)	**viejo** (adj)	['bjehɔ]
young (adj)	**joven** (adj)	['hɔβən]
old (adj)	**viejo** (adj)	['bjehɔ]
new (adj)	**nuevo** (adj)	[nu'ɛβɔ]

hard (adj)	duro (adj)	['durɔ]
soft (adj)	blando (adj)	['bʎandɔ]
warm (adj)	cálido (adj)	['kalidɔ]
cold (adj)	frío (adj)	['friɔ]
fat (adj)	gordo (adj)	['gɔrdɔ]
thin (adj)	delgado (adj)	[dɛʎ'gadɔ]
narrow (adj)	estrecho (adj)	[ɛst'rɛʧɔ]
wide (adj)	ancho (adj)	['anʧɔ]
good (adj)	bueno (adj)	[bu'ɛnɔ]
bad (adj)	malo (adj)	['malɜ]
brave (adj)	valiente (adj)	[ba'ʎjentɛ]
cowardly (adj)	cobarde (adj)	[kɔ'βardɛ]

24. Lines and shapes

square	cuadrado (m)	[kuad'radɔ]
square (as adj)	cuadrado (adj)	[kuad'radɔ]
circle	círculo (m)	['θirkulɔ]
round (adj)	redondo (adj)	[rɛ'dɔndɔ]
triangle	triángulo (m)	[tri'aŋulɔ]
triangular (adj)	triangular (adj)	[triaŋu'ʎar]
oval	óvalo (m)	['ɔβalɔ]
oval (as adj)	oval (adj)	[ɔ'βaʎ]
rectangle	rectángulo (m)	[rɛk'taŋulɜ]
rectangular (adj)	rectangular (adj)	[rɛktaŋu'ʎar]
pyramid	pirámide (f)	[pi'ramidɛ]
rhombus	rombo (m)	['rɔmbɔ]
trapezoid	trapecio (m)	[tra'pɛθiɔ]
cube	cubo (m)	['kuβɔ]
prism	prisma (m)	['prisma]
circumference	circunferencia (f)	[θirkunfɛ'rɛnsja]
sphere	esfera (f)	[ɛs'fɛra]
ball (solid sphere)	globo (m)	['glɜbɔ]
diameter	diámetro (m)	[di'amɛtrɔ]
radius	radio (f)	['radiɔ]
perimeter (circle's ~)	perímetro (m)	[pɛ'rimɛtrɔ]
center	centro (m)	['θæntrɔ]
horizontal (adj)	horizontal (adj)	[ɔriθɔn'taʎ]
vertical (adj)	vertical (adj)	[bɛrti'kaʎ]
parallel (n)	paralela (f)	[para'leʎa]
parallel (as adj)	paralelo (adj)	[para'lelɜ]

line	línea (f)	['linɛa]
stroke	trazo (m)	['traθɔ]
straight line	recta (f)	['rɛkta]
curve (curved line)	curva (f)	['kurva]
thin (line, etc.)	fino (adj)	['finɔ]
contour (outline)	contorno (m)	[kɔn'tɔrnɔ]

intersection	intersección (f)	[intɛrsɛk'θion]
right angle	ángulo (m) recto	['aŋulɔ 'rɛktɔ]
segment	segmento (m)	[sɛg'mɛntɔ]
sector	sector (m)	[sɛk'tɔr]
side (of triangle)	lado (m)	['ʎadɔ]
angle	ángulo (m)	['aŋulɔ]

25. Units of measurement

weight	peso (m)	['pɛsɔ]
length	longitud (f)	[lɔnhi'tud]
width	anchura (f)	[an'ʧura]
height	altura (f)	[aʎ'tura]
depth	profundidad (f)	[prɔfundi'dad]
volume	volumen (m)	[bɔ'lumɛn]
area	superficie (f), área (f)	[supɛr'fisiɛ], ['arɛa]

gram	gramo (m)	['gramɔ]
milligram	miligramo (m)	[milig'ramɔ]
kilogram	kilogramo (m)	[kilɔg'ramɔ]
ton	tonelada (f)	[tɔnɛ'ʎada]
pound	libra (f)	['libra]
ounce	onza (f)	['ɔnθa]

meter	metro (m)	['mɛtrɔ]
millimeter	milímetro (m)	[mi'limɛtrɔ]
centimeter	centímetro (m)	[θæn'timɛtrɔ]
kilometer	kilómetro (m)	[ki'lɔmɛtrɔ]
mile	milla (f)	['mija]

inch	pulgada (f)	[puʎ'gada]
foot	pie (m)	[pje]
yard	yarda (f)	['jarda]

| square meter | metro (m) cuadrado | ['mɛtrɔ kuad'radɔ] |
| hectare | hectárea (f) | [ɛk'tarɛa] |

liter	litro (m)	['litrɔ]
degree	grado (m)	['gradɔ]
volt	voltio (m)	['bɔʎtiɔ]
ampere	amperio (m)	[am'pɛriɔ]
horsepower	caballo (m) de fuerza	[ka'βajo dɛ fu'ɛrθa]
quantity	cantidad (f)	[kanti'dad]

a little bit of …	un poco de …	[un 'pɔkɔ dɛ]
half	mitad (f)	[mi'tad]
dozen	docena (f)	[dɔ'θæna]
piece (item)	pieza (f)	['pjeθa]

| size | dimensión (f) | [dimɛn'sɔn] |
| scale (map ~) | escala (f) | [ɛs'kaʎa] |

minimal (adj)	mínimo (adj)	['minimɔ]
the smallest (adj)	el menor (adj)	[ɛʎ mɛ'nɔr]
medium (adj)	medio (adj)	['mɛdiɔ]
maximal (adj)	máximo (adj)	['maksimɔ]
the largest (adj)	el más grande (adj)	[ɛʎ 'mas 'grandɛ]

26. Containers

jar (glass)	tarro (m) de vidrio	['tarrɔ dɛ 'widriɔ]
can	lata (f)	['ʎata]
bucket	cubo (m)	['kuβɔ]
barrel	barril (m)	[bar'riʎ]

basin (for washing)	palangana (f)	[pala'ŋana]
tank (for liquid, gas)	tanque (m)	['taŋke]
hip flask	petaca (f)	[pe'taka]
jerrycan	bidón (m) de gasolina	[bi'dɔn dɛ gasɔ'lina]
cistern (tank)	cisterna (f)	[θis'tɛrna]

mug	taza (f)	['taθa]
cup (of coffee, etc.)	taza (f)	['taθa]
saucer	platillo (m)	[pʎa'tijo]
glass (tumbler)	vaso (m)	['basɔ]
wineglass	copa (f)	['kɔpa]
saucepan	cacerola (f)	[kaθæ'rɔʎa]

| bottle (~ of wine) | botella (f) | [bɔ'tɛja] |
| neck (of the bottle) | cuello (m) de botella | [ku'ɛjo dɛ bɔ'tɛja] |

carafe	garrafa (f)	[gar'rafa]
pitcher (earthenware)	jarro (m)	['harrɔ]
vessel (container)	recipiente (m)	[rɛθi'pjentɛ]
pot (crock)	olla (f)	['ɔja]
vase	florero (m)	[flɔ'rɛrɔ]

bottle (~ of perfume)	frasco (m)	['fraskɔ]
vial, small bottle	frasquito (m)	[fras'kitɔ]
tube (of toothpaste)	tubo (m)	['tuβɔ]

sack (bag)	saco (m)	['sakɔ]
bag (paper ~, plastic ~)	bolsa (f)	['bɔʎsa]
pack (of cigarettes, etc.)	paquete (m)	[pa'ketɛ]

box (e.g., shoebox)	caja (f)	['kaha]
crate	cajón (m)	[ka'hɔn]
basket	cesta (f)	['θæsta]

27. Materials

material	material (f)	[ma'tɛrial]
wood	madera (f)	[ma'dɛra]
wooden (adj)	de madera (adj)	[dɛ ma'dɛra]

| glass (n) | cristal (m) | [kris'taʎ] |
| glass (as adj) | de cristal (adj) | [dɛ kris'taʎ] |

| stone (n) | piedra (f) | ['pjedra] |
| stone (as adj) | de piedra (adj) | [dɛ 'pjedra] |

| plastic (n) | plástico (m) | ['pʎastikɔ] |
| plastic (as adj) | de plástico (adj) | [dɛ 'pʎastikɔ] |

| rubber (n) | goma (f) | ['gɔma] |
| rubber (as adj) | de goma (adj) | [dɛ 'gɔma] |

| cloth, fabric (n) | tela (m) | ['tɛʎa] |
| fabric (as adj) | de tela (adj) | [dɛ 'teʎa] |

| paper (n) | papel (m) | [pa'pɛʎ] |
| paper (as adj) | de papel (adj) | [dɛ pa'pɛʎ] |

| cardboard (n) | cartón (m) | [kar'tɔn] |
| cardboard (as adj) | de cartón (adj) | [dɛ kar'tɔn] |

polyethylene	polietileno (m)	[pɔliɛti'lenɔ]
cellophane	celofán (m)	[θælɔ'fan]
linoleum	linóleo (m)	[li'nɔleɔ]
plywood	chapa (f) de madera	['tʃapa dɛ ma'dɛra]

porcelain (n)	porcelana (f)	[pɔrθæ'ʎana]
porcelain (as adj)	de porcelana (adj)	[dɛ pɔrθæ'ʎana]
clay (n)	arcilla (f)	[ar'θija]
clay (as adj)	de arcilla (adj)	[dɛ ar'θiʎja]
ceramics (n)	cerámica (f)	[θæ'ramika]
ceramic (as adj)	de cerámica (adj)	[dɛ θæ'ramika]

28. Metals

metal (n)	metal (m)	[mɛ'taʎ]
metal (as adj)	de metal (adj)	[dɛ mɛ'taʎ]
alloy (n)	aleación (f)	[alea'sɔn]

gold (n)	**oro** (m)	[ˈɔrɔ]
gold, golden (adj)	**de oro** (adj)	[dɛ ˈɔrɔ]
silver (n)	**plata** (f)	[ˈpʎata]
silver (as adj)	**de plata** (adj)	[dɛ ˈpʎata]
iron (n)	**hierro** (m)	[ˈjerrɔ]
iron (adj), made of iron	**de hierro** (adj)	[dɛ iˈerrɔ]
steel (n)	**acero** (m)	[aˈθæærɔ]
steel (as adj)	**de acero** (adj)	[dɛ aˈθæærɔ]
copper (n)	**cobre** (m)	[ˈkɔbrɛ]
copper (as adj)	**de cobre** (adj)	[dɛ ˈkɔbrɛ]
aluminum (n)	**aluminio** (m)	[alyˈminiɔ]
aluminum (as adj)	**de aluminio** (adj)	[dɛ alyˈminiɔ]
bronze (n)	**bronce** (m)	[ˈbrɔnθæ]
bronze (as adj)	**de bronce** (adj)	[dɛ ˈbrɔnθæ]
brass	**latón** (m)	[ʎaˈtɔn]
nickel	**níquel** (m)	[ˈnikeʎ]
platinum	**platino** (m)	[pʎaˈtinɔ]
mercury	**mercurio** (m)	[mɛrˈkuriɔ]
tin	**estaño** (m)	[ɛsˈtaɲɔ]
lead	**plomo** (m)	[ˈplɔmɔ]
zinc	**zinc** (m)	[θiŋk]

HUMAN BEING

Human being. The body

29. Humans. Basic concepts

human being	ser (m) humano	[sɛr u'manɔ]
man (adult male)	hombre (m)	['ɔmbrɛ]
woman	mujer (f)	[mu'hɛr]
child	niño -a (m, f)	['niɲ'ɔ], [a]
girl	niña (f)	['niɲja]
boy	niño (m)	['niɲ'ɔ]
teenager	adolescente (m)	[adɔle'θæntɛ]
old man	anciano (m)	[an'θjanɔ]
old woman	anciana (f)	[an'θjana]

30. Human anatomy

organism	organismo (m)	[ɔrga'nismɔ]
heart	corazón (m)	[kɔra'θɔn]
blood	sangre (f)	['saŋrɛ]
artery	arteria (f)	[ar'tɛria]
vein	vena (f)	['bɛna]
brain	cerebro (m)	[θæ'rɛbrɔ]
nerve	nervio (m)	['nɛrbiɔ]
nerves	nervios (m pl)	['nɛrbiɔs]
vertebra	vértebra (f)	['bɛrtɛbra]
spine	columna (f) vertebral	[kɔ'lumna bɛrtɛb'raʎ]
stomach (organ)	estómago (m)	[ɛs'tɔmagɔ]
intestines, bowel	intestinos (m pl)	[intɛs'tinɔs]
intestine (e.g., large ~)	intestino (m)	[intɛs'tinɔ]
liver	hígado (m)	['igadɔ]
kidney	riñón (m)	[ri'ɲ'ɔn]
bone	hueso (m)	[u'əsɔ]
skeleton	esqueleto (m)	[ɛske'lɛtɔ]
rib	costilla (f)	[kɔs'tija]
skull	cráneo (m)	['kranɛɔ]
muscle	músculo (m)	['muskulɔ]
biceps	bíceps (m)	['biθæps]

triceps	tríceps (m)	['triθæps]
tendon	tendón (m)	[tɛn'dɔn]
joint	articulación (f)	[artikuʎa'θʲon]
lungs	pulmones (m pl)	[puʎ'mɔnɛs]
genitals	genitales (m pl)	[hɛni'tales]
skin	piel (f)	[pjeʎ]

31. Head

head	cabeza (f)	[ka'βəθa]
face	cara (f)	['kara]
nose	nariz (f)	[na'riθ]
mouth	boca (f)	['bɔka]

eye	ojo (m)	['ɔhɔ]
eyes	ojos (m pl)	['ɔhɔs]
pupil	pupila (f)	[pu'piʎa]
eyebrow	ceja (f)	['θæha]
eyelash	pestaña (f)	[pɛs'taɲja]
eyelid	párpado (m)	['parpadɔ]

tongue	lengua (f)	['leŋua]
tooth	diente (m)	['djentɛ]
lips	labios (m pl)	['ʎabʲɔs]
cheekbones	pómulos (m pl)	['pɔmulɔs]
gum	encía (f)	[ɛn'θia]
palate	paladar (m)	[paʎa'dar]

nostrils	ventanas (f pl)	[bɛn'tanas]
chin	mentón (m)	[mɛn'tɔn]
jaw	mandíbula (f)	[man'diβuʎa]
cheek	mejilla (f)	[mɛ'hija]

forehead	frente (f)	['frɛntɛ]
temple	sien (f)	[θjen]
ear	oreja (f)	[ɔ'rɛha]
back of the head	nuca (f)	['nuka]
neck	cuello (m)	[ku'ɛjo]
throat	garganta (f)	[gar'ganta]

hair	cabello (m)	[ka'βəjo]
hairstyle	peinado (m)	[pɛj'nadɔ]
haircut	corte (m) de pelo	['kɔrtɛ dɛ 'pɛlɔ]
wig	peluca (f)	[pɛ'luka]

mustache	bigotes (m pl)	[bi'gɔtɛs]
beard	barba (f)	['barba]
to have (a beard, etc.)	tener (vt)	[tɛ'nɛr]
braid	trenza (f)	['trɛnθa]
sideburns	patillas (f pl)	[pa'tijas]

red-haired (adj)	**pelirrojo** (adj)	[peli'rɔhɔ]
gray (hair)	**canoso** (adj)	[ka'nɔsɔ]
bald (adj)	**calvo** (adj)	['kaʎvɔ]
bald patch	**calva** (f)	['kaʎva]
ponytail	**cola** (f) **de caballo**	['kɔʎa dɛ ka'βaʎɔ]
bangs	**flequillo** (m)	[fle'kiʎɔ]

32. Human body

hand	**mano** (f)	['manɔ]
arm	**brazo** (m)	['braθɔ]
finger	**dedo** (m)	['dɛdɔ]
thumb	**dedo** (m) **pulgar**	['dɛdɔ puʎ'gar]
little finger	**dedo** (m) **meñique**	['dɛdɔ mɛ'ɲ'ike]
nail	**uña** (f)	['uɲja]
fist	**puño** (m)	['puɲ'ɔ]
palm	**palma** (f)	['paʎma]
wrist	**muñeca** (f)	[mu'ɲjeka]
forearm	**antebrazo** (m)	[antɛb'raθɔ]
elbow	**codo** (m)	['kɔdɔ]
shoulder	**hombro** (m)	['ɔmbrɔ]
leg	**pierna** (f)	['pjerna]
foot	**planta** (f)	['pʎanta]
knee	**rodilla** (f)	[rɔ'dija]
calf (part of leg)	**pantorrilla** (f)	[pantɔr'rija]
hip	**cadera** (f)	[ka'dɛra]
heel	**talón** (m)	[ta'lɔn]
body	**cuerpo** (m)	[ku'ɛrpɔ]
stomach	**vientre** (m)	['bjentrɛ]
chest	**pecho** (m)	['pɛʧɔ]
breast	**seno** (m)	['sɛnɔ]
flank	**lado** (m), **costado** (m)	['ʎadɔ], [kɔs'tadɔ]
back	**espalda** (f)	[ɛs'paʎda]
lower back	**cintura** (f)	[θin'tura]
waist	**talle** (m)	['taje]
navel	**ombligo** (m)	[ɔmb'ligɔ]
buttocks	**nalgas** (f pl)	['naʎgas]
bottom	**trasero** (m)	[tra'sɛrɔ]
beauty mark	**lunar** (m)	[ly'nar]
birthmark	**marca** (f) **de nacimiento**	['marka dɛ nasi'mjentɔ]
tattoo	**tatuaje** (m)	[tatu'ahɛ]
scar	**cicatriz** (f)	[sikat'riθ]

Clothing & Accessories

33. Outerwear. Coats

clothes	ropa (f), vestido (m)	['rɔpa], [vɛs'tidɔ]
outer clothes	ropa (f) de calle	['rɔpa dɛ 'kaje]
winter clothes	ropa (f) de invierno	['rɔpa dɛ im'bjernɔ]
overcoat	abrigo (m)	[ab'rigɔ]
fur coat	abrigo (m) de piel	[ab'rigɔ dɛ pʲæʎ]
fur jacket	abrigo (m) corto de piel	[ab'rigɔ 'kortɔ dɛ pʲæʎ]
down coat	plumón (m)	[ply'mɔn]
jacket (e.g., leather ~)	cazadora (f)	[kaθa'dɔra]
raincoat	impermeable (m)	[impɛrme'able]
waterproof (adj)	impermeable (adj)	[impɛrme'able]

34. Men's & women's clothing

shirt	camisa (f)	[ka'misa]
pants	pantalones (m pl)	[panta'lɔnɛs]
jeans	vaqueros (m pl)	[ba'kɛrɔs]
jacket (of man's suit)	chaqueta (f), saco (m)	[ʧa'kɛta], ['sakɔ]
suit	traje (m)	['trahɛ]
dress (frock)	vestido (m)	[bɛs'tidɔ]
skirt	falda (f)	['faʎda]
blouse	blusa (f)	['blusa]
knitted jacket	rebeca (f)	[rɛ'bɛka]
jacket (of woman's suit)	chaqueta (f)	[ʧa'keta]
T-shirt	camiseta (f)	[kami'sɛta]
shorts (short trousers)	pantalón (m) corto	[panta'lɔn 'kortɔ]
tracksuit	traje (m) deportivo	['trahɛ dɛpɔr'tiβɔ]
bathrobe	bata (f) de baño	['bata dɛ 'baɲɔ]
pajamas	pijama (f)	[pi'hama]
sweater	jersey (m), suéter (m)	[hɛr'sɛj], [su'ɛtɛr]
pullover	pulóver (m)	[pu'lɔβər]
vest	chaleco (m)	[ʧa'lekɔ]
tailcoat	frac (m)	[frak]
tuxedo	esmoquin (m)	[ɛs'mɔkin]
uniform	uniforme (m)	[uni'fɔrmɛ]

workwear	ropa (f) de trabajo	['rɔpa dɛ tra'βaho]
overalls	mono (m)	['mɔnɔ]
coat (e.g., doctor's smock)	bata (f) blanca	['bata 'bʎaŋka]

35. Clothing. Underwear

underwear	ropa (f) interior	['rɔpa intɛ'rʲɔr]
undershirt (A-shirt)	camiseta (f) interior	[sami'θæta intɛ'rʲɔr]
socks	calcetines (m pl)	[kaʎθæ'tinɛs]
nightgown	camisón (m)	[kami'sɔn]
bra	sostén (m)	[sɔs'tɛn]
knee highs	calcetines (m pl) altos	[kaʎsɛ'tinɛs 'aʎtɔs]
tights	leotardos (m pl)	[leɔ'tardɔs]
stockings (thigh highs)	medias (f pl)	['mɛdjas]
bathing suit	traje (m) de baño	['trahɛ dɛ 'baɲɔ]

36. Headwear

hat	gorro (m)	['gɔrrɔ]
fedora	sombrero (m)	[sɔmb'rɛrɔ]
baseball cap	gorra (f) de béisbol	['gɔrra dɛ 'bɛjsbɔʎ]
flatcap	gorra (f) plana	['gɔrra 'pʎana]
beret	boina (f)	['bɔjna]
hood	capuchón (m)	[kapu'ʧɔn]
panama hat	panamá (m)	[pana'ma]
knitted hat	gorro (m) de punto	['gɔrrɔ dɛ 'puntɔ]
headscarf	pañuelo (m)	[paɲjy'ɛlɔ]
women's hat	sombrero (m) femenino	[sɔmb'rɛrɔ fɛme'ninɔ]
hard hat	casco (m)	['kaskɔ]
garrison cap	gorro (m) de campaña	['gɔrrɔ dɛ kam'paɲa]
helmet	casco (m)	['kaskɔ]
derby	bombín (m)	[bɔm'bin]
top hat	sombrero (m) de copa	[sɔmb'rɛrɔ dɛ 'kɔpa]

37. Footwear

footwear	calzado (m)	[kaʎ'θadɔ]
ankle boots	botas (f pl)	['bɔtas]
shoes (low-heeled ~)	zapatos (m pl)	[θa'patɔs]
boots (cowboy ~)	botas (f pl) altas	['bɔtas 'aʎtas]
slippers	zapatillas (f pl)	[θapa'tijas]

tennis shoes	zapatos (m pl) de tenis	[θa'patos dɛ 'tɛnis]
sneakers	zapatos (m pl) deportivos	[θa'patos dɛpɔr'tiβɔs]
sandals	sandalias (f pl)	[san'daʎjas]

cobbler	zapatero (m)	[θapa'tɛrɔ]
heel	tacón (m)	[ta'kɔn]
pair (of shoes)	par (m)	[par]

shoestring	cordón (m)	[kɔr'dɔn]
to lace (vt)	encordonar (vt)	[ɛŋkɔrdɔ'nar]
shoehorn	calzador (m)	[kaʎθa'dɔr]
shoe polish	betún (m)	[be'tun]

38. Textile. Fabrics

cotton (n)	algodón (m)	[aʎgɔ'dɔn]
cotton (as adj)	de algodón (adj)	[dɛ aʎgɔ'dɔn]
flax (n)	lino (m)	['linɔ]
flax (as adj)	de lino (adj)	[dɛ 'linɔ]

silk (n)	seda (f)	['sɛda]
silk (as adj)	de seda (adj)	[dɛ 'sɛda]
wool (n)	lana (f)	['ʎana]
woolen (adj)	de lana (adj)	[dɛ 'ʎana]

velvet	terciopelo (m)	[tɛrθiɔ'pɛlɔ]
suede	gamuza (f)	[ga'muθa]
corduroy	pana (f)	['pana]

nylon (n)	nylon (m)	[ni'lɔn]
nylon (as adj)	de nylon (adj)	[dɛ ni'lɔn]
polyester (n)	poliéster (m)	[pɔli'ɛstɛr]
polyester (as adj)	de poliéster (adj)	[dɛ pɔli'ɛstɛr]

leather (n)	piel (f)	[pjeʎ]
leather (as adj)	de piel	[dɛ 'pjeʎ]
fur (n)	piel (f)	[pjeʎ]
fur (e.g., ~ coat)	de piel (adj)	[dɛ 'pjeʎ]

39. Personal accessories

gloves	guantes (m pl)	[gu'antɛs]
mittens	manoplas (f pl)	[ma'nɔpʎas]
scarf (muffler)	bufanda (f)	[bu'fanda]

glasses	gafas (f pl)	['gafas]
frame (eyeglass ~)	montura (f)	[mɔn'tura]
umbrella	paraguas (m)	[pa'raguas]

walking stick	bastón (m)	[bas'tɔn]
hairbrush	cepillo (m) de pelo	[θæ'pijo dɛ 'pɛlɔ]
fan	abanico (m)	[aba'nikɔ]

necktie	corbata (f)	[kɔr'bata]
bow tie	pajarita (f)	[paha'rⁱita]
suspenders	tirantes (m pl)	[ti'rantɛs]
handkerchief	moquero (m)	[mɔ'kɛrɔ]

comb	peine (m)	['pɛjnɛ]
barrette	pasador (m)	[pasa'dɔr]
hairpin	horquilla (f)	[ɔr'kija]
buckle	hebilla (f)	[ɛ'bija]

| belt | cinturón (m) | [θintu'rɔn] |
| shoulder strap | correa (f) | [kɔr'rɛa] |

bag (handbag)	bolsa (f)	['bɔʎsa]
purse	bolso (m)	['bɔʎsɔ]
backpack	mochila (f)	[mɔ'ʧiʎa]

40. Clothing. Miscellaneous

fashion	moda (f)	['mɔda]
in vogue (adj)	de moda (adj)	[dɛ 'mɔda]
fashion designer	diseñador (m) de modas	[disɛɲja'dɔr dɛ 'mɔdas]

collar	cuello (m)	[ku'ɛjo]
pocket	bolsillo (m)	[bɔʎ'sijo]
pocket (as adj)	de bolsillo (adj)	[dɛ bɔʎ'sijo]
sleeve	manga (f)	['maŋa]
hanging loop	colgador (m)	[kɔʎga'dɔr]
fly (on trousers)	bragueta (f)	[bra'gɛta]

zipper (fastener)	cremallera (f)	[krɛma'jera]
fastener	cierre (m)	[si'ɛrrɛ]
button	botón (m)	[bɔ'tɔn]
buttonhole	ojal (m)	[ɔ'haʎ]
to come off (ab. button)	saltar (vi)	[saʎ'tar]

to sew (vi, vt)	coser (vi, vt)	[kɔ'sɛr]
to embroider (vi, vt)	bordar (vt)	[bɔr'dar]
embroidery	bordado (m)	[bɔr'dadɔ]
sewing needle	aguja (f)	[a'guha]
thread	hilo (m)	['ilɔ]
seam	costura (f)	[kɔs'tura]

to get dirty (vi)	ensuciarse (vr)	[ɛnsu'θjarsɛ]
stain (mark, spot)	mancha (f)	['manʧa]
to crease, crumple (vi)	arrugarse (vr)	[arru'garsɛ]

| to tear (vt) | rasgar (vt) | [ras'gar] |
| clothes moth | polilla (f) | [po'lija] |

41. Personal care. Cosmetics

toothpaste	pasta (f) de dientes	['pasta dɛ 'djentɛs]
toothbrush	cepillo (m) de dientes	[θæ'pijo dɛ 'djentɛs]
to brush one's teeth	limpiarse los dientes	[lim'pjarsɛ los 'djentɛs]

razor	maquinilla (f) de afeitar	[maki'niʎja dɛ afɛj'tar]
shaving cream	crema (f) de afeitar	['krɛma dɛ afɛj'tar]
to shave (vi)	afeitarse (vr)	[afɛj'tarsɛ]

| soap | jabón (m) | [ha'βon] |
| shampoo | champú (m) | [ʧam'pu] |

scissors	tijeras (f pl)	[ti'hɛras]
nail file	lima (f) de uñas	['lima dɛ 'uɲjas]
nail clippers	cortaúñas (m pl)	[korta'uɲjas]
tweezers	pinzas (f pl)	['pinθas]

cosmetics	cosméticos (m pl)	[kos'mɛtikɔs]
face mask	mascarilla (f)	[maska'rija]
manicure	manicura (f)	[mani'kura]
to have a manicure	hacer la manicura	[a'θær ʎa mani'kura]
pedicure	pedicura (f)	[pedi'kyra]

make-up bag	neceser (m) de maquillaje	[nɛsɛ'sɛr dɛ maki'jahe]
face powder	polvos (m pl)	['poʎvɔs]
powder compact	polvera (f)	[poʎ'vɛra]
blusher	colorete (m), rubor (m)	[kolo'retɛ], [ru'βor]

perfume (bottled)	perfume (m)	[pɛr'fumɛ]
toilet water (perfume)	agua (f) perfumada	['agua perfu'mada]
lotion	loción (f)	[lo'sjon]
cologne	agua (f) de colonia	['agua dɛ ko'lɔnia]

eyeshadow	sombra (f) de ojos	['sɔmbra dɛ 'ɔhɔs]
eyeliner	lápiz (m) de ojos	['ʎapiθ dɛ 'ɔhɔs]
mascara	rímel (m)	['rimeʎ]

lipstick	pintalabios (m)	[pinta'ʎaβiɔs]
nail polish, enamel	esmalte (m) de uñas	[ɛs'maʎte dɛ 'uɲjas]
hair spray	fijador (m) (para el pelo)	[fiha'dor]
deodorant	desodorante (m)	[dɛsodo'rantɛ]

cream	crema (f)	['krɛma]
face cream	crema (f) de belleza	['krɛma dɛ bɛ'ʎjeθa]
hand cream	crema (f) de manos	['krɛma dɛ 'manɔs]
anti-wrinkle cream	crema (f) antiarrugas	['krɛma 'antiar'rugas]

| day (as adj) | de día (adj) | [dɛ 'dia] |
| night (as adj) | de noche (adj) | [dɛ 'notʃe] |

tampon	tampón (m)	[tam'pɔn]
toilet paper	papel (m) higiénico	[pa'pɛʎ igi'ɛnikɔ]
hair dryer	secador (m) de pelo	[sɛka'dɔr dɛ 'pɛlɔ]

42. Jewelry

jewelry	joyas (f pl)	['hɔjas]
precious (e.g., ~ stone)	precioso (adj)	[prɛ'θiɔsɔ]
hallmark	contraste (m)	[kɔnt'rastɛ]
ring	anillo (m)	[a'nijo]
wedding ring	anillo (m) de boda	[a'nijo dɛ 'bɔda]
bracelet	pulsera (f)	[puʎ'sɛra]

earrings	pendientes (m pl)	[pɛn'djentɛs]
necklace (~ of pearls)	collar (m)	[kɔ'jar]
crown	corona (f)	[kɔ'rɔna]
bead necklace	collar (m) de abalorios	[kɔ'jar dɛ aba'lɔriɔs]

diamond	diamante (m)	[dja'mantɛ]
emerald	esmeralda (f)	[ɛsmɛ'raʎda]
ruby	rubí (m)	[ru'βɪ]
sapphire	zafiro (m)	[θa'firɔ]
pearl	perla (f)	['pɛrla]
amber	ámbar (m)	['ambar]

43. Watches. Clocks

watch (wristwatch)	reloj (m)	[rɛ'lɔh]
dial	esfera (f)	[ɛs'fɛra]
hand (of clock, watch)	aguja (f)	[a'guha]
metal watch band	pulsera (f)	[puʎ'sɛra]
watch strap	correa (f)	[kɔr'rɛa]

battery	pila (f)	['piʎa]
to be dead (battery)	descargarse (vr)	[dɛskar'garsɛ]
to change a battery	cambiar la pila	[kam'bjar ʎa 'piʎa]
to run fast	adelantarse (vr)	[adelan'tarθæ]
to run slow	retrasarse (vr)	[rɛtra'sarsɛ]

wall clock	reloj (m) de pared	[rɛ'lɔh dɛ pa'rɛd]
hourglass	reloj (m) de arena	[rɛ'lɔh dɛ a'rɛna]
sundial	reloj (m) de sol	[rɛ'lɔh dɛ 'sɔʎ]
alarm clock	despertador (m)	[dɛspɛrta'dɔr]
watchmaker	relojero (m)	[rɛlɔ'hɛrɔ]
to repair (vt)	reparar (vt)	[rɛpa'rar]

Food. Nutricion

44. Food

meat	carne (f)	['karnɛ]
chicken	gallina (f)	[ga'jɪna]
young chicken	pollo (m)	['pɔjo]
duck	pato (m)	['patɔ]
goose	ganso (m)	['gansɔ]
game	caza (f) menor	['kaθa mɛ'nɔr]
turkey	pava (f)	['paβa]
pork	carne (f) de cerdo	['karnɛ dɛ 'sɛrdɔ]
veal	carne (f) de ternera	['karnɛ dɛ tɛr'nɛra]
lamb	carne (f) de carnero	['karnɛ dɛ kar'nɛrɔ]
beef	carne (f) de vaca	['karnɛ dɛ 'baka]
rabbit	conejo (m)	[kɔ'nɛhɔ]
sausage (salami, etc.)	salchichón (m)	[saʎtʃi'tʃɔn]
vienna sausage	salchicha (f)	[saʎ'tʃitʃa]
bacon	beicon (m)	[ba'kɔn]
ham	jamón (m)	[ha'mɔn]
gammon (ham)	jamón (m) fresco	[ha'mɔn 'frɛskɔ]
pâté	paté (m)	[pa'tɛ]
liver	hígado (m)	['igadɔ]
lard	tocino (m)	[tɔ'θinɔ]
ground beef	carne (f) picada	['karnɛ pi'kada]
tongue	lengua (f)	['lenua]
egg	huevo (m)	[u'əβɔ]
eggs	huevos (m pl)	[u'əβɔs]
egg white	clara (f)	['kʎara]
egg yolk	yema (f)	['jəma]
fish	pescado (m)	[pɛs'kadɔ]
seafood	mariscos (m pl)	[ma'riskɔs]
crustaceans	crustáceos (m pl)	[krus'taθæɔs]
caviar	caviar (m)	[ka'vjar]
crab	cangrejo (m) de mar	[kaŋ'rɛhɔ dɛ 'mar]
shrimp	camarón (m)	[kama'rɔn]
oyster	ostra (f)	['ɔstra]
spiny lobster	langosta (f)	[ʎa'ŋɔsta]
octopus	pulpo (m)	['puʎpɔ]

squid	calamar (m)	[kaʎa'mar]
sturgeon	esturión (m)	[ɛsturi'ɔn]
salmon	salmón (m)	[saʎ'mɔn]
halibut	fletán (m)	[fle'tan]

cod	bacalao (m)	[baka'ʎaɔ]
mackerel	caballa (f)	[ka'βaja]
tuna	atún (m)	[a'tun]
eel	anguila (f)	[a'ŋiʎa]

| trout | trucha (f) | ['trutʃa] |
| sardine | sardina (f) | [sar'dina] |

| pike | lucio (m) | ['luθiɔ] |
| herring | arenque (m) | [a'rɛŋke] |

| bread | pan (m) | [pan] |
| cheese | queso (m) | ['kesɔ] |

| sugar | azúcar (m) | [a'θukar] |
| salt | sal (f) | [saʎ] |

rice	arroz (m)	[ar'rɔθ]
pasta	macarrones (m pl)	[makar'rɔnɛs]
noodles	tallarines (m pl)	[taja'rinɛs]

butter	mantequilla (f)	[mantɛ'kija]
vegetable oil	aceite (m) vegetal	[a'sɛjtɛ vɛhɛ'taʎ]
sunflower oil	aceite (m) de girasol	[a'sɛjtɛ dɛ hira'sɔʎ]
margarine	margarina (f)	[marga'rina]

| olives | olivas (f pl) | [ɔ'liβas] |
| olive oil | aceite (m) de oliva | [a'sɛjtɛ dɛ ɔ'liβa] |

milk	leche (f)	['letʃe]
condensed milk	leche (f) condensada	['letʃe kɔndɛn'sada]
yogurt	yogur (m)	[jo'gur]

| sour cream | nata (f) agria | ['nata 'agria] |
| cream (of milk) | nata (f) líquida | ['nata 'likida] |

| mayonnaise | mayonesa (f) | [majo'nɛsa] |
| buttercream | crema (f) de mantequilla | ['krɛma dɛ mantɛ'kija] |

cereal grain (wheat, etc.)	cereal molido grueso	[sɛrɛ'aʎ mɔ'lidɔ gru'ɛsɔ]
flour	harina (f)	[a'rina]
canned food	conservas (f pl)	[kɔn'sɛrvas]

cornflakes	copos (m pl) de maíz	['kɔpɔs dɛ ma'iθ]
honey	miel (f)	[mjeʎ]
jam	confitura (f)	[kɔnfi'tura]
chewing gum	chicle (m)	['tʃikle]

45. Drinks

water	agua (f)	['agua]
drinking water	agua (f) potable	['agua po'table]
mineral water	agua (f) mineral	['agua minɛ'raʎ]
still (adj)	sin gas	[sin 'gas]
carbonated (adj)	gaseoso (adj)	[gasɛ'ɔsɔ]
sparkling (adj)	con gas	[kɔn 'gas]
ice	hielo (m)	['jelɔ]
with ice	con hielo	[kɔn 'jelɔ]
non-alcoholic (adj)	sin alcohol	[sin aʎkɔ'ɔʎ]
soft drink	bebida (f) sin alcohol	[bɛ'bida sin aʎkɔ'ɔʎ]
cool soft drink	refresco (m)	[rɛf'rɛskɔ]
lemonade	limonada (f)	[limɔ'nada]
liquor	bebidas (f pl) alcohólicas	[bɛ'bidas aʎkɔ'ɔlikas]
wine	vino (m)	['binɔ]
white wine	vino (m) blanco	['binɔ 'bʎaŋkɔ]
red wine	vino (m) tinto	['binɔ 'tintɔ]
liqueur	licor (m)	[li'kɔr]
champagne	champaña (f)	[tʃam'paɲja]
vermouth	vermú (m)	[bɛr'mu]
whisky	whisky (m)	[u'iski]
vodka	vodka (m)	['bɔdka]
gin	ginebra (f)	[hi'nɛbra]
cognac	coñac (m)	[kɔ'ɲjak]
rum	ron (m)	[rɔn]
coffee	café (m)	[ka'fɛ]
black coffee	café (m) solo	[ka'fɛ 'sɔlɔ]
coffee with milk	café (m) con leche	[ka'fɛ kɔn 'letʃe]
cappuccino	capuchino (m)	[kapu'tʃinɔ]
instant coffee	café (m) soluble	[ka'fɛ sɔ'luble]
milk	leche (f)	['letʃe]
cocktail	cóctel (m)	['kɔktɛʎ]
milk shake	batido (m)	[ba'tidɔ]
juice	zumo (m)	['θumɔ]
tomato juice	jugo (m) de tomate	['hugɔ dɛ tɔ'matɛ]
orange juice	zumo (m) de naranja	['θumɔ dɛ na'ranha]
freshly squeezed juice	jugo (m) fresco	['hugɔ 'frɛskɔ]
beer	cerveza (f)	[sɛr'vɛθa]
light beer	cerveza (f) rubia	[sɛr'vɛθa 'ruβija]
dark beer	cerveza (f) negra	[sɛr'vɛθa 'nɛgra]
tea	té (m)	[tɛ]

| black tea | té (m) negro | ['tɛ 'nɛgrɔ] |
| green tea | té (m) verde | ['tɛ 'vɛrdɛ] |

46. Vegetables

vegetables	legumbres (f pl)	[le'gumbrɛs]
greens	verduras (f pl)	[bɛr'duras]
tomato	tomate (m)	[tɔ'matɛ]
cucumber	pepino (m)	[pɛ'pinɔ]
carrot	zanahoria (f)	[θana'ɔrija]
potato	patata (f)	[pa'tata]
onion	cebolla (f)	[θæ'bɔja]
garlic	ajo (m)	['ahɔ]
cabbage	col (f)	[kɔʎ]
cauliflower	coliflor (f)	[kɔlif'lɔr]
Brussels sprouts	col (f) de Bruselas	[kɔʎ dɛ bry'sɛlas]
broccoli	brócoli (m)	['brɔkɔli]
beetroot	remolacha (f)	[rɛmɔ'ʎatʃa]
eggplant	berenjena (f)	[bɛrɛn'hɛna]
zucchini	calabacín (m)	[kaʎaba'θin]
pumpkin	calabaza (f)	[kaʎa'βaθa]
turnip	nabo (m)	['naβɔ]
parsley	perejil (m)	[pɛrɛ'hiʎ]
dill	eneldo (m)	[ɛ'nɛʎdɔ]
lettuce	lechuga (f)	[le'tʃuga]
celery	apio (m)	['apiɔ]
asparagus	espárrago (m)	[ɛs'parragɔ]
spinach	espinaca (f)	[ɛspi'naka]
pea	guisante (m)	[gi'santɛ]
beans	habas (f pl)	['aβas]
corn (maize)	maíz (m)	[ma'iθ]
kidney bean	fréjol (m)	['frɛhɔʎ]
pepper	pimentón (m)	[pimen'tɔn]
radish	rábano (m)	['raβanɔ]
artichoke	alcachofa (f)	[aʎka'tʃofa]

47. Fruits. Nuts

fruit	fruto (m)	['frutɔ]
apple	manzana (f)	[man'θana]
pear	pera (f)	['pɛra]
lemon	limón (m)	[li'mɔn]

| orange | naranja (f) | [na'ranha] |
| strawberry | fresa (f) | ['frɛsa] |

mandarin	mandarina (f)	[manda'rina]
plum	ciruela (f)	[θiru'ɛʎa]
peach	melocotón (m)	[mɛlɔkɔ'tɔn]
apricot	albaricoque (m)	[aʎbari'kɔkɛ]
raspberry	frambuesa (f)	[frambu'ɛsa]
pineapple	ananás (m)	[ana'nas]

banana	banana (f)	[ba'nana]
watermelon	sandía (f)	[san'dia]
grape	uva (f)	['uβa]
sour cherry	guinda (f)	['ginda]
sweet cherry	cereza (f)	[θæ'rɛθa]
melon	melón (m)	[mɛ'lɔn]

grapefruit	pomelo (m)	[pɔ'mɛlɔ]
avocado	aguacate (m)	[agua'katɛ]
papaya	papaya (m)	[pa'paja]
mango	mango (m)	['maŋɔ]
pomegranate	granada (f)	[gra'nada]

redcurrant	grosella (f) roja	[grɔ'sɛja 'rɔha]
blackcurrant	grosella (f) negra	[grɔ'sɛja 'nɛgra]
gooseberry	grosella (f) espinosa	[grɔ'sɛja ɛspi'nɔsa]
bilberry	arándano (m)	[a'randanɔ]
blackberry	zarzamoras (f pl)	[θarθa'mɔras]

raisin	pasas (f pl)	['pasas]
fig	higo (m)	['igɔ]
date	dátil (m)	['datiʎ]

peanut	cacahuete (m)	[kakau'ətɛ]
almond	almendra (f)	[aʎ'mɛndra]
walnut	nuez (f)	[nu'ɛθ]
hazelnut	avellana (f)	[avɛ'ʎjana]
coconut	nuez (f) de coco	[nu'ɛθ dɛ 'kɔkɔ]
pistachios	pistachos (m pl)	[pis'tatʃɔs]

48. Bread. Candy

confectionery (pastry)	pasteles (m pl)	[pas'tɛles]
bread	pan (m)	[pan]
cookies	galletas (f pl)	[ga'jetas]

chocolate (n)	chocolate (m)	[tʃɔkɔ'ʎatɛ]
chocolate (as adj)	de chocolate (adj)	[dɛ tʃɔkɔ'ʎatɛ]
candy	caramelo (m)	[kara'mɛlɔ]
cake (e.g., cupcake)	tarta (f)	['tarta]

cake (e.g., birthday ~)	**tarta** (f)	['tarta]
pie (e.g., apple ~)	**pastel** (m)	[pas'tɛʎ]
filling (for cake, pie)	**relleno** (m)	[rɛ'jenɔ]

whole fruit jam	**confitura** (f)	[kɔnfi'tura]
marmalade	**mermelada** (f)	[mɛrmɛ'ʎada]
waffle	**gofre** (m)	['gɔfrɛ]
ice-cream	**helado** (m)	[ɛ'ʎadɔ]
pudding	**pudín** (f)	[pu'din]

49. Cooked dishes

course, dish	**plato** (m)	['pʎatɔ]
cuisine	**cocina** (f)	[kɔ'θina]
recipe	**receta** (f)	[rɛ'θæta]
portion	**porción** (f)	[pɔr'sʲɔn]

| salad | **ensalada** (f) | [ɛnsa'ʎada] |
| soup | **sopa** (f) | ['sɔpa] |

clear soup (broth)	**caldo** (m)	['kaʎdɔ]
sandwich (bread)	**bocadillo** (m)	[bɔka'dijo]
fried eggs	**huevos** (m pl) **fritos**	[u'əβɔs 'fritɔs]

cutlet (croquette)	**chuleta** (f)	[ʧu'leta]
hamburger (beefburger)	**hamburguesa** (f)	[ambur'gesa]
beefsteak	**bistec** (m)	[bis'tɛk]
stew	**asado** (m)	[a'sadɔ]

side dish	**guarnición** (f)	[guarni'sʲɔn]
spaghetti	**espagueti** (m)	[ɛspa'gɛtti]
mashed potatoes	**puré** (m) **de patatas**	[pu'rɛ dɛ pa'tatas]
pizza	**pizza** (f)	['pisθa]
porridge (oatmeal, etc.)	**gachas** (f pl)	['gaʧas]
omelet	**tortilla** (f) **francesa**	[tɔr'tiʎja fran'θæsa]

boiled (e.g., ~ beef)	**cocido en agua** (adj)	[kɔ'θidɔ ɛn 'agua]
smoked (adj)	**ahumado** (adj)	[au'madɔ]
fried (adj)	**frito** (adj)	['fritɔ]
dried (adj)	**seco** (adj)	['sɛkɔ]
frozen (adj)	**congelado** (adj)	[kɔnhɛ'ʎadɔ]
pickled (adj)	**marinado** (adj)	[mari'nadɔ]

sweet (sugary)	**azucarado, dulce** (adj)	[aθuka'radɔ], ['duʎθæ]
salty (adj)	**salado** (adj)	[sa'ʎadɔ]
cold (adj)	**frío** (adj)	['friɔ]
hot (adj)	**caliente** (adj)	[ka'ʎjentɛ]
bitter (adj)	**amargo** (adj)	[a'margɔ]
tasty (adj)	**sabroso** (adj)	[sab'rɔsɔ]
to cook in boiling water	**cocer** (vt) **en agua**	[kɔ'θær ɛn 'agua]

to cook (dinner)	preparar (vt)	[prɛpa'rar]
to fry (vt)	freír (vt)	[frɛ'ir]
to heat up (food)	calentar (vt)	[kalen'tar]

to salt (vt)	salar (vt)	[sa'ʎar]
to pepper (vt)	poner pimienta	[po'nɛr pi'mjenta]
to grate (vt)	rallar (vt)	[ra'ʎjar]
peel (n)	piel (f)	[pjeʎ]
to peel (vt)	pelar (vt)	[pɛ'ʎar]

50. Spices

salt	sal (f)	[saʎ]
salty (adj)	salado (adj)	[sa'ʎadɔ]
to salt (vt)	salar (vt)	[sa'ʎar]

black pepper	pimienta (f) negra	[pi'mjenta 'nɛgra]
red pepper	pimienta (f) roja	[pi'mjenta 'rɔha]
mustard	mostaza (f)	[mɔs'taθa]
horseradish	rábano (m) picante	['raβanɔ pi'kantɛ]

condiment	condimento (m)	[kɔndi'mɛntɔ]
spice	especia (f)	[ɛs'pɛθja]
sauce	salsa (f)	['saʎsa]
vinegar	vinagre (m)	[bi'nagrɛ]

anise	anís (m)	[a'nis]
basil	albahaca (f)	[aʎba'aka]
cloves	clavo (m)	['kʎaβɔ]
ginger	jengibre (m)	[hɛn'hibrɛ]
coriander	cilantro (m)	[θi'ʎantrɔ]
cinnamon	canela (f)	[ka'nɛʎa]

sesame	sésamo (m)	['sɛsamɔ]
bay leaf	hoja (f) de laurel	['ɔha dɛ ʎau'rɛʎ]
paprika	paprika (f)	[pap'rika]
caraway	comino (m)	[kɔ'minɔ]
saffron	azafrán (m)	[aθaf'ran]

51. Meals

| food | comida (f) | [kɔ'mida] |
| to eat (vi, vt) | comer (vi, vt) | [kɔ'mɛr] |

breakfast	desayuno (m)	[dɛsa'junɔ]
to have breakfast	desayunar (vi)	[dɛsaju'nar]
lunch	almuerzo (m)	[aʎmu'ɛrθɔ]
to have lunch	almorzar (vi)	[aʎmɔr'θar]

| dinner | cena (f) | ['θæna] |
| to have dinner | cenar (vi) | [θæ'nar] |

| appetite | apetito (m) | [apɛ'tito] |
| Enjoy your meal! | ¡Que aproveche! | [ke apro'βətʃe] |

to open (~ a bottle)	abrir (vt)	[ab'rir]
to spill (liquid)	derramar (vt)	[dɛrra'mar]
to spill out (vi)	derramarse (vr)	[dɛrra'marsɛ]

to boil (vi)	hervir (vi)	[ɛr'wir]
to boil (vt)	hervir (vt)	[ɛr'wir]
boiled (~ water)	hervido (adj)	[ɛr'wido]
to chill, cool down (vt)	enfriar (vt)	[ɛnfri'ar]
to chill (vi)	enfriarse (vr)	[ɛnfri'arsɛ]

| taste, flavor | sabor (m) | [sa'βor] |
| aftertaste | regusto (m) | [rɛ'gusto] |

to be on a diet	adelgazar (vi)	[adɛʎga'θar]
diet	dieta (f)	[di'ɛta]
vitamin	vitamina (f)	[bita'mina]
calorie	caloría (f)	[kalo'ria]
vegetarian (n)	vegetariano (m)	[bɛhɛta'rjano]
vegetarian (adj)	vegetariano (adj)	[bɛhɛta'rjano]

fats (nutrient)	grasas (f pl)	['grasas]
proteins	proteínas (f pl)	[protɛ'inas]
carbohydrates	carbohidratos (m pl)	[karboid'ratos]
slice (of lemon, ham)	loncha (f)	['lonha]
piece (of cake, pie)	pedazo (m)	[pɛ'daθo]
crumb (of bread)	miga (f)	['miga]

52. Table setting

spoon	cuchara (f)	[ku'tʃara]
knife	cuchillo (m)	[ku'tʃijo]
fork	tenedor (m)	[tɛnɛ'dor]
cup (of coffee)	taza (f)	['taθa]
plate (dinner ~)	plato (m)	['pʎato]
saucer	platillo (m)	[pʎa'tijo]
napkin (on table)	servilleta (f)	[sɛrwi'jeta]
toothpick	mondadientes (m)	[monda'djentɛs]

53. Restaurant

| restaurant | restaurante (m) | [rɛstau'rantɛ] |
| coffee house | cafetería (f) | [kafetɛ'rija] |

| pub, bar | **bar** (m) | [bar] |
| tearoom | **salón** (m) **de té** | [sa'lɔn dɛ 'tɛ] |

waiter	**camarero** (m)	[kama'rɛrɔ]
waitress	**camarera** (f)	[kama'rɛra]
bartender	**barman** (m)	['barman]

menu	**carta** (f), **menú** (m)	['karta], [me'nu]
wine list	**carta** (f) **de vinos**	['karta dɛ 'winɔs]
to book a table	**reservar una mesa**	[rɛsɛr'var 'una 'mɛsa]

course, dish	**plato** (m)	['pʎatɔ]
to order (meal)	**pedir** (vt)	[pɛ'dir]
to make an order	**hacer el pedido**	[a'θær ɛʎ pɛ'didɔ]

aperitif	**aperitivo** (m)	[apɛri'tiβɔ]
appetizer	**entremés** (m)	[ɛntrɛ'mɛs]
dessert	**postre** (m)	['pɔstrɛ]

check	**cuenta** (f)	[ku'ɛnta]
to pay the check	**pagar la cuenta**	[pa'gar ʎa ku'ɛnta]
to give change	**dar la vuelta**	['dar ʎa bu'ɛlta]
tip	**propina** (f)	[prɔ'pina]

Family, relatives and friends

54. Personal information. Forms

name, first name	**nombre** (m)	['nɔmbrɛ]
family name	**apellido** (m)	[apɛ'jido]
date of birth	**fecha** (f) **de nacimiento**	['fɛtʃa dɛ nasi'mjentɔ]
place of birth	**lugar** (m) **de nacimiento**	[ly'gar dɛ nasi'mjentɔ]
nationality	**nacionalidad** (f)	[nasʲɔnali'dad]
place of residence	**domicilio** (m)	[dɔmi'siʎɔ]
country	**país** (m)	[pa'is]
profession (occupation)	**profesión** (f)	[prɔfɛ'sʲɔn]
gender, sex	**sexo** (m)	['sɛksɔ]
height	**estatura** (f)	[ɛsta'tura]
weight	**peso** (m)	['pɛsɔ]

55. Family members. Relatives

mother	**madre** (f)	['madrɛ]
father	**padre** (m)	['padrɛ]
son	**hijo** (m)	['ihɔ]
daughter	**hija** (f)	['iha]
younger daughter	**hija** (f) **menor**	['iha mɛ'nɔr]
younger son	**hijo** (m) **menor**	['ihɔ mɛ'nɔr]
eldest daughter	**hija** (f) **mayor**	['iha ma'jɔr]
eldest son	**hijo** (m) **mayor**	['ihɔ ma'jɔr]
brother	**hermano** (m)	[ɛr'manɔ]
sister	**hermana** (f)	[ɛr'mana]
cousin (masc.)	**primo** (m)	['primɔ]
cousin (fem.)	**prima** (f)	['prima]
mom	**mamá** (f)	[ma'ma]
dad, daddy	**papá** (m)	[pa'pa]
parents	**padres** (m pl)	['padrɛs]
child	**niño -a** (m, f)	['niɲʲɔ], [a]
children	**niños** (m pl)	['niɲʲɔs]
grandmother	**abuela** (f)	[abu'ɛʎa]
grandfather	**abuelo** (m)	[abu'ɛlɔ]
grandson	**nieto** (m)	['ɲjetɔ]

| granddaughter | nieta (f) | ['njeta] |
| grandchildren | nietos (m pl) | ['njetɔs] |

uncle	tío (m)	['tiɔ]
aunt	tía (f)	['tia]
nephew	sobrino (m)	[sɔb'rinɔ]
niece	sobrina (f)	[sɔb'rina]

mother-in-law (wife's mother)	suegra (f)	[su'ɛgra]
father-in-law (husband's father)	suegro (m)	[su'ɛgrɔ]
son-in-law (daughter's husband)	yerno (m)	['jernɔ]
stepmother	madrastra (f)	[mad'rastra]
stepfather	padrastro (m)	[pad'rastrɔ]

infant	niño (m) de pecho	['ninjɔ dɛ 'pɛtʃɔ]
baby (infant)	bebé (m)	[bɛ'bɛ]
little boy, kid	chico (m)	['tʃikɔ]

wife	mujer (f)	[mu'hɛr]
husband	marido (m)	[ma'ridɔ]
spouse (husband)	esposo (m)	[ɛs'pɔsɔ]
spouse (wife)	esposa (f)	[ɛs'pɔsa]

married (masc.)	casado (adj)	[ka'sadɔ]
married (fem.)	casada (adj)	[ka'sada]
single (unmarried)	soltero (adj)	[sɔʎ'tɛrɔ]
bachelor	soltero (m)	[sɔʎ'tɛrɔ]
divorced (masc.)	divorciado (adj)	[divɔr'θjadɔ]
widow	viuda (f)	[bi'uda]
widower	viudo (m)	[bi'udɔ]

relative	pariente (m)	[pa'rjentɛ]
close relative	pariente (m) cercano	[pa'rjentɛ ser'kanɔ]
distant relative	pariente (m) lejano	[pa'rjentɛ le'hanɔ]
relatives	parientes (m pl)	[pa'rjentɛs]

orphan (boy)	huérfano (m)	[u'ərfanɔ]
orphan (girl)	huérfana (f)	[u'ərfana]
guardian (of minor)	tutor (m)	[tu'tɔr]
to adopt (a boy)	ahijar (vt)	[ai'har]
to adopt (a girl)	ahijar (vt)	[ai'har]

56. Friends. Coworkers

friend (masc.)	amigo (m)	[a'migɔ]
friend (fem.)	amiga (f)	[a'miga]
friendship	amistad (f)	[amis'tad]

to be friends	ser amigo	[sɛr a'migo]
buddy (masc.)	amigote (m)	[ami'gotɛ]
buddy (fem.)	amiguete (f)	[ami'getɛ]
partner	compañero (m)	[kompa'ɲjero]

chief (boss)	jefe (m)	['hɛfɛ]
superior	superior (m)	[supɛ'rʲor]
subordinate	subordinado (m)	[subordi'nado]
colleague	colega (m, f)	[ko'lɛga]

acquaintance (person)	conocido (m)	[kono'sido]
fellow traveler	compañero (m) de viaje	[kompa'ɲjero dɛ 'bjahɛ]
classmate	condiscípulo (m)	[kondi'sipulo]

neighbor (masc.)	vecino (m)	[bɛ'θino]
neighbor (fem.)	vecina (f)	[bɛ'θina]
neighbors	vecinos (m pl)	[bɛ'θinos]

57. Man. Woman

woman	mujer (f)	[mu'hɛr]
girl (young woman)	muchacha (f)	[mu'ʧaʧa]
bride	novia (f)	['noβia]

beautiful (adj)	guapa (adj)	[gu'apa]
tall (adj)	alta (adj)	['aʎta]
slender (adj)	esbelta (adj)	[ɛs'bɛʎta]
short (adj)	de estatura mediana	[dɛ ɛsta'tura mɛdi'ana]

| blonde (n) | rubia (f) | ['ruβia] |
| brunette (n) | morena (f) | [mo'rɛna] |

ladies' (adj)	de señora (adj)	[dɛ sɛ'ɲʲora]
virgin (girl)	virgen (f)	['birhɛn]
pregnant (adj)	embarazada (adj)	[ɛmbara'θada]

man (adult male)	hombre (m)	['ombrɛ]
blond (n)	rubio (m)	['ruβio]
brunet (n)	moreno (m)	[mo'rɛno]
tall (adj)	alto (adj)	['aʎto]
short (adj)	de estatura mediana	[dɛ ɛsta'tura mɛdi'ana]

rude (rough)	grosero (adj)	[gro'sɛro]
stocky (adj)	rechoncho (adj)	[rɛ'ʧonʧo]
robust (adj)	robusto (adj)	[ro'βusto]
strong (adj)	fuerte (adj)	[fu'ɛrtɛ]
strength	fuerza (f)	[fu'ɛrθa]

| stout, fat (adj) | gordo (adj) | ['gordo] |
| swarthy (adj) | moreno (adj) | [mo'rɛno] |

| well-built (adj) | esbelto (adj) | [ɛs'bɛʎtɔ] |
| elegant (adj) | elegante (adj) | [ɛle'gantɛ] |

58. Age

age	edad (f)	[ɛ'dad]
youth (young age)	juventud (f)	[huvɛn'tud]
young (adj)	joven (adj)	['hɔβən]

| younger (adj) | menor (adj) | [mɛ'nɔr] |
| older (adj) | mayor (adj) | [ma'jor] |

young man	joven (m)	['hɔβən]
teenager	adolescente (m)	[adɔle'θæntɛ]
guy, fellow	muchacho (m)	[mu'ʧaʧɔ]

| old man | anciano (m) | [an'θjanɔ] |
| old woman | anciana (f) | [an'θjana] |

adult	adulto	[a'duʎtɔ]
middle-aged (adj)	de edad media (adj)	[dɛ ɛ'dad 'mɛdja]
elderly (adj)	de edad, anciano (adj)	[dɛ ɛ'dad], [an'θjanɔ]
old (adj)	viejo (adj)	['bjehɔ]

| to retire (from job) | jubilarse (vr) | [hubi'ʎarsɛ] |
| retiree | jubilado (m) | [hubi'ʎadɔ] |

59. Children

child	niño -a (m, f)	['niɲɔ], [a]
children	niños (m pl)	['niɲɔs]
twins	gemelos (m pl)	[hɛ'mɛlɔs]

cradle	cuna (f)	['kuna]
rattle	sonajero (m)	[sɔna'hɛrɔ]
diaper	pañal (m)	[pa'ɲjaʎ]

pacifier	chupete (m)	[ʧu'pɛtɛ]
baby carriage	cochecito (m)	[kɔʧe'sitɔ]
kindergarten	jardín (m) de infancia	[har'din dɛ in'fansia]
babysitter	niñera (f)	[ni'ɲjera]

childhood	infancia (f)	[in'fansja]
doll	muñeca (f)	[mu'ɲjeka]
toy	juguete (m)	[hu'gɛtɛ]
construction set	mecano (m)	[mɛ'kanɔ]
well-bred (adj)	bien criado (adj)	[bjen kri'adɔ]
ill-bred (adj)	malcriado (adj)	[maʎkri'adɔ]

spoiled (adj)	mimado (adj)	[mi'mado]
to be naughty	hacer travesuras	[a'θær travɛ'suras]
mischievous (adj)	travieso (adj)	[tra'vjɛsɔ]
mischievousness	travesura (f)	[travɛ'sura]
mischievous child	travieso (m)	[tra'vjɛsɔ]
obedient (adj)	obediente (adj)	[ɔbɛdi'ɛntɛ]
disobedient (adj)	desobediente (adj)	[dɛsɔbɛdi'ɛntɛ]
docile (adj)	dócil (adj)	['dɔθiʎ]
clever (smart)	inteligente (adj)	[intɛli'hɛntɛ]
child prodigy	niño (m) prodigio	['niɲɔ prɔ'dihiɔ]

60. Married couples. Family life

to kiss (vt)	besar	[bɛ'sar]
to kiss (vi)	besarse	[bɛ'sarsɛ]
family (n)	familia (f)	[fa'milija]
family (as adj)	familiar (adj)	[fami'ʎjar]
couple	pareja (f)	[pa'rɛha]
marriage (state)	matrimonio (m)	[matri'mɔɲɔ]
hearth (home)	hogar (m) familiar	[ɔ'gar fami'ʎjar]
dynasty	dinastía (f)	[dinas'tia]
date	cita (f)	['θita]
kiss	beso (m)	['bɛsɔ]
love (for sb)	amor (m)	[a'mɔr]
to love (sb)	querer (vt)	[ke'rɛr]
beloved	querido (adj)	[ke'ridɔ]
tenderness	ternura (f)	[tɛr'nura]
tender (affectionate)	tierno (adj)	['tˈernɔ]
faithfulness	fidelidad (f)	[fidɛli'dad]
faithful (adj)	fiel (adj)	['fjeʎ]
care (attention)	cuidado (m)	[kui'dadɔ]
caring (~ father)	cariñoso (adj)	[kari'ɲɔsɔ]
newlyweds	recién casados (pl)	[rɛ'θjen ka'sadɔs]
honeymoon	luna (f) de miel	['lyna dɛ mjeʎ]
to get married (ab. woman)	estar casada	[ɛs'tar ka'sada]
to get married (ab. man)	casarse (vr)	[ka'sarsɛ]
wedding	boda (f)	['bɔda]
golden wedding	bodas (f pl) de oro	['bɔdas dɛ 'ɔrɔ]
anniversary	aniversario (m)	[anivɛr'sariɔ]
lover (masc.)	amante (m)	[a'mantɛ]
mistress	amante (f)	[a'mantɛ]

65

adultery	**adulterio** (m)	[aduʎ'tɛrio]
to cheat on ... (commit adultery)	**cometer adulterio**	[kome'tɛr aduʎ'tɛrio]
jealous (adj)	**celoso** (adj)	[θæ'loso]
to be jealous	**tener celos**	[tɛ'nɛr 'θælos]
divorce	**divorcio** (m)	[di'βorsio]
to divorce (vi)	**divorciarse** (vr)	[divor'θjarsɛ]
to quarrel (vi)	**reñir** (vi)	[rɛ'ɲir]
to be reconciled	**reconciliarse** (vr)	[rɛkonθi'ʎjarsɛ]
together (adv)	**juntos** (adv)	['huntos]
sex	**sexo** (m)	['sɛkso]
happiness	**felicidad** (f)	[fɛlisi'dad]
happy (adj)	**feliz** (adj)	[fɛ'liθ]
misfortune (accident)	**desgracia** (f)	[dɛsg'raθija]
unhappy (adj)	**desgraciado** (adj)	[dɛsgra'θjado]

Character. Feelings. Emotions

61. Feelings. Emotions

feeling (emotion)	sentimiento (m)	[sɛnti'mjentɔ]
feelings	sentimientos (m pl)	[sɛnti'mjentɔs]
to feel (vt)	sentir (vt)	[sɛn'tir]
hunger	hambre (f)	['ambrɛ]
to be hungry	tener hambre	[tɛ'nɛr 'ambrɛ]
thirst	sed (f)	[sɛd]
to be thirsty	tener sed	[tɛ'nɛr 'sɛd]
sleepiness	somnolencia (f)	[sɔmnɔ'lenθija]
to feel sleepy	tener sueño	[tɛ'nɛr su'ɛɲɔ]
tiredness	cansancio (m)	[kan'sanθiɔ]
tired (adj)	cansado (adj)	[kan'sadɔ]
to get tired	estar cansado	[ɛs'tar kan'sadɔ]
mood (humor)	humor (m)	[u'mɔr]
boredom	aburrimiento (m)	[aburri'mjentɔ]
to be bored	aburrirse (vr)	[abur'rirsɛ]
seclusion	soledad (f)	[sɔle'dad]
to seclude oneself	aislarse (vr)	[ais'ʎarsɛ]
to worry (make anxious)	inquietar (vt)	[inkje'tar]
to be worried	inquietarse (vr)	[inkje'tarsɛ]
worrying (n)	inquietud (f)	[inkje'tud]
anxiety	preocupación (f)	[preɔkupa'θion]
preoccupied (adj)	preocupado (adj)	[preɔku'padɔ]
to be nervous	estar nervioso	[ɛs'tar nɛr'viɔsɔ]
to panic (vi)	darse al pánico	['darsɛ aʎ 'panikɔ]
hope	esperanza (f)	[ɛspɛ'ranθa]
to hope (vi, vt)	esperar (vi)	[ɛspɛ'rar]
certainty	seguridad (f)	[sɛguri'dad]
certain, sure (adj)	seguro (adj)	[sɛ'gurɔ]
uncertainty	inseguridad (f)	[insɛguri'dad]
uncertain (adj)	inseguro (adj)	[insɛ'gurɔ]
drunk (adj)	borracho (adj)	[bɔr'ratʃɔ]
sober (adj)	sobrio (adj)	['sɔbriɔ]
weak (adj)	débil (adj)	['dɛβiʎ]
happy (adj)	feliz (adj)	[fɛ'liθ]
to scare (vt)	asustar (vt)	[asus'tar]

fury (madness)	**furia** (f)	[ˈfurija]
rage (fury)	**rabia** (f)	[ˈrabja]
depression	**depresión** (f)	[dɛprɛˈsʲɔn]
discomfort	**incomodidad** (f)	[iŋkɔmɔdiˈdad]
comfort	**comodidad** (f)	[kɔmɔdiˈdad]
to regret (be sorry)	**arrepentirse** (vr)	[arrɛpɛnˈtirsɛ]
regret	**arrepentimiento** (m)	[arrɛpɛntiˈmjentɔ]
bad luck	**mala suerte** (f)	[ˈmaʎa suˈɛrtɛ]
sadness	**tristeza** (f)	[trisˈtɛθa]
shame (remorse)	**vergüenza** (f)	[bɛrguˈɛnθa]
gladness	**júbilo** (m)	[ˈhuβilɔ]
enthusiasm, zeal	**entusiasmo** (m)	[ɛntusiˈjasmɔ]
enthusiast	**entusiasta** (m)	[ɛntusiˈjasta]
to show enthusiasm	**mostrar entusiasmo**	[mɔstˈrar ɛntuˈsjasmɔ]

62. Character. Personality

character	**carácter** (m)	[kaˈraktɛr]
character flaw	**defecto** (m)	[dɛˈfɛktɔ]
mind	**mente** (f)	[ˈmentɛ]
reason	**razón** (f)	[raˈθɔn]
conscience	**consciencia** (f)	[kɔnˈθjenθija]
habit (custom)	**hábito** (m)	[ˈaβitɔ]
ability	**habilidad** (f)	[abiliˈdad]
can (e.g., ~ swim)	**poder** (vt)	[pɔˈdɛr]
patient (adj)	**paciente** (adj)	[paˈθjentɛ]
impatient (adj)	**impaciente** (adj)	[impaˈθjentɛ]
curious (inquisitive)	**curioso** (adj)	[kuˈrʲɔsɔ]
curiosity	**curiosidad** (f)	[kuˈrʲɔsiˈdad]
modesty	**modestia** (f)	[mɔˈdɛstija]
modest (adj)	**modesto** (adj)	[mɔˈdɛstɔ]
immodest (adj)	**inmodesto** (adj)	[inmɔˈdɛstɔ]
lazy (adj)	**perezoso** (adj)	[pɛrɛˈθɔsɔ]
lazy person (masc.)	**perezoso** (m)	[pɛrɛˈθɔsɔ]
cunning (n)	**astucia** (f)	[asˈtuθija]
cunning (as adj)	**astuto** (adj)	[asˈtutɔ]
distrust	**desconfianza** (f)	[dɛskɔnˈfjanθa]
distrustful (adj)	**desconfiado** (adj)	[dɛskɔnˈfjadɔ]
generosity	**generosidad** (f)	[hɛnɛrɔsiˈdad]
generous (adj)	**generoso** (adj)	[hɛnɛˈrɔsɔ]
talented (adj)	**talentoso** (adj)	[talenˈtɔsɔ]
talent	**talento** (m)	[taˈlentɔ]

courageous (adj)	valiente (adj)	[ba'ʎjentɛ]
courage	coraje (m)	[kɔ'rahɛ]
honest (adj)	honesto (adj)	[ɔ'nɛstɔ]
honesty	honestidad (f)	[ɔnɛsti'dad]
careful (cautious)	prudente (adj)	[pru'dɛntɛ]
brave (courageous)	valeroso (adj)	[bale'rɔsɔ]
serious (adj)	serio (adj)	['sɛriɔ]
strict (severe, stern)	severo (adj)	[sɛ'vɛrɔ]
decisive (adj)	decidido (adj)	[dɛsi'didɔ]
indecisive (adj)	indeciso (adj)	[indɛ'θisɔ]
shy, timid (adj)	tímido (adj)	['timidɔ]
shyness, timidity	timidez (f)	[timi'dɛθ]
confidence (trust)	confianza (f)	[kɔn'fjanθa]
to believe (trust)	creer (vt)	[kre'ɛr]
trusting (naïve)	confiado (adj)	[kɔn'fjadɔ]
sincerely (adv)	sinceramente (adv)	[sinθæra'mɛntɛ]
sincere (adj)	sincero (adj)	[sin'θærɔ]
sincerity	sinceridad (f)	[sinθæri'dad]
open (person)	abierto (adj)	[a'bjertɔ]
calm (adj)	calmado (adj)	[kaʎ'madɔ]
frank (sincere)	franco (adj)	['fraŋkɔ]
naïve (adj)	ingenuo (adj)	[in'hɛnuɔ]
absent-minded (adj)	distraído (adj)	[distra'idɔ]
funny (odd)	gracioso (adj)	[gra'θʲosɔ]
greed	avaricia (f)	[ava'riθija]
greedy (adj)	avaro (adj)	[a'βarɔ]
stingy (adj)	tacaño (adj)	[ta'kaɲʲɔ]
evil (adj)	malvado (adj)	[maʎ'vadɔ]
stubborn (adj)	terco (adj)	['tɛrkɔ]
unpleasant (adj)	desagradable (adj)	[dɛsagra'dable]
selfish person (masc.)	egoísta (m)	[ɛgɔ'ista]
selfish (adj)	egoísta (adj)	[ɛgɔ'ista]
coward	cobarde (m)	[kɔ'βardɛ]
cowardly (adj)	cobarde (adj)	[kɔ'βardɛ]

63. Sleep. Dreams

to sleep (vi)	dormir (vi)	[dɔr'mir]
sleep, sleeping	sueño (m)	[su'ɛɲʲɔ]
dream	sueño (m)	[su'ɛɲʲɔ]
to dream (in sleep)	soñar (vi)	[sɔ'ɲjar]
sleepy (adj)	adormilado (adj)	[adɔrmi'ʎadɔ]
bed	cama (f)	['kama]

mattress	colchón (m)	[kɔʎ'tʃon]
blanket (comforter)	manta (f)	['manta]
pillow	almohada (f)	[aʎmɔ'ada]
sheet	sábana (f)	['saβana]

insomnia	insomnio (m)	[in'sɔmniɔ]
sleepless (adj)	de insomnio (adj)	[dɛ in'sɔmniɔ]
sleeping pill	somnífero (m)	[sɔm'nifɛrɔ]
to take a sleeping pill	tomar el somnífero	[tɔ'mar ɛʎ sɔm'nifɛrɔ]

to feel sleepy	tener sueño	[tɛ'nɛr su'ɛɲɔ]
to yawn (vi)	bostezar (vi)	[bɔstɛ'θar]
to go to bed	irse a la cama	['irsɛ a ʎa 'kama]
to make up the bed	hacer la cama	[a'θær ʎa 'kama]
to fall asleep	dormirse (vr)	[dɔr'mirsɛ]

nightmare	pesadilla (f)	[pɛsa'dija]
snoring	ronquido (m)	[rɔ'ŋkidɔ]
to snore (vi)	roncar (vi)	[rɔ'ŋkar]

alarm clock	despertador (m)	[dɛspɛrta'dɔr]
to wake (vt)	despertar (vt)	[dɛspɛr'tar]
to wake up	despertarse (vr)	[dɛspɛr'tarsɛ]
to get up (vi)	levantarse (vr)	[levan'tarsɛ]
to wash up (vi)	lavarse (vr)	[ʎa'βarsɛ]

64. Humour. Laughter. Gladness

humor (wit, fun)	humor (m)	[u'mɔr]
sense of humor	sentido (m) del humor	[sɛn'tidɔ dɛʎ u'mɔr]
to have fun	divertirse (vr)	[divɛr'tirsɛ]
cheerful (adj)	alegre (adj)	[a'legrɛ]
merriment, fun	júbilo (m)	['huβilɔ]

| smile | sonrisa (f) | [sɔn'risa] |
| to smile (vi) | sonreír (vi) | [sɔnrɛ'ir] |

to start laughing	echarse a reír	[ɛ'tʃarsɛ a rɛ'ir]
to laugh (vi)	reírse (vr)	[rɛ'irsɛ]
laugh, laughter	risa (f)	['risa]

anecdote	anécdota (f)	[a'nekdɔta]
funny (anecdote, etc.)	gracioso (adj)	[gra'θiɔsɔ]
funny (odd)	ridículo (adj)	[ri'dikulɔ]

to joke (vi)	bromear (vi)	[brɔmɛ'ar]
joke (verbal)	broma (f)	['brɔma]
joy (emotion)	alegría (f)	[aleg'rija]
to rejoice (vi)	alegrarse (vr)	[aleg'rarsɛ]
glad, cheerful (adj)	alegre (adj)	[a'legrɛ]

65. Discussion, conversation. Part 1

communication	comunicación (f)	[komunika'θion]
to communicate	comunicarse (vr)	[komuni'karsɛ]
conversation	conversación (f)	[konvɛrsa'θion]
dialog	diálogo (m)	['djalogo]
discussion (discourse)	discusión (f)	[disku'sion]
debate	debate (m)	[dɛ'batɛ]
to debate (vi)	debatir (vi)	[dɛba'tir]
interlocutor	interlocutor (m)	[intɛrloku'tor]
topic (theme)	tema (m)	['tɛma]
point of view	punto (m) de vista	['punto dɛ 'wista]
opinion (viewpoint)	opinión (f)	[opi'nion]
speech (talk)	discurso (m)	[dis'kurso]
discussion (of report, etc.)	discusión (f)	[disku'sion]
to discuss (vt)	discutir (vt)	[disku'tir]
talk (conversation)	conversación (f)	[konvɛrsa'θion]
to talk (vi)	conversar (vi)	[konvɛr'sar]
meeting	reunión (f)	[rɛu'nion]
to meet (vi, vt)	encontrarse (vr)	[ɛŋkont'rarsɛ]
proverb	proverbio (m)	[pro'βɛrbio]
saying	dicho (m)	['ditʃo]
riddle (poser)	adivinanza (f)	[adiwi'nanθa]
to ask a riddle	contar una adivinanza	[kon'tar una adiwi'nanθa]
password	contraseña (f)	[kontra'sɛnja]
secret	secreto (m)	[sɛk'rɛto]
oath (vow)	juramento (m)	[hura'mɛnto]
to swear (an oath)	jurar (vt)	[hu'rar]
promise	promesa (f)	[pro'mɛsa]
to promise (vt)	prometer (vt)	[promɛ'tɛr]
advice (counsel)	consejo (m)	[kon'sɛho]
to advise (vt)	aconsejar (vt)	[akonsɛ'har]
to listen to … (obey)	escuchar (vt)	[ɛsku'tʃar]
news	noticias (f pl)	[no'tiθijas]
sensation (news)	sensación (f)	[sɛnsa'θion]
information (data)	información (f)	[informa'θion]
conclusion (decision)	conclusión (f)	[koŋklu'sion]
voice	voz (f)	[boθ]
compliment	cumplido (m)	[kump'lido]
kind (nice)	amable (adj)	[a'mable]
word	palabra (f)	[pa'ʎabra]
phrase	frase (f)	['frasɛ]
answer	respuesta (f)	[rɛspu'ɛsta]

71

| truth | verdad (f) | [bɛr'dad] |
| lie | mentira (f) | [mɛn'tira] |

thought	pensamiento (m)	[pɛnsa'mjentɔ]
idea (inspiration)	idea (f)	[i'dea]
fantasy	fantasía (f)	[fanta'sia]

66. Discussion, conversation. Part 2

respected (adj)	respetado (adj)	[rɛspɛ'tadɔ]
to respect (vt)	respetar (vt)	[rɛspɛ'tar]
respect	respeto (m)	[rɛs'pɛtɔ]
Dear ... (letter)	Estimado ...	[ɛsti'madɔ]

to introduce (present)	presentar (vt)	[prɛsɛn'tar]
intention	intención (f)	[intɛn'θⁱon]
to intend (have in mind)	tener intención de ...	[te'nɛr intɛn'θⁱon dɛ]
wish	deseo (m)	[dɛ'sɛɔ]
to wish (~ good luck)	desear (vt)	[dɛsɛ'ar]

surprise (astonishment)	sorpresa (f)	[sɔrp'rɛsa]
to surprise (amaze)	sorprender (vt)	[sɔrprɛn'dɛr]
to be surprised	sorprenderse (vr)	[sɔrprɛn'dɛrsɛ]

to give (vt)	dar (vt)	[dar]
to take (get hold of)	tomar (vt)	[tɔ'mar]
to give back	devolver (vt)	[dɛvɔʎ'vɛr]
to return (give back)	retornar (vt)	[rɛtɔr'nar]

to apologize (vi)	disculparse (vr)	[diskuʎ'parsɛ]
apology	disculpa (f)	[dis'kuʎpa]
to forgive (vt)	perdonar (vt)	[pɛrdɔ'nar]

to talk (speak)	hablar (vi)	[ab'ʎar]
to listen (vi)	escuchar (vt)	[ɛsku'ʧar]
to hear out	escuchar hasta el final	[ɛsku'ʧar 'asta ɛʎ fi'naʎ]
to understand (vt)	comprender (vt)	[kɔmprɛn'dɛr]

to show (display)	mostrar (vt)	[mɔst'rar]
to look at ...	mirar a ...	[mi'rar a]
to call (with one's voice)	llamar (vt)	[ja'mar]
to disturb (vt)	molestar (vt)	[mɔles'tar]
to pass (to hand sth)	pasar (vt)	[pa'sar]

demand (request)	petición (f)	[pɛti'θⁱon]
to request (ask)	pedir (vt)	[pɛ'dir]
demand (firm request)	exigencia (f)	[ɛksi'hɛnθija]
to demand (request firmly)	exigir (vt)	[ɛksi'hir]
to tease (nickname)	motejar (vr)	[mɔtɛ'har]
to mock (make fun of)	burlarse (vr)	[bur'ʎarsɛ]

| mockery, derision | burla (f) | ['burʎa] |
| nickname | apodo (m) | [a'podɔ] |

allusion	alusión (f)	[aly'θion]
to allude (vi)	aludir (vi)	[aly'dir]
to imply (vt)	sobrentender (vt)	['sɔbrɛːntɛn'dɛr]

description	descripción (f)	[dɛskrip'θion]
to describe (vt)	describir (vt)	[dɛskri'βɪr]
praise (compliments)	elogio (m)	[ɛ'lɔhiɔ]
to praise (vt)	elogiar (vt)	[ɛlɔ'hjar]

disappointment	decepción (f)	[dɛθæp'θion]
to disappoint (vt)	decepcionar (vt)	[dɛθæpθio'nar]
to be disappointed	estar decepcionado	[ɛs'tar dɛθæpθio'nadɔ]

supposition	suposición (f)	[supɔsi'θion]
to suppose (assume)	suponer (vt)	[supɔ'nɛr]
warning (caution)	advertencia (f)	[adwer'tɛnθija]
to warn (vt)	prevenir (vt)	[prɛvɛ'nir]

67. Discussion, conversation. Part 3

| to talk into (convince) | convencer (vt) | [kɔmbɛn'sɛr] |
| to calm down (vt) | calmar (vt) | [kaʎ'mar] |

silence (~ is golden)	silencio (m)	[si'lenθiɔ]
to keep silent	no decir nada	[nɔ dɛ'θir 'nada]
to whisper (vi, vt)	susurrar (vt)	[susur'rar]
whisper	susurro (m)	[su'surrɔ]

| frankly, sincerely (adv) | francamente (adv) | [fraŋka'mɛntɛ] |
| in my opinion ... | en mi opinión ... | [ɛn mi ɔpiɲɔn] |

detail (of the story)	detalle (m)	[dɛ'taje]
detailed (adj)	detallado (adj)	[dɛta'jadɔ]
in detail (adv)	detalladamente (adv)	[dɛtajada'mɛntɛ]
hint, clue	pista (f)	['pista]
to give a hint	dar una pista	[dar 'una 'pista]

look (glance)	mirada (f)	[mi'rada]
to have a look	echar una mirada	[ɛ'ʧar 'una mi'rada]
fixed (look)	fija (adj)	['fiha]
to blink (vi)	parpadear (vi)	[parpadɛ'ar]
to wink (vi)	guiñar un ojo	[gi'ɲjar un 'ɔhɔ]
to nod (in assent)	asentir con la cabeza	[asɛn'tirkɔn ʎa ka'βəθa]

sigh	suspiro (m)	[sus'pirɔ]
to sigh (vi)	suspirar (vi)	[suspi'rar]
to shudder (vi)	estremecerse (vr)	[ɛstrɛme'sɛrsɛ]

gesture	gesto (m)	['hɛstɔ]
to touch (one's arm, etc.)	tocar (vt)	[tɔ'kar]
to seize (by the arm)	asir (vt)	[a'sir]
to tap (on the shoulder)	palmear (vt)	[paʎme'ar]

Look out!	¡Cuidado!	[kui'dadɔ]
Really?	¿De veras?	[dɛ 'vɛras]
Good luck!	¡Suerte!	[su'ɛrtɛ]
I see!	¡Ya veo!	[ja 'βəɔ]
It's a pity!	¡Es una lástima!	[ɛs 'una 'ʎastima]

68. Agreement. Refusal

consent (agreement)	acuerdo (m)	[aku'ɛrdɔ]
to agree (say yes)	estar de acuerdo	[ɛs'tar dɛ aku'ɛrdɔ]
approval	aprobación (f)	[aprɔba'θʲon]
to approve (vt)	aprobar (vt)	[aprɔ'βar]
refusal	rechazo (m)	[rɛ'ʧaθɔ]
to refuse (vi, vt)	negarse (vr)	[nɛ'garsɛ]

Great!	¡Excelente!	[ɛksɛ'lɛntɛ]
All right!	¡De acuerdo!	[dɛ aku'ɛrdɔ]
Okay! (I agree)	¡Vale!	['bale]

forbidden (adj)	prohibido (adj)	[prɔi'βidɔ]
it's forbidden	está prohibido	[ɛs'ta prɔi'βidɔ]
it's impossible	es imposible	[ɛs impɔ'sible]
incorrect (adj)	incorrecto (adj)	[iŋkɔr'rɛktɔ]
to reject (~ a demand)	rechazar (vt)	[rɛʧa'θar]
to support (cause, idea)	apoyar (vt)	[apɔ'jar]
to accept (~ an apology)	aceptar (vt)	[asɛp'tar]

to confirm (vt)	confirmar (vt)	[kɔnfir'mar]
confirmation	confirmación (f)	[kɔnfirma'θʲon]
permission	permiso (m)	[pɛr'misɔ]
to permit (vt)	permitir (vt)	[pɛrmi'tir]
decision	decisión (f)	[dɛsi'sʲon]
to say nothing	no decir nada	[nɔ dɛ'θir 'nada]

condition (term)	condición (f)	[kɔndi'θʲon]
excuse (pretext)	excusa (f)	[ɛks'kusa]
praise (compliments)	elogio (m)	[ɛ'lɔhiɔ]
to praise (vt)	elogiar (vt)	[ɛlɔ'hjar]

69. Success. Good luck. Failure

| success | éxito (m) | ['ɛksitɔ] |
| successfully (adv) | con éxito (adv) | [kɔn 'ɛksitɔ] |

successful (adj)	exitoso (adj)	[ɛksi'tɔsɔ]
good luck	suerte (f)	[su'ɛrtɛ]
Good luck!	¡Suerte!	[su'ɛrtɛ]
lucky (e.g., ~ day)	de suerte (adj)	[dɛ su'ɛrtɛ]
lucky (fortunate)	afortunado (adj)	[afɔrtu'nadɔ]
failure	fiasco (m)	[fi'askɔ]
misfortune	infortunio (m)	[infɔr'tuniɔ]
bad luck	mala suerte (f)	['maʎa su'ɛrtɛ]
unsuccessful (adj)	fracasado (adj)	[fraka'sadɔ]
catastrophe	catástrofe (f)	[ka'tastrɔfɛ]
pride	orgullo (m)	[ɔr'gujo]
proud (adj)	orgulloso (adj)	[ɔrgu'jɔsɔ]
to be proud	estar orgulloso	[ɛs'tar ɔrgu'jɔsɔ]
winner	ganador (m)	[gaɲia'dɔr]
to win (vi)	ganar (vi)	[ga'ɲar]
to lose (not win)	perder (vi)	[pɛr'dɛr]
try	tentativa (f)	[tɛnta'tiβa]
to try (vi)	intentar (vt)	[intɛn'tar]
chance (opportunity)	chance (f)	['ʧanθæ]

70. Quarrels. Negative emotions

shout (scream)	grito (m)	['gritɔ]
to shout (vi)	gritar (vi)	[gri'tar]
to start to cry out	comenzar a gritar	[kɔmen'θar a gri'tar]
quarrel	riña (f)	['riɲja]
to quarrel (vi)	reñir (vi)	[rɛ'ɲiɪr]
fight (scandal)	escándalo (m)	[ɛs'kandalɔ]
to have a fight	causar escándalo	[kau'sar ɛs'kandalɔ]
conflict	conflicto (m)	[kɔnf'liktɔ]
misunderstanding	malentendido (m)	[malentɛn'didɔ]
insult	insulto (m)	[in'suʎtɔ]
to insult (vt)	insultar (vt)	[insuʎ'tar]
insulted (adj)	insultado (adj)	[insuʎ'tadɔ]
resentment	ofensa (f)	[ɔ'fɛnsa]
to offend (vt)	ofender (vt)	[ɔfɛn'dɛr]
to take offense	ofenderse (vr)	[ɔfɛn'dɛrsɛ]
indignation	indignación (f)	[indigna'θiɔn]
to be indignant	indignarse (vr)	[indig'narsɛ]
complaint	queja (f)	['kɛha]
to complain (vi, vt)	quejarse (vr)	[kɛ'harsɛ]
apology	disculpa (f)	[dis'kuʎpa]
to apologize (vi)	disculparse (vr)	[diskuʎ'parsɛ]

to beg pardon	**pedir perdón**	[pɛ'dir pɛr'dɔn]
criticism	**crítica** (f)	['kritika]
to criticize (vt)	**criticar** (vt)	[kriti'kar]
accusation	**acusación** (f)	[akusa'θ'on]
to accuse (vt)	**acusar** (vt)	[aku'sar]
revenge	**venganza** (f)	[bɛ'ŋanθa]
to revenge (vt)	**vengar** (vt)	[bɛ'ŋar]
to pay back	**pagar** (vt)	[pa'gar]
disdain	**desprecio** (m)	[dɛsp'rɛθiɔ]
to despise (vt)	**despreciar** (vt)	[dɛsprɛ'θjar]
hatred, hate	**odio** (m)	['ɔdiɔ]
to hate (vt)	**odiar** (vt)	[ɔ'djar]
nervous (adj)	**nervioso** (adj)	[nɛr'v'ɔsɔ]
to be nervous	**estar nervioso**	[ɛs'tar nɛr'v'ɔsɔ]
angry (mad)	**enfadado** (adj)	[ɛnfa'dadɔ]
to make angry	**enfadar** (vt)	[ɛnfa'dar]
humiliation	**humillación** (f)	[umiʎja'θ'on]
to humiliate (vt)	**humillar** (vt)	[umi'ʎjar]
to humiliate oneself	**humillarse** (vr)	[umi'ʎjarsɛ]
shock	**choque** (m)	['ʧɔkɛ]
to shock (vt)	**chocar** (vi)	[ʧɔ'kar]
trouble (annoyance)	**molestia** (f)	[mɔ'lestija]
unpleasant (adj)	**desagradable** (adj)	[dɛsagra'dable]
fear (dread)	**miedo** (m)	['mjedɔ]
terrible (storm, heat)	**terrible** (adj)	[tɛr'rible]
scary (e.g., ~ story)	**de miedo** (adj)	[dɛ 'mjedɔ]
horror	**horror** (m)	[ɔr'rɔr]
awful (crime, news)	**horrible** (adj)	[ɔr'rible]
to begin to tremble	**empezar a temblar**	[ɛmpɛ'θar a tɛmb'ʎar]
to cry (weep)	**llorar** (vi)	[jo'rar]
to start crying	**comenzar a llorar**	[kɔmen'θar a jo'rar]
tear	**lágrima** (f)	['ʎagrima]
fault	**culpa** (f)	['kuʎpa]
guilt (feeling)	**remordimiento** (m)	[rɛmɔrdi'mjentɔ]
dishonor (disgrace)	**deshonra** (f)	[dɛ'sɔnra]
protest	**protesta** (f)	[prɔ'tɛsta]
stress	**estrés** (m)	[ɛst'rɛs]
to disturb (vt)	**molestar** (vt)	[mɔles'tar]
to be furious	**estar furioso**	[ɛs'tar fu'r'ɔθɔ]
mad, angry (adj)	**enfadado** (adj)	[ɛnfa'dadɔ]
to end (~ a relationship)	**terminar** (vt)	[tɛrmi'nar]
to swear (at sb)	**regañar** (vt)	[rɛga'ɲjar]

to be scared	**asustarse** (vr)	[asus'tarsɛ]
to hit (strike with hand)	**golpear** (vt)	[gɔʎpɛ'ar]
to fight (vi)	**pelear** (vi)	[pele'ar]
to settle (a conflict)	**regular** (vt)	[rɛgu'ʎar]
discontented (adj)	**descontento** (adj)	[dɛskɔn'tɛntɔ]
furious (adj)	**furioso** (adj)	[fu'rɔsɔ]
It's not good!	**¡No está bien!**	[nɔ ɛs'ta 'bjen]
It's bad!	**¡Está mal!**	[ɛs'ta 'maʎ]

Medicine

71. Diseases

sickness	enfermedad (f)	[ɛnfɛrmɛ'dad]
to be sick	estar enfermo	[ɛs'tar ɛn'fɛrmɔ]
health	salud (f)	[sa'lyd]
runny nose (coryza)	resfriado (m)	[rɛsfri'adɔ]
angina	angina (f)	[an'hina]
cold (illness)	resfriado (m)	[rɛsfri'adɔ]
to catch a cold	resfriarse (vr)	[rɛsfri'arsɛ]
bronchitis	bronquitis (f)	[brɔ'ŋkitis]
pneumonia	pulmonía (f)	[puʎmɔ'nia]
flu, influenza	gripe (f)	['gripɛ]
near-sighted (adj)	miope (adj)	[mi'ɔpɛ]
far-sighted (adj)	présbita (adj)	['prɛsbita]
strabismus (crossed eyes)	estrabismo (m)	[ɛstra'βismɔ]
cross-eyed (adj)	estrábico (m) (adj)	[ɛst'raβikɔ]
cataract	catarata (f)	[kata'rata]
glaucoma	glaucoma (f)	[gʎau'kɔma]
stroke	insulto (m)	[in'suʎtɔ]
heart attack	ataque (m) cardiaco	[a'take kardi'jakɔ]
myocardial infarction	infarto (m) de miocardio	[in'fartɔ dɛ miɔ'kardiɔ]
paralysis	parálisis (f)	[pa'ralisis]
to paralyze (vt)	paralizar (vt)	[parali'θar]
allergy	alergia (f)	[a'lerhija]
asthma	asma (f)	['asma]
diabetes	diabetes (m)	[dia'βətɛs]
toothache	dolor (m) de muelas	[dɔ'lɔr dɛ mu'ɛlas]
caries	caries (f)	['kariɛs]
diarrhea	diarrea (f)	[di'arrɛa]
constipation	estreñimiento (m)	[ɛstrɛnʲi'mjentɔ]
stomach upset	molestia (f) estomacal	[mɔ'lestija stɔma'kaʎ]
food poisoning	envenenamiento (m)	[ɛmbɛnɛna'mjentɔ]
to have a food poisoning	envenenarse (vr)	[ɛmbɛnɛ'narsɛ]
arthritis	artritis (f)	[art'ritis]
rickets	raquitismo (m)	[raki'tismɔ]
rheumatism	reumatismo (m)	[rɛuma'tismɔ]

atherosclerosis	ateroesclerosis (f)	[atɛroskle'rɔsis]
gastritis	gastritis (f)	[gast'ritis]
appendicitis	apendicitis (f)	[apɛndi'sitis]
cholecystitis	colecistitis (m)	[kɔlesis'titis]
ulcer	úlcera (f)	['uʌsɛra]

measles	sarampión (m)	[saram'pʲɔn]
German measles	rubeola (f)	[rube'ɔla]
jaundice	ictericia (f)	[iktɛ'risija]
hepatitis	hepatitis (f)	[ɛpa'titis]

schizophrenia	esquizofrenia (f)	[ɛskiθofrɛ'nia]
rabies (hydrophobia)	rabia (f)	['rabja]
neurosis	neurosis (f)	[nɛu'rɔsis]
concussion	conmoción (m) cerebral	[kɔnmɔ'θʲon θærɛb'raʌ]

| cancer | cáncer (m) | ['kanθær] |
| sclerosis | esclerosis (f) | [ɛskle'rɔsis] |

alcoholism	alcoholismo (m)	[aʌkɔ:'lismɔ]
alcoholic (n)	alcohólico (m)	[aʌkɔ'ɔlikɔ]
syphilis	sífilis (f)	['sifilis]
AIDS	SIDA (f)	['sida]

tumor	tumor (m)	[tu'mɔr]
fever	fiebre (f)	['fjebrɛ]
malaria	malaria (f)	[ma'ʌarija]
gangrene	gangrena (f)	[gaŋ'rɛna]
seasickness	mareo (m)	[ma'rɛɔ]
epilepsy	epilepsia (f)	[ɛpi'lɛpsija]

epidemic	epidemia (f)	[ɛpi'dɛmija]
typhus	tifus (m)	['tifus]
tuberculosis	tuberculosis (f)	[tubɛrku'lɔsis]
cholera	cólera (f)	['kɔlera]
plague (bubonic ~)	peste (f)	['pɛstɛ]

72. Symptoms. Treatments. Part 1

symptom	síntoma (m)	['sintɔma]
temperature	temperatura (f)	[tɛmpɛra'tura]
high temperature	fiebre (f)	['fjebrɛ]
pulse	pulso (m)	['puʌsɔ]

giddiness	mareo (m)	[ma'rɛɔ]
hot (adj)	caliente (adj)	[ka'ʌjentɛ]
shivering	escalofrío (m)	[ɛskalof'riɔ]
pale (e.g., ~ face)	pálido (adj)	['palidɔ]
cough	tos (f)	[tɔs]
to cough (vi)	toser (vi)	[tɔ'sɛr]

to sneeze (vi)	estornudar (vi)	[ɛstɔrnu'dar]
faint	desmayo (m)	[dɛs'majo]
to faint (vi)	desmayarse (vr)	[dɛsma'jarsɛ]

bruise (hématome)	moradura (f)	[mɔra'dura]
bump (lump)	chichón (m)	[tʃi'tʃon]
to bruise oneself	golpearse (vr)	[gɔʎpɛ'arsɛ]
bruise (contusion)	magulladura (f)	[maguja'dura]
to get bruised	magullarse (vr)	[magu'jarsɛ]

to limp (vi)	cojear (vi)	[kɔhɛ'ar]
dislocation	dislocación (f)	[dislɔka'θⁱon]
to dislocate (vt)	dislocar (vt)	[dislɔ'kar]
fracture	fractura (f)	[frak'tura]
to have a fracture	tener una fractura	[tɛ'nɛr 'una frak'tura]

cut (e.g., paper ~)	corte (m)	['kɔrtɛ]
to cut oneself	cortarse (vr)	[kɔr'tarsɛ]
bleeding	hemorragia (f)	[ɛmɔr'rahia]

| burn (injury) | quemadura (f) | [kema'dura] |
| to scald oneself | quemarse (vr) | [ke'marsɛ] |

to prick (vt)	pincharse (vr)	[pin'tʃarsɛ]
to prick oneself	pincharse (vr)	[pin'tʃarsɛ]
to injure (vt)	herir (vt)	[ɛ'rir]
injury	herida (f)	[ɛ'rida]
wound	lesión (f)	[le'sⁱon]
trauma	trauma (m)	['trauma]

to be delirious	delirar (vi)	[dɛli'rar]
to stutter (vi)	tartamudear (vi)	[tartamudɛ'ar]
sunstroke	insolación (f)	[insɔʎa'θⁱon]

73. Symptoms. Treatments. Part 2

| pain | dolor (m) | [dɔ'lɜr] |
| splinter (in foot, etc.) | astilla (f) | [as'tija] |

sweat (perspiration)	sudor (m)	[su'dɔr]
to sweat (perspire)	sudar (vi)	[su'dar]
vomiting	vómito (m)	['bɔmito]
convulsions	convulsiones (f)	[kɔnvuʎ'sⁱɔnɛs]

pregnant (adj)	embarazada (adj)	[ɛmbara'θada]
to be born	nacer (vi)	[na'θær]
delivery, labor	parto (m)	['partɔ]
to deliver (~ a baby)	dar a luz	[dar a 'luθ]
abortion	aborto (m)	[a'βɔrtɔ]
breathing, respiration	respiración (f)	[rɛspira'θⁱon]

inhalation	inspiración (f)	[inspira'θⁱon]
exhalation	espiración (f)	[εspira'θⁱon]
to exhale (vi)	espirar (vi)	[εspi'rar]
to inhale (vi)	inspirar (vi)	[inspi'rar]
disabled person	inválido (m)	[in'validɔ]
cripple	mutilado (m)	[muti'ʎadɔ]
drug addict	drogadicto (m)	[drɔga'diktɔ]
deaf (adj)	sordo (adj)	['sɔrdɔ]
dumb, mute	mudo (adj)	['mudɔ]
deaf-and-dumb (adj)	sordomudo (adj)	[sɔrdɔ'mudɔ]
mad, insane (adj)	loco (adj)	['lɔkɔ]
madman	loco (m)	['lɔkɔ]
madwoman	loca (f)	['lɔka]
to go insane	volverse loco	[bɔʎ'vεrsε 'lɔkɔ]
gene	gen (m)	[hεn]
immunity	inmunidad (f)	[inmuni'dad]
hereditary (adj)	hereditario (adj)	[εrεdi'tariɔ]
congenital (adj)	de nacimiento (adj)	[dε nasi'mjentɔ]
virus	virus (m)	['wirus]
microbe	microbio (m)	[mik'rɔβiɔ]
bacterium	bacteria (f)	[bak'tεrija]
infection	infección (f)	[infεk'θⁱon]

74. Symptoms. Treatments. Part 3

hospital	hospital (m)	[ɔspi'taʎ]
patient	paciente (m)	[pa'θjentε]
diagnosis	diagnosis (f)	[diag'nɔsis]
cure	cura (f)	['kura]
medical treatment	tratamiento (m)	[trata'mjentɔ]
to get treatment	curarse (vr)	[ku'rarsε]
to treat (vt)	tratar (vt)	[tra'tar]
to nurse (look after)	cuidar (vt)	[kui'dar]
care (nursing ~)	cuidados (m pl)	[kui'dadɔs]
operation, surgery	operación (f)	[ɔpεra'θⁱon]
to bandage (head, limb)	vendar (vt)	[bεn'dar]
bandaging	vendaje (m)	[bεn'dahε]
vaccination	vacunación (f)	[bakuna'θⁱon]
to vaccinate (vt)	vacunar (vt)	[baku'nar]
injection, shot	inyección (f)	[inʰek'θⁱon]
to give an injection	aplicar una inyección	[apli'kar 'una inʰek's'ɔn]
amputation	amputación (f)	[amputa'θⁱon]

to amputate (vt)	amputar (vt)	[ampu'tar]
coma	coma (m)	['kɔma]
to be in a coma	estar en coma	[ɛs'tar ɛn 'kɔma]
intensive care	revitalización (f)	[rɛwitaliθa'sʲɔn]

to recover (~ from flu)	recuperarse (vr)	[rɛkupe'rarsɛ]
state (patient's ~)	estado (m)	[ɛs'tadɔ]
consciousness	consciencia (f)	[kɔn'θjenθija]
memory (faculty)	memoria (f)	[mɛ'mɔrija]

to extract (tooth)	extraer (vt)	[ɛkstra'ɛr]
filling	empaste (m)	[ɛm'pastɛ]
to fill (a tooth)	empastar (vt)	[ɛmpas'tar]

| hypnosis | hipnosis (f) | [ip'nɔsis] |
| to hypnotize (vt) | hipnotizar (vt) | [ipnɔti'θar] |

75. Doctors

doctor	médico (m)	['mɛdikɔ]
nurse	enfermera (f)	[ɛnfɛr'mɛra]
private physician	médico (m) personal	['mɛdikɔ pɛrsɔ'naʎ]

dentist	dentista (m)	[dɛn'tista]
ophthalmologist	oftalmólogo (m)	[ɔftaʎ'mɔlɔgɔ]
internist	internista (m)	[intɛr'nista]
surgeon	cirujano (m)	[θiru'hanɔ]

psychiatrist	psiquiatra (m)	[siki'atra]
pediatrician	pediatra (m)	[pɛdi'atra]
psychologist	psicólogo (m)	[si'kɔlɔgɔ]
gynecologist	ginecólogo (m)	[hinɛ'kɔlɔgɔ]
cardiologist	cardiólogo (m)	[kardi'ɔlɔgɔ]

76. Medicine. Drugs. Accessories

medicine, drug	medicamento (m), droga (f)	[mɛdika'mɛntɔ, d'rɔga]
remedy	remedio (m)	[rɛ'mɛdiɔ]
to prescribe (vt)	prescribir	[prɛskri'βir]
prescription	receta (f)	[rɛ'θæta]

tablet, pill	tableta (f)	[tab'leta]
ointment	ungüento (m)	[uɲu'entɔ]
ampule	ampolla (f)	[am'pɔja]
mixture	mixtura (f), mezcla (f)	[miks'tura], ['mɛθkla]
syrup	sirope (m)	[si'rɔpɛ]
pill	píldora (f)	['piʎdɔra]

powder	polvo (m)	['poʎvɔ]
bandage	venda (f)	['bɛnda]
cotton wool	algodón (m)	[aʎgɔ'dɔn]
iodine	yodo (m)	['jodɔ]

Band-Aid	tirita (f), curita (f)	[ti'rita], [ku'rita]
eyedropper	pipeta (f)	[pi'pɛta]
thermometer	termómetro (m)	[tɛr'mɔmɛtrɔ]
syringe	jeringa (f)	[hɛ'riŋa]

wheelchair	silla (f) de ruedas	['siʎja dɛ ru'ɛdas]
crutches	muletas (f pl)	[mu'lɛtas]

painkiller	anestésico (m)	[anɛs'tɛsikɔ]
laxative	purgante (m)	[pur'gantɛ]
spirit (ethanol)	alcohol (m)	[aʎkɔ'ɔʎ]
medicinal herbs	hierba (f) medicinal	['jerba mediθi'naʎ]
herbal (~ tea)	de hierbas (adj)	[dɛ 'jerbas]

77. Smoking. Tobacco products

tobacco	tabaco (m)	[ta'βakɔ]
cigarette	cigarrillo (m)	[θigar'rijɔ]
cigar	cigarro (m)	[θi'garrɔ]
pipe	pipa (f)	['pipa]
pack (of cigarettes)	paquete (m)	[pa'ketɛ]

matches	cerillas (f pl)	[θæ'rijas]
matchbox	caja (f) de cerillas	['kaha dɛ sɛ'riʎjas]
lighter	encendedor (m)	[ɛnθændɛ'dɔr]
ashtray	cenicero (m)	[θæni'θærɔ]
cigarette case	pitillera (f)	[piti'jera]

cigarette holder	boquilla (f)	[bɔ'kija]
filter (cigarette tip)	filtro (m)	['fiʎtrɔ]

to smoke (vi, vt)	fumar (vi, vt)	[fu'mar]
to light a cigarette	encender un cigarrillo	[ɛnθæn'dɛr un sigar'rijɔ]
smoker	fumador (m)	[fuma'dɔr]

stub, butt (of cigarette)	colilla (f)	[kɔ'lija]
smoke, fumes	humo (m)	['umɔ]
ash	ceniza (f)	[sɛ'niθa]

HUMAN HABITAT

City

78. City. Life in the city

city, town	**ciudad** (f)	[θju'dad]
capital city	**capital** (f)	[kapi'taʎ]
village	**aldea** (f)	[aʎ'dɛa]
city map	**plano** (m) **de la ciudad**	['pʎanɔ dɛ ʎa θju'dad]
downtown	**centro** (m) **de la ciudad**	['θæntrɔ dɛ ʎa sju'dad]
suburb	**suburbio** (m)	[su'βurbiɔ]
suburban (adj)	**suburbano** (adj)	[subur'banɔ]
outskirts	**arrabal** (m)	[arra'βaʎ]
environs (suburbs)	**afueras** (f pl)	[afu'ɛras]
city block	**barrio** (m)	['barriɔ]
residential block	**zona** (f) **de viviendas**	['θɔna dɛ bi'bjendas]
traffic	**tráfico** (m)	['trafikɔ]
traffic lights	**semáforo** (m)	[sɛ'mafɔrɔ]
public transportation	**transporte** (m) **urbano**	[trans'pɔrtɛ ur'banɔ]
intersection	**cruce** (m)	['kruθæ]
crosswalk	**paso** (m) **de peatones**	['pasɔ dɛ pea'tɔnɛs]
pedestrian underpass	**paso** (m) **subterráneo**	['pasɔ subtɛr'ranɛɔ]
to cross (vt)	**cruzar** (vt)	[kru'θar]
pedestrian	**peatón** (m)	[pɛa'tɔn]
sidewalk	**acera** (f)	[a'θæra]
bridge	**puente** (m)	[pu'ɛntɛ]
bank (riverbank)	**muelle** (m)	[mu'ɛje]
allée	**alameda** (f)	[aʎa'mɛda]
park	**parque** (m)	['parke]
boulevard	**bulevar** (m)	[bule'βar]
square	**plaza** (f)	['pʎaθa]
avenue (wide street)	**avenida** (f)	[avɛ'nida]
street	**calle** (f)	['kaje]
side street	**callejón** (m)	[kaje'hɔn]
dead end	**callejón** (m) **sin salida**	[kajə'hɔn sin sa'lida]
house	**casa** (f)	['kasa]
building	**edificio** (m)	[ɛdi'fiθiɔ]

skyscraper	rascacielos (m)	[raska'θjelɔs]
facade	fachada (f)	[fa'tʃada]
roof	techo (m)	['tetʃɔ]
window	ventana (f)	[bɛn'tana]
arch	arco (m)	['arkɔ]
column	columna (f)	[kɔ'lumna]
corner	esquina (f)	[ɛs'kina]
store window	escaparate (f)	[ɛskapa'ratɛ]
store sign	letrero (m)	[let'rɛrɔ]
poster	cartel (m)	[kar'tɛʎ]
advertising poster	cartel (m) publicitario	[kar'tɛʎ publisi'tariɔ]
billboard	valla (f) publicitaria	['vaja publis'tarija]
garbage, trash	basura (f)	[ba'sura]
garbage can	cajón (m) de basura	[ka'hɔn dɛ ba'sura]
to litter (vi)	tirar basura	[ti'rar ba'sura]
garbage dump	basurero (m)	[basu'rɛrɔ]
phone booth	cabina (f) telefónica	[ka'βina tɛle'fonika]
lamppost	farola (f)	[fa'rɔʎa]
bench (park ~)	banco (m)	['baŋkɔ]
police officer	policía (m)	[pɔli'θija]
police	policía (f)	[pɔli'θija]
beggar	mendigo (m)	[mɛn'digɔ]
homeless, bum	persona (f) sin hogar	[pɛr'sɔna sin ɔ'gar]

79. Urban institutions

store	tienda (f)	['tˈenda]
drugstore, pharmacy	farmacia (f)	[far'maθia]
optical store	óptica (f)	['ɔptika]
shopping mall	centro (m) comercial	['θæntrɔ kɔmɛr'θjaʎ]
supermarket	supermercado (m)	[supɛrmɛr'kadɔ]
bakery	panadería (f)	[panadɛ'rija]
baker	panadero (m)	[pana'dɛrɔ]
candy store	pastelería (f)	[pastɛle'rija]
grocery store	tienda (f) de comestibles	['tˈenda dɛ kɔmes'tibles]
butcher shop	carnicería (f)	[karniθæ'rija]
produce store	verdulería (f)	[bɛrdule'rija]
market	mercado (m)	[mɛr'kadɔ]
coffee house	cafetería (f)	[kafetɛ'rija]
restaurant	restaurante (m)	[rɛstau'rantɛ]
pub	cervecería (f)	[θærvɛθæ'rija]
pizzeria	pizzería (f)	[pisθæ'rija]
hair salon	peluquería (f)	[pɛluke'rija]

post office	oficina (f) de correos	[ɔfi'θina dɛ kɔr'rɛɔs]
dry cleaners	tintorería (f)	[tintɔrɛ'rija]
photo studio	estudio (m) fotográfico	[ɛs'tudiɔ fotɔg'rafikɔ]

shoe store	zapatería (f)	[θapatɛ'rija]
bookstore	librería (f)	[librɛ'rija]
sporting goods store	tienda (f) deportiva	['tʲenda dɛpɔr'tiβa]

clothes repair	arreglos (m pl) de ropa	[ar'rɛglɔs dɛ 'rɔpa]
formal wear rental	alquiler (m) de ropa	[aʎki'ler dɛ 'rɔpa]
movie rental store	videoclub (m)	[wideɔk'lub]

circus	circo (m)	['θirkɔ]
zoo	zoo (m)	['θɔː]
movie theater	cine (m)	['θinɛ]
museum	museo (m)	[mu'sɛɔ]
library	biblioteca (f)	[bibliɔ'tɛka]

| theater | teatro (m) | [tɛ'atrɔ] |
| opera | ópera (f) | ['ɔpɛra] |

| nightclub | club (m) nocturno | [klub nɔk'turnɔ] |
| casino | casino (m) | [ka'sinɔ] |

mosque	mezquita (f)	[mɛθ'kita]
synagogue	sinagoga (f)	[sina'gɔga]
cathedral	catedral (f)	[katɛd'raʎ]

| temple | templo (m) | ['tɛmplɔ] |
| church | iglesia (f) | [ig'lesija] |

college	instituto (m)	[insti'tutɔ]
university	universidad (f)	[univɛrsi'dad]
school	escuela (f)	[ɛsku'ɛʎa]

| prefecture | prefectura (f) | [prɛfɛk'tura] |
| city hall | alcaldía (f) | [aʎkaʎ'dija] |

| hotel | hotel (m) | [ɔ'tɛʎ] |
| bank | banco (m) | ['baŋkɔ] |

| embassy | embajada (f) | [ɛmba'hada] |
| travel agency | agencia (f) de viajes | [a'hɛnθija dɛ 'bjahɛs] |

| information office | oficina (f) de información | [ɔfi'θina dɛ infɔrma'sʲɔn] |
| money exchange | oficina (f) de cambio | [ɔfi'θina dɛ 'kambiɔ] |

| subway | metro (m) | ['mɛtrɔ] |
| hospital | hospital (m) | [ɔspi'taʎ] |

| gas station | gasolinera (f) | [gasɔli'nɛra] |
| parking lot | aparcamiento (m) | [aparka'mjentɔ] |

80. Signs

store sign	letrero (m)	[let'rɛro]
notice (written text)	cartel (m)	[kar'tɛʎ]
poster	pancarta (f)	[pa'ŋkarta]
direction sign	signo (m) de dirección	['signo dɛ dirɛk'θⁱon]
arrow (sign)	flecha (f)	['fletʃa]
caution	advertencia (f)	[adwer'tɛnθija]
warning sign	aviso (m)	[a'βɪsɔ]
to warn (vt)	advertir (vt)	[advɛr'tir]
day off	día (m) de descanso	['dia dɛ dɛs'kansɔ]
timetable (schedule)	horario (m)	[ɔ'rarɪo]
opening hours	horario (m) de apertura	[ɔ'rarɪo dɛ aper'tura]
WELCOME!	¡BIENVENIDOS!	[bjenbe'nidɔs]
ENTRANCE	ENTRADA	[ɛnt'rada]
EXIT	SALIDA	[sa'lida]
PUSH	EMPUJAR	[ɛmpu'har]
PULL	TIRAR	[ti'rar]
OPEN	ABIERTO	[a'bjertɔ]
CLOSED	CERRADO	[θær'radɔ]
WOMEN	MUJERES	[mu'hɛrɛs]
MEN	HOMBRES	['ombrɛs]
DISCOUNTS	REBAJAS	[rɛ'bahas]
SALE	SALDOS	['saʎdɔs]
NEW!	NOVEDAD	[novɛ'dad]
FREE	GRATIS	['gratis]
ATTENTION!	¡ATENCIÓN!	[atɛn'θⁱon]
NO VACANCIES	COMPLETO	[kɔmp'letɔ]
RESERVED	RESERVADO	[rɛsɛr'vadɔ]
ADMINISTRATION	ADMINISTRACIÓN	[administra'θⁱon]
STAFF ONLY	SÓLO PERSONAL AUTORIZADO	['sɔlɔ pɛrsɔ'naʎ autori'ðadɔ]
BEWARE OF THE DOG!	CUIDADO CON EL PERRO	[kui'dadɔ kɔn ɛʎ 'pɛrrɔ]
NO SMOKING	PROHIBIDO FUMAR	[prɔi'βidɔ fu'mar]
DO NOT TOUCH!	NO TOCAR	[nɔ tɔ'kar]
DANGEROUS	PELIGROSO	[pɛlig'rɔsɔ]
DANGER	PELIGRO	[pɛ'ligrɔ]
HIGH TENSION	ALTA TENSIÓN	['aʎta tɛn's'on]
NO SWIMMING!	PROHIBIDO BAÑARSE	[prɔi'βidɔ ba'ɲarsɛ]
OUT OF ORDER	NO FUNCIONA	[nɔ fun'θⁱona]

FLAMMABLE	INFLAMABLE	[infʎaˈmable]
FORBIDDEN	PROHIBIDO	[prɔiˈβido]
NO TRESPASSING!	PROHIBIDO EL PASO	[prɔiˈβido εʎ ˈpaθɔ]
WET PAINT	RECIÉN PINTADO	[reˈθjen pinˈtadɔ]

81. Urban transportation

bus	autobús (m)	[autɔˈβus]
streetcar	tranvía (m)	[tramˈbija]
trolley	trolebús (m)	[trɔleˈβus]
route (of bus)	itinerario (m)	[itinεˈrariɔ]
number (e.g., bus ~)	número (m)	[ˈnumεrɔ]

to go by ...	ir en ...	[ir εn]
to get on (~ the bus)	tomar (vt)	[tɔˈmar]
to get off ...	bajar del ...	[baˈhar dεʎ]

stop (e.g., bus ~)	parada (f)	[paˈrada]
next stop	próxima parada (f)	[ˈprɔksima paˈrada]
terminus	parada (f) final	[paˈrada fiˈnaʎ]
schedule	horario (m)	[ɔˈrariɔ]
to wait (vt)	esperar (vt)	[εspεˈrar]

| ticket | billete (m) | [biˈjetε] |
| fare | precio (m) del billete | [ˈprεθiɔ dεʎ biˈjetε] |

cashier (ticket seller)	cajero (m)	[kaˈhεrɔ]
ticket inspection	control (m) de billetes	[kɔntˈrɔʎ dε biˈjetεs]
conductor	cobrador (m)	[kɔbraˈdɔr]

to be late (for ...)	llegar tarde (vi)	[jeˈgar ˈtardε]
to miss (~ the train, etc.)	perder (vt)	[pεrˈdεr]
to be in a hurry	tener prisa	[tεˈnεr ˈprisa]

taxi, cab	taxi (m)	[ˈtaksi]
taxi driver	taxista (m)	[takˈsista]
by taxi	en taxi	[εn ˈtaksi]
taxi stand	parada (f) de taxis	[paˈrada dε ˈtaksis]
to call a taxi	llamar un taxi	[jaˈmar un ˈtaksi]
to take a taxi	tomar un taxi	[tɔˈmar un ˈtaksi]

traffic	tráfico (m)	[ˈtrafikɔ]
traffic jam	atasco (m)	[aˈtaskɔ]
rush hour	horas (f pl) de punta	[ˈɔras dε ˈpunta]
to park (vi)	aparcar (vi)	[aparˈkar]
to park (vt)	aparcar (vt)	[aparˈkar]
parking lot	aparcamiento (m)	[aparkaˈmjentɔ]

| subway | metro (m) | [ˈmεtrɔ] |
| station | estación (f) | [εstaˈθ|on] |

to take the subway	ir en el metro	[ir ɛn ɛʎ 'mɛtrɔ]
train	tren (m)	[trɛn]
train station	estación (f)	[ɛsta'θ^jon]

82. Sightseeing

monument	monumento (m)	[mɔnu'mɛntɔ]
fortress	fortaleza (f)	[fɔrta'leθa]
palace	palacio (m)	[pa'ʎaθiɔ]
castle	castillo (m)	[kas'tijo]
tower	torre (f)	['tɔrrɛ]
mausoleum	mausoleo (m)	[mausɔ'leɔ]

architecture	arquitectura (f)	[arkitɛk'tura]
medieval (adj)	medieval (adj)	[mɛdiɛ'vaʎ]
ancient (adj)	antiguo (adj)	[an'tiguɔ]
national (adj)	nacional (adj)	[naθ^jo'naʎ]
well-known (adj)	conocido (adj)	[kɔnɔ'θidɔ]

tourist	turista (m)	[tu'rista]
guide (person)	guía (m)	['gija]
excursion, guided tour	excursión (f)	[ɛskur'θ^jon]
to show (vt)	mostrar (vt)	[mɔst'rar]
to tell (vt)	contar (vt)	[kɔn'tar]

to find (vt)	encontrar (vt)	[ɛŋkɔnt'rar]
to get lost (lose one's way)	perderse (vr)	[pɛr'dɛrsɛ]
map (e.g., subway ~)	plano (m), mapa (m)	['pʎanɔ], ['mapa]
map (e.g., city ~)	mapa (m)	['mapa]

souvenir, gift	recuerdo (m)	[rɛku'ɛrdɔ]
gift shop	tienda (f) de regalos	['t^jenda dɛ rɛ'galɔs]
to take pictures	hacer fotos	[a'θær 'fotɔs]
to be photographed	fotografiarse (vr)	[fotogra'fjarsɛ]

83. Shopping

to buy (purchase)	comprar (vt)	[kɔmp'rar]
purchase	compra (f)	['kɔmpra]
to go shopping	hacer compras	[a'θær 'kɔmpras]
shopping	compras (f pl)	['kɔmpras]

| to be open (ab. store) | estar abierto | [ɛs'tar a'bjertɔ] |
| to be closed | estar cerrado | [ɛs'tar sɛr'radɔ] |

footwear	calzado (m)	[kaʎ'θadɔ]
clothes, clothing	ropa (f), vestido (m)	['rɔpa], [vɛs'tidɔ]
cosmetics	cosméticos (m pl)	[kɔs'mɛtikɔs]

| food products | productos alimenticios | [prɔ'duktɔs alimen'tiθiɔs] |
| gift, present | regalo (m) | [rɛ'galɜ] |

| salesman | vendedor (m) | [bɛndɛ'dɔr] |
| saleswoman | vendedora (f) | [bɛndɛ'dɔra] |

check out, cash desk	caja (f)	['kaha]
mirror	espejo (m)	[ɛs'pɛhɔ]
counter (in shop)	mostrador (m)	[mɔstra'dɔr]
fitting room	probador (m)	[prɔba'dɔr]

to try on	probar (vt)	[prɔ'βar]
to fit (ab. dress, etc.)	quedar (vi)	[ke'dar]
to like (I like ...)	gustar (vi)	[gus'tar]

price	precio (m)	['prɛθiɔ]
price tag	etiqueta (f) de precio	[ɛti'keta dɛ 'prɛθiɔ]
to cost (vt)	costar (vt)	[kɔs'tar]
How much?	¿cuánto?	[ku'antɔ]
discount	descuento (m)	[desku'ɛntɔ]

inexpensive (adj)	no costoso (adj)	[nɔ kɔs'tɔsɔ]
cheap (adj)	barato (adj)	[ba'ratɔ]
expensive (adj)	caro (adj)	['karɔ]
It's expensive	Es caro	[ɛs 'karɔ]

rental (n)	alquiler (m)	[aʎki'ler]
to rent (~ a tuxedo)	alquilar (vt)	[aʎki'ʎar]
credit	crédito (m)	['krɛditɔ]
on credit (adv)	a crédito (adv)	[a 'krɛditɔ]

84. Money

money	dinero (m)	[di'nɛrɔ]
currency exchange	cambio (m)	['kambiɔ]
exchange rate	curso (m)	['kursɔ]
ATM	cajero (m) automático	[ka'hɛrɔ autɔ'matikɔ]
coin	moneda (f)	[mɔ'nɛda]

| dollar | dólar (m) | ['dɔʎar] |
| euro | euro (m) | ['ɛurɔ] |

lira	lira (f)	['lira]
Deutschmark	marco (m) alemán	['markɔ ale'man]
franc	franco (m)	['fraŋkɔ]
pound sterling	libra esterlina (f)	['libra ɛster'lina]
yen	yen (m)	[jen]

| debt | deuda (f) | ['dɛuda] |
| debtor | deudor (m) | [dɛu'dɔr] |

to lend (money)	**prestar** (vt)	[prɛs'tar]
to borrow (vi, vt)	**tomar prestado**	[to'mar a pres'tado]
bank	**banco** (m)	['baŋko]
account	**cuenta** (f)	[ku'ɛnta]
to deposit into the account	**ingresar en la cuenta**	[iŋre'sar ɛn ʎa ku'ɛnta]
to withdraw (vt)	**sacar de la cuenta**	[sa'kar dɛ ʎa ku'ɛnta]
credit card	**tarjeta** (f) **de crédito**	[tar'hɛta dɛ 'krɛdito]
cash	**dinero** (m) **en efectivo**	[di'nɛrɔ ɛn ɛfek'tiβo]
check	**cheque** (m)	['ʧɛkɛ]
to write a check	**sacar un cheque**	[sa'kar un 'ʧɛkɛ]
checkbook	**talonario** (m)	[talo'nario]
wallet	**cartera** (f)	[kar'tɛra]
change purse	**monedero** (m)	[mone'dɛrɔ]
billfold	**portamonedas** (m)	[portamo'nɛdas]
safe	**caja** (f) **fuerte**	['kaha fu'ɛrtɛ]
heir	**heredero** (m)	[ɛrɛ'dɛrɔ]
inheritance	**herencia** (f)	[ɛ'rɛnθija]
fortune (wealth)	**fortuna** (f)	[fɔr'tuna]
lease, rent	**arriendo** (m)	[ar'rjendo]
rent money	**alquiler** (m)	[aʎki'ler]
to rent (sth from sb)	**alquilar** (vt)	[aʎki'ʎar]
price	**precio** (m)	['prɛθio]
cost	**coste** (m)	['kɔstɛ]
sum	**suma** (f)	['suma]
to spend (vt)	**gastar** (vt)	[gas'tar]
expenses	**gastos** (m pl)	['gastɔs]
to economize (vi, vt)	**economizar** (vi, vt)	[ɛkonomi'θar]
economical	**económico** (adj)	[ɛko'nomikɔ]
to pay (vi, vt)	**pagar** (vi, vt)	[pa'gar]
payment	**pago** (m)	['pagɔ]
change (give the ~)	**cambio** (m)	['kambio]
tax	**impuesto** (m)	[impu'ɛstɔ]
fine	**multa** (f)	['muʎta]
to fine (vt)	**multar** (vt)	[muʎ'tar]

85. Post. Postal service

post office	**oficina** (f) **de correos**	[ɔfi'θina dɛ kɔr'rɛɔs]
mail (letters, etc.)	**correo** (m)	[kɔr'rɛɔ]
mailman	**cartero** (m)	[kar'tɛrɔ]
opening hours	**horario** (m) **de apertura**	[ɔ'rario dɛ aper'tura]

letter	**carta** (f)	[ˈkarta]
registered letter	**carta** (f) **certificada**	[ˈkarta θærtifiˈkada]
postcard	**tarjeta** (f) **postal**	[tarˈhɛta pɔsˈtaʎ]
telegram	**telegrama** (m)	[tɛlegˈrama]
parcel	**paquete** (m) **postal**	[paˈketɛ pɔsˈtaʎ]
money transfer	**giro** (m) **postal**	[ˈhirɔ pɔsˈtaʎ]
to receive (vt)	**recibir** (vt)	[rɛθiˈβir]
to send (vt)	**enviar** (vt)	[ɛmbiˈjar]
sending	**envío** (m)	[ɛmˈbiɔ]
address	**dirección** (f)	[dirɛkˈθⁱon]
ZIP code	**código** (m) **postal**	[ˈkɔdigɔ pɔsˈtaʎ]
sender	**expedidor** (m)	[ɛkspɛdiˈdɔr]
receiver, addressee	**destinatario** (m)	[dɛstinaˈtariɔ]
name	**nombre** (m)	[ˈnɔmbrɛ]
family name	**apellido** (m)	[apɛˈjⁱdɔ]
rate (of postage)	**tarifa** (f)	[taˈrifa]
standard (adj)	**ordinario** (adj)	[ɔrdiˈnariɔ]
economical (adj)	**económico** (adj)	[ɛkɔˈnɔmikɔ]
weight	**peso** (m)	[ˈpɛsɔ]
to weigh up (vt)	**pesar** (vt)	[pɛˈsar]
envelope	**sobre** (m)	[ˈsɔbrɛ]
postage stamp	**sello** (m)	[ˈsɛjo]
to stamp an envelope	**poner un sello**	[pɔˈnɛr un ˈsɛjo]

Dwelling. House. Home

86. House. Dwelling

house	casa (f)	['kasa]
at home (adv)	en casa (adv)	[ɛn 'kasa]
courtyard	patio (m)	['patiɔ]
fence	verja (f)	['bɛrha]
brick (n)	ladrillo (m)	[ʎad'rijo]
brick (as adj)	de ladrillo (adj)	[dɛ ʎad'rijo]
stone (n)	piedra (f)	['pjedra]
stone (as adj)	de piedra (adj)	[dɛ 'pjedra]
concrete (n)	hormigón (m)	[ɔrmi'gɔn]
concrete (as adj)	de hormigón (adj)	[dɛ ɔrmi'gɔn]
new (new-built)	nuevo (adj)	[nu'ɛβo]
old (adj)	viejo (adj)	['bjehɔ]
decrepit (house)	deteriorado (adj)	[dɛtɛriɔ'radɔ]
modern (adj)	moderno (adj)	[mo'dɛrnɔ]
multistory (adj)	de muchos pisos	[dɛ 'mutʃos 'pisɔs]
high (adj)	alto (adj)	['aʎtɔ]
floor, story	piso (m)	['pisɔ]
single-story (adj)	de un solo piso	[dɛ un 'sɔlɔ 'pisɔ]
ground floor	piso (m) bajo	['pisɔ 'βahɔ]
top floor	piso (m) alto	['pisɔ 'aʎtɔ]
roof	techo (m)	['tɛtʃɔ]
chimney (stack)	chimenea (f)	[tʃimɛ'nɛa]
roof tiles	tejas (f pl)	['tɛhas]
tiled (adj)	de tejas (adj)	[dɛ 'tɛhas]
loft (attic)	desván (m)	[dɛs'van]
window	ventana (f)	[bɛn'tana]
glass	vidrio (m)	['bidriɔ]
window ledge	alféizar (m)	[al'fɛjθar]
shutters	contraventanas (f pl)	['kɔntrabɛn'tanas]
wall	pared (f)	[pa'rɛd]
balcony	balcón (m)	[baʎ'kɔn]
downspout	gotera (f)	[gɔ'tɛra]
upstairs (to be ~)	arriba	[ar'riβa]
to go upstairs	subir (vi)	[su'βir]
to come down	descender (vi)	[dɛθɛn'dɛr]
to move (to new premises)	mudarse (vr)	[mu'darsɛ]

87. House. Entrance. Lift

entrance	**entrada** (f)	[ɛnt'rada]
stairs (stairway)	**escalera** (f)	[ɛska'lera]
steps	**escalones** (m)	[ɛska'lɔnɛs]
banisters	**baranda** (f)	[ba'randa]
lobby (hotel ~)	**vestíbulo** (m)	[bes'tiβulɔ]
mailbox	**buzón** (m)	[bu'θɔn]
trash container	**contenedor** (m) **de basura**	[kɔntɛnɛ'dɔr dɛ ba'sura]
trash chute	**bajante** (f) **de basura**	[ba'hantɛ dɛ ba'sura]
elevator	**ascensor** (m)	[aθæn'sɔr]
freight elevator	**ascensor** (m) **de carga**	[aθæn'sɔr dɛ 'karga]
elevator cage	**cabina** (f)	[ka'βina]
to take the elevator	**ir en el ascensor**	[ir ɛn ɛʎ aθæn'sɔr]
apartment	**apartamento** (m)	[aparta'mɛntɔ]
residents, inhabitants	**inquilinos** (m)	[iŋki'linɔs]
neighbors	**vecinos** (m pl)	[bɛ'θinɔs]

88. House. Electricity

electricity	**electricidad** (f)	[ɛlektriθi'dad]
light bulb	**bombilla** (f)	[bɔm'bija]
switch	**interruptor** (m)	[intɛrrup'tɔr]
fuse	**fusible** (m)	[fu'sible]
cable, wire (electric ~)	**hilo** (m)	['ilɔ]
wiring	**instalación** (f) **eléctrica**	[instaʎa'θion ɛ'lektrika]
electricity meter	**contador** (m) **de luz**	[kɔnta'dɔr dɛ luθ]
readings	**lectura** (f)	[lek'tura]

89. House. Doors. Locks

door	**puerta** (f)	[pu'ɛrta]
vehicle gate	**portón** (m)	[pɔr'tɔn]
handle, doorknob	**tirador** (m)	[tira'dɔr]
to unlock (unbolt)	**abrir el cerrojo**	[ab'rir ɛʎ θær'rɔhɔ]
to open (vt)	**abrir** (vt)	[ab'rir]
to close (vt)	**cerrar** (vt)	[θær'rar]
key	**llave** (f)	['jaβə]
bunch (of keys)	**manojo** (m) **de llaves**	[ma'nɔhɔ dɛ 'ʎjabɛs]
to creak (door hinge)	**crujir** (vi)	[kru'hir]
creak	**crujido** (m)	[kru'hidɔ]
hinge (of door)	**gozne** (m)	['gɔθnɛ]

doormat	felpudo (m)	[fɛʎ'puɔ]
door lock	cerradura (f)	[θæra'dura]
keyhole	ojo (m) de cerradura	['ɔhɔ dɛ sɛra'dura]
bolt (sliding bar)	cerrojo (m)	[θær'rɔhɔ]
door latch	pestillo (m)	[pɛs'tijo]
padlock	candado (m)	[kan'daɔ]

to ring (~ the door bell)	tocar el timbre	[tɔ'kar ɛʎ 'timbrɛ]
ringing (sound)	campanillazo (f)	[kampani'jaθɔ]
doorbell	timbre (m)	['timbrɛ]
doorbell button	botón (m)	[bɔ'tɔn]
knock (at the door)	llamada (f)	[ja'mada]
to knock (vi)	llamar (vi)	[ja'mar]

code	código (m)	['kɔdiɔ]
code lock	cerradura (f) de contraseña	[θæra'dura dɛ kɔntra'sɛɲa]
door phone	telefonillo (m)	[tɛlefɔ'nijo]
number (on the door)	número (m)	['numɛrɔ]
doorplate	placa (f) de puerta	['pʎaka dɛ pu'ɛrta]
peephole	mirilla (f)	[mi'rija]

90. Country house

village	aldea (f)	[aʎ'dɛa]
vegetable garden	huerta (f)	[u'ərta]
fence	empalizada (f)	[ɛmpali'θada]
picket fence	valla (f)	['vaja]
wicket gate	puertecilla (f)	[puɛrtɛ'sija]

granary	granero (m)	[gra'nɛrɔ]
cellar	sótano (m)	['sɔtanɔ]
shed (in garden)	cobertizo (m)	[kɔbɛr'tiθɔ]
well (water)	pozo (m)	['pɔθɔ]
stove (wood-fired ~)	estufa (f)	[ɛs'tufa]
to stoke the stove	calentar la estufa	[kalen'tar ʎa ɛs'tufa]
firewood	leña (f)	['leɲa]
log (firewood)	leño (m)	['leɲɔ]

veranda, stoop	veranda (f)	[bɛ'randa]
terrace (patio)	terraza (f)	[tɛr'raθa]
front steps	porche (m)	['pɔrtʃe]
swing (hanging seat)	columpio (m)	[kɔ'lumpɔ]

91. Villa. Mansion

| country house | casa (f) de campo | ['kasa dɛ 'kampɔ] |
| villa (by sea) | villa (f) | ['bija] |

wing (of building)	ala (f)	['aʎa]
garden	jardín (m)	[har'din]
park	parque (m)	['parke]
tropical greenhouse	invernadero (m)	[imbɛrna'dɛrɔ]
to look after (garden, etc.)	cuidar (vt)	[kui'dar]

swimming pool	piscina (f)	[pi'θina]
gym	gimnasio (m)	[him'nasiɔ]
tennis court	cancha (f) de tenis	['kantʃa dɛ 'tɛnis]
home theater room	sala (f) de cine	['saʎa dɛ 'sinɛ]
garage	garaje (m)	[ga'rahɛ]

| private property | propiedad (f) privada | [prɔpje'dad pri'βada] |
| private land | terreno (m) privado | [tɛr'rɛnɔ pri'βadɔ] |

| warning (caution) | advertencia (f) | [adwer'tɛnθija] |
| warning sign | letrero (m) de aviso | [let'rɛrɔ dɛ a'βiθɔ] |

security	seguridad (f)	[sɛguri'dad]
security guard	guardia (m) de seguridad	[gu'ardija dɛ sɛguri'dad]
burglar alarm	alarma (f) antirrobo	[a'ʎarma antir'rɔβɔ]

92. Castle. Palace

castle	castillo (m)	[kas'tijo]
palace	palacio (m)	[pa'ʎaθiɔ]
fortress	fortaleza (f)	[fɔrta'leθa]

wall (round castle)	muralla (f)	[mu'raja]
tower	torre (f)	['tɔrrɛ]
keep, donjon	torre (f) principal	['tɔrrɛ prinsi'paʎ]

portcullis	rastrillo (m)	[rast'rijo]
underground passage	pasaje (m) subterráneo	[pa'sahe subtɛr'ranɛɔ]
moat	foso (m) del castillo	['fɔsɔ dɛʎ kas'tijo]
chain	cadena (f)	[ka'dɛna]
arrow loop	aspillera (f)	[aspi'jera]

magnificent (adj)	magnífico (adj)	[mag'nifikɔ]
majestic (adj)	majestuoso (adj)	[mahɛstu'ɔsɔ]
impregnable (adj)	inexpugnable (adj)	[inɛspuk'nable]
medieval (adj)	medieval (adj)	[mɛdiɛ'vaʎ]

93. Apartment

apartment	apartamento (m)	[aparta'mɛntɔ]
room	habitación (f)	[abita'θion]
bedroom	dormitorio (m)	[dɔrmi'tɔriɔ]

dining room	comedor (m)	[kɔmɛ'dɔr]
living room	salón (m)	[sa'lɔn]
study (home office)	despacho (m)	[dɛs'patʃɔ]
entry room	antecámara (f)	[antɛ'kamara]
bathroom	cuarto (m) de baño	[ku'artɔ dɛ 'baɲɔ]
half bath	servicio (m)	[sɛr'wiθiɔ]
ceiling	techo (m)	['tɛtʃɔ]
floor	suelo (m)	[su'ɛlɔ]
corner	rincón (m)	[riɲ'kɔn]

94. Apartment. Cleaning

to clean (vi, vt)	hacer la limpieza	[a'θær ʎa lim'pjeθa]
to put away (to stow)	quitar (vt)	[ki'tar]
dust	polvo (m)	['pɔʎvɔ]
dusty (adj)	polvoriento (adj)	[pɔʎvɔ'rjentɔ]
to dust (vt)	limpiar el polvo	[lim'pjar ɛʎ 'pɔʎvɔ]
vacuum cleaner	aspirador (m)	[aspira'dɔr]
to vacuum (vt)	limpiar con la aspiradora	[lim'pjar kɔn ʎa aspira'dɔra]
to sweep (vi, vt)	barrer (vi, vt)	[bar'rɛr]
sweepings	barreduras (f pl)	[barrɛ'duras]
order	orden (m)	['ɔrdɛn]
disorder, mess	desorden (m)	[dɛ'sɔrdɛn]
mop	fregona (f)	[fre'gɔna]
dust cloth	trapo (m)	['trapɔ]
broom	escoba (f)	[ɛs'kɔβa]
dustpan	cogedor (m)	[kɔhɛ'dɔr]

95. Furniture. Interior

furniture	muebles (m pl)	[mu'ɛbles]
table	mesa (f)	['mɛsa]
chair	silla (f)	['sija]
bed	cama (f)	['kama]
couch, sofa	sofá (m)	[sɔ'fa]
armchair	sillón (m)	[si'jon]
bookcase	librería (f)	[librɛ'rija]
shelf	estante (m)	[ɛs'tantɛ]
set of shelves	estantería (f)	[ɛstantɛ'rija]
wardrobe	armario (m)	[ar'mariɔ]
coat rack	percha (f)	['pɛrtʃa]

coat stand	**perchero** (m) **de pie**	[pɛr'ʧero dɛ pje]
dresser	**cómoda** (f)	['komoda]
mirror	**espejo** (m)	[ɛs'pɛho]
carpet	**tapiz** (m)	[ta'piθ]
rug, small carpet	**alfombra** (f)	[aʎ'fombra]
fireplace	**chimenea** (f)	[ʧimɛ'nɛa]
candle	**candela** (f)	[kan'dɛʎa]
candlestick	**candelero** (m)	[kandɛ'lero]
drapes	**cortinas** (f pl)	[kor'tinas]
wallpaper	**empapelado** (m)	[ɛmpapɛ'ʎado]
blinds (jalousie)	**estor** (m) **de láminas**	[ɛs'tor dɛ 'ʎaminas]
table lamp	**lámpara** (f) **de mesa**	['ʎampara dɛ 'mɛsa]
wall lamp (sconce)	**candil** (m)	[kan'diʎ]
floor lamp	**lámpara** (f) **de pie**	['ʎampara dɛ pje]
chandelier	**lámpara** (f) **de araña**	['ʎampara dɛ a'raɲja]
leg (of chair, table)	**pata** (f)	['pata]
armrest	**brazo** (m)	['braθo]
back (backrest)	**espaldar** (m)	[ɛspaʎ'dar]
drawer	**cajón** (m)	[ka'hon]

96. Bedding

bedclothes	**ropa** (f) **de cama**	['ropa dɛ 'kama]
pillow	**almohada** (f)	[aʎmo'ada]
pillowcase	**funda** (f)	['funda]
blanket (comforter)	**manta** (f)	['manta]
sheet	**sábana** (f)	['saβana]
bedspread	**sobrecama** (f)	[sobrɛ'kama]

97. Kitchen

kitchen	**cocina** (f)	[ko'θina]
gas	**gas** (m)	[gas]
gas cooker	**cocina** (f) **de gas**	[ko'sina dɛ 'gas]
electric cooker	**cocina** (f) **eléctrica**	[ko'sina ɛ'lektrika]
oven	**horno** (m)	['orno]
microwave oven	**horno** (m) **microondas**	['orno mikro'ondas]
refrigerator	**frigorífico** (m)	[frigo'rifiko]
freezer	**congelador** (m)	[konhɛʎa'dor]
dishwasher	**lavavajillas** (m)	['ʎaβa ba'hiʎjas]
meat grinder	**picadora** (f) **de carne**	[pika'dora dɛ 'karnɛ]
juicer	**exprimidor** (m)	[ɛksprimi'dor]

| toaster | tostador (m) | [tɔsta'dɔr] |
| mixer | batidora (f) | [bati'dora] |

coffee maker	cafetera (f)	[kafɛ'tɛra]
coffee pot	cafetera (f)	[kafɛ'tɛra]
coffee grinder	molinillo (m) de café	[mɔli'nijo dɛ ka'fɛ]

kettle	hervidor (m) de agua	[ɛrwi'dɔr dɛ 'agua]
teapot	tetera (f)	[tɛ'tɛra]
lid	tapa (f)	['tapa]
tea strainer	colador (m) de té	[kɔʎa'dɔr dɛ tɛ]

spoon	cuchara (f)	[ku'ʧara]
teaspoon	cucharilla (f)	[kuʧa'rija]
tablespoon	cuchara (f) de sopa	[ku'ʧara dɛ 'sɔpa]
fork	tenedor (m)	[tɛnɛ'dɔr]
knife	cuchillo (m)	[ku'ʧijo]

tableware (dishes)	vajilla (f)	[ba'hija]
plate (dinner ~)	plato (m)	['pʎatɔ]
saucer	platillo (m)	[pʎa'tijo]

shot glass	vaso (m) de chupito	['basɔ dɛ ʧu'pitɔ]
glass (~ of water)	vaso (m)	['basɔ]
cup	taza (f)	['taθa]

| sugar bowl | azucarera (f) | [aθuka'rɛra] |
| salt shaker | salero (m) | [sa'lerɔ] |

| pepper shaker | pimentero (m) | [pimen'tɛrɔ] |
| butter dish | mantequera (f) | [mantɛ'kera] |

saucepan	cacerola (f)	[kaθæ'rɔʎa]
frying pan	sartén (f)	[sar'tɛn]
ladle	cucharón (m)	[kuʧa'rɔn]

| colander | colador (m) | [kɔʎa'dɔr] |
| tray | bandeja (f) | [ban'dɛha] |

bottle	botella (f)	[bɔ'tɛja]
jar (glass)	tarro (m) de vidrio	['tarrɔ dɛ 'widriɔ]
can	lata (f) de hojalata	['ʎata dɛ ɔ'haʎata]

bottle opener	abrebotellas (m)	[abrɛbɔ'tɛjas]
can opener	abrelatas (m)	[abrɛ'ʎatas]
corkscrew	sacacorchos (m)	[saka'kɔrʧɔs]

| filter | filtro (m) | ['fiʎtrɔ] |
| to filter (vt) | filtrar (vt) | [fiʎt'rar] |

| trash | basura (f) | [ba'sura] |
| trash can | cubo (m) de basura | ['kuβɔ dɛ ba'sura] |

98. Bathroom

bathroom	**cuarto** (m) **de baño**	[kuˈartɔ dɛ ˈbaɲʲɔ]
water	**agua** (f)	[ˈagua]
tap, faucet	**grifo** (m)	[ˈgrifɔ]
hot water	**agua** (f) **caliente**	[ˈagua kaˈʎjentɛ]
cold water	**agua** (f) **fría**	[ˈagua ˈfria]
toothpaste	**pasta** (f) **de dientes**	[ˈpasta dɛ ˈdjentɛs]
to brush one's teeth	**limpiarse los dientes**	[limˈpjarsɛ lɔs ˈdjentɛs]
to shave (vi)	**afeitarse** (vr)	[afɛjˈtarsɛ]
shaving foam	**espuma** (f) **de afeitar**	[ɛsˈpuma dɛ afɛjˈtar]
razor	**maquinilla** (f) **de afeitar**	[makiˈniʎja dɛ afɛjˈtar]
to wash (one's hands, etc.)	**lavar** (vt)	[ʎaˈβar]
to take a bath	**darse un baño**	[ˈdarsɛ un ˈbaɲʲɔ]
shower	**ducha** (f)	[ˈdutʃa]
to take a shower	**darse una ducha**	[ˈdarsɛ ˈuna ˈdutʃa]
bathtub	**baño** (m)	[ˈbaɲʲɔ]
toilet (toilet bowl)	**inodoro** (m)	[inɔˈdɔrɔ]
sink (washbasin)	**lavabo** (m)	[ʎaˈβabɔ]
soap	**jabón** (m)	[haˈβɔn]
soap dish	**jabonera** (f)	[habɔˈnɛra]
sponge	**esponja** (f)	[ɛsˈpɔnha]
shampoo	**champú** (m)	[tʃamˈpu]
towel	**toalla** (f)	[tɔˈaja]
bathrobe	**bata** (f) **de baño**	[ˈbata dɛ ˈbaɲʲɔ]
laundry (process)	**colada** (f), **lavado** (m)	[kɔˈʎada], [laˈβadɔ]
washing machine	**lavadora** (f)	[ʎavaˈdɔra]
to do the laundry	**lavar la ropa**	[ʎaˈβar ʎa ˈrɔpa]
laundry detergent	**detergente** (m) **en polvo**	[detɛrˈhentɛ ɛn ˈpɔʎvɔ]

99. Household appliances

TV set	**televisor** (m)	[tɛlewiˈsɔr]
tape recorder	**magnetófono** (m)	[magnɛˈtɔfɔnɔ]
video, VCR	**vídeo** (m)	[ˈwideɔ]
radio	**radio** (f)	[ˈradiɔ]
player (CD, MP3, etc.)	**reproductor** (m)	[rɛprɔdukˈtɔr]
video projector	**proyector** (m) **de vídeo**	[prɔjekˈtɔr dɛ ˈwideɔ]
home movie theater	**sistema** (m) **home cinema**	[sisˈtɛma ˈhɔum ˈsinɛma]
DVD player	**DVD grabador** (m)	[dɛ uvɛ ˈdɛ grabaˈdɔr]

| amplifier | amplificador (m) | [amplifika'dɔr] |
| video game console | videoconsola (f) | [wideɔkɔn'sɔʎa] |

video camera	cámara (f) de vídeo	['kamara dɛ 'wideɔ]
camera (photo)	cámara (f) fotográfica	['kamara fɔtɔg'rafika]
digital camera	cámara (f) digital	['kamara dihi'taʎ]

vacuum cleaner	aspirador (m)	[aspira'dɔr]
iron (e.g., steam ~)	plancha (f)	['pʎantʃa]
ironing board	tabla (f) de planchar	['tabʎa dɛ pʎan'tʃar]

telephone	teléfono (m)	[tɛ'lefɔnɔ]
mobile phone	teléfono (m) móvil	[tɛ'lefɔnɔ 'mɔβiʎ]
typewriter	máquina (f) de escribir	['makina dɛ ɛskri'βir]
sewing machine	máquina (f) de coser	['makina dɛ kɔ'sɛr]

microphone	micrófono (m)	[mik'rɔfɔnɔ]
headphones	auriculares (m pl)	[auriku'ʎarɛs]
remote control (TV)	mando (m) a distancia	['mandɔ a dis'tanθia]

CD, compact disc	disco compacto (m)	['diskɔ kɔm'paktɔ]
cassette	casete (m)	[ka'sɛtɛ]
vinyl record	disco (m) de vinilo	['diskɔ dɛ wi'nilɔ]

100. Repairs. Renovation

renovations	renovación (f)	[renɔva'θiɔn]
to renovate (vt)	renovar (vt)	[renɔ'βar]
to repair (vt)	reparar (vt)	[rɛpa'rar]
to put in order	poner en orden	[pɔ'nɛr ɛn 'ɔrdɛn]
to redo (do again)	rehacer (vt)	[rɛa'θær]

paint	pintura (f)	[pin'tura]
to paint (~ a wall)	pintar (vt)	[pin'tar]
house painter	pintor (m)	[pin'tɔr]
paintbrush	brocha (f)	['brɔtʃa]
whitewash	cal (f)	[kaʎ]
to whitewash (vt)	encalar (vt)	[ɛŋka'ʎar]

wallpaper	empapelado (m)	[ɛmpapɛ'ʎadɔ]
to wallpaper (vt)	empapelar (vt)	[ɛmpapɛ'ʎar]
varnish	barniz (m)	[bar'niθ]
to varnish (vt)	cubrir con barniz	[kub'rir kɔn bar'niθ]

101. Plumbing

| water | agua (f) | ['agua] |
| hot water | agua (f) caliente | ['agua ka'ʎjentɛ] |

| cold water | agua (f) fría | ['agua 'fria] |
| tap, faucet | grifo (m) | ['grifɔ] |

drop (of water)	gota (f)	['gɔta]
to drip (vi)	gotear (vi)	[gɔtɛ'ar]
to leak (ab. pipe)	gotear (vi)	[gɔtɛ'ar]
leak (pipe ~)	escape (f) de agua	[es'kapɛ dɛ 'agua]
puddle	charco (m)	['ʧarkɔ]

pipe	tubo (m)	['tuβɔ]
stop valve	válvula (f)	['baʎvuʎa]
to be clogged up	estar atascado	[es'tar atas'kadɔ]

tools	instrumentos (m pl)	[instru'mɛntɔs]
adjustable wrench	llave (f) inglesa	['jaβə iŋ'lesa]
to unscrew, untwist (vt)	destornillar (vt)	[dɛstɔrni'jar]
to screw (tighten)	atornillar (vt)	[atɔrni'jar]

to unclog (vt)	desatascar (vt)	[dɛsatas'kar]
plumber	fontanero (m)	[fɔnta'nɛrɔ]
basement	sótano (m)	['sɔtanɔ]
sewerage (system)	alcantarillado (m)	[aʎkantari'jadɔ]

102. Fire. Conflagration

fire (to catch ~)	fuego (m)	[fu'ɛgɔ]
flame	llama (f)	['ʎjama]
spark	chispa (f)	['ʧispa]
smoke (from fire)	humo (m)	['umɔ]
torch (flaming stick)	antorcha (f)	[an'tɔrʧa]
campfire	hoguera (f)	[ɔ'gɛra]

gas, gasoline	gasolina (f)	[gasɔ'lina]
kerosene (for aircraft)	queroseno (m)	[kɛrɔ'sɛnɛ]
flammable (adj)	inflamable (adj)	[infʎa'mable]
explosive (adj)	explosivo (adj)	[ɛksplɔ'siβɔ]
NO SMOKING	PROHIBIDO FUMAR	[prɔi'βidɔ fu'mar]

safety	seguridad (f)	[sɛguri'dad]
danger	peligro (m)	[pɛ'ligrɔ]
dangerous (adj)	peligroso (adj)	[pɛlig'rɔsɔ]

to catch fire	prenderse fuego	[prɛn'dɛrsɛ fu'ɛgɔ]
explosion	explosión (f)	[ɛksplɔ'sɔn]
to set fire	incendiar (vt)	[inθæn'djar]
incendiary (arsonist)	incendiario (m)	[inθæn'djariɔ]
arson	incendio (m) provocado	[in'θæendiɔ prɔvɔ'kadɔ]

| to blaze (vi) | estar en llamas | [es'tar ɛn 'jamas] |
| to burn (be on fire) | arder (vi) | [ar'dɛr] |

to burn down	**incendiarse**	[inθæn'dˈarsɛ]
to call the fire department	**llamar a los bomberos**	[ja'mar a lɔs bɔm'bɛrɔs]
fireman	**bombero** (m)	[bɔm'bɛrɔ]
fire truck	**coche** (m) **de bomberos**	['kɔʧe dɛ bɔm'bɛrɔs]
fire department	**cuerpo** (m) **de bomberos**	[ku'ɛrpɔ dɛ bɔm'bɛrɔs]
fire truck ladder	**escalera** (f) **de bomberos**	[ɛska'lera dɛ bɔm'bɛrɔs]
fire hose	**manguera** (f)	[ma'ŋɛra]
fire extinguisher	**extintor** (m)	[ɛkstin'tɔr]
helmet	**casco** (m)	['kaskɔ]
siren	**sirena** (f)	[si'rɛna]
to call out	**gritar** (vi)	[gri'tar]
to call for help	**pedir socorro**	[pɛ'dir sɔ'kɔrrɔ]
rescuer	**socorrista** (m)	[sɔkɔr'rista]
to rescue (vt)	**salvar** (vt)	[saʎ'var]
to arrive (vi)	**llegar** (vi)	[je'gar]
to extinguish (vt)	**apagar** (vt)	[apa'gar]
water	**agua** (f)	['agua]
sand	**arena** (f)	[a'rɛna]
ruins (destruction)	**ruinas** (f pl)	[ru'inas]
to collapse (building, etc.)	**colapsarse** (vr)	[kɔʎap'sarsɛ]
to fall down (vi)	**hundirse** (vr)	[un'dirsɛ]
to cave in (ceiling, floor)	**derrumbarse** (vr)	[dɛrrum'barsɛ]
piece of wreckage	**trozo** (m)	['trɔθɔ]
ash	**ceniza** (f)	[sɛ'niθa]
to suffocate (die)	**morir asfixiado**	[mɔ'rir asfik'sjadɔ]
to be killed (perish)	**perecer** (vi)	[pɛrɛ'θær]

HUMAN ACTIVITIES

Job. Business. Part 1

103. Office. Working in the office

office (of firm)	oficina (f)	[ɔfi'θina]
office (of director, etc.)	despacho (m)	[dɛs'patʃɔ]
front desk	recepción (f)	[rɛsɛp'θiˈon]
secretary	secretario (m)	[sɛkrɛ'tariɔ]
secretary (fem.)	secretaria (f)	[sɛkrɛ'taria]
director	director (m)	[dirɛk'tɔr]
manager	manager (m)	[manager]
accountant	contable (m)	[kɔn'table]
employee	colaborador (m)	[kɔʎabɔra'dɔr]
furniture	muebles (m pl)	[mu'ɛbles]
desk	escritorio (m)	[ɛskri'tɔriɔ]
desk chair	silla (f)	['sija]
chest of drawers	cajonera (f)	[kahɔ'nɛra]
coat stand	perchero (m) de pie	[pɛr'tʃɛrɔ dɛ pje]
computer	ordenador (m)	[ɔrdɛna'dɔr]
printer	impresora (f)	[imprɛ'sɔra]
fax machine	fax (m)	['faks]
photocopier	fotocopiadora (f)	[fɔtɔkɔpja'dɔra]
paper	papel (m)	[pa'pɛʎ]
office supplies	papelería (f)	[papɛle'rija]
mouse pad	alfombrilla (f) para ratón	[aʎfɔmb'rija 'para ra'tɔn]
sheet (of paper)	hoja (f)	['ɔha]
catalog	catálogo (m)	[ka'talɔgɔ]
phone book (directory)	directorio (m) telefónico	[dirɛk'tɔriɔ tele'fɔnikɔ]
documentation	documentación (f)	[dɔkumɛnta'θiˈon]
brochure	folleto (m)	[fɔ'jetɔ]
(e.g., 12 pages ~)		
leaflet	prospecto (m)	[prɔs'pɛktɔ]
sample	muestra (f)	[mu'ɛstra]
training meeting	entrenamiento (m)	[ɛntrɛna'mjentɔ]
meeting (of managers)	reunión (f)	[rɛu'ɲiˈon]
lunch time	pausa (f) de almuerzo	['pausa dɛ almu'ɛrθɔ]
to make a copy	hacer una copia	[a'sɛr una 'kɔpija]

to make copies	hacer copias	[a'sɛr 'kɔpijas]
to receive a fax	recibir un fax	[rɛθi'βɪr un 'faks]
to send a fax	enviar un fax	[ɛmbi'jar un 'faks]

to call (by phone)	llamar por teléfono	[ja'mar pɔr te'lefɔnɔ]
to answer (vt)	responder (vi, vt)	[rɛspɔn'dɛr]
to put through	poner en comunicación	[pɔ'nɛr ɛn kɔmunika'θion]

to arrange, to set up	fijar (vt)	[fi'har]
to demonstrate (vt)	demostrar (vt)	[dɛmɔst'rar]
to be absent	estar ausente	[ɛs'tar au'sɛntɛ]
absence	ausencia (f)	[au'sɛnθia]

104. Business processes. Part 1

occupation	ocupación (f)	[ɔkupa'θion]
firm	firma (f)	['firma]
company	compañía (f)	[kɔmpa'nija]
corporation	corporación (f)	[kɔrpɔra'θion]
enterprise	empresa (f)	[ɛmp'rɛsa]
agency	agencia (f)	[a'hɛnθija]

agreement (contract)	acuerdo (m)	[aku'ɛrdɔ]
contract	contrato (m)	[kɔnt'ratɔ]
deal	trato (m), acuerdo (m)	['tratɔ], [aku'ɛrdɔ]
order (to place an ~)	pedido (m)	[pɛ'didɔ]
term (of contract)	condición (f)	[kɔndi'θion]

wholesale (adv)	al por mayor (adv)	[aʎ pɔr ma'jor]
wholesale (adj)	al por mayor (adj)	[aʎ pɔr ma'jor]
wholesale (n)	venta (f) al por mayor	['bɛnta aʎ pɔr ma'jor]
retail (adj)	al por menor (adj)	[aʎ pɔr mɛ'nɔr]
retail (n)	venta (f) al por menor	['bɛnta aʎ pɔr mɛ'nɔr]

competitor	competidor (m)	[kɔmpɛti'dɔr]
competition	competencia (f)	[kɔmpɛ'tɛnθia]
to compete (vi)	competir (vi)	[kɔmpɛ'tir]

| partner (associate) | socio (m) | ['sɔθiɔ] |
| partnership | sociedad (f) | [sɔθje'dad] |

crisis	crisis (m)	['krisis]
bankruptcy	bancarrota (f)	[baŋkar'rɔta]
to go bankrupt	ir a la bancarrota	[ir a ʎa baŋkar'rɔta]
difficulty	dificultad (f)	[difikuʎ'tad]
problem	problema (m)	[prɔb'lema]
catastrophe	catástrofe (f)	[ka'tastrɔfɛ]

| economy | economía (f) | [ɛkɔnɔ'mija] |
| economic (~ growth) | económico (adj) | [ɛkɔ'nɔmikɔ] |

economic recession	recesión (f) económica	[rɛsɛ'θ^jon ɛkɔ'nɔmika]
goal (aim)	meta (f)	['mɛta]
task	objetivo (m)	[ɔbhɛ'tiβɔ]
to trade (vi)	comerciar (vi)	[kɔmɛr'θjar]
network (distribution ~)	red (f)	[rɛd]
inventory (stock)	existencias (f pl)	[ɛksis'tɛnθias]
assortment	surtido (m)	[sur'tidɔ]
leader (leading company)	líder (m)	['lidɛr]
large (~ company)	grande (adj)	['grandɛ]
monopoly	monopolio (m)	[mɔnɔ'pɔliɔ]
theory	teoría (f)	[tɛɔ'rija]
practice	práctica (f)	['praktika]
experience (in my ~)	experiencia (f)	[ɛkspɛ'rjensija]
trend (tendency)	tendencia (f)	[tɛn'dɛnsija]
development	desarrollo (m)	[dɛsa'rɔjɔ]

105. Business processes. Part 2

benefit, profit	rentabilidad (f)	[rɛntabili'dad]
profitable (adj)	rentable (adj)	[rɛn'table]
delegation (group)	delegación (f)	[dɛlega'θ^jon]
salary	salario (m)	[sa'ʎariɔ]
to correct (an error)	corregir (vt)	[kɔrrɛ'hir]
business trip	viaje (m) de negocios	['bjahɛ dɛ nɛ'gɔθiɔs]
commission	comisión (f)	[kɔmi's^jon]
to control (vt)	controlar (vt)	[kɔntrɔ'ʎar]
conference	conferencia (f)	[kɔnfɛ'rɛnsija]
license	licencia (f)	[li'sɛnsija]
reliable (~ partner)	fiable (adj)	['fjable]
initiative (undertaking)	iniciativa (f)	[inisja'tiβa]
norm (standard)	norma (f)	['nɔrma]
circumstance	circunstancia (f)	[θirkuns'tanθija]
duty (of employee)	deber (m)	[dɛ'bɛr]
organization (company)	empresa (f)	[ɛmp'rɛsa]
organization (process)	organización (f)	[ɔrganiθa's^jon]
organized (adj)	organizado (adj)	[ɔrgani'θadɔ]
cancellation	anulación (f)	[anuʎa'θ^jon]
to cancel (call off)	anular (vt)	[anu'ʎar]
report (official ~)	informe (m)	[in'fɔrmɛ]
patent	patente (m)	[pa'tɛntɛ]
to patent (obtain patent)	patentar (vt)	[patɛn'tar]
to plan (vt)	planear (vt)	[pʎanɛ'ar]

bonus (money)	premio (m)	['prɛmiɔ]
professional (adj)	profesional (adj)	[prɔfɛsⁱɔ'naʎ]
procedure	procedimiento (m)	[prɔθæðiˈmjentɔ]
to examine (contract, etc.)	examinar (vt)	[ɛksamiˈnar]
calculation	cálculo (m)	[ˈkaʎkulɔ]
reputation	reputación (f)	[rɛputaˈθⁱon]
risk	riesgo (m)	[ˈrjesgɔ]
to manage, to run	dirigir (vt)	[diriˈhir]
information	información (f)	[infɔrmaˈθⁱon]
property	propiedad (f)	[prɔpjeˈdad]
union	unión (f)	[uˈɲⁱon]
life insurance	seguro (m) de vida	[sɛˈgurɔ dɛ ˈwida]
to insure (vt)	asegurar (vt)	[asɛguˈrar]
insurance	seguro (m)	[sɛˈgurɔ]
auction (~ sale)	subasta (f)	[suˈβasta]
to notify (inform)	notificar (vt)	[nɔtifiˈkar]
management (process)	gestión (f)	[hɛsˈtⁱon]
service (~ industry)	servicio (m)	[sɛrˈwiθiɔ]
forum	foro (m)	[ˈfɔrɔ]
to function (vi)	funcionar (vi)	[funθⁱoˈnar]
stage (phase)	etapa (f)	[ɛˈtapa]
legal (~ services)	jurídico (adj)	[huˈridikɔ]
lawyer (legal expert)	jurista (m)	[huˈrista]

106. Production. Works

plant	planta (f)	[ˈpʎanta]
factory	fábrica (f)	[ˈfabrika]
workshop	taller (m)	[taˈjer]
works, production site	planta (f) de producción	[ˈplanta dɛ prɔdukˈθⁱon]
industry	industria (f)	[inˈdustrija]
industrial (adj)	industrial (adj)	[industriˈjaʎ]
heavy industry	industria (f) pesada	[inˈdustrija pɛˈsada]
light industry	industria (f) ligera	[inˈdustrija liˈhɛra]
products	producción (f)	[prɔdukˈθⁱon]
to produce (vt)	producir (vt)	[prɔduˈθir]
raw materials	materias (f pl) primas	[maˈtɛrjas ˈprimas]
foreman	jefe (m) de brigada	[ˈhɛfɛ dɛ briˈgada]
workers team	brigada (f)	[briˈgada]
worker	obrero (m)	[ɔbˈrɛrɔ]
working day	día (m) de trabajo	[ˈdia dɛ traˈβahɔ]
pause	descanso (m)	[dɛsˈkansɔ]

| meeting | reunión (f) | [rɛu'nᶦɔn] |
| to discuss (vt) | discutir (vt) | [disku'tir] |

plan	plan (m)	[pʎan]
to fulfill the plan	cumplir el plan	[kump'lir ɛʎ 'pʎan]
rate of output	tasa (f) de producción	['tasa dɛ produk'θᶦon]
quality	calidad (f)	[kali'dad]
checking (control)	revisión (f)	[rɛwi'sᶦɔn]
quality control	control (m) de calidad	[kɔnt'rɔʎ dɛ kali'dad]

work safety	seguridad (f) de trabajo	[sɛguri'dad dɛ tra'βahɔ]
discipline	disciplina (f)	[diθip'lina]
violation	infracción (f)	[infrak'θᶦon]
(of safety rules, etc.)		
to violate (rules)	violar (vt)	[bᶦɔ'ʎar]

strike	huelga (f)	[u'əʎga]
striker	huelguista (m)	[uəʎ'gista]
to be on strike	estar en huelga	[ɛs'tar ɛn u'əʎga]
labor union	sindicato (m)	[sindi'katɔ]

to invent (machine, etc.)	inventar (vt)	[inbɛn'tar]
invention	invención (f)	[imbɛn'θᶦon]
research	investigación (f)	[imbɛstiga'θᶦon]
to improve (make better)	mejorar (vt)	[mɛhɔ'rar]

| technology | tecnología (f) | [tɛknɔlɔ'hia] |
| technical drawing | dibujo (m) técnico | [di'βuhɔ 'tɛknikɔ] |

load, cargo	cargamento (m)	[karga'mentɔ]
loader (person)	cargador (m)	[karga'dɔr]
to load (vehicle, etc.)	cargar (vt)	[kar'gar]
loading (process)	carga (f)	['karga]

| to unload (vi, vt) | descargar (vt) | [dɛskar'gar] |
| unloading | descarga (f) | [dɛs'karga] |

transportation	transporte (m)	[trans'pɔrtɛ]
transportation company	compañía (f) de transporte	[kɔmpa'nija dɛ trans'pɔrtɛ]
to transport (vt)	transportar (vt)	[transpɔr'tar]

freight car	vagón (m)	[ba'gɔn]
cistern	cisterna (f)	[θis'tɛrna]
truck	camión (m)	[ka'mᶦon]

| machine tool | máquina (f) herramienta | ['makina erra'mjenta] |
| mechanism | mecanismo (m) | [mɛka'nismɔ] |

industrial waste	desperdicios (m pl)	[dɛspɛr'disᶦɔs]
packing (process)	empaquetado (m)	[ɛmpake'tadɔ]
to pack (vt)	embalar (vt)	[ɛmba'ʎar]

107. Contract. Agreement

contract	contrato (m)	[kɔnt'ratɔ]
agreement	acuerdo (m)	[aku'ɛrdɔ]
addendum	anexo (m)	[a'nɛksɔ]

to sign a contract	firmar un contrato	[fir'mar un kɔnt'ratɔ]
signature	firma (f)	['firma]
to sign (vt)	firmar (vt)	[fir'mar]
stamp (seal)	sello (m)	['sɛjɔ]

subject of contract	objeto (m) del acuerdo	[ɔb'hɛtɔ dɛʎ aku'ɛrdɔ]
clause	cláusula (f)	['klausuʎa]
parties (in contract)	partes (f pl)	['partɛs]
legal address	domicilio (m) legal	[dɔmi'θiliɔ le'gaʎ]

to break the contract	violar el contrato	[biɔ'ʎar ɛʎ kɔnt'ratɔ]
commitment	obligación (f)	[ɔbliga'θ'ɔn]
responsibility	responsabilidad (f)	[rɛspɔnsabili'dad]
force majeure	fuerza mayor (f)	[fu'ɛrθa ma'jɔr]
dispute	disputa (f)	[dis'puta]
penalties	penalidades (f pl)	[pɛnali'dadɛs]

108. Import & Export

import	importación (f)	[impɔrta'θ'ɔn]
importer	importador (m)	[impɔrta'dɔr]
to import (vt)	importar (vt)	[impɔr'tar]
import (e.g., ~ goods)	de importación (adj)	[dɛ impɔrta'θ'ɔn]

| exporter | exportador (m) | [ɛkspɔrta'dɔr] |
| to export (vi, vt) | exportar (vt) | [ɛkspɔr'tar] |

| goods | mercancía (f) | [mɛrkan'θija] |
| consignment, lot | lote (m) de mercancías | ['lɔtɛ dɛ merkan'θias] |

weight	peso (m)	['pɛsɔ]
volume	volumen (m)	[bɔ'lumɛn]
cubic meter	metro (m) cúbico	['mɛtrɔ 'kuβikɔ]

manufacturer	productor (m)	[prɔduk'tɔr]
transportation company	compañía (f) de transporte	[kɔmpa'nija dɛ trans'pɔrtɛ]
container	contenedor (m)	[kɔntɛnɛ'dɔr]

border	frontera (f)	[frɔn'tɛra]
customs	aduana (f)	[adu'ana]
customs duty	derechos (m pl) arancelarios	[dɛ'rɛtʃɔs aranθæ'ʎariɔs]

customs officer	aduanero (m)	[adua'nɛɾo]
smuggling	contrabandismo (m)	[kɔntraban'dismɔ]
contraband (goods)	contrabando (m)	[kɔntra'βandɔ]

109. Finances

stock (share)	acción (f)	[ak'θʲon]
bond (certificate)	bono (m), obligación (f)	['bɔnɔ], [ɔbliga'θʲon]
bill of exchange	letra (f) de cambio	['letra dɛ 'kambiɔ]

| stock exchange | bolsa (f) | ['bɔʎsa] |
| stock price | cotización (f) de valores | [kɔtiθasʲon dɛ va'lɔɾɛs] |

| to go down | abaratarse (vr) | [abar'tarsɛ] |
| to go up | encarecerse (vr) | [ɛŋkarɛ'sɛrsɛ] |

| shareholding | parte (f) | ['partɛ] |
| controlling interest | interés (m) mayoritario | [inte'rɛs majori'tariɔ] |

investment	inversiones (f pl)	[inwer'sʲonɛs]
to invest (vt)	invertir (vi, vt)	[invɛr'tir]
percent	porcentaje (m)	[pɔrsɛn'tahe]
interest (on investment)	interés (m)	[inte'rɛs]

profit	beneficio (m)	[bɛnɛ'fisiɔ]
profitable (adj)	beneficioso (adj)	[bɛnɛfisi'ɔsɔ]
tax	impuesto (m)	[impu'ɛstɔ]

currency (foreign ~)	divisa (f)	[di'βisa]
national (adj)	nacional (adj)	[naθʲo'naʎ]
exchange (currency ~)	cambio (m)	['kambiɔ]

| accountant | contable (m) | [kɔn'table] |
| accounting | contaduría (f) | [kɔntadu'ria] |

bankruptcy	bancarrota (f)	[baŋkar'rɔta]
collapse, crash	quiebra (f)	['kjebra]
ruin	ruina (f)	[ru'ina]
to be ruined	arruinarse (vr)	[arrui'narsɛ]
inflation	inflación (f)	[infʎa'θʲon]
devaluation	devaluación (f)	[dɛvalua'θʲon]

capital	capital (m)	[kapi'taʎ]
income	ingresos (m pl)	[iɲ'rɛsɔs]
turnover	volumen (m) de negocios	[vɔ'lumen dɛ ne'gɔsiɔs]
resources	recursos (m pl)	[rɛ'kursɔs]
monetary resources	recursos (m pl) monetarios	[rɛ'kursɔs mɔnɛ'tariɔs]

| overhead | gastos (m pl) accesorios | ['gastɔs aksɛ'sɔriɔs] |
| to reduce (expenses) | reducir (vt) | [rɛdu'θir] |

110. Marketing

marketing	mercadotecnia (f)	[merkadɔ'tehnija]
market	mercado (m)	[mɛr'kadɔ]
market segment	segmento (m) del mercado	[sɛg'mɛntɔ dɛʎ mɛr'kadɔ]
product	producto (m)	[prɔ'duktɔ]
goods	mercancía (f)	[mɛrkan'θija]
brand	marca (f)	['marka]
trademark	marca (f) comercial	['marka kɔmɛr'θjaʎ]
logotype	logotipo (m)	[lɔgɔ'tipɔ]
logo	logo (m)	['lɔgɔ]
demand	demanda (f)	[dɛ'manda]
supply	oferta (f)	[ɔ'fɛrta]
need	necesidad (f)	[nɛθæsi'dad]
consumer	consumidor (m)	[kɔnsumi'dɔr]
analysis	análisis (m)	[a'nalisis]
to analyze (vt)	analizar (vt)	[anali'θar]
positioning	posicionamiento (m)	[pɔsiθɪɔna'mjentɔ]
to position (vt)	posicionar (vt)	[pɔsiθɪo'nar]
price	precio (m)	['prɛθiɔ]
pricing policy	política (f) de precios	[pɔ'litika dɛ 'prɛθiɔs]
formation of price	formación (m) de precios	[fɔrma'θɪon dɛ 'prɛθiɔs]

111. Advertising

advertising	publicidad (f)	[publiθi'dad]
to advertise (vt)	publicitar (vt)	[publiθi'tar]
budget	presupuesto (m)	[prɛsupu'ɛstɔ]
ad, advertisement	anuncio (m)	[a'nunθiɔ]
TV advertising	publicidad (f) televisiva	[publiθi'dad tɛlɛwi'siβa]
radio advertising	publicidad (f) radiofónica	[publiθi'dad radiɔ'fɔnika]
outdoor advertising	publicidad (f) exterior	[publisi'dad ɛkstɛ'rjor]
mass media	medios (m pl) de comunicación de masas	['mɛdiɔs dɛ kɔmunika'sɪon dɛ 'masas]
periodical (n)	periódico (m)	[pɛri'ɔdikɔ]
image (public appearance)	imagen (f)	[i'mahɛn]
slogan	consigna (f)	[kɔn'signa]
motto (maxim)	divisa (f)	[di'βɪsa]
campaign	campaña (f)	[kam'paɲja]
advertising campaign	campaña (f) publicitaria	[kam'paɲja publisi'tarija]

target group	auditorio (m) objetivo	[audi'tɔriɔ ɔbhɛ'tiβɔ]
business card	tarjeta (f) de visita	[tar'hɛta dɛ wi'sita]
leaflet	prospecto (m)	[prɔs'pɛktɔ]
brochure (e.g., 12 pages ~)	folleto (m)	[fɔ'jetɔ]
pamphlet	panfleto (m)	[panf'letɔ]
newsletter	boletín (m)	[bɔle'tin]
store sign	letrero (m)	[let'rɛrɔ]
poster	pancarta (f)	[pa'ŋkarta]
billboard	valla (f) publicitaria	['vaja publis'tarija]

112. Banking

bank	banco (m)	['baŋkɔ]
branch (of bank, etc.)	sucursal (f)	[sukur'saʎ]
bank clerk, consultant	asesor (m)	[asɛ'sɔr]
manager (director)	gerente (m)	[hɛ'rɛntɛ]
banking account	cuenta (f)	[ku'ɛnta]
account number	numero (m) de la cuenta	['numɛrɔ dɛ ʎa 'kuɛnta]
checking account	cuenta (f) corriente	[ku'ɛnta kɔr'rjentɛ]
savings account	cuenta (f) de ahorros	[ku'ɛnta dɛ a:'ɔrrɔs]
to open an account	abrir una cuenta	[ab'rir una ku'ɛnta]
to close the account	cerrar la cuenta	[θær'rar ʎa ku'ɛnta]
to deposit into the account	ingresar en la cuenta	[iŋre'sar ɛn ʎa ku'ɛnta]
to withdraw (vt)	sacar de la cuenta	[sa'kar dɛ ʎa ku'ɛnta]
deposit	depósito (m)	[dɛ'pɔsitɔ]
to make a deposit	hacer un depósito	[a'θær un dɛ'pɔsitɔ]
wire transfer	giro (m)	['hirɔ]
to wire, to transfer	hacer un giro	[a'θær un 'hirɔ]
sum	suma (f)	['suma]
How much?	¿Cuánto?	[ku'antɔ]
signature	firma (f)	['firma]
to sign (vt)	firmar (vt)	[fir'mar]
credit card	tarjeta (f) de crédito	[tar'hɛta dɛ 'krɛditɔ]
code	código (m)	['kɔdigɔ]
credit card number	número (m) de tarjeta de crédito	['numɛrɔ dɛ tar'hɛta dɛ 'krɛditɔ]
ATM	cajero (m) automático	[ka'hɛrɔ autɔ'matikɔ]
check	cheque (m)	['ʧəkɛ]
to write a check	sacar un cheque	[sa'kar un 'ʧəkɛ]
checkbook	talonario (m)	[talɔ'nariɔ]

loan (bank ~)	crédito (m)	['krɛdito]
to apply for a loan	pedir el crédito	[pɛ'dir ɛʎ 'krɛdito]
to get a loan	obtener un crédito	[ɔbtɛ'nɛr un 'krɛdito]
to give a loan	conceder un crédito	[kɔnθæ'dɛr un 'krɛdito]
guarantee	garantía (f)	[garan'tija]

113. Telephone. Phone conversation

telephone	teléfono (m)	[tɛ'lefɔnɔ]
mobile phone	teléfono (m) móvil	[tɛ'lefɔnɔ 'mɔβiʎ]
answering machine	contestador (m)	[kɔntɛsta'dɔr]
to call (telephone)	llamar, telefonear	[ja'mar], [tɛlefɔnɛ'ar]
phone call	llamada (f)	[ja'mada]
to dial a number	marcar un número	[mar'kar un 'numɛrɔ]
Hello!	¿Sí?, ¿Dígame?	[si 'digamɛ]
to ask (vt)	preguntar (vt)	[prɛgun'tar]
to answer (vi, vt)	responder (vi, vt)	[rɛspon'dɛr]
to hear (vt)	oír (vt)	[ɔ'ir]
well (adv)	bien (adv)	[bjen]
not well (adv)	mal (adv)	[maʎ]
noises (interference)	ruidos (m pl)	[ru'idɔs]
receiver	auricular (m)	[auriku'ʎar]
busy (adj)	ocupado (adj)	[ɔku'padɔ]
to ring (ab. phone)	sonar (vi)	[sɔ'nar]
telephone book	guía (f) de teléfonos	['gija dɛ tɛ'lefɔnɔs]
local (adj)	local (adj)	[lɔ'kaʎ]
local call	llamada (f) local	[ja'mada lɔ'kaʎ]
long distance (~ call)	de larga distancia	[dɛ 'larga dis'tanθija]
long-distance call	llamada (f) interurbana	[ja'mada interur'bana]
international (adj)	internacional (adj)	[intɛrnaθio'naʎ]
international call	llamada (f) internacional	[ja'mada intɛrnaθio'naʎ]

114. Mobile telephone

mobile phone	teléfono (m) móvil	[tɛ'lefɔnɔ 'mɔβiʎ]
display	pantalla (f)	[pan'taja]
button	botón (m)	[bɔ'tɔn]
SIM card	tarjeta SIM (f)	[tar'hɛta sim]
battery	pila (f)	['piʎa]
to be dead (battery)	descargarse (vr)	[dɛskar'garsɛ]
charger	cargador (m)	[karga'dɔr]
menu	menú (m)	[mɛ'nu]

settings	preferencias (f pl)	[prefe'rɛnθias]
tune (melody)	melodía (f)	[mɛlɔ'dija]
to select (vt)	seleccionar (vt)	[selɛkθio'nar]

calculator	calculadora (f)	[kaʎkuʎa'dɔra]
voice mail	contestador (m)	[kɔntɛsta'dɔr]
alarm clock	despertador (m)	[dɛspɛrta'dɔr]
contacts	contactos (m pl)	[kɔn'taktɔs]

| SMS (text message) | mensaje (m) de texto | [men'sahɛ dɛ 'tɛkstɔ] |
| subscriber | abonado (m) | [abɔ'nadɔ] |

115. Stationery

| ballpoint pen | bolígrafo (m) | [bɔ'ligrafɔ] |
| fountain pen | pluma (f) estilográfica | ['plyma ɛstilɔg'rafika] |

pencil	lápiz (f)	['ʎapiθ]
highlighter	marcador (m)	[marka'dɔr]
felt-tip pen	rotulador (m)	[rɔtuʎa'dɔr]

| notepad | bloc (m) de notas | [blɔk dɛ 'nɔtas] |
| agenda (diary) | agenda (f) | [a'hɛnda] |

ruler	regla (f)	['rɛgʎa]
calculator	calculadora (f)	[kaʎkuʎa'dɔra]
eraser	goma (f) de borrar	['gɔma dɛ bɔr'rar]
thumbtack	chincheta (f)	[ʧin'ʧeta]
paper clip	clip (m)	[klip]

glue	cola (f), pegamento (m)	['kɔʎa], [pega'mentɔ]
stapler	grapadora (f)	[grapa'dɔra]
hole punch	perforador (m)	[pɛrfɔra'dɔr]
pencil sharpener	sacapuntas (m)	[saka'puntas]

116. Various kinds of documents

account (report)	informe (m)	[in'fɔrmɛ]
agreement	acuerdo (m)	[aku'ɛrdɔ]
application form	formulario (m) de solicitud	[fɔrmu'lariɔ dɛ sɔlisi'tud]
authentic (adj)	auténtico (adj)	[au'tɛntikɔ]
badge (identity tag)	tarjeta (f) de identificación	[tar'hɛta dɛ identifika'θiɔn]
business card	tarjeta (f) de visita	[tar'hɛta dɛ wi'sita]

| certificate (~ of quality) | certificado (m) | [θærtifi'kadɔ] |
| check (e.g., draw a ~) | cheque (m) | ['ʧəkɛ] |

check (in restaurant)	cuenta (f)	[ku'ɛnta]
constitution	constitución (f)	[kɔnstitu'θiᵒon]
contract	contrato (m)	[kɔnt'ratɔ]
copy	copia (f)	['kɔpja]
copy (of contract, etc.)	ejemplar (m)	[ɛhɛmp'ʎar]
customs declaration	declaración (f) de aduana	[dɛklara'θiᵒon dɛ adu'ana]
document	documento (m)	[dɔku'mɛntɔ]
driver's license	permiso (m) de conducir	[pɛr'misɔ dɛ kɔndu'θir]
addendum	anexo (m)	[a'nɛksɔ]
form	cuestionario (m)	[kuɛstiɔ'nariɔ]
identity card, ID	carnet (m) de identidad	[karnɛt dɛidɛnti'dad]
inquiry (request)	solicitud (f) de información	[sɔliθi'tud dɛ informa'θiᵒon]
invitation card	tarjeta (f) de invitación	[tar'hɛta dɛ inwita'θiᵒon]
invoice	factura (f)	[fak'tura]
law	ley (f)	[lej]
letter (mail)	carta (f)	['karta]
letterhead	membrete (m)	[memb'rɛtɛ]
list (of names, etc.)	lista (f)	['lista]
manuscript	manuscrito (m)	[manusk'ritɔ]
newsletter	boletín (m)	[bɔle'tin]
note (short message)	nota (f)	['nɔta]
pass (for worker, visitor)	pase (m)	['pasɛ]
passport	pasaporte (m)	[pasa'pɔrtɛ]
permit	permiso (m)	[pɛr'misɔ]
résumé	curriculum vitae (m)	[kur'rikulum bi'tae]
debt note, IOU	pagaré (m)	[paga'rɛ]
receipt (for purchase)	recibo (m)	[rɛ'θiβɔ]
sales slip, receipt	ticket (m) de compra	[ti'kɛt dɛ 'kɔmpra]
report	informe (m)	[in'fɔrmɛ]
to show (ID, etc.)	presentar (vt)	[prɛsɛn'tar]
to sign (vt)	firmar (vt)	[fir'mar]
signature	firma (f)	['firma]
stamp (seal)	sello (m)	['sɛjɔ]
text	texto (m)	['tɛkstɔ]
ticket (for entry)	billete (m)	[bi'jetɛ]
to cross out	tachar (vt)	[ta'tʃar]
to fill out (~ a form)	rellenar (vt)	[rɛje'nar]
waybill	guía (f) de embarque	['gija dɛ im'barke]
will (testament)	testamento (m)	[tɛsta'mɛntɔ]

117. Kinds of business

accounting services	contabilidad (f)	[kɔntabili'dad]
advertising	publicidad (f)	[publiθi'dad]
advertising agency	agencia (f) de publicidad	[a'hɛnθija dɛ publisi'dad]
air-conditioners	climatizadores (m pl)	[klimatiθa'dorɛs]
airline	compañía (f) aérea	[kɔmpa'nija a'ərɛa]
alcoholic drinks	bebidas (f pl) alcohólicas	[bɛ'bidas aʎkɔ'ɔlikas]
antiquities	antigüedad (f)	[antiguɛ'dad]
art gallery	galería (f) de arte	[gale'rija dɛ 'artɛ]
audit services	servicios (m pl) de auditoría	[sɛr'wiθiɔs dɛ auditɔ'rija]
banks	negocio (m) bancario	[nɛ'gɔsiɔ ba'ŋkariɔ]
bar	bar (m)	[bar]
beauty parlor	salón (m) de belleza	[sa'lɜn dɛ bɛ'ʎjeθa]
bookstore	librería (f)	[librɛ'rija]
brewery	fábrica (f) de cerveza	['fabrika dɛ θær'vɛθa]
business center	centro (m) de negocios	['θæntrɔ dɛ nɛ'gɔθiɔs]
business school	escuela (f) de negocios	[ɛsku'ɛʎa dɛ nɛ'gɔθiɔs]
casino	casino (m)	[ka'sinɔ]
construction	construcción (f)	[kɔnstruk'θiɔn]
consulting	consultoría (f)	[kɔnsuʎtɔ'rija]
dental clinic	estomatología (f)	[ɛstɔmatɔlɔ'hia]
design	diseño (m)	[di'sɛɲɔ]
drugstore, pharmacy	farmacia (f)	[far'maθia]
dry cleaners	tintorería (f)	[tintɔrɛ'rija]
employment agency	agencia (f) de empleo	[a'hɛnθija dɛ ɛmp'leɔ]
financial services	servicios (m pl) financieros	[sɛr'wisiɔs finan'sjerɔs]
food products	productos alimenticios	[prɔ'duktɔs alimen'tiθiɔs]
funeral home	funeraria (f)	[funɛ'rarija]
furniture (e.g., house ~)	muebles (m pl)	[mu'ɛbles]
garment	ropa (f), vestido (m)	['rɔpa], [vɛs'tidɔ]
hotel	hotel (m)	[ɔ'tɛʎ]
ice-cream	helado (m)	[ɛ'ʎadɔ]
industry	industria (f)	[in'dustrija]
insurance	seguro (m)	[sɛ'gurɔ]
Internet	internet (m)	[intɛr'nɛt]
investment	inversiones (f pl)	[inwer'sjɔnɛs]
jeweler	joyero (m)	[hɔ'jerɔ]
jewelry	joyería (f)	[hɔje'rija]
laundry (shop)	lavandería (f)	[ʎavandɛ'ria]
legal advisor	asesoría (f) jurídica	[asɛsɔ'rija hu'ridika]
light industry	industria (f) ligera	[in'dustrija li'hɛra]

magazine	revista (f)	[rɛ'wista]
mail-order selling	venta (f) por catálogo	['bɛnta pɔr ka'talɔgɔ]
medicine	medicina (f)	[mɛdi'θina]
movie theater	cine (m)	['θinɛ]
museum	museo (m)	[mu'sɛɔ]
news agency	agencia (f) de información	[a'hɛnθija dɛ infɔrma'sjɔn]
newspaper	periódico (m)	[pɛri'ɔdikɔ]
nightclub	club (m) nocturno	[klub nɔk'turnɔ]
oil (petroleum)	petróleo (m)	[pɛt'rɔleɔ]
parcels service	servicio (m) de entrega	[sɛr'wisiɔ dɛ ɛnt'rɛga]
pharmaceuticals	industria (f) farmacéutica	[in'dustria farma'seutika]
printing (industry)	poligrafía (f)	[pɔligra'fija]
publishing house	editorial (f)	[ɛditɔ'rjaʎ]
radio (~ station)	radio (f)	['radiɔ]
real estate	inmueble (m)	[inmu'ɛble]
restaurant	restaurante (m)	[rɛstau'rantɛ]
security agency	agencia (f) de seguridad	[a'hɛnθija dɛ sɛguri'dad]
sports	deporte (m)	[dɛ'pɔrtɛ]
stock exchange	bolsa (f) de comercio	['bɔʎsa dɛ kɔ'mɛrθiɔ]
store	tienda (f)	['tjenda]
supermarket	supermercado (m)	[supɛrmɛr'kadɔ]
swimming pool	piscina (f)	[pi'θina]
tailors	taller (m)	[ta'jer]
television	televisión (f)	[tɛlewi'θjon]
theater	teatro (m)	[tɛ'atrɔ]
trade	comercio (m)	[kɔ'mɛrsiɔ]
transportation	servicios de transporte	[sɛr'wiθiɔs dɛ trans'pɔrtɛ]
travel	turismo (m)	[tu'rismɔ]
veterinarian	veterinario (m)	[bɛtɛri'nariɔ]
warehouse	almacén (m)	[aʎma'θæn]
waste collection	recojo (m) de basura	[rɛ'kɔhɔ dɛ ba'sura]

Job. Business. Part 2

118. Show. Exhibition

exhibition, show	exposición (f)	[ɛksposi'θion]
trade show	feria (f) comercial	['fɛrja komɛr'θjaʎ]
participation	participación (f)	[partisipa'θion]
to participate (vi)	participar (vi)	[partisi'par]
participant (exhibitor)	participante (m)	[partisi'pantɛ]
director	director (m)	[dirɛk'tor]
organizer's office	dirección (f)	[dirɛk'θion]
organizer	organizador (m)	[organiθa'dor]
to organize (vt)	organizar (vt)	[organi'θar]
participation form	solicitud (f) de participación	[soliθi'tud dɛ partisipa'θion]
to fill out (vt)	rellenar (vt)	[rɛje'nar]
details	detalles (m pl)	[dɛ'tajes]
information	información (f)	[informa'θion]
price	precio (m)	['prɛθio]
including	incluso (adj)	[iŋk'luso]
to include (vt)	incluir (vt)	[iŋklu'ir]
to pay (vi, vt)	pagar (vi, vt)	[pa'gar]
registration fee	cuota (f) de registro	[ku'ota dɛ rɛ'histro]
entrance	entrada (f)	[ɛnt'rada]
pavilion, hall	pabellón (m)	[pabɛ'jon]
to register (vt)	registrar (vt)	[rɛhist'rar]
badge (identity tag)	tarjeta (f) de identificación	[tar'hɛta dɛ identifika'θion]
booth, stand	stand (m)	[stand]
to reserve, to book	reservar (vt)	[rɛsɛr'var]
display case	vitrina (f)	[wit'rina]
spotlight	lámpara (f)	['ʎampara]
design	diseño (m)	[di'sɛɲo]
to place (put, set)	poner (vt)	[po'nɛr]
to be placed	situarse (vr)	[situ'arsɛ]
distributor	distribuidor (m)	[distribui'dor]
supplier	proveedor (m)	[provɛ:'dor]
to supply (vt)	suministrar (vt)	[suminist'rar]

country	país (m)	[pa'is]
foreign (adj)	extranjero (adj)	[εkstran'hεrɔ]
product	producto (m)	[prɔ'duktɔ]

association	asociación (f)	[asɔθia'θion]
conference hall	sala (f) de conferencias	['saʎa dε kɔnfε'rεnθijas]
congress	congreso (m)	[kɔŋ'rεsɔ]
contest (competition)	concurso (m)	[kɔ'ŋkursɔ]

visitor	visitante (m)	[bisi'tantε]
to visit (attend)	visitar (vt)	[bisi'tar]
customer	cliente (m)	[kli'εntε]

119. Mass Media

newspaper	periódico (m)	[pεri'ɔdikɔ]
magazine	revista (f)	[rε'wista]
press (printed media)	prensa (f)	['prεnsa]
radio	radio (f)	['radiɔ]
radio station	estación (f) de radio	[εsta'θion dε 'radiɔ]
television	televisión (f)	[tεlewi'θion]

presenter, host	presentador (m)	[presεnta'dɔr]
newscaster	presentador (m) de noticias	[presεnta'dɔr dε nɔ'tisias]
commentator	comentarista (m)	[kɔmεnta'rista]

journalist	periodista (m)	[pεriɔ'dista]
correspondent (reporter)	corresponsal (m)	[kɔrrεspɔn'saʎ]
press photographer	corresponsal (m) fotográfico	[kɔrrεspɔn'saʎ fɔtɔg'rafikɔ]
reporter	reportero (m)	[rεpor'tεrɔ]

| editor | redactor (m) | [rεdak'tɔr] |
| editor-in-chief | redactor jefe (m) | [rεdak'tɔr 'hεfε] |

to subscribe (to ...)	suscribirse (vr)	[suskri'βirsε]
subscription	suscripción (f)	[suskrεp'θion]
subscriber	suscriptor (m)	[suskrip'tɔr]
to read (vi, vt)	leer (vi, vt)	[le'εr]
reader	lector (m)	[lek'tɔr]

circulation (of newspaper)	tirada (f)	[ti'rada]
monthly (adj)	mensual (adj)	[mεnsu'aʎ]
weekly (adj)	semanal (adj)	[sεma'naʎ]
issue (edition)	número (m)	['numεrɔ]
new (~ issue)	nuevo (adj)	[nu'εβɔ]

| headline | titular (m) | [titu'lar] |
| short article | noticia (f) | [nɔ'tiθia] |

column (regular article)	columna (f)	[kɔ'lumna]
article	artículo (m)	[ar'tikulɔ]
page	página (f)	['pahina]

reportage, report	reportaje (m)	[rɛpɔr'tahɛ]
event (happening)	evento (m)	[ɛ'vɛntɔ]
sensation (news)	sensación (f)	[sɛnsa'θiɔn]
scandal	escándalo (m)	[ɛs'kandalɔ]
scandalous (adj)	escandaloso (adj)	[ɛskanda'lɔsɔ]
great (~ scandal)	gran (adj)	[gran]

program	emisión (f)	[ɛmi'siɔn]
interview	entrevista (f)	[ɛntrɛ'wista]
live broadcast	transmisión (f) en vivo	[transmi'siɔn ɛn 'biβɔ]
channel	canal (m)	[ka'naʎ]

120. Agriculture

agriculture	agricultura (f)	[agrikuʎ'tura]
peasant (masc.)	campesino (m)	[kampɛ'sinɔ]
peasant (fem.)	campesina (f)	[kampɛ'sina]
farmer	granjero (m)	[gran'hɛrɔ]

| tractor | tractor (m) | [trak'tɔr] |
| combine, harvester | cosechadora (f) | [kɔsetʃa'dɔra] |

plow	arado (m)	[a'radɔ]
to plow (vi, vt)	arar (vi, vt)	[a'rar]
plowland	labrado (m)	[ʎab'radɔ]
furrow (in field)	surco (m)	['surkɔ]

to sow (vi, vt)	sembrar (vi, vt)	[sɛmb'rar]
seeder	sembradora (f)	[sɛmbra'dɔra]
sowing (process)	siembra (f)	['sjembra]

| scythe | guadaña (f) | [gua'daɲa] |
| to mow, to scythe | segar (vi, vt) | [sɛ'gar] |

| spade (tool) | pala (f) | ['paʎa] |
| to dig (to till) | layar (vt) | [la'jar] |

hoe	azada (f)	[a'θada]
to hoe, to weed	sachar, escardar	[sa'tʃar], [ɛskar'dar]
weed (plant)	mala hierba (f)	['maʎa 'jerba]

watering can	regadera (f)	[rɛgar'dɛra]
to water (plants)	regar (vt)	[rɛ'gar]
watering (act)	riego (m)	['rjegɔ]
pitchfork	horquilla (f)	[ɔr'kija]
rake	rastrillo (m)	[rast'rijɔ]

fertilizer	fertilizante (m)	[fɛrtili'ðantɛ]
to fertilize (vt)	abonar (vt)	[abɔ'nar]
manure (fertilizer)	estiércol (m)	[ɛs'tⁱerkɔʎ]

field	campo (m)	['kampɔ]
meadow	prado (m)	['pradɔ]
vegetable garden	huerta (f)	[u'ərta]
orchard (e.g., apple ~)	jardín (m)	[har'din]

to pasture (vt)	pacer (vt)	[pa'sɛr]
herdsman	pastor (m)	[pas'tɔr]
pastureland	pastadero (m)	[pasta'dɛrɔ]

| cattle breeding | ganadería (f) | [ganadɛ'rija] |
| sheep farming | cría (f) de ovejas | ['krija dɛ ɔ'βəhas] |

plantation	plantación (f)	[pʎanta'θⁱon]
row (garden bed ~s)	hilera (f)	[i'lera]
hothouse	invernadero (m)	[imbɛrna'dɛrɔ]

| drought (lack of rain) | sequía (f) | [sɛ'kia] |
| dry (~ summer) | seco, árido (adj) | ['sɛkɔ], ['aridɔ] |

| cereal crops | cereales (m pl) | [θærɛ'ales] |
| to harvest, to gather | recolectar (vt) | [rɛkɔlek'tar] |

miller (person)	molinero (m)	[mɔli'nɛrɔ]
mill (e.g., gristmill)	molino (m)	[mɔ'linɔ]
to grind (grain)	moler (vt)	[mɔ'lɛr]
flour	harina (f)	[a'rina]
straw	paja (f)	['paha]

121. Building. Building process

construction site	obra (f)	['ɔbra]
to build (vt)	construir (vt)	[kɔnstru'ir]
construction worker	albañil (m)	[aʎba'niʎ]

project	proyecto (m)	[prɔ'jəktɔ]
architect	arquitecto (m)	[arki'tɛktɔ]
worker	obrero (m)	[ɔb'rɛrɔ]

foundation (of building)	cimientos (m pl)	[θi'mjentɔs]
roof	techo (m)	['tɛʧɔ]
foundation pile	pila (f) de cimentación	['pila dɛ θimenta'θⁱon]
wall	muro (m)	['murɔ]

reinforcing bars	armadura (f)	[arma'dura]
scaffolding	andamio (m)	[an'damiɔ]
concrete	hormigón (m)	[ɔrmi'gɔn]

granite	granito (m)	[gra'nitɔ]
stone	piedra (f)	['pjedra]
brick	ladrillo (m)	[ʎad'rijo]

sand	arena (f)	[a'rɛna]
cement	cemento (m)	[θæ'mɛntɔ]
plaster (for walls)	estuco (m)	[ɛs'tukɔ]
to plaster (vt)	estucar (vt)	[ɛstu'kar]
paint	pintura (f)	[pin'tura]
to paint (~ a wall)	pintar (vt)	[pin'tar]
barrel	barril (m)	[bar'riʎ]

crane	grúa (f)	['grua]
to lift (vt)	levantar (vt)	[levan'tar]
to lower (vt)	bajar (vt)	[ba'har]

bulldozer	bulldózer (m)	[buʎ'dɔθær]
excavator	excavadora (f)	[ɛkskava'dɔra]
scoop, bucket	cuchara (f)	[ku'ʧara]
to dig (excavate)	cavar (vt)	[ka'βar]
hard hat	casco (m)	['kaskɔ]

122. Science. Research. Scientists

science	ciencia (f)	['sjenθija]
scientific (adj)	científico (adj)	[sjen'tifikɔ]
scientist	científico (m)	[sjen'tifikɔ]
theory	teoría (f)	[tɛɔ'rija]

axiom	axioma (m)	[aksi'ɔma]
analysis	análisis (m)	[a'nalisis]
to analyze (vt)	analizar (vt)	[anali'θar]
argument (strong ~)	argumento (m)	[argu'mɛntɔ]
substance (matter)	sustancia (f)	[sus'tanθija]

hypothesis	hipótesis (f)	[i'pɔtɛsis]
dilemma	dilema (m)	[di'lema]
dissertation	tesis (f) de grado	['tɛsis dɛ 'gradɔ]
dogma	dogma (m)	['dɔgma]

doctrine	doctrina (f)	[dɔkt'rina]
research	investigación (f)	[imbɛstiga'θiɔn]
to do research	investigar (vt)	[imbɛsti'gar]
testing	prueba (f)	[pru'ɛβa]
laboratory	laboratorio (m)	[ʎabɔra'tɔriɔ]

method	método (m)	['mɛtɔdɔ]
molecule	molécula (f)	[mɔ'lɛkuʎa]
monitoring	seguimiento (m)	[segi'mjentɔ]
discovery (act, event)	descubrimiento (m)	[dɛskubri'mjentɔ]

postulate	**postulado** (m)	[pɔstu'ʎadɔ]
principle	**principio** (m)	[prin'sipiɔ]
forecast	**pronóstico** (m)	[prɔ'nɔstikɔ]
prognosticate (vt)	**pronosticar** (vt)	[prɔnɔsti'kar]
synthesis	**síntesis** (f)	['sintɛsis]
trend (tendency)	**tendencia** (f)	[tɛn'dɛnsija]
theorem	**teorema** (m)	[tɛɔ'rɛma]
teachings	**enseñanzas** (f pl)	[ɛnsɛ'njanθas]
fact	**hecho** (m)	['ɛʧɔ]
expedition	**expedición** (f)	[ɛkspɛdi'θiɔn]
experiment	**experimento** (m)	[ɛkspɛri'mɛntɔ]
academician	**académico** (m)	[aka'dɛmikɔ]
bachelor (e.g., ~ of Arts)	**bachiller** (m)	[baʧi'jer]
doctor (PhD)	**doctorado** (m)	[dɔktɔ'radɔ]
Associate Professor	**docente** (m)	[dɔ'θæntɛ]
Master (e.g., ~ of Arts)	**Master** (m)	['mastɛr]
professor	**profesor** (m)	[prɔfɛ'sɔr]

Professions and occupations

123. Job search. Dismissal

job	trabajo (m)	[tra'βaho]
staff (work force)	empleados (pl)	[ɛmple'aðɔs]
personnel	personal (m)	[pɛrsɔ'naʎ]
career	carrera (f)	[kar'rɛra]
prospects	perspectiva (f)	[pɛrspɛk'tiβa]
skills (mastery)	maestría (f)	[maɛst'rija]
selection (screening)	selección (f)	[selek'θʲon]
employment agency	agencia (f) de empleo	[a'hɛnθija dɛ ɛmp'leɔ]
résumé	curriculum vitae (m)	[kur'rikulum bi'taɛ]
interview (for job)	entrevista (f)	[ɛntrɛ'wista]
vacancy, opening	vacancia (f)	[va'kansija]
salary, pay	salario (m)	[sa'ʎariɔ]
fixed salary	salario (m) fijo	[sa'ʎariɔ 'fihɔ]
pay, compensation	remuneración (f)	[rɛmunɛra'θʲon]
position (job)	puesto (m)	[pu'ɛstɔ]
duty (of employee)	deber (m)	[dɛ'bɛr]
range of duties	gama (f) de deberes	['gama dɛ dɛ'bɛrɛs]
busy (I'm ~)	ocupado (adj)	[ɔku'paðɔ]
to fire (dismiss)	despedir (vt)	[dɛspɛ'dir]
dismissal	despido (m)	[dɛs'pidɔ]
unemployment	desempleo (m)	[dɛsɛmp'leɔ]
unemployed (n)	desempleado (m)	[dɛsɛmple'aðɔ]
retirement	jubilación (f)	[hubiʎa'θʲon]
to retire (from job)	jubilarse (vr)	[hubi'ʎarsɛ]

124. Business people

director	director (m)	[dirɛk'tɔr]
manager (director)	gerente (m)	[hɛ'rɛntɛ]
boss	jefe (m)	['hɛfɛ]
superior	superior (m)	[supɛ'rʲor]
superiors	superiores (m pl)	[supɛri'ɔrɛs]
president	presidente (m)	[prɛsi'dɛntɛ]

chairman	presidente (m)	[prɛsi'dɛntɛ]
deputy (substitute)	adjunto (m)	[ad'huntɔ]
assistant	asistente (m)	[asis'tɛntɛ]
secretary	secretario, -a (m, f)	[sɛkrɛ'tariɔ] / [a]
personal assistant	secretario (m) particular	[sɛkrɛ'tariɔ partiku'ʎar]

businessman	hombre (m) de negocios	['ɔmbrɛ dɛ nɛ'gɔθiɔs]
entrepreneur	emprendedor (m)	[ɛmprɛndɛ'dɔr]
founder	fundador (m)	[funda'dɔr]
to found (vt)	fundar (vt)	[fun'dar]

incorporator	institutor (m)	[institu'tɔr]
partner	compañero (m)	[kɔmpa'ɲjerɔ]
stockholder	accionista (m)	[akθｊo'nista]

millionaire	millonario (m)	[mijo'nariɔ]
billionaire	multimillonario (m)	[muʎtimijo'nariɔ]
owner, proprietor	propietario (m)	[prɔpje'tariɔ]
landowner	terrateniente (m)	[tɛrratɛ'ɲjentɛ]

client	cliente (m)	[kli'ɛntɛ]
regular client	cliente (m) habitual	[kli'ɛntɛ abitu'aʎ]
buyer (customer)	comprador (m)	[kɔmpra'dɔr]
visitor	visitante (m)	[bisi'tantɛ]

professional (n)	profesional (m)	[prɔfɛsｊo'naʎ]
expert	experto (m)	[ɛks'pɛrtɔ]
specialist	especialista (m)	[ɛspɛθja'lista]

| banker | banquero (m) | [ba'ŋkɛrɔ] |
| broker | broker (m) | ['brɔker] |

cashier, teller	cajero (m)	[ka'hɛrɔ]
accountant	contable (m)	[kɔn'tablɛ]
security guard	guardia (m) de seguridad	[gu'ardija dɛ sɛguri'dad]

investor	inversionista (m)	[invɛrsｊo'nista]
debtor	deudor (m)	[dɛu'dɔr]
creditor	acreedor (m)	[akrɛ:'dɔr]
borrower	prestatario (m)	[prɛsta'tarｊo]

| importer | importador (m) | [impɔrta'dɔr] |
| exporter | exportador (m) | [ɛkspɔrta'dɔr] |

manufacturer	productor (m)	[prɔduk'tɔr]
distributor	distribuidor (m)	[distribui'dɔr]
middleman	intermediario (m)	[intɛrmɛ'djariɔ]

consultant	asesor (m)	[asɛ'sɔr]
sales representative	representante (m)	[rɛprɛsɛn'tantɛ]
agent	agente (m)	[a'hɛntɛ]
insurance agent	agente (m) de seguros	[a'hɛntɛ dɛ sɛ'gurɔs]

125. Service professions

cook	**cocinero** (m)	[koθi'nɛɾo]
chef (kitchen chef)	**jefe** (m) **de cocina**	['hɛfɛ dɛ ko'θina]
baker	**panadero** (m)	[pana'dɛɾo]
bartender	**barman** (m)	['barman]
waiter	**camarero** (m)	[kama'rɛɾo]
waitress	**camarera** (f)	[kama'rɛɾa]
lawyer, attorney	**abogado** (m)	[abo'gadɔ]
lawyer (legal expert)	**jurista** (m)	[hu'rista]
notary	**notario** (m)	[nɔ'tariɔ]
electrician	**electricista** (m)	[ɛlektri'θista]
plumber	**fontanero** (m)	[fɔnta'nɛɾo]
carpenter	**carpintero** (m)	[karpin'tɛɾo]
masseur	**masajista** (m)	[masa'hista]
masseuse	**masajista** (f)	[masa'hista]
doctor	**médico** (m)	['mɛdikɔ]
taxi driver	**taxista** (m)	[tak'sista]
driver	**chófer** (m)	['ʧofɛr]
delivery man	**repartidor** (m)	[rɛparti'dɔr]
chambermaid	**camarera** (f)	[kama'rɛɾa]
security guard	**guardia** (m) **de seguridad**	[gu'ardija dɛ sɛguri'dad]
flight attendant	**azafata** (f)	[aθa'fata]
teacher (in primary school)	**profesor** (m)	[prɔfɛ'sɔr]
librarian	**bibliotecario** (m)	[bibliotɛ'kariɔ]
translator	**traductor** (m)	[traduk'tor]
interpreter	**intérprete** (m)	[in'tɛrprɛtɛ]
guide	**guía** (m)	['gija]
hairdresser	**peluquero** (m)	[pɛlu'kero]
mailman	**cartero** (m)	[kar'tɛɾo]
salesman (store staff)	**vendedor** (m)	[bɛndɛ'dɔr]
gardener	**jardinero** (m)	[hardi'nɛɾo]
domestic servant	**servidor** (m)	[sɛrwi'dɔr]
maid	**criada** (f)	[kri'ada]
cleaner (cleaning lady)	**mujer** (f) **de la limpieza**	[mu'hɛr dɛ ʎa lim'pjeθa]

126. Military professions and ranks

private	**soldado** (m) **raso**	[sɔʎ'dadɔ 'rasɔ]
sergeant	**sargento** (m)	[sar'hɛntɔ]

| lieutenant | teniente (m) | [tɛ'ɲjentɛ] |
| captain | capitán (m) | [kapi'tan] |

major	mayor (m)	[ma'jor]
colonel	coronel (m)	[kɔrɔ'nɛʎ]
general	general (m)	[hɛnɛ'raʎ]
marshal	mariscal (m)	[maris'kaʎ]
admiral	almirante (m)	[aʎmi'rantɛ]

military man	militar (m)	[mili'tar]
soldier	soldado (m)	[sɔʎ'dadɔ]
officer	oficial (m)	[ɔfi'θjaʎ]
commander	comandante (m)	[kɔman'dantɛ]

border guard	guardafronteras (m)	[guardafrɔn'tɛras]
radio operator	radio-operador (m)	['radʲo ɔpera'dɔr]
scout (searcher)	explorador (m)	[ɛksplɔra'dɔr]
pioneer (sapper)	zapador (m)	[θapa'dɔr]
marksman	tirador (m)	[tira'dɔr]
navigator	navegador (m)	[navɛga'dɔr]

127. Officials. Priests

| king | rey (m) | [rɛj] |
| queen | reina (f) | ['rɛjna] |

| prince | príncipe (m) | ['prinθipɛ] |
| princess | princesa (f) | [prin'θæsa] |

| tsar, czar | zar (m) | [θar] |
| czarina | zarina (f) | [θa'rina] |

president	presidente (m)	[prɛsi'dɛntɛ]
Secretary (~ of State)	ministro (m)	[mi'nistrɔ]
prime minister	primer ministro (m)	[pri'mɛr mi'nistrɔ]
senator	senador (m)	[sɛna'dɔr]

diplomat	diplomático (m)	[diplɔ'matikɔ]
consul	cónsul (m)	['kɔnsuʎ]
ambassador	embajador (m)	[ɛmbaha'dɔr]
advisor (military ~)	consejero (m)	[kɔnsɛ'hɛrɔ]

official (civil servant)	funcionario (m)	[funθio'nario]
prefect	prefecto (m)	[prɛ'fɛktɔ]
mayor	alcalde (m)	[aʎ'kaʎdɛ]

judge	juez (m)	[hu'ɛθ]
district attorney (prosecutor)	fiscal (m)	[fis'kaʎ]
missionary	misionero (m)	[misʲo'nɛrɔ]

monk	monje (m)	['monhɛ]
abbot	abad (m)	[a'βad]
rabbi	rabino (m)	[ra'βino]

vizier	visir (m)	[bi'sir]
shah	sha (m), shah (m)	[ʃa]
sheikh	jeque (m)	['hɛke]

128. Agricultural professions

beekeeper	apicultor (m)	[apikuʎ'tor]
herder, shepherd	pastor (m)	[pas'tor]
agronomist	agrónomo (m)	[ag'ronomo]
cattle breeder	ganadero (m)	[gana'dɛro]
veterinarian	veterinario (m)	[bɛtɛri'nario]

farmer	granjero (m)	[gran'hɛro]
winemaker	vinicultor (m)	[binikuʎ'tor]
zoologist	zoólogo (m)	[θo'ologo]
cowboy	cowboy (m)	[kov'boj]

129. Art professions

| actor | actor (m) | [ak'tor] |
| actress | actriz (f) | [akt'riθ] |

| singer (masc.) | cantante (m) | [kan'tantɛ] |
| singer (fem.) | cantante (f) | [kan'tantɛ] |

| dancer (masc.) | bailarín (m) | [bajʎa'rin] |
| dancer (fem.) | bailarina (f) | [bajʎa'rina] |

| performing artist (masc.) | artista (m) | [ar'tista] |
| performing artist (fem.) | artista (f) | [ar'tista] |

musician	músico (m)	['musiko]
pianist	pianista (m)	[pja'nista]
guitar player	guitarrista (m)	[gitar'rista]

conductor (orchestra ~)	director (m) de orquesta	[dirɛk'tor dɛ or'kɛsta]
composer	compositor (m)	[komposi'tor]
impresario	empresario (m)	[ɛmprɛ'sario]

movie director	director (m) de cine	[direk'tor dɛ 'θinɛ]
producer	productor (m)	[produk'tor]
scriptwriter	guionista (m)	[gijo'nista]
critic	crítico (m)	['kritiko]
writer	escritor (m)	[ɛskri'tor]

poet	poeta (m)	[po'ɛta]
sculptor	escultor (m)	[ɛskuʎ'tɔr]
artist (painter)	pintor (m)	[pin'tɔr]

juggler	malabarista (m)	[maʎaba'rista]
clown	payaso (m)	[pa'jasɔ]
acrobat	acróbata (m)	[ak'rɔβata]
magician	ilusionista (m)	[ilysɔ'nista]

130. Various professions

doctor	médico (m)	['mɛdikɔ]
nurse	enfermera (f)	[ɛnfɛr'mɛra]
psychiatrist	psiquiatra (m)	[siki'atra]
dentist	estomatólogo (m)	[ɛstɔma'tɔlɔgɔ]
surgeon	cirujano (m)	[θiru'hanɔ]

| astronaut | astronauta (m) | [astrɔ'nauta] |
| astronomer | astrónomo (m) | [ast'rɔnɔmɔ] |

driver (of taxi, etc.)	conductor (m)	[kɔnduk'tɔr]
engineer (train driver)	maquinista (m)	[maki'nista]
mechanic	mecánico (m)	[mɛ'kanikɔ]

miner	minero (m)	[mi'nɛrɔ]
worker	obrero (m)	[ɔb'rɛrɔ]
metalworker	cerrajero (m)	[θærra'hɛrɔ]
joiner (carpenter)	carpintero (m)	[karpin'tɛrɔ]
turner	tornero (m)	[tɔr'nɛrɔ]
construction worker	albañil (m)	[aʎba'niʎ]
welder	soldador (m)	[sɔʎda'dɔr]

professor (title)	profesor (m)	[prɔfɛ'sɔr]
architect	arquitecto (m)	[arki'tɛktɔ]
historian	historiador (m)	[istɔria'dɔr]
scientist	científico (m)	[sjen'tifikɔ]
physicist	físico (m)	['fisikɔ]
chemist (scientist)	químico (m)	['kimikɔ]

archeologist	arqueólogo (m)	[arke'ɔlɔgɔ]
geologist	geólogo (m)	[hɛ'ɔlɔgɔ]
researcher	investigador (m)	[imbɛstiga'dɔr]

| babysitter | niñera (f) | [ni'ɲjera] |
| teacher, educator | pedagogo (m) | [pɛda'gɔgɔ] |

editor	redactor (m)	[rɛdak'tɔr]
editor-in-chief	redactor jefe (m)	[rɛdak'tɔr 'hɛfɛ]
correspondent	corresponsal (m)	[kɔrrɛspɔn'saʎ]
typist (fem.)	mecanógrafa (f)	[mɛka'nɔgrafa]

designer	diseñador (m)	[disɛɲja'dɔr]
computer expert	especialista (m) en ordenadores	[ɛspɛsja'lista ɛn ɔrdɛna'dɔrɛs]
programmer	programador (m)	[prɔgrama'dɔr]
engineer (designer)	ingeniero (m)	[inhɛ'ɲjerɔ]

sailor	marino (m)	[ma'rinɔ]
seaman	marinero (m)	[mari'nɛrɔ]
rescuer	socorrista (m)	[sɔkɔr'rista]

fireman	bombero (m)	[bɔm'bɛrɔ]
policeman	policía (m)	[pɔli'θija]
watchman	vigilante (m) nocturno	[wihi'ʎantɛ nɔk'turnɔ]
detective	detective (m)	[dɛtɛk'tiβə]

customs officer	aduanero (m)	[adua'nɛrɔ]
bodyguard	guardaespaldas (m)	[guardaɛs'paʎdas]
prison guard	guardia (m) de prisiones	[gu'ardija dɛ pri'sjɔnɛs]
inspector	inspector (m)	[inspɛk'tɔr]

sportsman	deportista (m)	[dɛpɔr'tista]
trainer, coach	entrenador (m)	[ɛntrɛna'dɔr]
butcher	carnicero (m)	[karni'θærɔ]
cobbler	zapatero (m)	[θapa'tɛrɔ]
merchant	comerciante (m)	[kɔmer'θjantɛ]
loader (person)	cargador (m)	[karga'dɔr]

| fashion designer | diseñador (m) de modas | [disɛɲja'dɔr dɛ 'mɔdas] |
| model (fem.) | modelo (f) | [mɔ'dɛlɔ] |

131. Occupations. Social status

| schoolboy | escolar (m) | [ɛskɔ'ʎar] |
| student (college ~) | estudiante (m) | [ɛstu'djantɛ] |

philosopher	filósofo (m)	[fi'lɔsɔfɔ]
economist	economista (m)	[ɛkɔnɔ'mista]
inventor	inventor (m)	[imbɛn'tɔr]

unemployed (n)	desempleado (m)	[dɛsɛmple'adɔ]
retiree	jubilado (m)	[hubi'ʎadɔ]
spy, secret agent	espía (m)	[ɛs'pia]

prisoner	prisionero (m)	[prisjɔ'nɛrɔ]
striker	huelguista (m)	[uəʎ'gista]
bureaucrat	burócrata (m)	[bu'rɔkrata]
traveler	viajero (m)	[bja'hɛrɔ]

| homosexual | homosexual (m) | [ɔmɔsɛksu'aʎ] |
| hacker | pirata (m) informático | [pi'rata infɔr'matikɔ] |

hippie	**hippie** (m)	['hippi]
bandit	**bandido** (m)	[ban'dido]
hit man, killer	**sicario** (m)	[si'kario]
drug addict	**drogadicto** (m)	[droga'dikto]
drug dealer	**narcotraficante** (m)	[narkotrafi'kantɛ]
prostitute (fem.)	**prostituta** (f)	[prosti'tuta]
pimp	**chulo** (m), **proxeneta** (m)	['tʃulɔ], [prokse'nɛta]
sorcerer	**brujo** (m)	['bruhɔ]
sorceress	**bruja** (f)	['bruha]
pirate	**pirata** (m)	[pi'rata]
slave	**esclavo** (m)	[ɛsk'ʎaβɔ]
samurai	**samurai** (m)	[samu'raj]
savage (primitive)	**salvaje** (m)	[saʎ'vahɛ]

Sports

132. Kinds of sports. Sportspersons

sportsman	**deportista** (m)	[dɛpɔr'tista]
kind of sports	**tipo** (m) **de deporte**	['tipɔ dɛ dɛ'pɔrtɛ]
basketball	**baloncesto** (m)	[balɔn'θæstɔ]
basketball player	**baloncestista** (m)	[balɔnθæs'tista]
baseball	**béisbol** (m)	['bɛjsbɔl]
baseball player	**beisbolista** (m)	[bɛjsbɔ'lista]
soccer	**fútbol** (m)	['futbɔʎ]
soccer player	**futbolista** (m)	[futbɔ'lista]
goalkeeper	**portero** (m)	[pɔr'tɛrɔ]
hockey	**hockey** (m)	['ɔkɛj]
hockey player	**jugador** (m) **de hockey**	[huga'dɔr dɛ 'ɔkɛj]
volleyball	**voleibol** (m)	[vɔlej'bɔʎ]
volleyball player	**voleibolista** (m)	[vɔlejbɔ'lista]
boxing	**boxeo** (m)	[bɔk'sɛɔ]
boxer	**boxeador** (m)	[bɔksɛa'dɔr]
wrestling	**lucha** (f)	['lytʃa]
wrestler	**luchador** (m)	[lytʃa'dɔr]
karate	**kárate** (m)	['karatɛ]
karate fighter	**karateka** (m)	[kara'tɛka]
judo	**judo** (m)	['judɔ]
judo athlete	**judoka** (m)	[ju'dɔka]
tennis	**tenis** (m)	['tɛnis]
tennis player	**tenista** (m)	[tɛ'nista]
swimming	**natación** (f)	[nata'sɔn]
swimmer	**nadador** (m)	[nada'dɔr]
fencing	**esgrima** (f)	[ɛsg'rima]
fencer	**esgrimidor** (m)	[ɛsgrimi'dɔr]
chess	**ajedrez** (m)	[ahɛd'rɛθ]
chess player	**ajedrecista** (m)	[ahɛdrɛ'θista]

alpinism	alpinismo (m)	[aʎpi'nismo]
alpinist	alpinista (m)	[aʎpi'nista]
running	carrera (f)	[kar'rɛra]
runner	corredor (m)	[korrɛ'dor]
athletics	atletismo (m)	[atlɛ'tismo]
athlete	atleta (m)	[at'leta]
horseback riding	deporte (m) hípico	[dɛ'portɛ 'hipiko]
horse rider	jinete (m)	[hi'nɛtɛ]
figure skating	patinaje (m) artístico	[pati'nahɛ ar'tistiko]
figure skater (masc.)	patinador (m)	[patina'dor]
figure skater (fem.)	patinadora (f)	[patina'dora]
weightlifting	levantamiento (m) de pesas	[levanta'mjento dɛ 'pesas]
car racing	carreras (f pl) de coches	[kar'rɛras dɛ 'kotʃes]
racing driver	piloto (m) de carreras	[pi'loto dɛ kar'rɛras]
cycling	ciclismo (m)	[sik'lismo]
cyclist	ciclista (m)	[sik'lista]
broad jump	salto (m) de longitud	['saʎto dɛ loŋhi'tud]
pole vault	salto (m) con pértiga	['saʎto kon 'pɛrtiga]
jumper	saltador (m)	[saʎta'dor]

133. Kinds of sports. Miscellaneous

football	fútbol (m) americano	['futboʎ amɛri'kano]
badminton	bádminton (m)	['badminton]
biathlon	biatlón (m)	[biat'lon]
billiards	billar (m)	[bi'jar]
bobsled	bobsleigh (m)	['bobslej]
bodybuilding	culturismo (m)	[kuʎtu'rismo]
water polo	waterpolo (m)	[vatɛr'polɜ]
handball	balonmano (m)	[balon'mano]
golf	golf (m)	[goʎf]
rowing	remo (m)	['rɛmo]
scuba diving	buceo (m)	[by'θæo]
cross-country skiing	esquí (m) de fondo	[ɛs'ki dɛ 'fondo]
ping-pong	tenis (m) de mesa	['tɛnis dɛ 'mɛsa]
sailing	vela (f)	['bɛʎa]
rally racing	rally (m)	['raʎi]
rugby	rugby (m)	['rugbi]
snowboarding	snowboarding (m)	[snou'βordin]
archery	tiro (m) con arco	['tiro kon 'arko]

134. Gym

barbell	**barra** (f) **de pesas**	['barra dɛ 'pɛsas]
dumbbells	**pesas** (f pl)	['pɛsas]
training machine	**aparato** (m) **de ejercicios**	[apa'ratɔ dɛ ɛhɛr'siθiɔs]
bicycle trainer	**bicicleta** (f) **estática**	[bisik'leta ɛs'tatika]
treadmill	**cinta** (f) **de correr**	['θinta dɛ kɔr'rɛr]
horizontal bar	**barra** (f) **fija**	['barra 'fiha]
parallel bars	**barras** (f pl) **paralelas**	['barras para'leʎas]
vaulting horse	**potro** (m)	['pɔtrɔ]
mat (in gym)	**colchoneta** (f)	[kɔʎtʃɔ'nɛta]
jump rope	**comba** (f)	['kɔmba]
aerobics	**aeróbica** (f)	[aɛ'rɔβika]
yoga	**yoga** (m)	['jɔga]

135. Hockey

hockey	**hockey** (m)	['ɔkɛj]
hockey player	**jugador** (m) **de hockey**	[huga'dɔr dɛ 'ɔkɛj]
to play hockey	**jugar al hockey**	[hu'gar aʎ 'ɔkɛj]
ice	**hielo** (m)	['jelɔ]
puck	**disco** (m)	['diskɔ]
hockey stick	**palo** (m) **de hockey**	['palɔ dɛ 'ɔkɛj]
ice skates	**patines** (m pl)	[pa'tinɛs]
board	**muro** (m)	['murɔ]
shot	**tiro** (m)	['tirɔ]
goaltender	**portero** (m)	[pɔr'tɛrɔ]
goal (score)	**gol** (m)	[gɔʎ]
to score a goal	**marcar un gol**	[mar'kar un 'gɔʎ]
period	**período** (m)	[pɛ'riɔdɔ]
second period	**segundo período** (m)	[sɛ'gundɔ pɛ'riɔdɔ]
substitutes bench	**banquillo** (m) **de reserva**	[ba'ŋkijɔ dɛ rɛ'sɛrva]

136. Football

soccer	**fútbol** (m)	['futbɔʎ]
soccer player	**futbolista** (m)	[futbɔ'lista]
to play soccer	**jugar al fútbol**	[hu'gar aʎ 'futbɔʎ]
major league	**liga** (f) **superior**	['liga supɛr'ɔr]
soccer club	**club** (m) **de fútbol**	[klub dɛ 'futbɔʎ]

| coach | entrenador (m) | [ɛntrɛna'dɔr] |
| owner, proprietor | propietario (m) | [prɔpje'tarjɔ] |

team	equipo (m)	[ɛ'kipɔ]
team captain	capitán (m) del equipo	[kapi'tan dɛʎ ɛ'kipɔ]
player	jugador (m)	[huga'dɔr]
substitute	reserva (m)	[rɛ'sɛrva]

forward	delantero (m)	[dɛʎan'tɛrɔ]
center forward	delantero centro (m)	[deʎan'tɛrɔ 'sɛntrɔ]
striker, scorer	goleador (m)	[gɔlea'dɔr]
defender, back	defensa (m)	[dɛ'fɛnsa]
halfback	medio (m)	['mɛdjɔ]

match	match (m)	[matʃ]
to meet (vi, vt)	encontrarse (vr)	[ɛŋkɔnt'rarsɛ]
final	final (m)	[fi'naʎ]
semi-final	semifinal (f)	[sɛmifi'naʎ]
championship	campeonato (m)	[kampɛɔ'natɔ]

period, half	tiempo (m)	['tʲempɔ]
first period	primer tiempo (m)	[pri'mɛr 'tʲempɔ]
half-time	descanso (m)	[dɛs'kansɔ]

goal	puerta (f)	[pu'ɛrta]
goalkeeper	portero (m)	[pɔr'tɛrɔ]
goalpost	poste (m)	['pɔstɛ]
crossbar	larguero (m)	[ʎar'gɛrɔ]
net	red (f)	[rɛd]
to concede a goal	recibir un gol	[rɛθi'βir un gɔʎ]

ball	balón (m)	[ba'lɔn]
pass	pase (m)	['pasɛ]
kick	tiro (m)	['tirɔ]
to kick (~ the ball)	lanzar un tiro	[ʎan'θar un 'tirɔ]
free kick	tiro (m) de castigo	['tirɔ dɛ kas'tigɔ]
corner kick	saque (m) de esquina	['sake dɛ ɛs'kina]

attack	ataque (m)	[a'take]
counterattack	contraataque (m)	[kɔntra:'take]
combination	combinación (f)	[kɔmbina'θʲon]

referee	árbitro (m)	['arbitrɔ]
to whistle (vi)	silbar (vi)	[siʎ'bar]
whistle (sound)	silbato (m)	[siʎ'batɔ]
foul, misconduct	infracción (f)	[infrak'θʲon]
to commit a foul	cometer una infracción	[kɔme'tɛr una infrak'θʲon]
to send off	expulsar del campo	[ɛkspuʎ'sar dɛʎ 'kampɔ]

yellow card	tarjeta (f) amarilla	[tar'hɛta ama'rija]
red card	tarjeta (f) roja	[tar'hɛta 'rɔha]
disqualification	descalificación (f)	[dɛskalifika'θʲon]

to disqualify (vt)	descalificar (vt)	[dɛskalifi'kar]
penalty kick	penalti (m)	[pɛ'naʎti]
wall	barrera (f)	[bar'rɛra]
to score (vi, vt)	meter un gol	[me'tɛr un gɔʎ]
goal (score)	gol (m)	[gɔʎ]
to score a goal	marcar un gol	[mar'kar un 'gɔʎ]
substitution	reemplazo (m)	[rɛ:mp'ʎaθɔ]
to replace (vt)	reemplazar (vt)	[rɛ:mpʎa'θar]
rules	reglas (f pl)	['rɛgʎas]
tactics	táctica (f)	['taktika]
stadium	estadio (m)	[ɛs'tadiɔ]
stand (bleachers)	gradería (f)	[gradɛ'rija]
fan, supporter	hincha (m)	['intʃa]
to shout (vi)	gritar (vi)	[gri'tar]
scoreboard	tablero (m)	[tab'lerɔ]
score	tanteo (m)	[tan'tɛɔ]
defeat	derrota (f)	[dɛr'rɔta]
to lose (not win)	perder (vi)	[pɛr'dɛr]
draw	empate (m)	[ɛm'patɛ]
to draw (vi)	empatar (vi)	[ɛmpa'tar]
victory	victoria (f)	[bik'tɔrija]
to win (vi, vt)	ganar (vi)	[ga'ɲar]
champion	campeón (m)	[kampɛ'ɔn]
best (adj)	mejor (adj)	[mɛ'hɔr]
to congratulate (vt)	felicitar (vt)	[fɛliθi'tar]
commentator	comentarista (m)	[kɔmɛnta'rista]
to commentate (vt)	comentar (vt)	[kɔmɛn'tar]
broadcast	transmisión (f)	[transmi'θion]

137. Alpine skiing

skis	esquís (m pl)	[ɛs'kis]
to ski (vi)	esquiar (vi)	[ɛski'jar]
mountain-ski resort	estación (f) de esquí	[ɛsta'θion dɛ ɛs'ki]
ski lift	telesquí (m)	[teles'ki]
ski poles	bastones (m pl)	[bas'tonɛs]
slope	cuesta (f)	[ku'ɛsta]
slalom	eslalon (m)	[ɛsla'lɔn]

138. Tennis. Golf

golf	golf (m)	[gɔʎf]
golf club	club (m) de golf	['klub dɛ 'gɔʎf]

golfer	**jugador** (m) **de golf**	[huga'dɔr dɛ 'gɔʎf]
hole	**hoyo** (m)	['ɔjo]
club	**palo** (m)	['palɜ]
tennis	**tenis** (m)	['tɛnis]
tennis court	**cancha** (f) **de tenis**	['kantʃa dɛ 'tɛnis]
serve	**saque** (m)	['sake]
to serve (vt)	**sacar** (vi)	[sa'kar]
racket	**raqueta** (f)	[ra'keta]
net	**red** (f)	[rɛd]
ball	**pelota** (f)	[pɛ'lɜta]

139. Chess

chess	**ajedrez** (m)	[ahɛd'rɛθ]
chessmen	**piezas** (f pl)	['pjeθas]
chess player	**ajedrecista** (m)	[ahɛdrɛ'θista]
chessboard	**tablero** (m) **de ajedrez**	[tab'lerɔ dɛ ahɛd'rɛθ]
chessman	**pieza** (f)	['pjeθa]
White (white pieces)	**blancas** (f pl)	['bʎaŋkas]
Black (black pieces)	**negras** (f pl)	['nɛgras]
pawn	**peón** (m)	[pɛ'ɔn]
bishop	**alfil** (m)	[aʎ'fiʎ]
knight	**caballo** (m)	[ka'βajo]
rook (castle)	**torre** (f)	['tɔrrɛ]
queen	**reina** (f)	['rɛjna]
king	**rey** (m)	[rɛj]
move	**jugada** (f)	[hu'gada]
to move (vi, vt)	**jugar** (vt)	[hu'gar]
to sacrifice (vt)	**sacrificar** (vt)	[sakrifi'kar]
castling	**enroque** (m)	[ɛn'rɔke]
check	**jaque** (m)	['hake]
checkmate	**mate** (m)	['matɛ]
chess tournament	**torneo** (m) **de ajedrez**	[tɔr'nɛɔ dɛ ahɛd'rɛθ]
Grand Master	**gran maestro** (m)	[gran ma'ɛstrɔ]
combination	**combinación** (f)	[kɔmbina'θʲon]
game (in chess)	**partida** (f)	[par'tida]
checkers	**damas** (f pl)	['damas]

140. Boxing

boxing	**boxeo** (m)	[bɔk'sɛɔ]
fight (bout)	**combate** (m)	[kɔm'batɛ]
boxing match	**pelea** (f) **de boxeo**	[pe'lɛa dɛ bɔk'sɛɔ]

round (in boxing)	**asalto** (m)	[a'saʎtɔ]

ring	**cuadrilátero** (m)	[kuadri'ʎatɛrɔ]
gong	**gong** (m)	[gɔŋ]

punch	**golpe** (m)	['gɔʎpɛ]
knock-down	**knockdown** (m)	[nɔk'daun]
knockout	**nocaut** (m)	[nɔ'kaut]
to knock out	**noquear** (vt)	[nɔkɛ'ar]

boxing glove	**guante** (m) **de boxeo**	[gu'antɛ dɛ bɔk'sɛɔ]
referee	**árbitro** (m)	['arbitrɔ]

lightweight	**peso** (m) **ligero**	['pɛsɔ li'hɛrɔ]
middleweight	**peso** (m) **medio**	['pɛsɔ 'mɛdiɔ]
heavyweight	**peso** (m) **pesado**	['pɛsɔ pɛ'sadɔ]

141. Sports. Miscellaneous

Olympic Games	**Juegos** (m pl) **Olímpicos**	[hu'ɛgɔs ɔ'limpikɔs]
winner	**vencedor** (m)	[bɛnθæ'dɔr]
to be winning	**vencer** (vi)	[bɛn'θær]
to win (vi)	**ganar** (vi)	[ga'ɲar]

leader	**líder** (m)	['lidɛr]
to lead (vi)	**llevar la delantera**	[je'βar ʎa deʎan'tɛra]

first place	**primer puesto** (m)	[pri'mɛr pu'ɛstɔ]
second place	**segundo puesto** (m)	[sɛ'gundɔ pu'ɛstɔ]
third place	**tercer puesto** (m)	[tɛr'θær pu'ɛstɔ]

medal	**medalla** (f)	[mɛ'daja]
trophy	**trofeo** (m)	[trɔ'fɛɔ]
prize cup (trophy)	**copa** (f)	['kɔpa]
prize (in game)	**premio** (m)	['prɛmiɔ]
main prize	**premio** (m) **principal**	['prɛmiɔ prinθi'paʎ]

record	**record** (m)	['rɛkɔrd]
to set a record	**establecer un record**	[ɛstable'θær un 'rɛkɔrd]

final	**final** (m)	[fi'naʎ]
final (adj)	**de final** (adj)	[dɛ fi'naʎ]

champion	**campeón** (m)	[kampɛ'ɔn]
championship	**campeonato** (m)	[kampɛɔ'natɔ]

stadium	**estadio** (m)	[ɛs'tadiɔ]
stand (bleachers)	**gradería** (f)	[gradɛ'rija]
fan, supporter	**hincha** (m)	['intʃa]
opponent, rival	**adversario** (m)	[advɛr'sariɔ]

| start | arrancadero (m) | [arraŋka'dɛrɔ] |
| finish line | línea (f) de meta | ['linea dɛ 'meta] |

| defeat | derrota (f) | [dɛr'rɔta] |
| to lose (not win) | perder (vi) | [pɛr'dɛr] |

referee	árbitro (m)	['arbitrɔ]
jury	jurado (m)	[hu'radɔ]
score	cuenta (f)	[ku'ɛnta]
draw	empate (m)	[ɛm'patɛ]
to draw (vi)	empatar (vi)	[ɛmpa'tar]
point	punto (m)	['puntɔ]
result (final score)	resultado (m)	[rɛsuʎ'tadɔ]

half-time	descanso (m)	[dɛs'kansɔ]
doping	droga (f), doping (m)	['drɔga], ['dɔpin]
to penalize (vt)	penalizar (vt)	[penali'θar]
to disqualify (vt)	descalificar (vt)	[dɛskalifi'kar]

apparatus	aparato (m)	[apa'ratɔ]
javelin	jabalina (f)	[haba'lina]
shot put ball	peso (m)	['pɛsɔ]
ball (snooker, etc.)	bola (f)	['bɔʎa]

aim (target)	objetivo (m)	[ɔbhɛ'tiβɔ]
target	blanco (m)	['bʎaŋkɔ]
to shoot (vi)	tirar (vi)	[ti'rar]
precise (~ shot)	preciso (adj)	[prɛ'sisɔ]

trainer, coach	entrenador (m)	[ɛntrɛna'dɔr]
to train (sb)	entrenar (vt)	[ɛntrɛ'nar]
to train (vi)	entrenarse (vr)	[ɛntrɛ'narsɛ]
training	entrenamiento (m)	[ɛntrɛna'mjentɔ]

gym	gimnasio (m)	[him'nasiɔ]
exercise (physical)	ejercicio (m)	[ɛhɛr'θisiɔ]
warm-up (of athlete)	calentamiento (m)	[kalenta'mjentɔ]

Education

142. School

school	escuela (f)	[ɛsku'ɛʎa]
headmaster	director (m) de escuela	[direk'tɔr dɛ ɛsku'ɛla]
pupil (boy)	alumno (m)	[a'lymnɔ]
pupil (girl)	alumna (f)	[a'lymna]
schoolboy	escolar (m)	[ɛskɔ'ʎar]
schoolgirl	escolar (f)	[ɛskɔ'ʎar]
to teach (sb)	enseñar (vt)	[ɛnsɛ'ɲjar]
to learn (language, etc.)	aprender (vt)	[aprɛn'dɛr]
to learn by heart	aprender de memoria	[aprɛn'dɛr dɛ mɛ'mɔrija]
to study (work to learn)	aprender (vt)	[aprɛn'dɛr]
to be in school	estar en la escuela	[ɛs'tar ɛn ʎa ɛsku'ɛla]
to go to school	ir a la escuela	[ir a la ɛsku'ɛla]
alphabet	alfabeto (m)	[aʎfa'βətɔ]
subject (at school)	materia (f)	[ma'tɛrija]
classroom	clase (f), aula (f)	['kʎasɛ], [auʎa]
lesson	lección (f)	[lek'θⁱon]
recess	recreo (m)	[rɛk'rɛɔ]
school bell	campana (f)	[kam'pana]
school desk	pupitre (m)	[pu'pitrɛ]
chalkboard	pizarra (f)	[pi'θarra]
grade	nota (f)	['nɔta]
good grade	buena nota (f)	[bu'ɛna 'nɔta]
bad grade	mala nota (f)	['maʎa 'nɔta]
to give a grade	poner una nota	[pɔ'nɛr 'una 'nɔta]
mistake, error	falta (f)	['faʎta]
to make mistakes	hacer faltas	[a'θær 'faʎtas]
to correct (an error)	corregir (vt)	[kɔrrɛ'hir]
cheat sheet	chuleta (f)	[ʧu'leta]
homework	deberes (m pl) de casa	[dɛ'bɛrɛs dɛ 'kasa]
exercise (in education)	ejercicio (m)	[ɛhɛr'θisiɔ]
to be present	estar presente	[ɛs'tar prɛ'sɛntɛ]
to be absent	estar ausente	[ɛs'tar au'sɛntɛ]
to miss school	faltar a las clases	[faʎ'tar a ʎas 'kʎasɛs]

to punish (vt)	castigar (vt)	[kasti'gar]
punishment	castigo (m)	[kas'tigɔ]
conduct (behavior)	conducta (f)	[kɔn'dukta]

report card	libreta (f) de notas	[lib'rɛta dɛ 'nɔtas]
pencil	lápiz (f)	['ʎapiθ]
eraser	goma (f) de borrar	['gɔma dɛ bɔr'rar]
chalk	tiza (f)	['tiθa]
pencil case	cartuchera (f)	[kartu'tʃəra]

schoolbag	mochila (f)	[mɔ'tʃiʎa]
pen	bolígrafo (m)	[bɔ'ligrafɔ]
school notebook	cuaderno (m)	[kua'dɛrnɔ]
textbook	manual (m)	[manu'aʎ]
compasses	compás (m)	[kɔm'pas]

to draw (a blueprint, etc.)	trazar (vi, vt)	[tra'θar]
technical drawing	dibujo (m) técnico	[di'βuhɔ 'tɛknikɔ]

poem	poema (m), poesía (f)	[pɔ'ɛma], [pɔɛ'sija]
by heart (adv)	de memoria (adv)	[dɛ mɛ'mɔrija]
to learn by heart	aprender de memoria	[aprɛn'dɛr dɛ mɛ'mɔrija]

school vacation	vacaciones (f pl)	[baka'θⁱɔnɛs]
to be on vacation	estar de vacaciones	[ɛs'tar dɛ baka'sⁱɔnɛs]
to spend one's vacation	pasar las vacaciones	[pa'sar ʎas baka'sⁱɔnɛs]

test (written math ~)	prueba (f) escrita	[pru'ɛβa ɛsk'rita]
essay (composition)	composición (f)	[kɔmpɔsi'θⁱɔn]
dictation	dictado (m)	[dik'tadɔ]
exam	examen (m)	[ɛk'samɛn]
to take an exam	hacer un examen	[a'θær un ɛk'samɛn]
experiment (chemical ~)	experimento (m)	[ɛkspɛri'mɛntɔ]

143. College. University

academy	academia (f)	[aka'dɛmja]
university	universidad (f)	[univɛrsi'dad]
faculty (section)	facultad (f)	[fakuʎ'tad]

student (masc.)	estudiante (m)	[ɛstu'djantɛ]
student (fem.)	estudiante (f)	[ɛstu'djantɛ]
lecturer (teacher)	profesor (m)	[prɔfɛ'sɔr]

lecture hall, room	aula (f)	['auʎa]
graduate	graduado (m)	[gradu'adɔ]
diploma	diploma (m)	[dip'lɔma]
dissertation	tesis (f) de grado	['tɛsis dɛ 'gradɔ]
study (report)	estudio (m)	[ɛs'tudiɔ]
laboratory	laboratorio (m)	[ʎabɔra'tɔriɔ]

lecture	clase (f)	[ˈkʎasɛ]
course mate	compañero (m) de curso	[kɔmpaˈɲjerɔ dɛ ˈkursɔ]
scholarship	beca (f)	[ˈbɛka]
academic degree	grado (m) académico	[ˈgradɔ akaˈdemikɔ]

144. Sciences. Disciplines

mathematics	matemáticas (f pl)	[matɛˈmatikas]
algebra	álgebra (f)	[ˈalhɛbra]
geometry	geometría (f)	[hɛɔmetˈrija]
astronomy	astronomía (f)	[astrɔnɔˈmija]
biology	biología (f)	[biɔlɔˈhija]
geography	geografía (f)	[hɛɔgraˈfija]
geology	geología (f)	[hɛɔlɔˈhija]
history	historia (f)	[isˈtɔrja]
medicine	medicina (f)	[mɛdiˈθina]
pedagogy	pedagogía (f)	[pɛdagɔˈhija]
law	derecho (m)	[dɛˈrɛʧɔ]
physics	física (f)	[ˈfisika]
chemistry	química (f)	[ˈkimika]
philosophy	filosofía (f)	[filɔsɔˈfija]
psychology	psicología (f)	[sikɔlɔˈhija]

145. Writing system. Orthography

grammar	gramática (f)	[graˈmatika]
vocabulary	vocabulario (m)	[vɔkabuˈlariɔ]
phonetics	fonética (f)	[fɔˈnɛtika]
noun	sustantivo (m)	[sustanˈtiβɔ]
adjective	adjetivo (m)	[adhɛˈtiβɔ]
verb	verbo (m)	[ˈvɛrbɔ]
adverb	adverbio (m)	[adˈvɛrbiɔ]
pronoun	pronombre (m)	[prɔˈnɔmbrɛ]
interjection	interjección (f)	[intɛrhɛkˈθʲon]
preposition	preposición (f)	[prɛpɔsiˈθʲon]
root	raíz (f), radical (m)	[raˈiθ], [radiˈkal]
ending	desinencia (f)	[dɛsiˈnɛnθija]
prefix	prefijo (m)	[prɛˈfihɔ]
syllable	sílaba (f)	[ˈsiʎaba]
suffix	sufijo (m)	[suˈfihɔ]
stress mark	acento (m)	[aˈθæntɔ]
apostrophe	apóstrofo (m)	[aˈpɔstrɔfɔ]

period, dot	punto (m)	['puntɔ]
comma	coma (f)	['kɔma]
semicolon	punto y coma	['puntɔ i 'kɔma]
colon	dos puntos (m pl)	[dɔs 'puntɔs]
ellipsis	puntos (m pl) suspensivos	['puntɔs suspɛn'siβɔs]

| question mark | signo (m) de interrogación | ['signɔ dɛ intɛrrɔga'θʲon] |
| exclamation point | signo (m) de admiración | ['signɔ dɛ admira'θʲon] |

quotation marks	comillas (f pl)	[kɔ'mijas]
in quotation marks	entre comillas	['ɛntrɛ kɔ'mijas]
parenthesis	paréntesis (m)	[pa'rɛntɛsis]
in parenthesis	entre paréntesis	['ɛntrɛ pa'rɛntɛsis]

hyphen	guión (m)	[gi'jon]
dash	raya (f)	['raja]
space (between words)	blanco (m)	['bʎaŋkɔ]

| letter | letra (f) | ['letra] |
| capital letter | letra (f) mayúscula | ['letra ma'juskuʎa] |

| vowel (n) | vocal (f) | [bɔ'kaʎ] |
| consonant (n) | consonante (m) | [kɔnsɔ'nantɛ] |

sentence	oración (f)	[ɔra'θʲon]
subject	sujeto (m)	[su'hɛtɔ]
predicate	predicado (m)	[prɛdi'kadɔ]

line	línea (f)	['linɛa]
on a new line	en una nueva línea	[ɛn 'una nu'ɛβa 'linɛa]
paragraph	párrafo (m)	['parrafɔ]

word	palabra (f)	[pa'ʎabra]
group of words	combinación (f) de palabras	[kɔmbina'θʲon dɛ pa'ʎabras]
expression	expresión (f)	[ɛksprɛ'θʲon]

| synonym | sinónimo (m) | [si'nɔnimɔ] |
| antonym | antónimo (m) | [an'tɔnimɔ] |

rule	regla (f)	['rɛgʎa]
exception	excepción (f)	[ɛksɛp'θʲon]
correct (adj)	correcto (adj)	[kɔr'rɛktɔ]

conjugation	conjugación (f)	[kɔnhuga'θʲon]
declension	declinación (f)	[dɛklina'sjon]
nominal case	caso (m)	['kasɔ]
question	pregunta (f)	[prɛ'gunta]
to underline (vt)	subrayar (vt)	[subra'jar]
dotted line	línea (f) de puntos	['linɛa dɛ 'puntɔs]

146. Foreign languages

language	**lengua** (f)	['leŋua]
foreign (adj)	**extranjero** (adj)	[ɛkstran'hɛrɔ]
to study (vt)	**estudiar** (vt)	[ɛstu'djar]
to learn (language, etc.)	**aprender** (vt)	[aprɛn'dɛr]
to read (vi, vt)	**leer** (vi, vt)	[le'ɛr]
to speak (vi, vt)	**hablar** (vi, vt)	[ab'ʎar]
to understand (vt)	**comprender** (vt)	[kɔmprɛn'dɛr]
to write (vt)	**escribir** (vt)	[ɛskri'βir]
fast (adv)	**rápidamente** (adv)	['rapida'mɛntɛ]
slowly (adv)	**lentamente** (adv)	[lenta'mɛntɛ]
fluently (adv)	**con fluidez** (adv)	[kɔn flyi'dɛθ]
rules	**reglas** (f pl)	['rɛgʎas]
grammar	**gramática** (f)	[gra'matika]
vocabulary	**vocabulario** (m)	[vɔkabu'lariɔ]
phonetics	**fonética** (f)	[fɔ'nɛtika]
textbook	**manual** (m)	[manu'aʎ]
dictionary	**diccionario** (m)	[dikθiɔ'nariɔ]
teach-yourself book	**manual** (m) **autodidáctico**	[manu'aʎ autɔdi'daktikɔ]
phrasebook	**guía** (f) **de conversación**	['gija dɛ kɔnwersa'θiɔn]
cassette	**casete** (m)	[ka'sɛtɛ]
videotape	**videocasete** (f)	[widɛɔka'sɛtɛ]
CD, compact disc	**disco compacto** (m)	['diskɔ kɔm'paktɔ]
DVD	**DVD** (m)	[dɛ uvɛ 'dɛ]
alphabet	**alfabeto** (m)	[aʎfa'βɛtɔ]
to spell (vt)	**deletrear** (vt)	[dɛletrɛ'ar]
pronunciation	**pronunciación** (f)	[prɔnunθja'θiɔn]
accent	**acento** (m)	[a'θæntɔ]
with an accent	**con acento**	[kɔn a'θæntɔ]
without an accent	**sin acento**	[sin a'θæntɔ]
word	**palabra** (f)	[pa'ʎabra]
meaning	**significado** (m)	[signifi'kadɔ]
course (e.g., a French ~)	**cursos** (m pl)	['kursɔs]
to sign up	**inscribirse** (vr)	[inskri'βirsɛ]
teacher	**profesor** (m)	[prɔfɛ'sɔr]
translation (process)	**traducción** (f)	[traduk'θiɔn]
translation (text, etc.)	**traducción** (f)	[traduk'θiɔn]
translator	**traductor** (m)	[traduk'tɔr]
interpreter	**intérprete** (m)	[in'tɛrprɛtɛ]
polyglot	**políglota** (m)	[pɔ'liglɔta]
memory	**memoria** (f)	[mɛ'mɔrija]

147. Fairy tale characters

Santa Claus	Papá Noel (m)	[pa'pa nɔ'ɛʎ]
Cinderella	Cenicienta	[θæni'θjenta]
mermaid	sirena (f)	[si'rɛna]
Neptune	Neptuno	[nɛp'tunɔ]
magician, wizard	mago (m)	['magɔ]
fairy	maga (f)	['maga]
magic (adj)	mágico (adj)	['mahikɔ]
magic wand	varita (f) mágica	[ba'rita 'mahika]
fairy tale	cuento (m) de hadas	[ku'ɛntɔ dɛ 'adas]
miracle	milagro (m)	[mi'ʎagrɔ]
dwarf	enano (m)	[ɛ'nanɔ]
to turn into ...	transformarse en ...	[transfɔr'marsɛ ɛn]
ghost	espíritu (m)	[ɛs'piritu]
phantom	fantasma (m)	[fan'tasma]
monster	monstruo (m)	['mɔnstruɔ]
dragon	dragón (m)	[dra'gɔn]
giant	gigante (m)	[hi'gantɛ]

148. Zodiac Signs

Aries	Aries (m)	['ariɛs]
Taurus	Tauro (m)	['taurɔ]
Gemini	Géminis (m pl)	['hɛminis]
Cancer	Cáncer (m)	['kanθær]
Leo	Leo (m)	['leɔ]
Virgo	Virgo (m)	['birgɔ]
Libra	Libra (f)	['libra]
Scorpio	Escorpio (m)	[ɛs'kɔrpiɔ]
Sagittarius	Sagitario (m)	[sahi'tariɔ]
Capricorn	Capricornio (m)	[kapri'kɔrniɔ]
Aquarius	Acuario (m)	[aku'ariɔ]
Pisces	Piscis (m pl)	['piθis]
character	carácter (m)	[ka'raktɛr]
features of character	rasgos (m pl) de carácter	['rasgɔs dɛ ka'raktɛr]
behavior	conducta (f)	[kɔn'dukta]
to tell fortunes	decir la buenaventura	[dɛ'θir ʎa buɛnavɛn'tura]
fortune-teller	adivinadora (f)	[adiwina'dɔra]
horoscope	horóscopo (m)	[ɔ'rɔskɔpɔ]

Arts

149. Theater

theater	teatro (m)	[tɛ'atrɔ]
opera	ópera (f)	['ɔpɛra]
operetta	opereta (f)	[ɔpɛ'rɛta]
ballet	ballet (m)	[ba'let]
theater poster	cartelera (f)	[kartɛ'lera]
theatrical company	compañía (f)	[kɔmpa'nija]
tour	gira (f) artística	['hira ar'tistika]
to be on tour	hacer una gira artística	[a'θær una 'hira ar'tistika]
to rehearse (vi, vt)	ensayar (vi, vt)	[ɛnsa'jar]
rehearsal	ensayo (m)	[ɛn'sajo]
repertoire	repertorio (m)	[rɛpɛr'tɔriɔ]
performance	representación (f)	[rɛprɛsɛnta'θiɔn]
theatrical show	espectáculo (m)	[ɛspɛk'takulɔ]
play	pieza (f) de teatro	['pjeθa dɛ te'atrɔ]
ticket	billet (m)	[bi'je]
Box office	taquilla (f)	[ta'kija]
lobby, foyer	vestíbulo (m)	[bes'tiβulɔ]
coat check	guardarropa (f)	[guardar'rɔpa]
coat check tag	ficha (f) de guardarropa	['fitʃa dɛ guardar'rɔpa]
binoculars	gemelos (m pl)	[hɛ'mɛlɔs]
usher	acomodador (m)	[akɔmɔda'dɔr]
orchestra seats	patio (m) de butacas	['patiɔ dɛ bu'takas]
balcony	balconcillo (m)	[balkɔn'sijo]
dress circle	entresuelo (m)	[ɛntrɛsu'ɛlɔ]
box	palco (m)	['paʎkɔ]
row	fila (f)	['fiʎa]
seat	asiento (m)	[a'sjentɔ]
audience	público (m)	['publikɔ]
spectator	espectador (m)	[ɛspɛkta'dɔr]
to clap (vi, vt)	aplaudir (vi, vt)	[apʎau'dir]
applause	aplausos (m pl)	[ap'ʎausɔs]
ovation	ovación (f)	[ɔva'θiɔn]
stage	escenario (m)	[ɛsθæ'nariɔ]
curtain	telón (m)	[tɛ'lɔn]
scenery	decoración (f)	[dɛkɔra'θiɔn]
backstage	bastidores (m pl)	[basti'dɔrɛs]

scene (e.g., the last ~)	escena (f)	[εθ'sεna]
act	acto (m)	['aktɔ]
intermission	entreacto (m)	[εntrε'aktɔ]

150. Cinema

| actor | actor (m) | [ak'tɔr] |
| actress | actriz (f) | [akt'riθ] |

movies (industry)	cine (m)	['θinε]
movie	película (f)	[pε'likuʎa]
episode	episodio (m)	[εpi'sɔdiɔ]

detective	película (f) policíaca	[pε'likuʎa pɔli'siaka]
action movie	película (f) de acción	[pε'likuʎa dε ak'θion]
adventure movie	película (f) de aventura	[pε'likuʎa dε avεn'tura]
science fiction movie	película (f) de ciencia ficción	[pε'likuʎa dε 'sʲænθia fik'θion]

| horror movie | película (f) de horror | [pε'likuʎa dε ɔr'rɔr] |

comedy movie	película (f) cómica	[pε'likuʎa 'kɔmika]
melodrama	melodrama (m)	[mεlɔd'rama]
drama	drama (m)	['drama]

fictional movie	película (f) de ficción	[pe'likuʎa dε fik'θion]
documentary	documental (m)	[dɔkumεn'taʎ]
cartoon	dibujos (m pl) animados	[di'βuhɔs ani'madɔs]
silent movies	cine (m) mudo	['θinε 'mudɔ]

role (part)	papel (m)	[pa'pεʎ]
leading role	papel (m) principal	[pa'pεʎ prinθi'paʎ]
to play (vi, vt)	interpretar (vt)	[intεrprε'tar]

movie star	estrella (f) de cine	[εst'rεja dε 'θinε]
well-known (adj)	conocido (adj)	[kɔnɔ'θidɔ]
famous (adj)	famoso (adj)	[fa'mɔsɔ]
popular (adj)	popular (adj)	[pɔpu'ʎar]

script (screenplay)	guión (m) de cine	[gi'jon dε 'θinε]
scriptwriter	guionista (m)	[gijo'nista]
movie director	director (m) de cine	[dirεk'tɔr dε 'θinε]
producer	productor (m)	[prɔduk'tɔr]
assistant	asistente (m)	[asis'tεntε]
cameraman	operador (m)	[ɔpεra'dɔr]
double	doble (m)	['dɔble]

to shoot a movie	filmar una película	[fiʎ'mar una pe'likuʎa]
audition, screen test	audición (f)	[audi'θion]
shooting	rodaje (m)	[rɔ'dahε]
movie crew	equipo (m) de rodaje	[ε'kipɔ dε rɔ'dahe]

movie set	plató (m) de rodaje	[pʎa'tɔ dɛ rɔ'dahe]
camera	cámara (f)	['kamara]
movie theater	cine (m)	['θinɛ]
screen (e.g., big ~)	pantalla (f)	[pan'taja]
to show a movie	mostrar la película	[mɔst'rar ʎa pɛ'likuʎa]
soundtrack	pista (f) sonora	['pista sɔ'nɔra]
special effects	efectos (m pl) especiales	[ɛ'fɛktɔs ɛspɛ'θjales]
subtitles	subtítulos (m pl)	[sub'titulɔs]
credits	créditos (m pl)	['krɛditɔs]
translation	traducción (f)	[traduk'θⁱon]

151. Painting

art	arte (m)	['artɛ]
fine arts	bellas artes (f pl)	['bɛjas 'artɛs]
art gallery	galería (f) de arte	[gale'rija dɛ 'artɛ]
art exhibition	exposición (f) de arte	[ɛkspɔsi'θⁱon dɛ 'artɛ]
painting (art)	pintura (f)	[pin'tura]
graphic art	gráfica (f)	['grafika]
abstract art	abstraccionismo (m)	[abstrakθⁱo'nismɔ]
impressionism	impresionismo (m)	[imprɛsⁱo'nismɔ]
picture (painting)	pintura (f)	[pin'tura]
drawing	dibujo (m)	[di'βuhɔ]
poster	pancarta (f)	[pa'ŋkarta]
illustration (picture)	ilustración (f)	[ilystra'θⁱon]
miniature	miniatura (f)	[minia'tura]
copy (of painting, etc.)	copia (f)	['kɔpja]
reproduction	reproducción (f)	[rɛprɔduk'θⁱon]
mosaic	mosaico (m)	[mɔ'saikɔ]
stained glass	vidriera (f)	[widri'era]
fresco	fresco (m)	['frɛskɔ]
engraving	grabado (m)	[gra'βadɔ]
bust (sculpture)	busto (m)	['bustɔ]
sculpture	escultura (f)	[ɛskuʎ'tura]
statue	estatua (f)	[ɛs'tatua]
plaster of Paris	yeso (m)	['jesɔ]
plaster (as adj)	en yeso (adj)	[ɛn 'jesɔ]
portrait	retrato (m)	[rɛt'ratɔ]
self-portrait	autorretrato (m)	[autɔrrɛt'ratɔ]
landscape painting	paisaje (m)	[paj'sahɛ]
still life	naturaleza (f) muerta	[natura'leθa mu'ɛrta]
caricature	caricatura (f)	[karika'tura]

sketch	boceto (m)	[bo'sɛto]
paint	pintura (f)	[pin'tura]
watercolor	acuarela (f)	[akua'rɛʎa]
oil (paint)	óleo (m)	['ɔleo]
pencil	lápiz (f)	['ʎapiθ]
Indian ink	tinta (f) china	['tinta 'ʧina]
charcoal	carboncillo (m)	[karbon'θijo]

to draw (vi, vt)	dibujar (vi, vt)	[dibu'har]
to paint (vi, vt)	pintar (vi, vt)	[pin'tar]

to pose (vi)	posar (vi)	[pɔ'sar]
artist's model (masc.)	modelo (m)	[mɔ'dɛlɔ]
artist's model (fem.)	modelo (f)	[mɔ'dɛlɔ]

artist (painter)	pintor (m)	[pin'tɔr]
work of art	obra (f) de arte	['ɔbra dɛ 'artɛ]
masterpiece	obra (f) maestra	['ɔbra ma'ɛstra]
artist's workshop	estudio (m)	[ɛs'tudiɔ]

canvas (cloth)	lienzo (m)	['ʎjenθɔ]
easel	caballete (m)	[kaba'jetɛ]
palette	paleta (f)	[pa'leta]

frame (of picture, etc.)	marco (m)	['markɔ]
restoration	restauración (f)	[rɛstaura'θion]
to restore (vt)	restaurar (vt)	[rɛstau'rar]

152. Literature & Poetry

literature	literatura (f)	[litɛra'tura]
author (writer)	autor (m)	[au'tɔr]
pseudonym	seudónimo (m)	[sɛu'dɔnimɔ]

book	libro (m)	['librɔ]
volume	tomo (m)	['tɔmɔ]
table of contents	tabla (f) de contenidos	['tabla dɛ kɔntɛ'nidɔs]
page	página (f)	['pahina]
main character	héroe (m) principal	['ɛrɔɛ prinθi'paʎ]
autograph	autógrafo (m)	[au'tɔgrafɔ]

short story	relato (m) corto	[rɛ'ʎatɔ 'kɔrtɔ]
story (novella)	cuento (m)	[ku'ɛntɔ]
novel	novela (f)	[nɔ'βɵʎa]
work (writing)	obra (f) literaria	['ɔbra lite'rarija]
fable	fábula (f)	['faβuʎa]
detective novel	novela (f) policíaca	[nɔ'βɵʎa poli'θijaka]

poem (verse)	verso (m)	['vɛrsɔ]
poetry	poesía (f)	[pɔɛ'sija]

| poem (epic, ballad) | poema (f) | [po'ɛma] |
| poet | poeta (m) | [po'ɛta] |

fiction	bellas letras (f pl)	['bɛjas 'letras]
science fiction	ciencia ficción (f)	['sjenθija fik'θion]
adventures	aventuras (f pl)	[avɛn'turas]
educational literature	literatura (f) didáctica	[litɛra'tura di'daktika]
children's literature	literatura (f) infantil	[litɛra'tura infan'tiʎ]

153. Circus

circus	circo (m)	['θirkɔ]
chapiteau circus	circo (m) ambulante	['θirkɔ ambu'ʎantɛ]
program	programa (m)	[prɔg'rama]
performance	representación (f)	[rɛprɛsɛnta'θion]

| act (circus ~) | número (m) | ['numɛrɔ] |
| circus ring | arena (f) | [a'rɛna] |

| pantomime (act) | pantomima (f) | [pantɔ'mima] |
| clown | payaso (m) | [pa'jasɔ] |

acrobat	acróbata (m)	[ak'rɔβata]
acrobatics	acrobacia (f)	[akrɔ'βaθija]
gymnast	gimnasta (m)	[him'nasta]
gymnastics	gimnasia (f)	[him'nasija]
somersault	salto (m)	['saʎtɔ]

athlete (strongman)	forzudo (m)	[fɔr'θudɔ]
animal-tamer	domador (m)	[dɔma'dɔr]
equestrian	caballista (m)	[kaba'jista]
assistant	asistente (m)	[asis'tɛntɛ]

stunt	truco (m)	['trukɔ]
magic trick	truco (m) de magia	['trukɔ dɛ 'mahia]
conjurer, magician	ilusionista (m)	[ilysiɔ'nista]

juggler	malabarista (m)	[maʎaba'rista]
to juggle (vi, vt)	hacer malabarismos	[a'sɛr maʎaba'rismɔs]
animal trainer	amaestrador (m)	[amaɛstra'dɔr]
animal training	amaestramiento (m)	[amaɛstra'mɛntɔ]
to train (animals)	amaestrar (vt)	[amaɛst'rar]

154. Music. Pop music

music	música (f)	['musika]
musician	músico (m)	['musikɔ]
musical instrument	instrumento (m) musical	[instru'mɛntɔ musi'kaʎ]

to play …	tocar …	[tɔ'kar]
guitar	guitarra (f)	[gi'tarra]
violin	violín (m)	[bʲɔ'lin]
cello	violonchelo (m)	[bʲɔlɔn'ʧɛlɜ]
double bass	contrabajo (m)	[kɔntra'βahɔ]
harp	arpa (f)	['arpa]
piano	piano (m)	['pjanɔ]
grand piano	piano (m) de cola	['pjanɔ dɛ 'kɔʎa]
organ	órgano (m)	['ɔrganɔ]
wind instruments	instrumentos (m pl) de viento	[instru'mɛntɔs dɛ 'bjentɔ]
oboe	oboe (m)	[ɔ'βɔɛ]
saxophone	saxofón (m)	[saksɔ'fɔn]
clarinet	clarinete (m)	[kʎari'nɛtɛ]
flute	flauta (f)	['fʎauta]
trumpet	trompeta (f)	[trɔm'pɛta]
accordion	acordeón (m)	[akɔrdɛ'ɔn]
drum	tambor (m)	[tam'bɔr]
duo	dúo (m)	['duɔ]
trio	trío (m)	['triɔ]
quartet	cuarteto (m)	[kuar'tɛtɔ]
choir	coro (m)	['kɔrɔ]
orchestra	orquesta (f)	[ɔr'kesta]
pop music	música (f) pop	['musika pɔp]
rock music	música (f) rock	['musika rɔk]
rock group	grupo (m) de rock	['grupo dɛ rɔk]
jazz	jazz (m)	[dʒas]
idol	ídolo (m)	['idɔlɜ]
admirer, fan	admirador (m)	[admira'dɔr]
concert	concierto (m)	[kɔn'θjertɔ]
symphony	sinfonía (f)	[sinfɔ'nia]
composition	composición (f)	[kɔmpɔsi'θʲɔn]
to compose (write)	escribir (vt)	[ɛskri'βɪr]
singing	canto (m)	['kantɔ]
song	canción (f)	[kan'θʲon]
tune (melody)	melodía (f)	[mɛlɔ'dija]
rhythm	ritmo (m)	['ritmɔ]
blues	blues (m)	[blys]
sheet music	notas (f pl)	['nɔtas]
baton	batuta (f)	[ba'tuta]
bow	arco (m)	['arkɔ]
string	cuerda (f)	[ku'ɛrda]
case (e.g., guitar ~)	estuche (m)	[ɛs'tuʧe]

Rest. Entertainment. Travel

155. Trip. Travel

tourism	**turismo** (m)	[tu'rismɔ]
tourist	**turista** (m)	[tu'rista]
trip, voyage	**viaje** (m)	['bjahɛ]
adventure	**aventura** (f)	[avɛn'tura]
trip, journey	**viaje** (m)	['bjahɛ]
vacation	**vacaciones** (f pl)	[baka'θɪonɛs]
to be on vacation	**estar de vacaciones**	[ɛs'tar dɛ baka'sɪonɛs]
rest	**descanso** (m)	[dɛs'kansɔ]
train	**tren** (m)	[trɛn]
by train	**en tren**	[ɛn 'trɛn]
airplane	**avión** (m)	[a'bɪon]
by airplane	**en avión**	[ɛn a'vɪon]
by car	**en coche**	[ɛn 'kɔʧə]
by ship	**en barco**	[ɛn 'barkɔ]
luggage	**equipaje** (m)	[ɛki'pahɛ]
suitcase, luggage	**maleta** (f)	[ma'leta]
luggage cart	**carrito** (m) **de equipaje**	[kar'ritɔ dɛ ɛki'pahe]
passport	**pasaporte** (m)	[pasa'pɔrtɛ]
visa	**visado** (m)	[bi'sadɔ]
ticket	**billete** (m)	[bi'jetɛ]
air ticket	**billete** (m) **de avión**	[bi'jetɛ dɛ a'bɪon]
guidebook	**guía** (f)	['gija]
map	**mapa** (m)	['mapa]
area (rural ~)	**área** (m)	['area]
place, site	**lugar** (m)	[ly'gar]
exotic (n)	**exotismo** (m)	[ɛksɔ'tismɔ]
exotic (adj)	**exótico** (adj)	[ɛk'sɔtikɔ]
amazing (adj)	**asombroso** (adj)	[asɔmb'rɔsɔ]
group	**grupo** (m)	['grupɔ]
excursion	**excursión** (f)	[ɛskur'θɪon]
guide (person)	**guía** (m)	['gija]

156. Hotel

hotel	**hotel** (m)	[ɔ'tɛʎ]
motel	**motel** (m)	[mɔ'tɛʎ]
three-star	**de tres estrellas**	[dɛ 'trɛs ɛst'rɛjas]
five-star	**de cinco estrellas**	[dɛ 'θiŋkɔ ɛst'rɛjas]
to stay (in hotel, etc.)	**hospedarse** (vr)	[ɔspɛ'darsɛ]
room	**habitación** (f)	[abita'θɪon]
single room	**habitación** (f) **individual**	[abita'θɪon indiwidu'aʎ]
double room	**habitación** (f) **doble**	[abita'θɪon 'dɔble]
to book a room	**reservar una habitación**	[rɛsɛr'var una abita'θɪon]
half board	**media pensión** (f)	['mɛdja pɛn'θɪon]
full board	**pensión** (f) **completa**	[pɛn'θɪon kɔmp'lɛta]
with bath	**con baño** (adj)	[kɔn 'baɲɔ]
with shower	**con ducha**	[kɔn 'dutʃa]
satellite television	**televisión** (f) **satélite**	[tɛlewi'θɪon sa'tɛlitɛ]
air-conditioner	**climatizador** (m)	[klimatiða'dɔr]
towel	**toalla** (f)	[tɔ'aja]
key	**llave** (f)	['jaβə]
administrator	**administrador** (m)	[administra'dɔr]
chambermaid	**camarera** (f)	[kama'rɛra]
porter, bellboy	**maletero** (m)	[male'tɛrɔ]
doorman	**portero** (m)	[pɔr'tɛrɔ]
restaurant	**restaurante** (m)	[rɛstau'rantɛ]
pub, bar	**bar** (m)	[bar]
breakfast	**desayuno** (m)	[dɛsa'junɔ]
dinner	**cena** (f)	['θæna]
buffet	**buffet** (m) **libre**	[buf'fɛt 'librɛ]
lobby	**vestíbulo** (m)	[bes'tiβulɔ]
elevator	**ascensor** (m)	[aθæn'sɔr]
DO NOT DISTURB	**NO MOLESTAR**	[nɔ mɔles'tar]
NO SMOKING	**PROHIBIDO FUMAR**	[prɔi'βıdɔ fu'mar]

157. Books. Reading

book	**libro** (m)	['librɔ]
author	**autor** (m)	[au'tɔr]
writer	**escritor** (m)	[ɛskri'tɔr]
to write (~ a book)	**escribir** (vt)	[ɛskri'βır]
reader	**lector** (m)	[lek'tɔr]
to read (vi, vt)	**leer** (vi, vt)	[le'ɛr]

reading (activity)	**lectura** (f)	[lek'tura]
silently (to oneself)	**en silencio**	[ɛn si'lenθio]
aloud (adv)	**en voz alta**	[ɛn 'boθ 'aʎta]
to publish (vt)	**editar** (vt)	[ɛdi'tar]
publishing (process)	**edición** (f)	[ɛdi'θion]
publisher	**editor** (m)	[ɛdi'tɔr]
publishing house	**editorial** (f)	[ɛditɔ'rjaʎ]
to come out (be released)	**salir** (vt)	[sa'lir]
release (of a book)	**salida** (f)	[sa'lida]
print run	**tirada** (f)	[ti'rada]
bookstore	**librería** (f)	[librɛ'rija]
library	**biblioteca** (f)	[bibliɔ'tɛka]
story (novella)	**cuento** (m)	[ku'ɛntɔ]
short story	**relato** (m) **corto**	[rɛ'ʎatɔ 'kɔrtɔ]
novel	**novela** (f)	[nɔ'βəʎa]
detective novel	**novela** (f) **policíaca**	[nɔ'βəʎa pɔli'θijaka]
memoirs	**memorias** (f pl)	[mɛ'mɔrijas]
legend	**leyenda** (f)	[le'jenda]
myth	**mito** (m)	['mitɔ]
poetry, poems	**versos** (m pl)	['bɛrsɔs]
autobiography	**autobiografía** (f)	[autɔbiɔgra'fija]
selected works	**obras** (f pl) **escogidas**	['ɔbras ɛskɔ'hidas]
science fiction	**ciencia ficción** (f)	['sjenθija fik'θion]
title	**título** (m)	['titulɔ]
introduction	**introducción** (f)	[intrɔduk'θion]
title page	**portada** (f)	[pɔr'tada]
chapter	**capítulo** (m)	[ka'pitulɔ]
extract	**extracto** (m)	[ɛkst'raktɔ]
episode	**episodio** (m)	[ɛpi'sɔdiɔ]
plot (storyline)	**sujeto** (m)	[su'hɛtɔ]
contents	**contenido** (m)	[kɔntɛ'nidɔ]
main character	**héroe** (m) **principal**	['ɛrɔɛ prinθi'paʎ]
volume	**tomo** (m)	['tɔmɔ]
cover	**cubierta** (f)	[ku'bjerta]
binding	**encuadernado** (m)	[ɛŋkuadɛr'nadɔ]
bookmark	**marcador** (m) **de libro**	[marka'dɔr dɛ 'librɔ]
page	**página** (f)	['pahina]
to flick through	**hojear** (vt)	[ɔhɛ'ar]
margins	**márgenes** (m pl)	['marhɛnɛs]
annotation	**anotación** (f)	[anɔta'θion]
footnote	**nota** (f) **a pie de página**	['nɔta a pje dɛ 'pahina]

text	texto (m)	['tɛkstɔ]
type, font	fuente (f)	[fu'ɛntɛ]
misprint, typo	errata (f)	[ɛr'rata]

translation	traducción (f)	[traduk'θiɔn]
to translate (vt)	traducir (vt)	[tradu'θir]
original (n)	original (m)	[ɔrihi'naʎ]

famous (adj)	famoso (adj)	[fa'mɔsɔ]
unknown (adj)	desconocido (adj)	[dɛskɔnɔ'θidɔ]
interesting (adj)	interesante (adj)	[intɛrɛ'santɛ]
bestseller	best-seller (m)	[bɛs'tsɛller]

dictionary	diccionario (m)	[dikθiɔ'nariɔ]
textbook	manual (m)	[manu'aʎ]
encyclopedia	enciclopedia (f)	[ɛnθiklɔ'pɛdija]

158. Hunting. Fishing

hunting	caza (f)	['kaθa]
to hunt (vi, vt)	cazar (vi, vt)	[ka'θar]
hunter	cazador (m)	[kaθa'dɔr]

to shoot (vi)	tirar (vi)	[ti'rar]
rifle	fusil (m)	[fu'siʎ]
bullet (shell)	cartucho (m)	[kar'tutʃɔ]
shot (lead balls)	perdigón (m)	[pɛrdi'gɔn]

trap (e.g., bear ~)	cepo (m)	['θæpɔ]
snare (for birds, etc.)	trampa (f)	['trampa]
to fall into the trap	caer en la trampa	[ka'ɛr ɛn ʎa 'trampa]
to lay a trap	poner una trampa	[pɔ'nɛr 'una 'trampa]

poacher	cazador (m) furtivo	[kaθa'dɔr fur'tiβɔ]
game (in hunting)	caza (f) menor	['kaθa mɛ'nɔr]
hound dog	perro (m) de caza	['pɛrrɔ dɛ 'kaθa]
safari	safari (m)	[sa'fari]
mounted animal	animal (m) disecado	[ani'maʎ disɛ'kadɔ]

fisherman	pescador (m)	[pɛska'dɔr]
fishing	pesca (f)	['pɛska]
to fish (vi)	pescar (vi)	[pɛs'kar]

fishing rod	caña (f) de pescar	['kaɲja dɛ pɛs'kar]
fishing line	sedal (m)	[sɛ'daʎ]
hook	anzuelo (m)	[anθu'ɛlɔ]
float	flotador (m)	[flɔta'dɔr]
bait	cebo (m)	['θæβɔ]
to cast a line	lanzar el anzuelo	[ʎan'θar ɛʎ anθu'ɛlɔ]
to bite (ab. fish)	picar (vt)	[pi'kar]

| catch (of fish) | **pesca** (f) | ['pɛska] |
| ice-hole | **agujero** (m) **en el hielo** | [agu'hɛrɔ ɛn ɛʎ jelɔ] |

| fishing net | **red** (f) | [rɛd] |
| boat | **barca** (f) | ['barka] |

to net (catch with net)	**pescar con la red**	[pɛs'kar kɔn ʎa 'rɛd]
to cast the net	**tirar la red**	[ti'rar ʎa 'rɛd]
to haul in the net	**sacar la red**	[sa'kar ʎa 'rɛd]
to fall into the net	**caer en la red**	[ka'ɛr ɛn ʎa 'rɛd]

whaler (person)	**ballenero** (m)	[baje'nɛrɔ]
whaleboat	**ballenero** (m)	[baje'nɛrɔ]
harpoon	**arpón** (m)	[ar'pɔn]

159. Games. Billiards

billiards	**billar** (m)	[bi'jar]
billiard room, hall	**sala** (f) **de billar**	['saʎa dɛ bi'jar]
ball	**bola** (f) **de billar**	['bɔʎa dɛ bi'jar]

to pocket a ball	**entronerar la bola**	[ɛntrɔne'rar ʎa 'βɔla]
cue	**taco** (m)	['takɔ]
pocket	**tronera** (f)	[trɔ'nɛra]

160. Games. Playing cards

diamonds	**cuadrados** (m pl)	[kuad'radɔs]
spades	**picas** (f pl)	['pikas]
hearts	**corazones** (m pl)	[kɔra'θɔnɛs]
clubs	**tréboles** (m pl)	['trɛβɔles]

ace	**as** (m)	[as]
king	**rey** (m)	[rɛj]
queen	**dama** (f)	['dama]
jack, knave	**sota** (f)	['sɔta]

| playing card | **carta** (f) | ['karta] |
| cards | **cartas** (f pl) | ['kartas] |

| trump | **triunfo** (m) | [tri'unfɔ] |
| deck of cards | **baraja** (f) | [ba'raha] |

point	**punto** (m)	['puntɔ]
to deal (vi, vt)	**dar** (vt)	[dar]
to shuffle (cards)	**barajar** (vt)	[bara'har]
lead, turn (n)	**jugada** (f)	[hu'gada]
cardsharp	**fullero** (m)	[fu'ʎjerɔ]

161. Casino. Roulette

casino	casino (m)	[ka'sinɔ]
roulette (game)	ruleta (f)	[ru'leta]
bet, stake	puesta (f)	[pu'ɛsta]
to place bets	apostar (vt)	[apɔs'tar]
red	rojo (m)	['rɔhɔ]
black	negro (m)	['nɛgrɔ]
to bet on red	apostar al rojo	[apɔs'tar aʎ 'rɔhɔ]
to bet on black	apostar al negro	[apɔs'tar aʎ 'nɛgrɔ]
croupier (dealer)	crupier (m, f)	[kru'pje]
to turn the wheel	girar la ruleta	[hi'rar ʎa ru'leta]
rules (of game)	reglas (f pl) de juego	['rɛgʎas dɛ hu'ɛgɔ]
chip	ficha (f)	['fitʃa]
to win (vi, vt)	ganar (vi, vt)	[ga'ɲar]
winnings	ganancia (f)	[ga'nansija]
to lose (~ 100 dollars)	perder (vi)	[pɛr'dɛr]
loss	pérdida (f)	['pɛrdida]
player	jugador (m)	[huga'dɔr]
blackjack (card game)	black jack (m)	[blɛk 'dʒɛk]
craps (dice game)	juego (m) de dados	[hu'ɛgɔ dɛ 'dadɔs]
dice	dados (m pl)	['dadɔs]
slot machine	tragaperras (f)	[traga'pɛrras]

162. Rest. Games. Miscellaneous

to walk, to stroll (vi)	pasear (vi)	[pasɛ'ar]
walk, stroll	paseo (m)	[pa'sɛɔ]
road trip	paseo (m)	[pa'sɛɔ]
adventure	aventura (f)	[avɛn'tura]
picnic	picnic (m)	['piknik]
game (chess, etc.)	juego (m)	[hu'ɛgɔ]
player	jugador (m)	[huga'dɔr]
game (one ~ of chess)	partido (m)	[par'tidɔ]
collector (e.g., philatelist)	coleccionista (m)	[kɔlekθio'nista]
to collect (vt)	coleccionar (vt)	[kɔlekθio'nar]
collection	colección (f)	[kɔlek'θion]
crossword puzzle	crucigrama (m)	[kruθig'rama]
racetrack (hippodrome)	hipódromo (m)	[i'pɔdrɔmɔ]
discotheque	discoteca (f)	[diskɔ'tɛka]
sauna	sauna (f)	['sauna]

lottery	lotería (f)	[lɔtɛ'ria]
camping trip	marcha (f)	['martʃa]
camp	campo (m)	['kampɔ]
tent (for camping)	tienda (f) de campaña	['tⁱenda dɛ kam'paɲja]
compass	brújula (f)	['bruhuʎa]
camper	campista (m)	[kam'pista]

to watch (movie, etc.)	ver (vt)	[bɛr]
viewer	telespectador (m)	[tɛlespɛkta'dɔr]
TV show	programa (m) de televisión	[prɔg'rama dɛ tɛlɛwi'sⁱɔn]

163. Photography

| camera (photo) | cámara (f) fotográfica | ['kamara fɔtɔg'rafika] |
| photo, picture | foto (f) | ['fɔtɔ] |

photographer	fotógrafo (m)	[fɔ'tɔgrafɔ]
photo studio	estudio (m) fotográfico	[ɛs'tudiɔ fɔtɔg'rafikɔ]
photo album	álbum (m) de fotos	['aʎbum dɛ 'fɔtɔs]

camera lens	objetivo (m)	[ɔbhɛ'tiβɔ]
telephoto lens	teleobjetivo (m)	[tɛleɔbhɛ'tiβɔ]
filter	filtro (m)	['fiʎtrɔ]
lens	lente (m)	['lentɛ]

optics (high-quality ~)	óptica (f)	['ɔptika]
diaphragm (aperture)	diafragma (m)	[diaf'ragma]
exposure time	tiempo (m) de exposición	['tⁱempɔ dɛ ɛkspɔsi'θⁱɔn]
viewfinder	visor (m)	[wi'sɔr]

digital camera	cámara (f) digital	['kamara dihi'taʎ]
tripod	trípode (m)	['tripɔdɛ]
flash	flash (m)	[fʎaʃ]

to photograph (vt)	fotografiar (vt)	[fɔtɔgra'fjar]
to take pictures	hacer fotos	[a'θær 'fɔtɔs]
to be photographed	fotografiarse (vr)	[fɔtɔgra'fjarsɛ]

focus	foco (m)	['fɔkɔ]
to adjust the focus	enfocar (vt)	[ɛnfɔ'kar]
sharp, in focus (adj)	nítido (adj)	['nitidɔ]
sharpness	nitidez (f)	[niti'dɛθ]

| contrast | contraste (m) | [kɔnt'rastɛ] |
| contrasty (adj) | contrastante (adj) | [kɔntras'tantɛ] |

picture (photo)	foto (f)	['fɔtɔ]
negative (n)	negativo (m)	[nɛga'tiβɔ]
film (a roll of ~)	película (f) fotográfica	[pɛ'likuʎa fɔtɔg'rafika]

| frame (still) | fotograma (m) | [fɔtɔg'rama] |
| to print (photos) | imprimir (vt) | [impri'mir] |

164. Beach. Swimming

beach	playa (f)	['pʎaja]
sand	arena (f)	[a'rɛna]
deserted (beach)	desierto (adj)	[dɛ'sjertɔ]
suntan	bronceado (m)	[bronθæ'adɔ]
to get a tan	broncearse (vr)	[bronθæ'arsɛ]
tan (adj)	bronceado (adj)	[bronθæ'adɔ]
sunscreen	protector (m) solar	[prɔtɛk'tɔr sɔ'ʎar]
bikini	bikini (m)	[bi'kini]
bathing suit	traje (m) de baño	['trahɛ dɛ 'baɲɔ]
swim briefs	bañador (m)	[baɲa'dɔr]
swimming pool	piscina (f)	[pi'θina]
to swim (vi)	nadar (vi)	[na'dar]
shower	ducha (f)	['dutʃa]
to change (one's clothes)	cambiarse (vr)	[kam'bjarsɛ]
towel	toalla (f)	[tɔ'aja]
boat	barca (f)	['barka]
motorboat	lancha (f) motora	['ʎantʃa mɔ'tɔra]
water ski	esquís (m pl) acuáticos	[ɛs'kis aku'atikɔs]
paddle boat	bicicleta (f) acuática	[bisik'lɛta aku'atika]
surfing	surf (m)	[surf]
surfer	surfista (m)	[sur'fista]
scuba set	equipo (m) de buceo	[ɛ'kipɔ dɛ bu'sɛɔ]
flippers (swimfins)	aletas (f pl)	[a'letas]
mask	máscara (f) de buceo	['maskara dɛ bu'θæɔ]
diver	buceador (m)	[busɛa'dɔr]
to dive (vi)	bucear (vi)	[buθæ'ar]
underwater (adv)	bajo el agua (adv)	['bahɔ ɛʎ 'agua]
beach umbrella	sombrilla (f)	[sɔmb'rija]
beach chair	tumbona (f)	[tum'bɔna]
sunglasses	gafas (f pl) de sol	['gafas dɛ 'sɔʎ]
air mattress	colchoneta (f) inflable	[kɔʎtʃɔ'neta inf'ʎable]
to play (amuse oneself)	jugar (vi)	[hu'gar]
to go for a swim	bañarse (vr)	[ba'ɲarsɛ]
beach ball	pelota (f) de playa	[pe'lɔta dɛ 'pʎaja]
to inflate (vt)	inflar (vt)	[inf'ʎar]
inflatable, air- (adj)	inflable (adj)	[inf'lable]

wave	**ola** (f)	['ɔʎa]
buoy	**boya** (f)	['bɔja]
to drown (ab. person)	**ahogarse** (vr)	[aɔ'garsɛ]

to save, to rescue	**salvar** (vt)	[saʎ'var]
life vest	**chaleco** (m) **salvavidas**	[ʧa'lekɔ saʎva'βɪdas]
to observe, to watch	**observar** (vt)	[ɔbsɛr'var]
lifeguard	**socorrista** (m)	[sɔkɔr'rista]

TECHNICAL EQUIPMENT. TRANSPORTATION

Technical equipment

165. Computer

computer	ordenador (m)	[ɔrdɛna'dɔr]
notebook, laptop	ordenador (m) portátil	[ɔrdɛna'dɔr pɔr'tatiʎ]
to turn on	encender (vt)	[ɛnθæn'dɛr]
to turn off	apagar (vt)	[apa'gar]
keyboard	teclado (m)	[tɛk'ʎadɔ]
key	tecla (f)	['tɛkʎa]
mouse	ratón (m)	[ra'tɔn]
mouse pad	alfombrilla (f) para ratón	[aʎfɔmb'rija 'para ra'tɔn]
button	botón (m)	[bɔ'tɔn]
cursor	cursor (m)	[kur'sɔr]
monitor	monitor (m)	[mɔni'tɔr]
screen	pantalla (f)	[pan'taja]
hard disk	disco (m) duro	['diskɔ 'durɔ]
hard disk volume	volumen (m)	[bɔ'lymɛn
	de disco duro	dɛ 'diskɔ 'durɔ]
memory	memoria (f)	[mɛ'mɔrija]
random access memory	memoria (f) operativa	[mɛ'mɔrija ɔpera'tiβa]
file	archivo, fichero (m)	[ar'ʧiβɔ], [fi'ʧerɔ]
folder	carpeta (f)	[kar'peta]
to open (vt)	abrir (vt)	[ab'rir]
to close (vt)	cerrar (vt)	[θær'rar]
to save (vt)	guardar (vt)	[guar'dar]
to delete (vt)	borrar (vt)	[bɔr'rar]
to copy (vt)	copiar (vt)	[kɔ'pʲar]
to sort (vt)	ordenar (vt)	[ɔrdɛ'nar]
to transfer (copy)	copiar (vt)	[kɔ'pʲar]
program	programa (m)	[prɔg'rama]
software	software (m)	['sɔftvɛa]
programmer	programador (m)	[prɔgrama'dɔr]
to program (vt)	programar (vt)	[prɔgra'mar]
hacker	pirata (m) informático	[pi'rata infɔr'matikɔ]

password	contraseña (f)	[kɔntra'seɲja]
virus	virus (m)	['wirus]
to find, to detect	detectar (vt)	[dɛtɛk'tar]

| byte | octeto (m) | [ɔk'tɛtɔ] |
| megabyte | megaocteto (m) | [megaɔk'tɛtɔ] |

| data | datos (m pl) | ['datɔs] |
| database | base (f) de datos | ['basɛ dɛ 'datɔs] |

cable (USB, etc.)	cable (m)	['kable]
to disconnect (vt)	desconectar (vt)	[dɛskɔnɛk'tar]
to connect (sth to sth)	conectar (vt)	[kɔnɛk'tar]

166. Internet. E-mail

Internet	internet (m), red (f)	[inter'nɛt], [rɛd]
browser	navegador (m)	[navɛga'dɔr]
search engine	buscador (m)	[buska'dɔr]
provider	proveedor (m)	[prɔvɛː'dɔr]

web master	webmaster (m)	[vɛb'master]
website	sitio (m) web	['sitiɔ vɛb]
web page	página (f) web	['pahina vɛb]

| address | dirección (f) | [dirɛk'θion] |
| address book | libro (m) de direcciones | ['librɔ dɛ dirɛk'θionɛs] |

mailbox	buzón (m)	[bu'θon]
mail	correo (m)	[kɔr'rɛɔ]
full (adj)	lleno (adj)	['jenɔ]

message	mensaje (m)	[mɛn'sahɛ]
incoming messages	correo (m) entrante	[kɔr'rɛɔ ɛnt'rantɛ]
outgoing messages	correo (m) saliente	[kɔr'rɛɔ sali'ɛntɛ]

sender	expedidor (m)	[ɛkspɛdi'dɔr]
to send (vt)	enviar (vt)	[ɛmbi'jar]
sending (of mail)	envío (m)	[ɛm'biɔ]

| receiver | destinatario (m) | [dɛstina'tariɔ] |
| to receive (vt) | recibir (vt) | [rɛθi'βir] |

| correspondence | correspondencia (f) | [kɔrrɛspɔn'dɛnsija] |
| to correspond (vi) | escribirse con ... | [ɛskri'βirsɛ kɔn] |

file	archivo, fichero (m)	[ar'tʃiβɔ], [fi'tʃerɔ]
to download (vt)	descargar (vt)	[dɛskar'gar]
to create (vt)	crear (vt)	[kre'ar]
to delete (vt)	borrar (vt)	[bɔr'rar]

deleted (adj)	borrado (adj)	[bɔr'radɔ]
connection (ADSL, etc.)	conexión (f)	[kɔnɛk'θiⁱon]
speed	velocidad (f)	[bɛloθi'dad]
modem	módem (m)	['mɔdɛm]
access	acceso (m)	[ak'θæsɔ]
port (e.g., input ~)	puerto (m)	[pu'ɛrtɔ]
connection (make a ~)	conexión (f)	[kɔnɛk'θiⁱon]
to connect to … (vi)	conectarse a …	[kɔnɛk'tarsɛ a]
to select (vt)	seleccionar (vt)	[selɛkθiⁱo'nar]
to search (for …)	buscar (vt)	[bus'kar]

167. Electricity

electricity	electricidad (f)	[ɛlektriθi'dad]
electrical (adj)	eléctrico (adj)	[ɛ'lektrikɔ]
electric power station	central (f) eléctrica	[θænt'raʎ ɛ'lektrika]
energy	energía (f)	[ɛnɛr'hija]
electric power	energía (f) eléctrica	[ɛnɛr'hija ɛ'lektrika]
light bulb	bombilla (f)	[bɔm'bija]
flashlight	linterna (f)	[lin'tɛrna]
street light	farola (f)	[fa'rɔʎa]
light	luz (f)	[lyθ]
to turn on	encender (vt)	[ɛnθæn'dɛr]
to turn off	apagar (vt)	[apa'gar]
to turn off the light	apagar la luz	[apa'gar ʎa lyθ]
to burn out (vi)	quemarse (vr)	[ke'marsɛ]
short circuit	circuito (m) corto	[θir'kuitɔ 'kɔrtɔ]
broken wire	ruptura (f)	[rup'tura]
contact	contacto (m)	[kɔn'taktɔ]
light switch	interruptor (m)	[intɛrrup'tɔr]
wall socket	enchufe (m)	[ɛn'ʧufe]
plug	clavija (f)	[kʎa'βiha]
extension cord	alargador (m)	[aʎarga'dɔr]
fuse	fusible (m)	[fu'sible]
cable, wire	hilo (m)	['ilɔ]
wiring	instalación (f) eléctrica	[instaʎa'θiⁱon ɛ'lektrika]
ampere	amperio (m)	[am'pɛriɔ]
amperage	amperaje (m)	[ampɛ'rahɛ]
volt	voltio (m)	['bɔʎtiɔ]
voltage	voltaje (m)	[bɔʎ'tahɛ]
electrical device	aparato (m) eléctrico	[apa'ratɔ ɛ'lektrikɔ]
indicator	indicador (m)	[indika'dɔr]

electrician	electricista (m)	[ɛlektri'θista]
to solder (vt)	soldar (vt)	[sɔʎ'dar]
soldering iron	soldador (m)	[sɔʎda'dɔr]
electric current	corriente (f)	[kɔr'rjentɛ]

168. Tools

tool, instrument	instrumento (m)	[instru'mentɔ]
tools	instrumentos (m pl)	[instru'mɛntɔs]
equipment (factory ~)	maquinaria (f)	[maki'narija]

hammer	martillo (m)	[mar'tijo]
screwdriver	destornillador (m)	[dɛstɔrnija'dɔr]
ax	hacha (f)	['atʃa]

saw	sierra (f)	['sjerra]
to saw (vt)	serrar (vt)	[sɛr'rar]
plane (tool)	cepillo (m)	[θæ'pijo]
to plane (vt)	cepillar (vt)	[θæpi'jar]
soldering iron	soldador (m)	[sɔʎda'dɔr]
to solder (vt)	soldar (vt)	[sɔʎ'dar]

file (for metal)	lima (f)	['lima]
carpenter pincers	tenazas (f pl)	[tɛ'naθas]
lineman's pliers	alicates (m pl)	[ali'katɛs]
chisel	escoplo (m)	[ɛs'kɔplɔ]

drill bit	broca (f)	['brɔka]
electric drill	taladro (m)	[ta'ʎadrɔ]
to drill (vi, vt)	taladrar (vi, vt)	[taʎad'rar]

knife	cuchillo (m)	[ku'tʃijo]
pocket knife	navaja (f)	[na'βaha]
folding (~ knife)	plegable (adj)	[ple'gable]
blade	filo (m)	['filo]

sharp (blade, etc.)	agudo (adj)	[a'gudɔ]
blunt (adj)	embotado (adj)	[ɛmbo'tadɔ]
to become blunt	embotarse (vr)	[ɛmbo'tarsɛ]
to sharpen (vt)	afilar (vt)	[afi'ʎar]

bolt	perno (m)	['pɛrnɔ]
nut	tuerca (f)	[tu'ɛrka]
thread (of a screw)	filete (m)	[fi'letɛ]
wood screw	tornillo (m)	[tɔr'nijo]

nail	clavo (m)	['kʎaβɔ]
nailhead	cabeza (f) del clavo	[ka'βəθa dɛʎ 'kʎaβɔ]
ruler (for measuring)	regla (f)	['rɛgʎa]
tape measure	cinta (f) métrica	['θinta 'mɛtrika]

| spirit level | nivel (m) de burbuja | [ni'βɐʎ dɛ bur'buha] |
| magnifying glass | lupa (f) | ['lypa] |

measuring instrument	aparato (m) de medida	[apa'ratɔ dɛ mɛ'dida]
to measure (vt)	medir (vt)	[mɛ'dir]
scale	escala (f)	[ɛs'kaʎa]
(of thermometer, etc.)		
readings	lectura (f)	[lek'tura]

| compressor | compresor (m) | [kɔmprɛ'sɔr] |
| microscope | microscopio (m) | [mikrɔs'kɔpiɔ] |

pump (e.g., water ~)	bomba (f)	['bɔmba]
robot	robot (m)	[rɔ'βɔt]
laser	láser (m)	['ʎasɛr]

wrench	llave (f) de tuerca	['jaβə dɛ tu'ɛrka]
adhesive tape	cinta (f) adhesiva	['θinta adɛ'siβa]
glue	pegamento (m)	[pega'mentɔ]

emery paper	papel (m) de lija	[pa'pɛʎ dɛ 'liha]
spring	resorte (m)	[rɛ'sɔrtɛ]
magnet	imán (m)	[i'man]
gloves	guantes (m pl)	[gu'antɛs]

rope	cuerda (f)	[ku'ɛrda]
cord	cordón (m)	[kɔr'dɔn]
wire (e.g., telephone ~)	hilo (m)	['ilɔ]
cable	cable (m)	['kable]

sledgehammer	almádana (f)	[aʎ'madana]
crowbar	barra (f)	['barra]
ladder	escalera (f) portátil	[ɛkska'lera pɔr'tatiʎ]
stepladder	escalera (f) de tijera	[ɛkska'lera dɛ ti'hɛra]

to screw (tighten)	atornillar (vt)	[atɔrni'jar]
to unscrew, untwist (vt)	destornillar (vt)	[dɛstɔrni'jar]
to tighten (vt)	apretar (vt)	[aprɛ'tar]
to glue, to stick	pegar (vt)	[pɛ'gar]
to cut (vt)	cortar (vt)	[kɔr'tar]

malfunction (fault)	fallo (m)	['fajɔ]
repair (mending)	reparación (f)	[rɛpara'θʲon]
to repair, to mend (vt)	reparar (vt)	[rɛpa'rar]
to adjust (machine, etc.)	regular, ajustar (vt)	[rɛgu'lar], [ahus'tar]

to check (to examine)	verificar (vt)	[bɛrifi'kar]
checking	control (m)	[kɔnt'rɔʎ]
readings	lectura (f)	[lek'tura]

| reliable (machine) | fiable (adj) | ['fjable] |
| complicated (adj) | complicado (adj) | [kɔmpli'kadɔ] |

to rust (get rusted)   **oxidarse** (vr)   [ɔksi'darsɛ]
rusty, rusted (adj)   **oxidado** (adj)   [ɔksi'dadɔ]
rust   **óxido** (m)   ['ɔksidɔ]

Transportation

169. Airplane

airplane	avión (m)	[a'bɔn]
air ticket	billete (m) de avión	[bi'jetɛ dɛ a'bɔn]
airline	compañía (f) aérea	[kɔmpa'nija a'ərɛa]
airport	aeropuerto (m)	[aərɔpu'ɛrtɔ]
supersonic (adj)	supersónico (adj)	[supɛr'sɔnikɔ]
captain	comandante (m)	[kɔman'dantɛ]
crew	tripulación (f)	[tripuʎa'θɪon]
pilot	piloto (m)	[pi'lɔtɔ]
flight attendant	azafata (f)	[aθa'fata]
navigator	navegador (m)	[navɛga'dɔr]
wings	alas (f pl)	['aʎas]
tail	cola (f)	['kɔʎa]
cockpit	cabina (f)	[ka'βɪna]
engine	motor (m)	[mɔ'tɔr]
undercarriage	tren (m) de aterrizaje	['trɛn dɛ atɛrri'θahɛ]
turbine	turbina (f)	[tur'bina]
propeller	hélice (f)	['ɛlisɛ]
black box	caja (f) negra	['kaha 'nɛgra]
control column	timón (m)	[ti'mɔn]
fuel	combustible (m)	[kɔmbus'tible]
safety card	instructivo (m) de seguridad	[instruk'tiβɔ dɛ sɛguri'dad]
oxygen mask	respirador (m) de oxígeno	[rɛspira'dɔr dɛ ɔk'sihɛnɔ]
uniform	uniforme (m)	[uni'fɔrmɛ]
life vest	chaleco (m) salvavidas	[ʧa'lekɔ saʎva'βɪdas]
parachute	paracaídas (m)	[paraka'idas]
takeoff	despegue (m)	[dɛs'pɛgɛ]
to take off (vi)	despegar (vi)	[dɛspɛ'gar]
runway	pista (f) de despegue	['pista dɛ dɛs'pɛgɛ]
visibility	visibilidad (f)	[wisibili'dad]
flight (act of flying)	vuelo (m)	[bu'ɛlɔ]
altitude	altura (f)	[aʎ'tura]
air pocket	pozo (m) de aire	['pɔθɔ dɛ 'airɛ]
seat	asiento (m)	[a'sjentɔ]
headphones	auriculares (m pl)	[auriku'ʎarɛs]

folding tray	mesita (f) plegable	[mε'sita ple'gable]
airplane window	ventana (f)	[bεn'tana]
aisle	pasillo (m)	[pa'sijo]

170. Train

train	tren (m)	[trεn]
suburban train	tren (m) eléctrico	['trεn ε'lektrikɔ]
express train	tren (m) rápido	['trεn 'rapidɔ]
diesel locomotive	locomotora (f) diésel	[lɔkɔmɔ'tɔra di'εsεʎ]
steam engine	tren (m) de vapor	[trεn dε va'pɔr]

| passenger car | coche (m) | ['kɔʧe] |
| dining car | coche (m) restaurante | ['kɔʧe rεstau'rantε] |

rails	rieles (m pl)	['rjeles]
railroad	ferrocarril (m)	[fεrrɔkar'riʎ]
railway tie	traviesa (f)	[tra'vjesa]

platform (railway ~)	plataforma (f)	[pʎata'fɔrma]
track (~ 1, 2, etc.)	vía (f)	['bija]
semaphore	semáforo (m)	[sε'mafɔrɔ]
station	estación (f)	[εsta'θʲon]

engineer	maquinista (m)	[maki'nista]
porter (of luggage)	maletero (m)	[male'tεrɔ]
train steward	mozo (m) del vagón	['mɔθɔ dεʎ ba'gɔn]
passenger	pasajero (m)	[pasa'hεrɔ]
conductor	revisor (m)	[rεwi'sɔr]

| corridor (in train) | corredor (m) | [kɔrrε'dɔr] |
| emergency break | freno (m) de urgencia | ['frεnɔ dε ur'hεnsija] |

compartment	compartimiento (m)	[kɔmparti'mjentɔ]
berth	litera (f)	[li'tεra]
upper berth	litera (f) de arriba	[li'tεra dε ar'riβa]
lower berth	litera (f) de abajo	[li'tεra dε a'βahɔ]
bed linen	ropa (f) de cama	['rɔpa dε 'kama]

ticket	billete (m)	[bi'jetε]
schedule	horario (m)	[ɔ'rariɔ]
information display	pantalla (f) de información	[pan'taja dε infɔrma'θʲon]

to leave, to depart	partir (vi)	[par'tir]
departure (of train)	partida (f)	[par'tida]
to arrive (ab. train)	llegar (vi)	[je'gar]
arrival	llegada (f)	[je'gada]
to arrive by train	llegar en tren	[je'gar εn 'trεn]
to get on the train	tomar el tren	[tɔ'mar εʎ 'trεn]

to get off the train	bajar del tren	[ba'har dεʎ trεn]
train wreck	descarrilamiento (m)	[dεskarriʎa'mjentɔ]
to be derailed	descarrilarse (vr)	[dεskari'ʎarsε]

steam engine	tren (m) de vapor	[trεn dε va'pɔr]
stoker, fireman	fogonero (m)	[fɔgɔ'nεrɔ]
firebox	hogar (m)	[ɔ'gar]
coal	carbón (m)	[kar'bɔn]

171. Ship

| ship | buque (m) | ['buke] |
| vessel | navío (m) | ['naβiɔ] |

steamship	buque (m) de vapor	['bukε dε va'pɔr]
riverboat	motonave (m)	[mɔtɔ'naβə]
ocean liner	trasatlántico (m)	[trasat'ʎantikɔ]
cruiser	crucero (m)	[kru'θærɔ]

yacht	yate (m)	['jatε]
tugboat	remolcador (m)	[rεmɔʎka'dɔr]
barge	barcaza (f)	[bar'kaθa]
ferry	ferry (m)	['fεrri]

sailing ship	velero (m)	[bε'lεrɔ]
brigantine	bergantín (m)	[bergan'tin]
ice breaker	rompehielos (m)	[rɔmpε'jelɔs]
submarine	submarino (m)	[subma'rinɔ]

boat (flat-bottomed ~)	bote (m)	['bɔtε]
dinghy	bote (m)	['bɔtε]
lifeboat	bote (m) salvavidas	['bɔtε saʎva'βɪdas]
motorboat	lancha (f) motora	['ʎantʃa mɔ'tɔra]

captain	capitán (m)	[kapi'tan]
seaman	marinero (m)	[mari'nεrɔ]
sailor	marino (m)	[ma'rinɔ]
crew	tripulación (f)	[tripuʎa'θiɔn]

boatswain	contramaestre (m)	[kɔntrama'εstrε]
ship's boy	grumete (m)	[gry'mεtε]
cook	cocinero (m) de a bordo	[kɔθi'njerɔ dε a'βɔrdɔ]
ship's doctor	médico (m) del buque	['mεdikɔ dεʎ 'buke]

deck	cubierta (f)	[ku'bjerta]
mast	mástil (m)	['mastiʎ]
sail	vela (f)	['bεʎa]
hold	bodega (f)	[bɔ'dεga]
bow (prow)	proa (f)	['prɔa]
stern	popa (f)	['pɔpa]

| oar | remo (m) | ['rɛmɔ] |
| screw propeller | hélice (f) | ['ɛlisɛ] |

cabin	camarote (m)	[kama'rɔtɛ]
wardroom	sala (f) de oficiales	['saʎa dɛ ɔfi'sjales]
engine room	sala (f) de máquinas	['saʎa dɛ 'makinas]
bridge	puente (m) de mando	[pu'ɛntɛ dɛ 'mandɔ]
wave (radio)	onda (f)	['ɔnda]
logbook	cuaderno (m) de bitácora	[kua'dɛrnɔ dɛ bi'takɔra]

spyglass	anteojo (m)	[antɛ'ɔhɔ]
bell	campana (f)	[kam'pana]
flag	bandera (f)	[ban'dɛra]

| rope (mooring ~) | cabo (m) | ['kaβɔ] |
| knot (bowline, etc.) | nudo (m) | ['nudɔ] |

| deckrail | pasamano (m) | [pasa'manɔ] |
| gangway | pasarela (f) | [pasa'rɛʎa] |

anchor	ancla (f)	['aŋkʎa]
to weigh anchor	levar ancla	[le'βar 'aŋkʎa]
to drop anchor	echar ancla	[ɛ'ʧar 'aŋkla]
anchor chain	cadena (f) del ancla	[ka'dɛna dɛʎ 'aŋkʎa]

port (harbor)	puerto (m)	[pu'ɛrtɔ]
berth, wharf	embarcadero (m)	[ɛmbarka'dɛrɔ]
to berth (moor)	amarrar (vt)	[amar'rar]
to cast off	desamarrar (vt)	[dɛsamar'rar]

trip, voyage	viaje (m)	['bjahɛ]
cruise (sea trip)	crucero (m)	[kru'θærɔ]
course (route)	derrota (f)	[dɛr'rɔta]
route (itinerary)	itinerario (m)	[itinɛ'rarjɔ]

fairway	canal (m) navegable	[ka'naʎ navɛ'gable]
shallows (shoal)	bajío (m)	[ba'hiɔ]
to run aground	encallar (vi)	[ɛŋka'jar]

storm	tempestad (f)	[tɛmpɛs'tad]
signal	señal (f)	[sɛ'ɲjaʎ]
to sink (vi)	hundirse (vr)	[un'dirsɛ]
Man overboard!	¡Hombre al agua!	['ɔmbrɛ aʎ 'agua]
SOS	SOS	['ɛsɛ ɔ 'ɛsɛ]
ring buoy	aro (m) salvavidas	['arɔ saʎva'βɪdas]

172. Airport

| airport | aeropuerto (m) | [aərɔpu'ɛrtɔ] |
| airplane | avión (m) | [a'bɔn] |

airline	compañía (f) aérea	[kɔmpa'nija a'ərɛa]
air-traffic controller	controlador (m) aéreo	[kɔntrɔʎa'dɔr a'ərɛɔ]
departure	despegue (m)	[dɛs'pɛgɛ]
arrival	llegada (f)	[je'gada]
to arrive (by plane)	llegar (vi)	[je'gar]
departure time	hora (f) de salida	['ɔra dɛ sa'lida]
arrival time	hora (f) de llegada	['ɔra dɛ je'gada]
to be delayed	retrasarse (vr)	[rɛtra'sarsɛ]
flight delay	retraso (m) de vuelo	[rɛt'rasɔ dɛ bu'ɛlɔ]
information board	pantalla (f) de información	[pan'taja dɛ infɔrma'θiɔn]
information	información (f)	[infɔrma'θiɔn]
to announce (vt)	anunciar (vt)	[anun'θjar]
flight (e.g., next ~)	vuelo (m)	[bu'ɛlɔ]
customs	aduana (f)	[adu'ana]
customs officer	aduanero (m)	[adua'nɛrɔ]
customs declaration	declaración (f) de aduana	[dɛklara'θiɔn dɛ adu'ana]
to fill out (vt)	rellenar (vt)	[rɛje'nar]
to fill out the declaration	rellenar la declaración	[rɛje'nar ʎa dɛklara'θiɔn]
passport control	control (m) de pasaportes	[kɔnt'rɔʎ dɛ pasa'pɔrtɛs]
luggage	equipaje (m)	[ɛki'pahɛ]
hand luggage	equipaje (m) de mano	[ɛki'pahɛ dɛ 'manɔ]
Lost Luggage Desk	objetos perdidos	[ɔb'hetɔs per'didɔs]
luggage cart	carrito (m) de equipaje	[kar'ritɔ dɛ ɛki'pahe]
landing	aterrizaje (m)	[atɛrri'θahɛ]
landing strip	pista (f) de aterrizaje	['pista dɛ atɛrri'θahɛ]
to land (vi)	aterrizar (vi)	[atɛrri'θar]
airstairs	escaleras (f pl)	[ɛska'leras]
check-in	facturación (f), check-in (m)	[faktura'θiɔn, ʧə'kin]
check-in desk	mostrador (m) de facturación	[mɔstra'dɔr dɛ faktyra'θiɔn]
to check-in (vi)	hacer el check-in	[a'θær ɛʎ ʧə'kin]
boarding pass	tarjeta (f) de embarque	[tar'hɛta dɛ ɛm'barkɛ]
departure gate	puerta (f) de embarque	[pu'ɛrta dɛ ɛm'barkɛ]
transit	tránsito (m)	['transitɔ]
to wait (vt)	esperar (vt)	[ɛspɛ'rar]
departure lounge	zona (f) de preembarque	['θɔna dɛ prɛ:m'barkɛ]
to see off	despedir (vt)	[dɛspɛ'dir]
to say goodbye	despedirse (vr)	[dɛspɛ'dirsɛ]

171

173. Bicycle. Motorcycle

bicycle	**bicicleta** (f)	[biθik'leta]
scooter	**scooter** (f)	['skutɛr]
motorcycle, bike	**motocicleta** (f)	[mɔtɔθik'leta]
to go by bicycle	**ir en bicicleta**	[ir ɛn biθik'lɛta]
handlebars	**manillar** (m)	[mani'jar]
pedal	**pedal** (m)	[pɛ'daʎ]
brakes	**frenos** (m pl)	['frɛnɔs]
bicycle seat	**sillín** (m)	[si'jɪn]
pump	**bomba** (f)	['bɔmba]
luggage rack	**portaequipajes** (m)	[pɔrtaɛki'pahɛs]
front lamp	**linterna** (f)	[lin'tɛrna]
helmet	**casco** (m)	['kaskɔ]
wheel	**rueda** (f)	[ru'ɛda]
fender	**guardabarros** (m)	[guarda'βarrɔs]
rim	**llanta** (f)	['janta]
spoke	**rayo** (m)	['rajo]

Cars

174. Types of cars

automobile, car	**coche** (m)	['kɔtʃe]
sports car	**coche** (m) **deportivo**	['kɔtʃe dɛpɔr'tiβɔ]
limousine	**limusina** (f)	[limu'sina]
off-road vehicle	**todoterreno** (m)	['tɔdɔtɛr'rɛnɔ]
convertible	**cabriolé** (m)	[kabriɔ'le]
minibus	**microbús** (m)	[mikrɔ'βus]
ambulance	**ambulancia** (f)	[ambu'ʎansija]
snowplow	**quitanieves** (m)	[kita'njevɛs]
truck	**camión** (m)	[ka'mɔn]
tank truck	**camión** (m) **cisterna**	[ka'mɔn sis'tɛrna]
van (small truck)	**camioneta** (f)	[kamiɔ'neta]
tractor (big rig)	**remolcador** (m)	[rɛmɔʎka'dɔr]
trailer	**remolque** (m)	[rɛ'mɔʎke]
comfortable (adj)	**confortable** (adj)	[kɔnfɔr'table]
second hand (adj)	**de ocasión** (adj)	[dɛ ɔka'θɔn]

175. Cars. Bodywork

hood	**capó** (m)	[ka'pɔ]
fender	**guardabarros** (m)	[guarda'βarrɔs]
roof	**techo** (m)	['tɛtʃɔ]
windshield	**parabrisas** (m)	[parab'risas]
rear-view mirror	**espejo** (m) **retrovisor**	[ɛs'pɛhɔ rɛtrɔwi'sɔr]
windshield washer	**limpiador** (m)	[limpja'dɔr]
windshield wipers	**limpiaparabrisas** (m)	[limpjaparab'risas]
side window	**ventana** (f) **lateral**	[ben'tana late'raʎ]
window lift	**elevalunas** (m)	[ɛleva'lunas]
antenna	**antena** (f)	[an'tɛna]
sun roof	**techo** (m) **solar**	['tɛtʃɔ sɔ'ʎar]
bumper	**parachoques** (m)	[para'tʃɔkɛs]
trunk	**maletero** (m)	[male'tɛrɔ]
door	**puerta** (f)	[pu'ɛrta]
door handle	**tirador** (m) **de puerta**	[tira'dɔr dɛ pu'ɛrta]

door lock	cerradura (f)	[θærra'dura]
license plate	matrícula (f)	[mat'rikuʎa]
muffler	silenciador (m)	[silensja'dɔr]
gas tank	tanque (m) de gasolina	['taŋke dɛ gasɔ'lina]
tail pipe	tubo (m) de escape	['tuβɔ dɛ ɛs'kapɛ]

gas, accelerator	acelerador (m)	[aθælera'dɔr]
pedal	pedal (m)	[pɛ'daʎ]
gas pedal	pedal (m) de acelerador	[pɛ'daʎ dɛ aθelera'dɔr]
brake	freno (m)	['frɛnɔ]
brake pedal	pedal (m) de freno	[pɛ'daʎ dɛ 'frenɔ]
to slow down (to brake)	frenar (vi)	[frɛ'nar]
parking brake	freno (m) de mano	['frɛnɔ dɛ 'manɔ]

clutch	embrague (m)	[ɛmb'rage]
clutch pedal	pedal (m) de embrague	[pɛ'daʎ dɛ ɛmb'ragɛ]
clutch plate	disco (m) de embrague	['diskɔ dɛ ɛmb'ragɛ]
shock absorber	amortiguador (m)	[amɔrtigua'dɔr]

wheel	rueda (f)	[ru'ɛda]
spare tire	rueda (f) de repuesto	[ru'ɛda dɛ rɛpu'ɛstɔ]
hubcap	tapacubo (m)	[tapa'kuβɔ]

driving wheels	ruedas (f pl) motrices	[ru'ɛdas mɔt'risɛs]
front-wheel drive (as adj)	de tracción delantera	[dɛ trak'θion delan'tɛra]
rear-wheel drive (as adj)	de tracción trasera	[dɛ trak'θion tra'sɛra]
all-wheel drive (as adj)	de tracción integral	[dɛ trak'θion intɛg'raʎ]
gearbox	caja (f) de cambios	['kaha dɛ 'kambiɔs]
automatic (adj)	automático (adj)	[autɔ'matikɔ]
mechanical (adj)	mecánico (adj)	[mɛ'kanikɔ]
gear shift	palanca (f) de cambios	[pa'laŋka dɛ 'kambiɔs]

| headlight | faro (m) | ['farɔ] |
| headlights | faros (m pl) | ['farɔs] |

low beam	luz (f) de cruce	[lyθ dɛ 'kruθæ]
high beam	luz (f) de carretera	['lyθ dɛ karrɛ'tɛra]
brake light	luz (f) de freno	[lyθ dɛ 'frɛnɔ]

parking lights	luz (f) de posición	[lyθ dɛ pɔsi'θion]
hazard lights	luces (f pl) de emergencia	['lysɛs dɛ ɛmer'hensija]
fog lights	luces (f pl) antiniebla	['lyθæs anti'njebla]
turn signal	intermitente (m)	[intɛrmi'nɛntɛ]
back-up light	luz (f) de marcha atrás	[lyθ dɛ 'martʃa at'ras]

176. Cars. Passenger compartment

| car inside | habitáculo (m) | [abi'takulɔ] |
| leather (as adj) | de cuero (adj) | [dɛ ku'ɛrɔ] |

velour (as adj)	de felpa (adj)	[dɛ 'feʎpa]
upholstery	revestimiento (m)	[rɛbɛsti'mjentɔ]
instrument (gage)	instrumento (m)	[instru'mentɔ]
dashboard	salpicadero (m)	[saʎpika'dɛrɔ]
speedometer	velocímetro (m)	[bɛlɔ'simɛtrɔ]
needle (pointer)	aguja (f)	[a'guha]
odometer	cuentakilómetros (m)	[kuɛntaki'lɔmɛtrɔs]
indicator (sensor)	indicador (m)	[indika'dɔr]
level	nivel (m)	[ni'βəʎ]
warning light	testigo (m)	[tɛs'tigɔ]
steering wheel	volante (m)	[bɔ'ʎantɛ]
horn	bocina (f)	[bɔ'θina]
button	botón (m)	[bɔ'tɔn]
switch	interruptor (m)	[intɛrrup'tɔr]
seat	asiento (m)	[a'sjentɔ]
backrest	respaldo (m)	[rɛs'paʎdɔ]
headrest	reposacabezas (m)	[repɔsaka'βeθas]
seat belt	cinturón (m) de seguridad	[θintu'rɔn dɛ seguri'dad]
to fasten the belt	abrocharse el cinturón	[abrɔ'ʧarsɛ ɛʎ sintu'rɔn]
adjustment (of seats)	reglaje (m)	[rɛg'ʎahɛ]
airbag	bolsa (f) de aire	['bɔʎsa dɛ 'airɛ]
air-conditioner	climatizador (m)	[klimatiθa'dɔr]
radio	radio (f)	['radiɔ]
CD player	lector (m) de CD	[lek'tɔr dɛ sɛ'dɛ]
to turn on	encender (vt)	[ɛnθæn'dɛr]
antenna	antena (f)	[an'tɛna]
glove box	guantera (f)	[guan'tɛra]
ashtray	cenicero (m)	[θæni'θærɔ]

177. Cars. Engine

engine, motor	motor (m)	[mɔ'tɔr]
diesel (as adj)	diesel (adj)	[dje'sɛʎ]
gasoline (as adj)	a gasolina (adj)	[a gasɔ'lina]
engine volume	volumen (m) del motor	[bɔ'lumɛn dɛʎ mɔ'tɔr]
power	potencia (f)	[pɔ'tɛnsija]
horsepower	caballo (m) de fuerza	[ka'βajo dɛ fu'ɛrθa]
piston	pistón (m)	[pis'tɔn]
cylinder	cilindro (m)	[θi'lindrɔ]
valve	válvula (f)	['baʎvuʎa]
injector	inyector (m)	[inʰek'tɔr]
generator	generador (m)	[hɛnɛra'dɔr]

carburetor	carburador (m)	[karbura'dɔr]
engine oil	aceite (m) de motor	[a'sɛjte dɛ mɔ'tɔr]
radiator	radiador (m)	[radia'dɔr]
coolant	liquido (m) refrigerante	[li'kidɔ rɛfrihe'rantɛ]
cooling fan	ventilador (m)	[bɛntiʎa'dɔr]
battery (accumulator)	batería (f)	[batɛ'rija]
starter	estárter (m)	[ɛs'tartɛr]
ignition	encendido (m)	[ɛnθæn'didɔ]
spark plug	bujía (f) de ignición	[bu'hija dɛ igni'sʲɔn]
terminal (of battery)	terminal (f)	[termi'naʎ]
positive terminal	terminal (f) positiva	[termi'naʎ pɔsi'tiβa]
negative terminal	terminal (f) negativa	[termi'naʎ nɛga'tiβa]
fuse	fusible (m)	[fu'sible]
air filter	filtro (m) de aire	['fiʎtrɔ dɛ 'ajrɛ]
oil filter	filtro (m) de aceite	['fiʎtrɔ dɛ a'θæjtɛ]
fuel filter	filtro (m) de combustible	['fiʎtrɔ dɛ kɔmbus'tible]

178. Cars. Crash. Repair

car accident	accidente (m)	[aksi'dɛntɛ]
road accident	accidente (m) de tráfico	[aksi'dɛntɛ dɛ 'trafikɔ]
to run into …	chocar contra …	[tʃɔ'kar 'kɔntra]
to have an accident	tener un accidente	[tɛ'nɛr un aksi'dɛntɛ]
damage	daño (m)	['daɲɔ]
intact (adj)	intacto (adj)	[in'taktɔ]
to break down (vi)	averiarse (vr)	[avɛ'rjarsɛ]
towrope	remolque (m)	[rɛ'mɔʎke]
puncture	pinchazo (m)	[pin'tʃaθɔ]
to be flat	desinflarse (vr)	[dɛsinf'ʎarsɛ]
to pump up	inflar (vt)	[inf'ʎar]
pressure	presión (f)	[prɛ'sʲɔn]
to check (to examine)	verificar (vt)	[bɛrifi'kar]
repair	reparación (f)	[rɛpara'θʲɔn]
auto repair shop	taller (m)	[ta'jer]
spare part	parte (f) de repuesto	['partɛ dɛ rɛpu'ɛstɔ]
part	parte (f)	['partɛ]
bolt (with nut)	perno (m)	['pɛrnɔ]
screw bolt (without nut)	tornillo (m)	[tɔr'nijo]
nut	tuerca (f)	[tu'ɛrka]
washer	arandela (f)	[aran'dɛʎa]
bearing	rodamiento (m)	[rɔda'mjentɔ]
tube	tubo (m)	['tuβɔ]

| gasket (head ~) | junta (f) | ['hunta] |
| cable, wire | hilo (m) | ['ilɔ] |

jack	gato (m)	['gatɔ]
wrench	llave (f) de tuerca	['jaβə dɛ tu'ɛrka]
hammer	martillo (m)	[mar'tijo]
pump	bomba (f)	['bɔmba]
screwdriver	destornillador (m)	[dɛstɔrnija'dɔr]

| fire extinguisher | extintor (m) | [ɛkstin'tɔr] |
| warning triangle | triángulo (m) de avería | [tri'aŋulɔ dɛ awe'rija] |

to stall (vi)	calarse (vr)	[ka'ʎarsɛ]
stalling	parada (f)	[pa'rada]
to be broken	estar averiado	[ɛs'tar awe'rjadɔ]

to overheat (vi)	recalentarse (vr)	[rɛkalen'tarsɛ]
to be clogged up	estar atascado	[ɛs'tar atas'kadɔ]
to freeze up (pipes, etc.)	congelarse (vr)	[kɔnhɛ'ʎarsɛ]
to burst (vi, ab. tube)	reventar (vi)	[rɛvɛn'tar]

pressure	presión (f)	[prɛ'siɔn]
level	nivel (m)	[ni'βəʎ]
slack (~ belt)	flojo (adj)	['flɔhɔ]

dent	abolladura (f)	[abɔja'dura]
abnormal noise (motor)	ruido (m)	[ru'idɔ]
crack	grieta (f)	[gri'ɛta]
scratch	rozadura (f)	[rɔθa'dura]

179. Cars. Road

road	camino (m)	[ka'minɔ]
highway	autovía (f)	[autɔ'βia]
freeway	carretera (f)	[karrɛ'tɛra]
direction (way)	dirección (f)	[dirɛk'θiɔn]
distance	distancia (f)	[dis'tansija]

bridge	puente (m)	[pu'ɛntɛ]
parking lot	aparcamiento (m)	[aparka'mjentɔ]
square	plaza (f)	['pʎaθa]
interchange	intercambiador (m)	[intɛrkambia'dɔr]
tunnel	túnel (m)	['tunɛʎ]

gas station	gasolinera (f)	[gasɔli'nɛra]
parking lot	aparcamiento (m)	[aparka'mjentɔ]
gas pump	surtidor (m)	[surti'dɔr]
auto repair shop	taller (m)	[ta'jer]
to get gas	cargar gasolina	[kar'gar gasɔ'lina]
fuel	combustible (m)	[kɔmbus'tible]

jerrycan	**bidón** (m) **de gasolina**	[bi'dɔn dɛ gasɔ'lina]
asphalt	**asfalto** (m)	[as'faʎtɔ]
road markings	**señalización** (f) **vial**	[seɲjaliθa'sʲɔn bi'jaʎ]
curb	**bordillo** (m)	[bɔr'dijo]
guardrail	**barrera** (f) **de seguridad**	[barrɛra dɛ sɛguri'dad]
ditch	**cuneta** (f)	[ku'nɛta]
roadside (shoulder)	**borde** (m) **de la carretera**	['bɔrdɛ dɛ ʎa karrɛ'tɛra]
lamppost	**farola** (f)	[fa'rɔʎa]
to drive (a car)	**conducir** (vi, vt)	[kɔndu'sir]
to turn (~ to the left)	**girar** (vi)	[hi'rar]
to make a U-turn	**dar la vuelta en U**	[dar ʎa vu'ɛʎta ɛn u]
reverse (~ gear)	**marcha** (f) **atrás**	[''martʃa at'ras]
to honk (vi)	**tocar la bocina**	[tɔ'kar ʎa bɔ'θina]
honk (sound)	**bocinazo** (m)	[bɔθi'naðɔ]
to get stuck	**atascarse** (vr)	[atas'karsɛ]
to spin (in mud)	**patinar** (vi)	[pati'nar]
to cut, to turn off	**parar** (vt)	[pa'rar]
speed	**velocidad** (f)	[bɛlɔθi'dad]
to exceed the speed limit	**exceder la velocidad**	[ɛkθæ'dɛr ʎa bɛlɔθi'dad]
to give a ticket	**multar** (vt)	[muʎ'tar]
traffic lights	**semáforo** (m)	[sɛ'mafɔrɔ]
driver's license	**permiso** (m) **de conducir**	[pɛr'misɔ dɛ kɔndu'θir]
grade crossing	**paso** (m) **a nivel**	['pasɔ a ni'βeʎ]
intersection	**cruce** (m)	['kruθæ]
crosswalk	**paso** (m) **de peatones**	['pasɔ dɛ pea'tɔnɛs]
bend, curve	**curva** (f)	['kurva]
pedestrian zone	**zona** (f) **de peatones**	['θona dɛ pɛa'tɔnɛs]

180. Traffic signs

rules of the road	**reglas** (f pl) **de tránsito**	['rɛgʎas dɛ 'transitɔ]
traffic sign	**señal** (m) **de tráfico**	[sɛ'ɲjaʎ dɛ 'trafikɔ]
passing (overtaking)	**adelantamiento** (m)	[adɛʎanta'mjentɔ]
curve	**curva** (f)	['kurva]
U-turn	**vuelta** (f) **en U**	[bu'ɛʎta ɛn 'ju]
traffic circle	**rotonda** (f)	[rɔ'tɔnda]
No entry	**prohibido el paso**	[prɔi'βidɔ eʎ 'paθɔ]
No vehicles allowed	**circulación prohibida**	[θirkyʎa'sʲɔn prɔi'βida]
No passing	**prohibido adelantar**	[prɔi'βidɔ adɛʎan'tar]
No parking	**prohibido aparcar**	[prɔi'βidɔ apar'kar]
No stopping	**prohibido parar**	[prɔi'βidɔ pa'rar]
dangerous turn	**curva** (f) **peligrosa**	['kurva pɛlig'rɔsa]
steep descent	**bajada con fuerte pendiente**	[ba'hada kɔn fu'ɛrtɛ pɛn'djentɛ]

one-way traffic	**sentido** (m) **único**	[sɛn'tidɔ 'unikɔ]
crosswalk	**paso** (m) **de peatones**	['pasɔ dɛ pea'tɔnɛs]
slippery road	**pavimento** (m) **deslizante**	[pavli'mentɔ dɛsli'ðantɛ]
YIELD	**ceda el paso**	['θæda ɛʎ 'pasɔ]

PEOPLE. LIFE EVENTS

Life events

181. Holidays. Event

celebration, holiday	**fiesta** (f)	['fjesta]
national day	**fiesta** (f) **nacional**	['fjesta nasɔ'naʎ]
public holiday	**día** (m) **de fiesta**	['dia dɛ 'fjesta]
to commemorate (vt)	**festejar** (vt)	[feste'har]
event (happening)	**evento** (m)	[ɛ'vɛntɔ]
event (organized activity)	**medida** (f)	[mɛ'dida]
banquet (party)	**banquete** (m)	[ba'ŋkɛtɛ]
reception (formal party)	**recepción** (f)	[rɛsɛp'θɔon]
feast	**festín** (m)	[fɛs'tin]
anniversary	**aniversario** (m)	[anivɛr'sarɔ]
jubilee	**jubileo** (m)	[hubi'leɔ]
to celebrate (vt)	**celebrar** (vt)	[θæleb'rar]
New Year	**Año** (m) **Nuevo**	['aɲɔ nu'ɛβɔ]
Happy New Year!	**¡Feliz Año Nuevo!**	[fɛ'liθ 'aɲɔ nu'ɛβɔ]
Christmas	**Navidad** (f)	[nawi'dad]
Merry Christmas!	**¡Feliz Navidad!**	[fɛ'liθ nawi'dad]
Christmas tree	**árbol** (m) **de Navidad**	['arbɔʎ dɛ nawi'dad]
fireworks	**fuegos** (m pl) **artificiales**	[fu'ɛgɔs artifi'θjales]
wedding	**boda** (f)	['bɔda]
groom	**novio** (m)	['nɔβɔ]
bride	**novia** (f)	['nɔβia]
to invite (vt)	**invitar** (vt)	[inbi'tar]
invitation card	**tarjeta** (f) **de invitación**	[tar'hɛta dɛ inwita'θɔon]
guest	**invitado** (m)	[imbi'tadɔ]
to visit	**visitar** (vt)	[bisi'tar]
(~ your parents, etc.)		
to greet the guests	**recibir a los invitados**	[rɛθi'βir a lɔs imbi'tadɔs]
gift, present	**regalo** (m)	[rɛ'galɔ]
to give (sth as present)	**regalar** (vt)	[rɛga'ʎar]
to receive gifts	**recibir regalos**	[rɛθi'βir rɛ'galɔs]
bouquet (of flowers)	**ramo** (m) **de flores**	['ramɔ dɛ 'flɔrɛs]

| congratulations | felicitación (f) | [fɛliθita'sʲon] |
| to congratulate (vt) | felicitar (vt) | [fɛliθi'tar] |

greeting card	tarjeta (f) de felicitación	[tar'hɛta dɛ fɛlisita'θʲon]
to send a postcard	enviar una tarjeta	[ɛmbi'jar una tar'hɛta]
to get a postcard	recibir una tarjeta	[rɛθi'βir una tar'hɛta]

toast	brindis (m)	['brindis]
to offer (a drink, etc.)	ofrecer (vt)	[ɔfrɛ'sɛr]
champagne	champaña (f)	[ʧam'paɲja]

to have fun	divertirse (vr)	[divɛr'tirsɛ]
fun, merriment	diversión (f)	[diwer'sʲon]
joy (emotion)	alegría (f)	[aleg'rija]

| dance | baile (m) | ['bajle] |
| to dance (vi, vt) | bailar (vi, vt) | [baj'ʎar] |

| waltz | vals (m) | [baʎs] |
| tango | tango (m) | ['taŋɔ] |

182. Funerals. Burial

cemetery	cementerio (m)	[θæmɛn'tɛrɔ]
grave, tomb	tumba (f)	['tumba]
gravestone	lápida (f)	['ʎapida]
fence	verja (f)	['bɛrha]
chapel	capilla (f)	[ka'pija]

death	muerte (f)	[mu'ɛrtɛ]
to die (vi)	morir (vi)	[mɔ'rir]
the deceased	difunto (m)	[di'funtɔ]
mourning	luto (m)	['lytɔ]

to bury (vt)	enterrar (vt)	[ɛntɛr'rar]
funeral home	funeraria (f)	[funɛ'rarija]
funeral	entierro (m)	[ɛn'tʲerrɔ]

wreath	corona (f) funeraria	[kɔ'rɔna fynɛ'rarija]
casket	ataúd (m)	[ata'ud]
hearse	coche (m) fúnebre	['kɔʧe 'funɛbrɛ]
shroud	mortaja (f)	[mɔr'taha]

funeral procession	cortejo (m) fúnebre	[kɔr'tɛhɔ 'funɛbrɛ]
cremation urn	urna (f) funeraria	['urna funɛ'raria]
crematory	crematorio (m)	[krɛma'tɔrɔ]

obituary	necrología (f)	[nɛkrɔlɔ'hia]
to cry (weep)	llorar (vi)	[jo'rar]
to sob (vi)	sollozar (vi)	[sɔjo'θar]

181

183. War. Soldiers

platoon	sección (f)	[sɛk'θion]
company	compañía (f)	[kɔmpa'nija]
regiment	regimiento (m)	[rɛhi'mjentɔ]
army	ejército (m)	[ɛ'hɛrθitɔ]
division	división (f)	[diwi'θion]

| section, squad | destacamento (m) | [dɛstaka'mentɔ] |
| host (army) | hueste (f) | [u'əstɛ] |

| soldier | soldado (m) | [sɔʎ'dadɔ] |
| officer | oficial (m) | [ɔfi'θjaʎ] |

private	soldado (m) raso	[sɔʎ'dadɔ 'rasɔ]
sergeant	sargento (m)	[sar'hɛntɔ]
lieutenant	teniente (m)	[tɛ'njentɛ]
captain	capitán (m)	[kapi'tan]
major	mayor (m)	[ma'jor]
colonel	coronel (m)	[kɔrɔ'nɛʎ]
general	general (m)	[hɛnɛ'raʎ]

sailor	marino (m)	[ma'rinɔ]
captain	capitán (m)	[kapi'tan]
boatswain	contramaestre (m)	[kɔntrama'ɛstrɛ]

artilleryman	artillero (m)	[arti'ʎjerɔ]
paratrooper	paracaidista (m)	[parakai'dista]
pilot	piloto (m)	[pi'lotɔ]
navigator	navegador (m)	[navɛga'dor]
mechanic	mecánico (m)	[mɛ'kanikɔ]

pioneer (sapper)	zapador (m)	[θapa'dor]
parachutist	paracaidista (m)	[parakai'dista]
reconnaissance scout	explorador (m)	[ɛksplɔra'dor]
sniper	francotirador (m)	['fraŋkɔtiradɔr]

patrol (group)	patrulla (f)	[pat'ruja]
to patrol (vt)	patrullar (vi, vt)	[patru'jar]
sentry, guard	centinela (m)	[θænti'nɛʎa]

warrior	guerrero (m)	[gɛr'rɛrɔ]
hero	héroe (m)	['ɛrɔɛ]
heroine	heroína (f)	[ɛrɔ'ina]
patriot	patriota (m)	[pat'riota]

| traitor | traidor (m) | [trai'dor] |
| to betray (vt) | traicionar (vt) | [traiθio'nar] |

| deserter | desertor (m) | [dɛsɛr'tor] |
| to desert (vi) | desertar (vi) | [dɛsɛr'tar] |

mercenary	mercenario (m)	[mɛrθæ'narɔ]
recruit	recluta (m)	[rɛk'lyta]
volunteer	voluntario (m)	[bɔlun'tarɔ]

dead (n)	muerto (m)	[mu'ɛrtɔ]
wounded (n)	herido (m)	[ɛ'ridɔ]
prisoner of war	prisionero (m)	[prisɔ'nɛrɔ]

184. War. Military actions. Part 1

war	guerra (f)	['gɛrra]
to be at war	estar en guerra	[ɛs'tar ɛn 'gɛrra]
civil war	guerra (f) civil	['gɛrra θi'βiʎ]

treacherously (adv)	pérfidamente (adv)	['pɛrfida'mɛntɛ]
declaration of war	declaración (f) de guerra	[dɛklara'θiɔn dɛ 'gɛrra]
to declare (~ war)	declarar (vt)	[dɛkʎa'rar]
aggression	agresión (f)	[agrɛ'siɔn]
to attack (invade)	atacar (vt)	[ata'kar]

to invade (vt)	invadir (vt)	[inva'dir]
invader	invasor (m)	[inva'sɔr]
conqueror	conquistador (m)	[kɔŋkista'dɔr]

defense	defensa (f)	[dɛ'fɛnsa]
to defend (a country, etc.)	defender (vt)	[dɛfɛn'dɛr]
to defend oneself	defenderse (vr)	[dɛfɛn'dɛrsɛ]

enemy	enemigo (m)	[ɛnɛ'migɔ]
foe, adversary	adversario (m)	[advɛr'sariɔ]
enemy (as adj)	enemigo (adj)	[ɛnɛ'migɔ]

| strategy | estrategia (f) | [ɛstra'tɛhija] |
| tactics | táctica (f) | ['taktika] |

order	orden (f)	['ɔrdɛn]
command (order)	comando (m)	[kɔ'mandɔ]
to order (vt)	ordenar (vt)	[ɔrdɛ'nar]
mission	misión (f)	[mi'siɔn]
secret (adj)	secreto (adj)	[sɛk'rɛtɔ]

| battle | batalla (f) | [ba'taja] |
| combat | combate (m) | [kɔm'batɛ] |

attack	ataque (m)	[a'takɛ]
storming (assault)	asalto (m)	[a'saʎtɔ]
to storm (vt)	tomar por asalto	[tɔ'mar pɔr a'saʎtɔ]
siege (to be under ~)	asedio (m), sitio (m)	[a'sɛdiɔ], ['sitiɔ]
offensive (n)	ofensiva (f)	[ɔfɛn'siβa]
to go on the offensive	tomar la ofensiva	[tɔ'mar ʎa ɔfɛn'siβa]

| retreat | retirada (f) | [rɛti'rada] |
| to retreat (vi) | retirarse (vr) | [rɛti'rarsɛ] |

| encirclement | envolvimiento (m) | [ɛnvɔʎwi'mjentɔ] |
| to encircle (vt) | cercar (vt) | [θær'kar] |

bombing (by aircraft)	bombardeo (m)	[bɔmbar'dɛɔ]
to drop a bomb	lanzar una bomba	[ʎan'θar 'una 'βɔmba]
to bomb (vt)	bombear (vt)	[bɔmbe'ar]
explosion	explosión (f)	[ɛksplɔ's'ɔn]

shot	tiro (m), disparo (m)	['tirɔ], [dis'parɔ]
to fire a shot	disparar (vi)	[dispa'rar]
firing (burst of ~)	tiroteo (m)	[tirɔ'tɛɔ]

| to take aim (at ...) | apuntar a ... | [apun'tar a] |
| to point (a gun) | encarar (vt) | [ɛŋka'rar] |

to sink (~ a ship)	hundir (vt)	[un'dir]
hole (in a ship)	brecha (f)	['brɛʧa]
to founder, to sink (vi)	hundirse (vr)	[un'dirsɛ]

front (war ~)	frente (m)	['frɛntɛ]
rear (homefront)	retaguardia (f)	[rɛtagu'ardija]
evacuation	evacuación (f)	[ɛvakua'θ'ɔn]
to evacuate (vt)	evacuar (vt)	[ɛvaku'ar]

trench	trinchera (f)	[trin'ʧera]
barbwire	alambre (m) de púas	[a'ʎambrɛ dɛ 'puas]
barrier (anti tank ~)	barrera (f)	[bar'rɛra]
watchtower	torre (f) de vigilancia	['tɔrrɛ dɛ wihi'lanθia]

hospital	hospital (m)	[ɔspi'taʎ]
to wound (vt)	herir (vi, vt)	[ɛ'rir]
wound	herida (f)	[ɛ'rida]
wounded (n)	herido (m)	[ɛ'ridɔ]
to be wounded	recibir una herida	[rɛθi'βir 'una ɛ'rida]
serious (wound)	grave (adj)	['graβə]

185. War. Military actions. Part 2

captivity	cautiverio (m)	[kauti'βəriɔ]
to take captive	capturar (vt)	[kaptu'rar]
to be in captivity	estar en cautiverio	[ɛs'tar ɛn kauti'βəriɔ]
to be taken prisoner	caer prisionero	[ka'ɛr pris'ɔ'nɛrɔ]

| concentration camp | campo (m) de concentración | ['kampɔ dɛ kɔnθæntra's'ɔn] |

| prisoner of war | prisionero (m) | [pris'ɔ'nɛrɔ] |
| to escape (vi) | escapar (vi) | [ɛska'par] |

to betray (vt)	traicionar (vt)	[traiθˈnar]
betrayer	traidor (m)	[traiˈdɔr]
betrayal	traición (f)	[traiˈθon]

to execute (shoot)	fusilar (vt)	[fusiˈʎar]
execution (by firing squad)	fusilamiento (m)	[fusiʎaˈmjentɔ]

equipment (military gear)	equipo (m)	[ɛˈkipɔ]
shoulder board	hombrera (f)	[ɔmbˈrɛra]
gas mask	máscara (f) antigás	[ˈmaskara antiˈgas]

radio transmitter	radio transmisor (m)	[ˈradiɔ transmiˈsɔr]
cipher, code	cifra (f)	[ˈθifra]
secrecy	conspiración (f)	[kɔnspiraˈθon]
password	contraseña (f)	[kɔntraˈsɛɲa]

land mine	mina (f) terrestre	[ˈmina tɛrˈrɛstrɛ]
to mine (road, etc.)	minar (vt)	[miˈnar]
minefield	campo (m) minado	[ˈkampɔ miˈnadɔ]

air-raid warning	alarma (f) aérea	[aˈʎarma aˈərɛa]
alarm (warning)	alarma (f)	[aˈʎarma]
signal	señal (f)	[sɛˈɲjaʎ]
signal flare	cohete (m) de señales	[kɔˈɛtɛ dɛ sɛˈɲjales]

headquarters	estado (m) mayor	[ɛsˈtadɔ maˈjor]
reconnaissance	reconocimiento (m)	[rɛkɔnɔθiˈmjentɔ]
situation	situación (f)	[situaˈθon]
report	informe (m)	[inˈfɔrmɛ]
ambush	emboscada (f)	[ɛmbɔsˈkada]
reinforcement (of army)	refuerzo (m)	[rɛfuˈɛrθɔ]

target	blanco (m)	[ˈbʎaŋkɔ]
proving ground	terreno (m) de prueba	[tɛrˈrɛnɔ dɛ pruˈɛβa]
military exercise	maniobras (f pl)	[maniˈɔbras]

panic	pánico (m)	[ˈpanikɔ]
devastation	devastación (f)	[dɛvastaˈθon]
destruction, ruins	destrucciones (f pl)	[dɛstrukθˈonɛs]
to destroy (vt)	destruir (vt)	[dɛstruˈir]

to survive (vi, vt)	sobrevivir (vi, vt)	[sɔbrɛwiˈβir]
to disarm (vt)	desarmar (vt)	[dɛsarˈmar]
to handle (~ a gun)	manejar (vt)	[manɛˈhar]

Attention!	¡Firmes!	[ˈfirmɛs]
At ease!	¡Descanso!	[dɛsˈkansɔ]

feat (of courage)	hazaña (f)	[aˈθaɲja]
oath (vow)	juramento (m)	[huraˈmɛntɔ]
to swear (an oath)	jurar (vt)	[huˈrar]
decoration (medal, etc.)	condecoración (f)	[kɔndekɔraˈsˈon]

to award (give medal to)	condecorar (vt)	[kɔndɛkɔˈrar]
medal	medalla (f)	[mɛˈdaja]
order (e.g., ~ of Merit)	orden (f)	[ˈɔrdɛn]
victory	victoria (f)	[bikˈtɔrija]
defeat	derrota (f)	[dɛrˈrɔta]
armistice	armisticio (m)	[armisˈtisiɔ]
banner (standard)	bandera (f)	[banˈdɛra]
glory (honor, fame)	gloria (f)	[ˈglɔrija]
parade	desfile (m) militar	[dɛsfiˈle miliˈtar]
to march (on parade)	marchar (vi)	[marˈʧar]

186. Weapons

weapons	arma (f)	[ˈarma]
firearm	arma (f) de fuego	[ˈarma dɛ fuˈɛgɔ]
cold weapons (knives, etc.)	arma (f) blanca	[ˈarma ˈbʎaŋka]
chemical weapons	arma (f) química	[ˈarma ˈkimika]
nuclear (adj)	nuclear (adj)	[nukleˈar]
nuclear weapons	arma (f) nuclear	[ˈarma nukleˈar]
bomb	bomba (f)	[ˈbɔmba]
atomic bomb	bomba (f) atómica	[ˈbɔmba aˈtɔmika]
pistol (gun)	pistola (f)	[pisˈtɔʎa]
rifle	fusil (m)	[fuˈsiʎ]
submachine gun	metralleta (f)	[mɛtraˈjeta]
machine gun	ametralladora (f)	[amɛtrajaˈdɔra]
muzzle	boca (f)	[ˈbɔka]
barrel	cañón (m)	[kaˈɲɔn]
caliber	calibre (m)	[kaˈlibrɛ]
trigger	gatillo (m)	[gaˈtiˈjo]
sight (aiming device)	alza (f)	[ˈaʎθa]
magazine	cargador (m)	[kargaˈdɔr]
butt (of rifle)	culata (f)	[kuˈʎata]
hand grenade	granada (f)	[graˈnada]
explosive	explosivo (m)	[ɛksplɔˈsiβɔ]
bullet	bala (f)	[ˈbaʎa]
cartridge	cartucho (m)	[karˈtuʧɔ]
charge	carga (f)	[ˈkarga]
ammunition	pertrechos (m pl)	[pɛrtˈrɛʧɔs]
bomber (aircraft)	bombardero (m)	[bɔmbarˈdɛrɔ]
fighter	avión (m) de caza	[aˈvɔn dɛ ˈkaθa]

helicopter	helicóptero (m)	[ɛli'kɔptɛrɔ]
anti-aircraft gun	antiaéreo (m)	[antia'ərɛɔ]
tank	tanque (m)	['taŋke]
tank gun	cañón (m)	[ka'ɲɔn]

artillery	artillería (f)	[artije'rija]
cannon	cañón (m)	[ka'ɲɔn]
to lay (a gun)	dirigir (vt)	[diri'hir]

shell (projectile)	obús (m)	[ɔ'βys]
mortar bomb	bomba (f) de mortero	['bɔmba dɛ mar'tɛrɔ]
mortar	mortero (m)	[mɔr'tɛrɔ]
splinter (shell fragment)	trozo (m) de obús	['trɔθɔ dɛ ɔ'βus]

submarine	submarino (m)	[subma'rinɔ]
torpedo	torpedo (m)	[tɔr'pɛdɔ]
missile	misil (m)	[mi'siʎ]

to load (gun)	cargar (vt)	[kar'gar]
to shoot (vi)	tirar (vi)	[ti'rar]
to point at (the cannon)	apuntar a ...	[apun'tar a]
bayonet	bayoneta (f)	[bajo'nɛta]

epee	espada (f)	[ɛs'pada]
saber (e.g., cavalry ~)	sable (m)	['sable]
spear (weapon)	lanza (f)	['ʎanθa]
bow	arco (m)	['arkɔ]
arrow	flecha (f)	['fletʃa]
musket	mosquete (m)	[mɔs'kɛtɛ]
crossbow	ballesta (f)	[ba'jesta]

187. Ancient people

primitive (prehistoric)	primitivo (adj)	[primi'tiβɔ]
prehistoric (adj)	prehistórico (adj)	[prɛis'tɔrikɔ]
ancient (~ civilization)	antiguo (adj)	[an'tiguɔ]

Stone Age	Edad (f) de Piedra	[ɛ'dad dɛ 'pjedra]
Bronze Age	Edad (f) de Bronce	[ɛ'dad dɛ 'brɔnθæ]
Ice Age	Edad (f) de Hielo	[ɛ'dad dɛ 'jəlɔ]

tribe	tribu (f)	['triβu]
cannibal	caníbal (m)	[ka'niβaʎ]
hunter	cazador (m)	[kaθa'dɔr]
to hunt (vi, vt)	cazar (vi, vt)	[ka'θar]
mammoth	mamut (m)	[ma'mut]

cave	caverna (f)	[ka'βərna]
fire	fuego (m)	[fu'ɛgɔ]
campfire	hoguera (f)	[ɔ'gɛra]

rock painting	pintura (f) rupestre	[pin'tura ru'pɛstrɛ]
tool (e.g., stone ax)	útil (m)	['utiʎ]
spear	lanza (f)	['ʎanθa]
stone ax	hacha (f) de piedra	['atʃa dɛ 'pjedra]
to be at war	estar en guerra	[ɛs'tar ɛn 'gɛrra]
to domesticate (vt)	domesticar (vt)	[dɔmɛsti'kar]

idol	ídolo (m)	['idɔlɜ]
to worship (vt)	adorar (vt)	[adɔ'rar]
superstition	superstición (f)	[supɛrsti'θiˡon]

evolution	evolución (f)	[ɛvɔlu'θiˡon]
development	desarrollo (m)	[dɛsa'rɔjo]
disappearance (extinction)	desaparición (f)	[dɛsapari'θiˡon]
to adapt oneself	adaptarse (vr)	[adap'tarsɛ]

archeology	arqueología (f)	[arkeɔlɔ'hija]
archeologist	arqueólogo (m)	[arke'ɔlɔgɔ]
archeological (adj)	arqueológico (adj)	[arkeɔ'lɔhikɔ]

excavation site	sitio (m) de excavación	[sitiɔ dɛ ɛkskava'θiˡon]
excavations	excavaciones (f pl)	[ɛkskava'siˡonɛs]
find (object)	hallazgo (m)	[a'jaᴢgɔ]
fragment	fragmento (m)	[frag'mɛntɔ]

188. Middle Ages

people (ethnic group)	pueblo (m)	[pu'ɛblɜ]
peoples	pueblos (m pl)	[pu'ɛblɜs]
tribe	tribu (f)	['triβu]
tribes	tribus (f pl)	['triβus]

barbarians	bárbaros (m pl)	['barbarɔs]
Gauls	galos (m pl)	['galɜs]
Goths	godos (m pl)	['gɔdɔs]
Slavs	eslavos (m pl)	[ɛs'ʎaβɔs]
Vikings	vikingos (m pl)	[wi'kiŋɔs]

| Romans | romanos (m pl) | [rɔ'manɔs] |
| Roman (adj) | romano (adj) | [rɔ'manɔ] |

Byzantines	bizantinos (m pl)	[biθan'tinɔs]
Byzantium	Bizancio (m)	[bi'θansiɔ]
Byzantine (adj)	bizantino (adj)	[biθan'tinɔ]

emperor	emperador (m)	[ɛmpera'dɔr]
leader, chief	jefe (m)	['hɛfɛ]
powerful (~ king)	poderoso (adj)	[pɔdɛ'rɔsɔ]
king	rey (m)	['rɛj]
ruler (sovereign)	gobernador (m)	[gɔbɛrna'dɔr]

knight	caballero (m)	[kaba'jero]
feudal lord	señor (m) feudal	[sɛ'ɲʲor fɛu'daʎ]
feudal (adj)	feudal (adj)	[fɛu'daʎ]
vassal	vasallo (m)	[bas'sajo]

duke	duque (m)	['dukɛ]
earl	conde (m)	['kondɛ]
baron	barón (m)	[ba'rɔn]
bishop	obispo (m)	[ɔ'βɪspɔ]

armor	armadura (f)	[arma'dura]
shield	escudo (m)	[ɛs'kudɔ]
sword	espada (f)	[ɛs'pada]
visor	visera (f)	[wi'sɛra]
chainmail	cota (f) de malla	['kɔta ɛ 'maja]

| crusade | cruzada (f) | [kru'θada] |
| crusader | cruzado (m) | [kru'θadɔ] |

territory	territorio (m)	[tɛrri'tɔriɔ]
to attack (invade)	atacar (vt)	[ata'kar]
to conquer (vt)	conquistar (vt)	[kɔŋkis'tar]
to occupy (invade)	ocupar (vt)	[ɔku'par]

siege (to be under ~)	asedio (m), sitio (m)	[a'sɛdiɔ], ['sitiɔ]
besieged (adj)	sitiado (adj)	[si'tiadɔ]
to besiege (vt)	asediar, sitiar	[asɛ'djar], [siti'ar]

inquisition	inquisición (f)	[iŋkisi'θʲon]
inquisitor	inquisidor (m)	[iŋkisi'dɔr]
torture	tortura (f)	[tɔr'tura]
cruel (adj)	cruel (adj)	[kru'ɛʎ]

| heretic | hereje (m) | [ɛ'rɛhɛ] |
| heresy | herejía (f) | [ɛrɛ'hija] |

seafaring	navegación (f) marítima	[navɛga'θʲon ma'ritima]
pirate	pirata (m)	[pi'rata]
piracy	piratería (f)	[piratɛ'rija]
boarding (attack)	abordaje (m)	[abɔr'dahɛ]

| loot, booty | botín (m) | [bɔ'tin] |
| treasures | tesoros (m pl) | [tɛ'sɔrɔs] |

discovery	descubrimiento (m)	[dɛskubri'mjentɔ]
to discover (new land, etc.)	descubrir (vt)	[dɛskub'rir]
expedition	expedición (f)	[ɛkspɛdi'θʲon]

musketeer	mosquetero (m)	[mɔske'tɛrɔ]
cardinal	cardenal (m)	[kardɛ'naʎ]
heraldry	heráldica (f)	[ɛ'raʎdika]
heraldic (adj)	heráldico (adj)	[ɛ'raʎdikɔ]

189. Leader. Chief. Authorities

king	**rey** (m)	[rɛj]
queen	**reina** (f)	[ˈrɛjna]
royal (adj)	**real** (adj)	[rɛˈaʎ]
kingdom	**reino** (m)	[ˈrɛjnɔ]
prince	**príncipe** (m)	[ˈprinθipɛ]
princess	**princesa** (f)	[prinˈθæsa]
president	**presidente** (m)	[prɛsiˈdɛntɛ]
vice-president	**vicepresidente** (m)	[bisɛprɛsiˈdɛntɛ]
senator	**senador** (m)	[sɛnaˈdɔr]
monarch	**monarca** (m)	[mɔˈnarka]
ruler (sovereign)	**gobernador** (m)	[gɔbɛrnaˈdɔr]
dictator	**dictador** (m)	[diktaˈdɔr]
tyrant	**tirano** (m)	[tiˈranɔ]
magnate	**magnate** (m)	[magˈnatɛ]
director	**director** (m)	[dirɛkˈtɔr]
chief	**jefe** (m)	[ˈhɛfɛ]
manager (director)	**gerente** (m)	[hɛˈrɛntɛ]
boss	**amo** (m)	[ˈamɔ]
owner	**dueño** (m)	[duˈɛɲɔ]
head (~ of delegation)	**jefe** (m)	[ˈhɛfɛ]
authorities	**autoridades** (f pl)	[autoriˈdadɛs]
superiors	**superiores** (m pl)	[supɛriˈɔrɛs]
governor	**gobernador** (m)	[gɔbɛrnaˈdɔr]
consul	**cónsul** (m)	[ˈkɔnsuʎ]
diplomat	**diplomático** (m)	[diplɔˈmatikɔ]
mayor	**alcalde** (m)	[aʎˈkaʎdɛ]
sheriff	**sheriff** (m)	[ʃɛˈrif]
emperor	**emperador** (m)	[ɛmperaˈdɔr]
tsar, czar	**zar** (m)	[θar]
pharaoh	**faraón** (m)	[faraˈɔn]
khan	**jan** (m), **kan** (m)	[han]

190. Road. Way. Directions

road	**camino** (m)	[kaˈminɔ]
way (direction)	**vía** (f)	[ˈbija]
freeway	**carretera** (f)	[karrɛˈtɛra]
highway	**autovía** (f)	[autɔˈβia]
interstate	**camino** (m) **nacional**	[kaˈminɔ nasiɔˈnaʎ]

| main road | camino (m) principal | [ka'minɔ prinsi'paʎ] |
| dirt road | camino (m) de tierra | [ka'minɔ dɛ 'tʲerra] |

| pathway | sendero (m) | [sɛn'dɛrɔ] |
| footpath (troddenpath) | senda (f) | ['sɛnda] |

Where?	¿Dónde?	['dɔndɛ]
Where (to)?	¿A dónde?	[a 'dɔndɛ]
Where ... from?	¿De dónde?	[dɛ 'dɔndɛ]

| direction (way) | dirección (f) | [dirɛk'θʲon] |
| to point (~ the way) | mostrar (vt) | [mɔst'rar] |

to the left	a la izquierda	[a ʎa iθ'kjerda]
to the right	a la derecha	[a ʎa dɛ'rɛtʃa]
straight ahead (adv)	todo recto (adv)	['tɔdo 'rɛktɔ]
back (e.g., to turn ~)	atrás (adv)	[at'ras]

bend, curve	curva (f)	['kurva]
to turn (~ to the left)	girar (vi)	[hi'rar]
to make a U-turn	girar en U	[hi'rar ɛn 'ju:]

| to be visible | divisarse (vr) | [diwi'sarsɛ] |
| to appear (come into view) | aparecer (vi) | [aparɛ'sɛr] |

stop, halt (in journey)	alto (m)	['aʎtɔ]
to rest, to halt (vi)	descansar (vi)	[dɛskan'sar]
rest (pause)	reposo (m)	[rɛ'pɔsɔ]

to lose one's way	perderse (vr)	[pɛr'dɛrsɛ]
to lead to ... (ab. road)	llevar a ...	[je'βar a]
to arrive at ...	llegar a ...	[je'gar a]
stretch (of road)	tramo (m)	['tramɔ]

asphalt	asfalto (m)	[as'faʎtɔ]
curb	bordillo (m)	[bɔr'dijo]
ditch	cuneta (f)	[ku'nɛta]
manhole	pozo (m) de alcantarillado	['pɔθɔ dɛ alkantari'jadɔ]

| roadside (shoulder) | borde (m) de la carretera | ['bɔrdɛ dɛ ʎa karrɛ'tɛra] |
| pit, pothole | bache (m) | ['batʃə] |

| to go (on foot) | ir (vi) | [ir] |
| to pass (overtake) | adelantar (vt) | [adɛʎan'tar] |

| step (footstep) | paso (m) | ['pasɔ] |
| on foot (adv) | a pie | [a 'pje] |

to block (road)	bloquear (vt)	[blɔke'ar]
boom barrier	barrera (f)	[bar'rɛra]
dead end	callejón (m) sin salida	[kajə'hɔn sin sa'lida]

191. Breaking the law. Criminals. Part 1

bandit	bandido (m)	[ban'didɔ]
crime	crimen (m)	['krimɛn]
criminal (person)	criminal (m)	[krimi'naʎ]
thief	ladrón (m)	[ʎad'rɔn]
to steal (vi, vt)	robar (vt)	[rɔ'βar]
stealing, theft	robo (m)	['rɔβɔ]
to kidnap (vt)	secuestrar (vt)	[sɛkuɛst'rar]
kidnapping	secuestro (m)	[sɛku'ɛstrɔ]
kidnapper	secuestrador (m)	[sɛkuɛstra'dɔr]
ransom	rescate (m)	[rɛs'katɛ]
to demand ransom	exigir un rescate	[ɛksi'hir un rɛs'katɛ]
to rob (vt)	robar (vt)	[rɔ'βar]
robbery	robo (m)	['rɔβɔ]
robber	atracador (m)	[atraka'dɔr]
to extort (vt)	extorsionar (vt)	[ɛkstɔrsɔ'nar]
extortionist	extorsionista (m)	[ɛkstɔrsɔ'nista]
extortion	extorsión (f)	[ɛkstɔr'sɔn]
to murder, to kill	matar, asesinar (vt)	[ma'tar], [asɛsi'nar]
murder	asesinato (m)	[asɛsi'natɔ]
murderer	asesino (m)	[asɛ'sinɔ]
gunshot	tiro (m), disparo (m)	['tirɔ], [dis'parɔ]
to fire a shot	disparar (vi)	[dispa'rar]
to shoot to death	matar (vt)	[ma'tar]
to shoot (vi)	tirar (vi)	[ti'rar]
shooting	tiroteo (m)	[tirɔ'tɛɔ]
incident (fight, etc.)	incidente (m)	[insi'dɛntɛ]
fight, brawl	pelea (f)	[pe'lɛa]
Help!	¡Socorro!	[sɔ'kɔrrɔ]
victim	víctima (f)	['biktima]
to damage (vt)	perjudicar (vt)	[pɛrhudi'kar]
damage	daño (m)	['daɲɔ]
dead body	cadáver (m)	[ka'daβər]
grave (~ crime)	grave (adj)	['graβə]
to attack (vt)	atacar (vt)	[ata'kar]
to beat (dog, person)	pegar (vt)	[pɛ'gar]
to beat up	apporear (vt)	[appɔre'ar]
to take (rob of sth)	quitar (vt)	[ki'tar]
to stab to death	acuchillar (vt)	[akuʧi'jar]
to maim (vt)	mutilar (vt)	[muti'ʎar]

to wound (vt)	herir (vt)	[ɛ'rir]
blackmail	chantaje (m)	[ʧan'tahɛ]
to blackmail (vt)	hacer chantaje	[a'θær ʧan'tahɛ]
blackmailer	chantajista (m)	[ʧanta'hista]

protection racket	extorsión (f)	[ɛkstor'sʲon]
racketeer	extorsionador (m)	[ɛkstorsʲona'dor]
gangster	gángster (m)	['gaŋstɛr]
mafia, Mob	mafia (f)	['mafia]

pickpocket	carterista (m)	[kartɛ'rista]
burglar	ladrón (m) de viviendas	[lad'rɔn dɛ wi'vjendas]
smuggling	contrabandismo (m)	[kɔntraban'dismɔ]
smuggler	contrabandista (m)	[kɔntraban'dista]

forgery	falsificación (f)	[faʎsifika'θʲon]
to forge (counterfeit)	falsificar (vt)	[faʎsifi'kar]
fake (forged)	falso, falsificado	['faʎsɔ], [faʎsifi'kadɔ]

192. Breaking the law. Criminals. Part 2

rape	violación (f)	[bʲɔʎa'sʲɔn]
to rape (vt)	violar (vt)	[bʲɔ'ʎar]
rapist	violador (m)	[bʲɔʎa'dor]
maniac	maníaco (m)	[ma'niakɔ]

prostitute (fem.)	prostituta (f)	[prɔsti'tuta]
prostitution	prostitución (f)	[prɔstitu'θʲon]
pimp	chulo (m), proxeneta (m)	['ʧulɔ], [prɔkse'nɛta]

| drug addict | drogadicto (m) | [drɔga'diktɔ] |
| drug dealer | narcotraficante (m) | [narkɔtrafi'kantɛ] |

to blow up (bomb)	hacer explotar	[a'θær ɛksplɔ'tar]
explosion	explosión (f)	[ɛksplɔ'sʲon]
to set fire	incendiar (vt)	[inθæn'djar]
incendiary (arsonist)	incendiario (m)	[inθæn'djariɔ]

terrorism	terrorismo (m)	[tɛrrɔ'rismɔ]
terrorist	terrorista (m)	[tɛrrɔ'rista]
hostage	rehén (m)	[rɛ'ɛn]

to swindle (vt)	estafar (vt)	[ɛsta'far]
swindle	estafa (f)	[ɛs'tafa]
swindler	estafador (m)	[ɛstafa'dor]

to bribe (vt)	sobornar (vt)	[sɔbɔr'nar]
bribery	soborno (m)	[sɔ'βɔrnɔ]
bribe	soborno (m)	[sɔ'βɔrnɔ]
poison	veneno (m)	[bɛ'nɛnɔ]

to poison (vt)	envenenar (vt)	[ɛmbɛnɛ'nar]
to poison oneself	envenenarse (vr)	[ɛmbɛnɛ'narsɛ]
suicide (act)	suicidio (m)	[sui'θidiɔ]
suicide (person)	suicida (m, f)	[sui'θida]
to threaten (vt)	amenazar (vt)	[amɛna'θar]
threat	amenaza (f)	[amɛ'nasa]
to make an attempt	atentar (vi)	[atɛn'tar]
attempt (attack)	atentado (m)	[atɛn'tadɔ]
to steal (a car)	robar (vt)	[rɔ'βar]
to hijack (a plane)	secuestrar (vt)	[sɛkuɛst'rar]
revenge	venganza (f)	[bɛ'ŋanθa]
to revenge (vt)	vengar (vt)	[bɛ'ŋar]
to torture (vt)	torturar (vt)	[tɔrtu'rar]
torture	tortura (f)	[tɔr'tura]
to torment (vt)	atormentar (vt)	[atɔrmɛn'tar]
pirate	pirata (m)	[pi'rata]
hooligan	gamberro (m)	[gam'bɛrrɔ]
armed (adj)	armado (adj)	[ar'madɔ]
violence	violencia (f)	[bʲɔ'lɛnsija]
spying (n)	espionaje (m)	[ɛspʲɔ'nahɛ]
to spy (vi)	espiar (vi, vt)	[ɛspi'jar]

193. Police. Law. Part 1

justice	justicia (f)	[hus'tiθija]
court (court room)	tribunal (m)	[tribu'naʎ]
judge	juez (m)	[hu'ɛθ]
jurors	jurados (m pl)	[hu'radɔs]
jury trial	tribunal (m) de jurados	[tribu'naʎ dɛ hu'radɔs]
to judge (vt)	juzgar (vt)	[huθ'gar]
lawyer, attorney	abogado (m)	[abɔ'gadɔ]
accused	acusado (m)	[aku'sadɔ]
dock	banquillo (m) de los acusados	[ba'ŋkijo dɛ lɔs aku'sadɔs]
charge	inculpación (f)	[iŋkuʎpa'θʲon]
accused	inculpado (m)	[iŋkuʎ'padɔ]
sentence	sentencia (f)	[sɛn'tɛnθija]
to sentence (vt)	sentenciar (vt)	[sɛntɛn'sjar]
guilty (culprit)	culpable (m)	[kuʎ'pable]

| to punish (vt) | castigar (vt) | [kasti'gar] |
| punishment | castigo (m) | [kas'tigɔ] |

fine (penalty)	multa (f)	['muʎta]
life imprisonment	cadena (f) perpetua	[ka'dɛna pɛr'pɛtua]
death penalty	pena (f) de muerte	['pɛna dɛ mu'ɛrtɛ]
electric chair	silla (f) eléctrica	['sija ɛ'lektrika]
gallows	horca (f)	['ɔrka]

| to execute (vt) | ejecutar (vt) | [ɛhɛku'tar] |
| execution | ejecución (f) | [ɛhɛku'θʲon] |

| prison, jail | prisión (f) | [pri'sʲon] |
| cell | celda (f) | ['θæʎda] |

escort	escolta (f)	[ɛs'kɔʎta]
prison guard	guardia (m) de prisiones	[gu'ardija dɛ pri'sʲonɛs]
prisoner	prisionero (m)	[prisʲo'nɛro]

| handcuffs | esposas (f pl) | [ɛs'pɔsas] |
| to handcuff (vt) | esposar (vt) | [ɛspɔ'sar] |

prison break	escape (m)	[ɛs'kapɛ]
to break out (vi)	escaparse (vr)	[ɛska'parsɛ]
to disappear (vi)	desaparecer (vi)	[dɛsaparɛ'θær]
to release (from prison)	liberar (vt)	[libɛ'rar]
amnesty	amnistía (f)	[amnis'tia]

police	policía (f)	[pɔli'θija]
police officer	policía (m)	[pɔli'θija]
police station	comisaría (f) de policía	[kɔmisa'ria dɛ pɔli'θia]
billy club	porra (f)	['pɔrra]
bullhorn	megáfono (m)	[me'gafɔnɔ]

patrol car	coche (m) patrulla	['kotʃe pat'ruja]
siren	sirena (f)	[si'rɛna]
to turn on the siren	poner la sirena	[pɔ'nɛr ʎa si'rɛna]
siren call	canto (m) de la sirena	['kantɔ dɛ ʎa si'rɛna]

crime scene	escena (f) del delito	[ɛs'θænɔ dɛʎ dɛ'litɔ]
witness	testigo (m)	[tɛs'tigɔ]
freedom	libertad (f)	[libɛr'tad]
accomplice	cómplice (m)	['kompliθæ]
to flee (vi)	escapar de …	[ɛska'par dɛ]
trace (to leave a ~)	rastro (m)	['rastrɔ]

194. Police. Law. Part 2

| search (investigation) | búsqueda (f) | ['buskeda] |
| to look for … | buscar (vt) | [bus'kar] |

suspicion	**sospecha** (f)	[sɔs'petʃa]
suspicious (suspect)	**sospechoso** (adj)	[sɔspɛ'tʃɔsɔ]
to stop (cause to halt)	**parar** (vt)	[pa'rar]
to detain (keep in custody)	**retener** (vt)	[rɛtɛ'nɛr]
case (lawsuit)	**causa** (f)	['kausa]
investigation	**investigación** (f)	[imbɛstiga'θion]
detective	**detective** (m)	[dɛtɛk'tiβe]
investigator	**investigador** (m)	[imbɛstiga'dɔr]
hypothesis	**versión** (f)	[bɛr'sion]
motive	**motivo** (m)	[mɔ'tiβɔ]
interrogation	**interrogatorio** (m)	[intɛrrɔga'tɔriɔ]
to interrogate (vt)	**interrogar** (vt)	[intɛrrɔ'gar]
to question (vt)	**interrogar** (vt)	[intɛrrɔ'gar]
check (identity ~)	**control** (m)	[kɔnt'rɔʎ]
round-up	**redada** (f)	[rɛ'dada]
search (~ warrant)	**registro** (m)	[rɛ'histrɔ]
chase (pursuit)	**persecución** (f)	[pɛrsɛku'θion]
to pursue, to chase	**perseguir** (vt)	[pɛrsɛ'gir]
to track (a criminal)	**rastrear** (vt)	[rastrɛ'ar]
arrest	**arresto** (m)	[ar'rɛstɔ]
to arrest (sb)	**arrestar** (vt)	[arrɛs'tar]
to catch (thief, etc.)	**capturar** (vt)	[kaptu'rar]
capture	**captura** (f)	[kap'tura]
document	**documento** (m)	[dɔku'mɛntɔ]
proof (evidence)	**prueba** (f)	[pru'ɛβa]
to prove (vt)	**probar** (vt)	[prɔ'βar]
footprint	**huella** (f)	[u'eja]
fingerprints	**huellas** (f pl) **digitales**	[u'ejas dihi'tales]
piece of evidence	**elemento** (m) **de prueba**	[ele'mɛntɔ dɛ pru'ɛβa]
alibi	**coartada** (f)	[kɔar'tada]
innocent (not guilty)	**inocente** (adj)	[inɔ'θæntɛ]
injustice	**injusticia** (f)	[inhus'tiθija]
unjust, unfair (adj)	**injusto** (adj)	[in'hustɔ]
criminal (adj)	**criminal** (adj)	[krimi'naʎ]
to confiscate (vt)	**confiscar** (vt)	[kɔnfis'kar]
drug (illegal substance)	**narcótico** (f)	[nar'kɔtikɔ]
weapon, gun	**arma** (f)	['arma]
to disarm (vt)	**desarmar** (vt)	[dɛsar'mar]
to order (command)	**ordenar** (vt)	[ɔrdɛ'nar]
to disappear (vi)	**desaparecer** (vi)	[dɛsaparɛ'θær]
law	**ley** (f)	[lej]
legal, lawful (adj)	**legal** (adj)	[le'gaʎ]
illegal, illicit (adj)	**ilegal** (adj)	[ile'gaʎ]
responsibility (blame)	**responsabilidad** (f)	[rɛspɔnsabili'dad]
responsible (adj)	**responsable** (adj)	[rɛspɔn'sable]

NATURE

The Earth. Part 1

195. Outer space

cosmos	cosmos (m)	['kɔsmɔs]
space (as adj)	espacial, cósmico (adj)	[ɛspa'sjaʎ], ['kɔsmikɔ]
outer space	espacio (m) cósmico	[ɛs'pa'sʲɔ 'kɔsmikɔ]
world	mundo (m)	['mundɔ]
universe	universo (m)	[uni'βɜrsɔ]
galaxy	Galaxia (f)	[ga'ʎaksija]
star	estrella (f)	[ɛst'rɛja]
constellation	constelación (f)	[kɔnstɛʎa'θʲon]
planet	planeta (m)	[pʎa'nɛta]
satellite	satélite (m)	[sa'tɛlitɛ]
meteorite	meteorito (m)	[mɛtɛɔ'ritɔ]
comet	cometa (f)	[kɔ'mɛta]
asteroid	asteroide (m)	[astɛ'rɔidɛ]
orbit	órbita (f)	['ɔrbita]
to revolve	girar (vi)	[hi'rar]
(~ around the Earth)		
atmosphere	atmósfera (f)	[at'mɔsfɛra]
the Sun	Sol (m)	[sɔʎ]
solar system	Sistema (m) Solar	[sis'tɛma sɔ'ʎar]
solar eclipse	eclipse (m) de Sol	[ɛk'lipsɛ dɛ sɔʎ]
the Earth	Tierra (f)	['tʲerra]
the Moon	Luna (f)	['lyna]
Mars	Marte (m)	['martɛ]
Venus	Venus (f)	['bɛnus]
Jupiter	Júpiter (m)	['hupitɛr]
Saturn	Saturno (m)	[sa'turnɔ]
Mercury	Mercurio (m)	[mɛr'kuriɔ]
Uranus	Urano (m)	[u'ranɔ]
Neptune	Neptuno (m)	[nɛp'tunɔ]
Pluto	Plutón (m)	[ply'tɔn]
Milky Way	la Vía Láctea	[ʎa 'βɪja 'ʎaktɛa]
Great Bear	la Osa Mayor	[ʎa 'ɔsa ma'jor]

North Star	la Estrella Polar	[ʎa εst'rεja pɔ'ʎar]
Martian	marciano (m)	[marsi'janɔ]
extraterrestrial (n)	extraterrestre (m)	[εkstratεr'rεstrε]
alien	planetícola (m)	[pʎanε'tikɔʎa]
flying saucer	platillo (m) volante	[pʎa'tijo bɔ'ʎantε]

spaceship	nave (f) espacial	['naβə εspa'θjaʎ]
space station	estación (f) orbital	[εsta'θᶦon ɔrbi'taʎ]
blast-off	despegue (m)	[dεs'pεgε]

engine	motor (m)	[mɔ'tɔr]
nozzle	tobera (f)	[tɔ'βəra]
fuel	combustible (m)	[kɔmbus'tible]

cockpit, flight deck	carlinga (f)	[kar'liŋa]
antenna	antena (f)	[an'tεna]
porthole	ventana (f)	[bεn'tana]
solar battery	batería (f) solar	[batε'rija sɔ'ʎar]
spacesuit	escafandra (f)	[εska'fandra]

| weightlessness | ingravidez (f) | [iŋrawi'dεs] |
| oxygen | oxígeno (m) | [ɔk'sihεnɔ] |

| docking (in space) | atraque (m) | [at'rake] |
| to dock (vi, vt) | realizar el atraque | [rεali'θar εʎ at'rakε] |

observatory	observatorio (m)	[ɔbsεrva'tɔriɔ]
telescope	telescopio (m)	[tεles'kɔpiɔ]
to observe (vt)	observar (vt)	[ɔbsεr'var]
to explore (vt)	explorar (vt)	[εksplɔ'rar]

196. The Earth

the Earth	Tierra (f)	['tᶦerra]
globe (the Earth)	globo (m) terrestre	['glɔbɔ tεr'rεstrε]
planet	planeta (m)	[pʎa'nεta]

atmosphere	atmósfera (f)	[at'mɔsfεra]
geography	geografía (f)	[hεogra'fija]
nature	naturaleza (f)	[natura'leθa]

globe (table ~)	globo (m) terráqueo	['glɔbɔ tεr'rakeɔ]
map	mapa (m)	['mapa]
atlas	atlas (m)	['atʎas]

Europe	Europa (f)	[əu'rɔpa]
Asia	Asia (f)	['asija]
Africa	África (f)	['afrika]
Australia	Australia (f)	[aust'ralija]
America	América (f)	[a'mεrika]

North America	América (f) del Norte	[a'mɛrika dɛʎ 'nɔrtɛ]
South America	América (f) del Sur	[a'mɛrika dɛʎ 'sur]
Antarctica	Antártida (f)	[an'tartida]
the Arctic	Ártico (m)	['artikɔ]

197. Cardinal directions

north	norte (m)	['nɔrtɛ]
to the north	al norte	[aʎ 'nɔrtɛ]
in the north	en el norte	[ɛn ɛʎ 'nɔrtɛ]
northern (adj)	del norte (adj)	[dɛʎ 'nɔrtɛ]
south	sur (m)	[sur]
to the south	al sur	[aʎ sur]
in the south	en el sur	[ɛn ɛʎ sur]
southern (adj)	del sur (adj)	[dɛʎ sur]
west	oeste (m)	[ɔ'əstɛ]
to the west	al oeste	[aʎ ɔ'əstɛ]
in the west	en el oeste	[ɛn ɛʎ ɔ'əstɛ]
western (adj)	del oeste (adj)	[dɛʎ ɔ'əstɛ]
east	este (m)	['ɛstɛ]
to the east	al este	[aʎ 'ɛstɛ]
in the east	en el este	[ɛn ɛʎ 'ɛstɛ]
eastern (adj)	del este (adj)	[dɛʎ 'ɛstɛ]

198. Sea. Ocean

sea	mar (m)	[mar]
ocean	océano (m)	[ɔ'θæanɔ]
gulf (bay)	golfo (m)	['gɔʎfɔ]
straits	estrecho (m)	[ɛst'rɛtʃɔ]
solid ground	tierra (f) firme	['tʲerra 'firmɛ]
continent (mainland)	continente (m)	[kɔnti'nɛntɛ]
island	isla (f)	['isʎa]
peninsula	península (f)	[pɛ'ninsuʎa]
archipelago	archipiélago (m)	[artʃipi'ɛʎagɔ]
bay, cove	bahía (f)	[ba'ija]
harbor	puerto (m)	[pu'ɛrtɔ]
lagoon	laguna (f)	[ʎa'guna]
cape	cabo (m)	['kaβɔ]
atoll	atolón (m)	[atɔ'lɔn]
reef	arrecife (m)	[arrɛ'θifɛ]

coral	coral (m)	[kɔ'raʎ]
coral reef	arrecife (m) de coral	[arrɛ'θifɛ dɛ kɔ'raʎ]
deep (adj)	profundo (adj)	[prɔ'fundɔ]
depth (deep water)	profundidad (f)	[prɔfundi'dad]
abyss	abismo (m)	[a'βismɔ]
trench (e.g., Mariana ~)	fosa (f) oceánica	['fɔsa ɔsɛ'anika]
current, stream	corriente (f)	[kɔr'rjentɛ]
to surround (bathe)	bañar (vt)	[ba'ɲiar]
shore	orilla (f)	[ɔ'rija]
coast	costa (f)	['kɔsta]
high tide	flujo (m)	['flyhɔ]
low tide	reflujo (m)	[rɛf'lyhɔ]
sandbank	banco (m) de arena	['baŋkɔ dɛ a'rɛna]
bottom	fondo (m)	['fɔndɔ]
wave	ola (f)	['ɔʎa]
crest (~ of a wave)	cresta (f) de la ola	['krɛsta dɛ ʎa 'ɔʎa]
froth (foam)	espuma (f)	[ɛs'puma]
storm	tempestad (f)	[tɛmpɛs'tad]
hurricane	huracán (m)	[ura'kan]
tsunami	tsunami (m)	[ʦu'nami]
calm (dead ~)	bonanza (f)	[bɔ'nanθa]
quiet, calm (adj)	calmo, tranquilo (adj)	['kaʎmɔ], [tra'ŋkilʒ]
pole	polo (m)	['pɔlɔ]
polar (adj)	polar (adj)	[pɔ'ʎar]
latitude	latitud (f)	[ʎati'tud]
longitude	longitud (f)	[lɔnhi'tud]
parallel	paralelo (m)	[para'lelʒ]
equator	ecuador (m)	[ɛkua'dɔr]
sky	cielo (m)	['sjelʒ]
horizon	horizonte (m)	[ɔri'θɔntɛ]
air	aire (m)	['ajrɛ]
lighthouse	faro (m)	['farɔ]
to dive (vi)	bucear (vi)	[buθæ'ar]
to sink (ab. boat)	hundirse (vr)	[un'dirsɛ]
treasures	tesoros (m pl)	[tɛ'sɔrɔs]

199. Seas' and Oceans' names

Atlantic Ocean	océano (m) Atlántico	[ɔ'θæœanɔ at'ʎantikɔ]
Indian Ocean	océano (m) Índico	[ɔ'θæœanɔ 'indikɔ]

Pacific Ocean	océano (m) Pacífico	[ɔ'θæænɔ pa'sifikɔ]
Arctic Ocean	océano (m) Glacial Ártico	[ɔ'θæænɔ gʎa'sjaʎ 'artikɔ]
Black Sea	mar (m) Negro	[mar 'nɛgrɔ]
Red Sea	mar (m) Rojo	[mar 'rɔhɔ]
Yellow Sea	mar (m) Amarillo	[mar ama'rijo]
White Sea	mar (m) Blanco	[mar 'bʎaŋkɔ]
Caspian Sea	mar (m) Caspio	[mar 'kaspiɔ]
Dead Sea	mar (m) Muerto	[mar mu'ɛrtɔ]
Mediterranean Sea	mar (m) Mediterráneo	[mar mɛditɛr'ranɛɔ]
Aegean Sea	mar (m) Egeo	[mar ɛ'hɛɔ]
Adriatic Sea	mar (m) Adriático	[mar adri'atikɔ]
Arabian Sea	mar (m) Arábigo	[mar a'raβigɔ]
Sea of Japan	mar (m) del Japón	[mar dɛʎ ha'pɔn]
Bering Sea	mar (m) de Bering	[mar dɛ 'bɛrin]
South China Sea	mar (m) de la China Meridional	[mar dɛ ʎa 'ʃina mɛridˈɔ'naʎ]
Coral Sea	mar (m) del Coral	[mar dɛʎ kɔ'raʎ]
Tasman Sea	mar (m) de Tasmania	[mar dɛ tas'manija]
Caribbean Sea	mar (m) Caribe	[mar kari'βə]
Barents Sea	mar (m) de Barents	[mar dɛ ba'rɛnts]
Kara Sea	mar (m) de Kara	[mar dɛ 'kara]
North Sea	mar (m) del Norte	['mar dɛʎ 'nɔrtɛ]
Baltic Sea	mar (m) Báltico	[mar 'baltikɔ]
Norwegian Sea	mar (m) de Noruega	[mar dɛ nɔru'ɛga]

200. Mountains

mountain	montaña (f)	[mɔn'taɲja]
mountain range	cadena (f) de montañas	[ka'dɛna dɛ mɔn'taɲias]
mountain ridge	cresta (f) de montañas	['krɛsta dɛ mɔn'taɲias]
summit, top	cima (f)	['θima]
peak	pico (m)	['pikɔ]
foot (of mountain)	pie (m)	[pje]
slope (mountainside)	cuesta (f)	[ku'ɛsta]
volcano	volcán (m)	[bɔʎ'kian]
active volcano	volcán (m) activo	[bɔʎ'kian ak'tiβɔ]
dormant volcano	volcán (m) apagado	[bɔʎ'kian apa'gadɔ]
eruption	erupción (f)	[ɛrup'θion]
crater	cráter (m)	['kratɛr]
magma	magma (f)	['magma]

lava	**lava** (f)	['ʎaβa]
molten (~ lava)	**fundido** (adj)	[fun'didɔ]
canyon	**cañón** (m)	[ka'ɲɔn]
gorge	**desfiladero** (m)	[dɛsfiʎa'dɛrɔ]
crevice	**grieta** (f)	[gri'ɛta]
abyss (chasm)	**precipicio** (m)	[prɛθi'pisɔ]
pass, col	**puerto** (m)	[pu'ɛrtɔ]
plateau	**meseta** (f)	[mɛ'sɛta]
cliff	**roca** (f)	['rɔka]
hill	**colina** (f)	[kɔ'lina]
glacier	**glaciar** (m)	[gʎa'sjar]
waterfall	**cascada** (f)	[kas'kada]
geyser	**geiser** (m)	['hɛjsɛr]
lake	**lago** (m)	['ʎagɔ]
plain	**llanura** (f)	[ja'nura]
landscape	**paisaje** (m)	[paj'sahɛ]
echo	**eco** (m)	['ɛkɔ]
alpinist	**alpinista** (m)	[aʎpi'nista]
rock climber	**escalador** (m)	[ɛskaʎa'dɔr]
to conquer (in climbing)	**conquistar** (vt)	[kɔŋkis'tar]
climb (an easy ~)	**ascensión** (f)	[aθæn'sɔn]

201. Mountains names

Alps	**Alpes** (m pl)	['aʎpɛs]
Mont Blanc	**Montblanc** (m)	[mɔnbʎan]
Pyrenees	**Pirineos** (m pl)	[piri'nɛɔs]
Carpathians	**Cárpatos** (m pl)	['karpatɔs]
Ural Mountains	**Urales** (m pl)	[u'rales]
Caucasus	**Cáucaso** (m)	['kaukasɔ]
Elbrus	**Elbrus** (m)	['ɛʎbrus]
Altai	**Altai** (m)	[aʎ'taj]
Tien Shan	**Tian-Shan** (m)	['tjan 'ʃan]
Pamir Mountains	**Pamir** (m)	[pa'mir]
Himalayas	**Himalayos** (m pl)	[ima'ʎajos]
Everest	**Everest** (m)	[ɛvɛ'rɛst]
Andes	**Andes** (m pl)	['andɛs]
Kilimanjaro	**Kilimanjaro** (m)	[kiliman'harɔ]

202. Rivers

river	río (m)	['rio]
spring (natural source)	manantial (m)	[manan'tjaʎ]
riverbed	lecho (m)	['letʃɔ]
basin	cuenca (f) fluvial	[ku'ɛŋka flu'vjaʎ]
to flow into …	desembocar en …	[dɛsɛmbɔ'kar ɛn]

tributary	afluente (m)	[aflu'ɛntɛ]
bank (of river)	orilla (f), ribera (f)	[ɔ'rija], [ri'βəra]

current, stream	corriente (f)	[kɔr'rjentɛ]
downstream (adv)	río abajo (adv)	['riɔ a'βahɔ]
upstream (adv)	río arriba (adv)	['riɔ ar'riβa]

inundation	inundación (f)	[inunda'θiˈon]
flooding	riada (f)	[ri'ada]
to overflow (vi)	desbordarse (vr)	[dɛsbɔr'darsɛ]
to flood (vt)	inundar (vt)	[inun'dar]

shallows (shoal)	bajo (m) arenoso	['bahɔ are'nɔsɔ]
rapids	rápido (m)	['rapidɔ]

dam	presa (f)	['presa]
canal	canal (m)	[ka'naʎ]
artificial lake	lago (m) artificiale	['lagɔ artifi'sjale]
sluice, lock	esclusa (f)	[ɛsk'lysa]

water body (pond, etc.)	cuerpo (m) de agua	[ku'ɛrpɔ dɛ 'agua]
swamp, bog	pantano (m)	[pan'tanɔ]
marsh	ciénaga (m)	['sjenaga]
whirlpool	remolino (m)	[rɛmɔ'linɔ]

stream (brook)	arroyo (m)	[ar'rɔjo]
drinking (ab. water)	potable (adj)	[pɔ'table]
fresh (~ water)	dulce (adj)	['duʎθæ]

ice	hielo (m)	['jelɜ]
to freeze (ab. river, etc.)	helarse (vr)	[ɛ'ʎarsɛ]

203. Rivers' names

Seine	Sena (m)	['sɛna]
Loire	Loira (m)	[lu'ara]

Thames	Támesis (m)	['tamɛsis]
Rhine	Rin (m)	[rin]
Danube	Danubio (m)	[da'nuβiɔ]
Volga	Volga (m)	['bɔʎga]

| Don | **Don** (m) | [dɔn] |
| Lena | **Lena** (m) | ['lena] |

Yellow River	**Río** (m) **Amarillo**	['riɔ ama'rijo]
Yangtze	**Río** (m) **Azul**	['riɔ a'θuʎ]
Mekong	**Mekong** (m)	[mɛ'kɔŋ]
Ganges	**Ganges** (m)	['gaŋɛs]

Nile River	**Nilo** (m)	['nilɔ]
Congo	**Congo** (m)	['kɔŋɔ]
Okavango	**Okavango** (m)	[ɔka'βaŋɔ]
Zambezi	**Zambeze** (m)	[sam'bɛθæ]
Limpopo	**Limpopo** (m)	[limpɔ'pɔ]

204. Forest

| forest | **bosque** (m) | ['bɔske] |
| forest (as adj) | **de bosque** (adj) | [dɛ 'bɔske] |

thick forest	**espesura** (f)	[ɛspɛ'sura]
grove	**bosquecillo** (m)	[bɔksɛ'sijo]
forest clearing	**claro** (m)	['kʎarɔ]

| thicket | **maleza** (f) | [ma'leθa] |
| scrubland | **matorral** (m) | [matɔr'raʎ] |

| footpath (troddenpath) | **senda** (f) | ['sɛnda] |
| gully | **barranco** (m) | [bar'raŋkɔ] |

tree	**árbol** (m)	['arbɔʎ]
leaf	**hoja** (f)	['ɔha]
leaves	**follaje** (m)	[fɔ'jahɛ]

fall of leaves	**caída** (f) **de hojas**	[ka'ida dɛ 'ɔhas]
to fall (ab. leaves)	**caer** (vi)	[ka'ɛr]
top (of the tree)	**cima** (f)	['θima]

branch	**rama** (f)	['rama]
bough	**rama** (f)	['rama]
bud (on shrub, tree)	**brote** (m)	['brɔte]
needle (of pine tree)	**aguja** (f)	[a'guha]
pine cone	**piña** (f)	['piɲja]

hollow (in a tree)	**agujero** (m)	[agu'hɛrɔ]
nest	**nido** (m)	['nidɔ]
burrow (animal hole)	**madriguera** (f)	[madri'gɛra]

trunk	**tronco** (m)	['trɔŋkɔ]
root	**raíz** (f)	[ra'iθ]
bark	**corteza** (f)	[kɔr'tɛθa]

moss	musgo (m)	['musgɔ]
to uproot (vt)	extirpar (vt)	[ɛstir'par]
to chop down	talar (vt)	[ta'ʎar]
to deforest (vt)	deforestar (vt)	[dɛfɔrɛs'tar]
tree stump	tocón (m)	[tɔ'kɔn]
campfire	hoguera (f)	[ɔ'gɛra]
forest fire	incendio (m)	[in'sɛndiɔ]
to extinguish (vt)	apagar (vt)	[apa'gar]
forest ranger	guarda (m) forestal	[gu'arda fɔrɛs'taʎ]
protection	protección (f)	[prɔtɛk'θiɔn]
to protect (~ nature)	proteger (vt)	[prɔtɛ'hɛr]
poacher	cazador (m) furtivo	[kaθa'dɔr fur'tiβɔ]
trap (e.g., bear ~)	cepo (m)	['θæpɔ]
to gather, to pick (vt)	recoger (vt)	[rɛkɔ'hɛr]
to lose one's way	perderse (vr)	[pɛr'dɛrsɛ]

205. Natural resources

natural resources	recursos (m pl) naturales	[rɛ'kursɔs natu'rales]
minerals	minerales (m pl)	[minɛ'rales]
deposits	depósitos (m pl)	[dɛ'pɔsitɔs]
field (e.g., oilfield)	yacimiento (m)	[jasi'mjentɔ]
to mine (extract)	extraer (vt)	[ɛkstra'ɛr]
mining (extraction)	extracción (f)	[ɛkstrak'θiɔn]
ore	mineral (m)	[minɛ'raʎ]
mine (e.g., for coal)	mina (f)	['mina]
mine shaft, pit	pozo (m) de mina	['pɔθɔ dɛ 'mina]
miner	minero (m)	[mi'nɛrɔ]
gas	gas (m)	[gas]
gas pipeline	gasoducto (m)	[gasɔ'duktɔ]
oil (petroleum)	petróleo (m)	[pɛt'rɔleɔ]
oil pipeline	oleoducto (m)	[ɔleɔ'duktɔ]
oil well	torre (f) petrolera	['tɔrrɛ pɛtrɔ'lera]
derrick	torre (f) de sondeo	['tɔrrɛ dɛ sɔn'dɛɔ]
tanker	petrolero (m)	[pɛtrɔ'lerɔ]
sand	arena (f)	[a'rɛna]
limestone	caliza (f)	[ka'liθa]
gravel	grava (f)	['graβa]
peat	turba (f)	['turba]
clay	arcilla (f)	[ar'θija]
coal	carbón (m)	[kar'bɔn]
iron	hierro (m)	['jerrɔ]
gold	oro (m)	['ɔrɔ]

silver	**plata** (f)	[ˈpʎata]
nickel	**níquel** (m)	[ˈnikeʎ]
copper	**cobre** (m)	[ˈkɔbrɛ]

zinc	**zinc** (m)	[θiŋk]
manganese	**manganeso** (m)	[maɲaˈnɛsɔ]
mercury	**mercurio** (m)	[mɛrˈkuriɔ]
lead	**plomo** (m)	[ˈplɔmɔ]

mineral	**mineral** (m)	[minɛˈraʎ]
crystal	**cristal** (m)	[krisˈtaʎ]
marble	**mármol** (m)	[ˈmarmɔʎ]
uranium	**uranio** (m)	[uˈraniɔ]

The Earth. Part 2

206. Weather

weather	tiempo (m)	['tʲempɔ]
weather forecast	previsión (m) del tiempo	[prɛwi'sʲɔn dɛʎ 'tʲempɔ]
temperature	temperatura (f)	[tɛmpɛra'tura]
thermometer	termómetro (m)	[tɛr'mɔmɛtrɔ]
barometer	barómetro (m)	[ba'rɔmɛtrɔ]
humidity	humedad (f)	[umɛ'dad]
heat (extreme ~)	calor (m) intenso	[ka'lɔr in'tɛnsɔ]
hot (torrid)	tórrido (adj)	['tɔrridɔ]
it's hot	hace mucho calor	['asɛ 'mutʃɔ ka'lɔr]
it's warm	hace calor	['aθæ ka'lɔr]
warm (moderately hot)	templado (adj)	[tɛmp'ladɔ]
it's cold	hace frío	['aθæ 'friɔ]
cold (adj)	frío (adj)	['friɔ]
sun	sol (m)	[sɔʎ]
to shine (vi)	brillar (vi)	[bri'jar]
sunny (day)	soleado (adj)	[sole'adɔ]
to come up (vi)	elevarse (vr)	[ɛle'βarsɛ]
to set (vi)	ponerse (vr)	[pɔ'nɛrsɛ]
cloud	nube (f)	['nuβə]
cloudy (adj)	nuboso (adj)	[nu'βɔsɔ]
rain cloud	nubarrón (m)	[nybar'rɔn]
somber (gloomy)	nublado (adj)	[nub'ʎadɔ]
rain	lluvia (f)	['juβɪja]
it's raining	está lloviendo	[ɛs'ta jo'vjendɔ]
rainy (day)	lluvioso (adj)	[juwi'ɔsɔ]
to drizzle (vi)	lloviznar (vi)	[jowiθ'nar]
pouring rain	aguacero (m)	[agua'θæɾɔ]
downpour	chaparrón (m)	[tʃapar'rɔn]
heavy (e.g., ~ rain)	fuerte (adj)	[fu'ɛrtɛ]
puddle	charco (m)	['tʃarkɔ]
to get wet (in rain)	mojarse (vr)	[mɔ'harsɛ]
fog (mist)	niebla (f)	['njebʎa]
foggy	nebuloso (adj)	[nebu'lɔsɔ]
snow	nieve (f)	['njebɛ]
it's snowing	está nevando	[ɛs'ta ne'βandɔ]

207. Severe weather. Natural disasters

thunderstorm	tormenta (f)	[tɔr'mɛnta]
lightning (~ strike)	relámpago (m)	[rɛ'ʎampagɔ]
to flash (vi)	relampaguear (vi)	[rɛlampagɛ'ar]
thunder	trueno (m)	[tru'ɛnɔ]
to thunder (vi)	tronar (vi)	[trɔ'nar]
it's thundering	está tronando	[ɛs'ta trɔ'nandɔ]
hail	granizo (m)	[gra'niθɔ]
it's hailing	está granizando	[ɛs'ta grani'θandɔ]
to flood (vt)	inundar (vt)	[inun'dar]
flood, inundation	inundación (f)	[inunda'θʲon]
earthquake	terremoto (m)	[tɛrrɛ'mɔtɔ]
tremor, quake	sacudida (f)	[saku'dida]
epicenter	epicentro (m)	[ɛpi'θæntrɔ]
eruption	erupción (f)	[ɛrup'θʲon]
lava	lava (f)	['ʎaβa]
twister	torbellino (m)	[tɔrbɛ'ʎɪnɔ]
tornado	tornado (m)	[tɔr'nadɔ]
typhoon	tifón (m)	[ti'fɔn]
hurricane	huracán (m)	[ura'kan]
storm	tempestad (f)	[tɛmpɛs'tad]
tsunami	tsunami (m)	[ʦu'nami]
cyclone	ciclón (m)	[sik'lɔn]
bad weather	mal tiempo (m)	[maʎ 'tʲempɔ]
fire (accident)	incendio (m)	[in'sɛndɪɔ]
disaster	catástrofe (f)	[ka'tastrɔfɛ]
meteorite	meteorito (m)	[mɛtɛɔ'ritɔ]
avalanche	avalancha (f)	[ava'ʎanʧa]
snowslide	alud (m) de nieve	[alyð dɛ 'nʲævɛ]
blizzard	ventisca (f)	[bɛn'tiska]
snowstorm	nevasca (f)	[nɛ'vaska]

208. Noises. Sounds

silence (quiet)	silencio (m)	[si'lɛnθɪɔ]
sound	sonido (m)	[sɔ'nidɔ]
noise	ruido (m)	[ru'idɔ]
to make noise	hacer ruido	[a'θɛr ru'idɔ]
noisy (adj)	ruidoso (adj)	[rui'dɔsɔ]

loudly (to speak, etc.)	**alto** (adv)	['aʌto]
loud (voice, etc.)	**fuerte** (adj)	[fu'ɛrtɛ]
constant (continuous)	**constante** (adj)	[kɔns'tantɛ]
shout (n)	**grito** (m)	['gritɔ]
to shout (vi)	**gritar** (vi)	[gri'tar]
whisper	**susurro** (m)	[su'surrɔ]
to whisper (vi, vt)	**susurrar** (vi, vt)	[susur'rar]
barking (of dog)	**ladrido** (m)	[ʌad'ridɔ]
to bark (vi)	**ladrar** (vi)	[ʌad'rar]
groan (of pain)	**gemido** (m)	[hɛ'midɔ]
to groan (vi)	**gemir** (vi)	[hɛ'mir]
cough	**tos** (f)	[tɔs]
to cough (vi)	**toser** (vi)	[tɔ'sɛr]
whistle	**silbido** (m)	[siʌ'bidɔ]
to whistle (vi)	**silbar** (vi)	[siʌ'bar]
knock (at the door)	**llamada** (f)	[ja'mada]
to knock (at the door)	**golpear** (vt)	[gɔʌpɛ'ar]
to crack (vi)	**crepitar** (vi)	[krɛpi'tar]
crack (plank, etc.)	**crepitación** (f)	[krɛpita'θіon]
siren	**sirena** (f)	[si'rɛna]
whistle (factory ~)	**pito** (m)	['pitɔ]
to whistle (ship, train)	**pitar** (vi)	[pi'tar]
honk (signal)	**bocinazo** (m)	[bɔθi'naðɔ]
to honk (vi)	**tocar la bocina**	[tɔ'kar ʌa bɔ'θina]

209. Winter

winter (n)	**invierno** (m)	[im'bjernɔ]
winter (as adj)	**de invierno** (adj)	[dɛ im'bjernɔ]
in winter	**en invierno**	[ɛn im'bjernɔ]
snow	**nieve** (f)	['njebɛ]
it's snowing	**está nevando**	[ɛs'ta ne'βandɔ]
snowfall	**nevada** (f)	[nɛ'vada]
snowdrift	**montón** (m) **de nieve**	[mɔn'tɔn dɛ 'njebɛ]
snowflake	**copo** (m) **de nieve**	['kɔpɔ dɛ 'njebɛ]
snowball	**bola** (f) **de nieve**	['bɔla dɛ 'njewe]
snowman	**monigote** (m) **de nieve**	[mɔni'gɔtɛ dɛ 'njebɛ]
icicle	**carámbano** (m)	[ka'rambanɔ]
December	**diciembre** (m)	[di'sjembrɛ]
January	**enero** (m)	[ɛ'nɛrɔ]
February	**febrero** (m)	[fɛb'rɛrɔ]

severe frost	**helada** (f)	[e'lada]
frosty (weather, air)	**helado** (adj)	[e'laðo]
below zero (adv)	**bajo cero** (adv)	['baho 'sɛɾɔ]
first frost	**primeras heladas** (f pl)	[pri'mɛras ɛ'ʎadas]
hoarfrost	**escarcha** (f)	[ɛs'kartʃa]
cold (cold weather)	**frío** (m)	['friɔ]
it's cold	**hace frío**	['aθæ 'friɔ]
fur coat	**abrigo** (m) **de piel**	[ab'riɡɔ dɛ pʲæʎ]
mittens	**manoplas** (f pl)	[ma'nɔpʎas]
to get sick	**enfermarse** (vr)	[ɛnfɛr'marsɛ]
cold (illness)	**resfriado** (m)	[rɛsfri'aðɔ]
to catch a cold	**resfriarse** (vr)	[rɛsfri'arsɛ]
ice	**hielo** (m)	['jelɔ]
black ice	**hielo** (m) **en la carretera**	['jelɔ ɛn la karrɛ'tɛra]
to freeze (ab. river, etc.)	**helarse** (vr)	[ɛ'ʎarsɛ]
ice floe	**bloque** (m) **de hielo**	['blɔkɛ dɛ 'jelɔ]
skis	**esquís** (m pl)	[ɛs'kis]
skier	**esquiador** (m)	[ɛskija'dɔr]
to ski (vi)	**esquiar** (vi)	[ɛski'jar]
to skate (vi)	**patinar** (vi)	[pati'nar]

Fauna

210. Mammals. Predators

predator	carnívoro (m)	[kar'niβɔrɔ]
tiger	tigre (m)	['tigrɛ]
lion	león (m)	[le'ɔn]
wolf	lobo (m)	['lɔβɔ]
fox	zorro (m)	['θɔrrɔ]
jaguar	jaguar (m)	[hagu'ar]
leopard	leopardo (m)	[leɔ'pardɔ]
cheetah	guepardo (m)	[ge'pardɔ]
black panther	pantera (f)	[pan'tɛra]
puma	puma (f)	['puma]
snow leopard	leopardo (m) de las nieves	[leɔ'pardɔ dɛ ʎas 'njebɛs]
lynx	lince (m)	['linsɛ]
coyote	coyote (m)	[kɔ'jotɛ]
jackal	chacal (m)	[ʧa'kaʎ]
hyena	hiena (f)	['jena]

211. Wild animals

animal	animal (m)	[ani'maʎ]
beast (animal)	bestia (f)	['bɛstja]
squirrel	ardilla (f)	[ar'dija]
hedgehog	erizo (m)	[ɛ'riθɔ]
hare	liebre (f)	['ʎjebrɛ]
rabbit	conejo (m)	[kɔ'nɛhɔ]
badger	tejón (m)	[tɛ'hɔn]
raccoon	mapache (m)	[ma'paʧə]
hamster	hámster (m)	['amstɛr]
marmot	marmota (f)	[mar'mɔta]
mole	topo (m)	['tɔpɔ]
mouse	ratón (m)	[ra'tɔn]
rat	rata (f)	['rata]
bat	murciélago (m)	[mur'θjeʎagɔ]
ermine	armiño (m)	[ar'miɲɔ]

sable	cebellina (f)	[θæbɛ'jɪna]
marten	marta (f)	['marta]
weasel	comadreja (f)	[kɔmad'rɛha]
mink	visón (m)	[bi'sɔn]

| beaver | castor (m) | [kas'tɔr] |
| otter | nutria (f) | ['nutrija] |

horse	caballo (m)	[ka'βajo]
moose	alce (m)	['aʎθæ]
deer	ciervo (m)	['θjervɔ]
camel	camello (m)	[ka'mɛʎjo]
bison	bisonte (m)	[bi'sɔntɛ]
aurochs	uro (m)	['urɔ]
buffalo	búfalo (m)	['bufalɔ]

zebra	cebra (f)	['θæbra]
antelope	antílope (m)	[an'tilɔpɛ]
roe deer	corzo (m)	['kɔrθɔ]
fallow deer	gamo (m)	['gamɔ]
chamois	gamuza (f)	[ga'muθa]
wild boar	jabalí (m)	[haba'li]

whale	ballena (f)	[ba'jena]
seal	foca (f)	['fɔka]
walrus	morsa (f)	['mɔrsa]
fur seal	oso (m) marino	['ɔsɔ ma'rinɔ]
dolphin	delfín (m)	[dɛʎ'fin]

bear	oso (m)	['ɔsɔ]
polar bear	oso (m) blanco	['ɔsɔ 'bʎaŋkɔ]
panda	panda (f)	['panda]

monkey	mono (m)	['mɔnɔ]
chimpanzee	chimpancé (m)	[tʃimpan'sɛ]
orangutan	orangután (m)	[ɔraŋu'tan]
gorilla	gorila (m)	[gɔ'riʎja]
macaque	macaco (m)	[ma'kakɔ]
gibbon	gibón (m)	[hi'βɔn]

elephant	elefante (m)	[ɛle'fantɛ]
rhinoceros	rinoceronte (m)	[rinɔsɛ'rɔntɛ]
giraffe	jirafa (f)	[hi'rafa]
hippopotamus	hipopótamo (m)	[ipɔ'pɔtamɔ]

| kangaroo | canguro (m) | [ka'ŋurɔ] |
| koala (bear) | koala (f) | [kɔ'aʎa] |

mongoose	mangosta (f)	[ma'ŋɔsta]
chinchilla	chinchilla (f)	[tʃin'tʃiʎja]
skunk	mofeta (f)	[mɔ'feta]
porcupine	espín (m)	[ɛs'pin]

212. Domestic animals

tomcat	**gato** (m)	['gatɔ]
dog	**perro** (m)	['pɛrrɔ]
horse	**caballo** (m)	[ka'βajo]
stallion	**garañón** (m)	[gara'ɲɔn]
mare	**yegua** (f)	['jegua]
cow	**vaca** (f)	['vaka]
bull	**toro** (m)	['tɔrɔ]
ox	**buey** (m)	[bu'ɛj]
sheep	**oveja** (f)	[ɔ'βəha]
ram	**carnero** (m)	[kar'nɛrɔ]
goat	**cabra** (f)	['kabra]
billy goat, he-goat	**cabrón** (m)	[kab'rɔn]
donkey	**asno** (m)	['asnɔ]
mule	**mulo** (m)	['mulɔ]
pig	**cerdo** (m)	['θærdɔ]
piglet	**cerdito** (m)	[θær'ditɔ]
rabbit	**conejo** (m)	[kɔ'nɛhɔ]
hen (chicken)	**gallina** (f)	[ga'jɪna]
rooster	**gallo** (m)	['gajo]
duck	**pato** (m)	['patɔ]
drake	**ánade** (m)	['anadɛ]
goose	**ganso** (m)	['gansɔ]
tom turkey	**pavo** (m)	['paβɔ]
turkey (hen)	**pava** (f)	['paβa]
domestic animals	**animales** (m pl) **domésticos**	[ani'males dɔ'mɛstikɔs]
tame (e.g., ~ hamster)	**domesticado** (adj)	[dɔmɛsti'kadɔ]
to tame (vt)	**domesticar** (vt)	[dɔmɛsti'kar]
to breed (vt)	**criar** (vt)	[kri'ar]
farm	**granja** (f)	['granha]
poultry	**aves** (f pl) **de corral**	['aβəs dɛ kɔ'raʎ]
cattle	**ganado** (m)	[ga'ɲadɔ]
herd (cattle)	**rebaño** (m)	[rɛ'baɲɔ]
stable	**caballeriza** (f)	[kabaje'riθa]
pigsty	**porqueriza** (f)	[pɔrke'riθa]
cowshed	**vaquería** (f)	[bake'rija]
rabbit hutch	**conejal** (m)	[kɔnɛ'haʎ]
hen house	**gallinero** (m)	[gajɪ'nɛrɔ]

213. Dogs. Dog breeds

dog	**perro** (m)	['pɛrrɔ]
sheepdog	**perro** (m) **pastor**	['pɛrrɔ pas'tɔr]
poodle	**perro** (m) **maltés**	['pɛrrɔ maʎ'tɛs]
dachshund	**teckel** (m)	['tɛkeʎ]
bulldog	**buldog** (m)	[buʎ'dɔg]
boxer	**bóxer** (m)	['bɔksɛr]
mastiff	**Mastín** (m) **inglés**	[mas'tin iŋ'les]
rottweiler	**rottweiler** (m)	[rɔtu'ɛler]
Doberman	**Dobermann** (m)	[dɔbɛr'maŋ]
basset	**basset hound** (m)	['bassɛt 'haund]
bobtail	**Bobtail** (m)	[bɔb'tajl]
Dalmatian	**dálmata** (m)	['daʎmata]
cocker spaniel	**cocker** (m) **spaniel**	['kɔker spani'ɛʎ]
Newfoundland	**Terranova** (m)	[tɛrra'nɔβa]
Saint Bernard	**San Bernardo** (m)	[san bɛr'nardɔ]
husky	**husky** (m)	['aski]
Chow Chow	**Chow Chow** (m)	['ʧɔu 'ʧɔu]
spitz	**pomerania** (m)	[pɔmɛ'ranija]
pug	**Pug** (m), **Carlino** (m)	[pag], [kar'linɔ]

214. Sounds made by animals

barking (n)	**ladrido** (m)	[ʎad'ridɔ]
to bark (vi)	**ladrar** (vi)	[ʎad'rar]
to meow (vi)	**maullar** (vi)	[mau'ʎjar]
to purr (vi)	**ronronear** (vi)	[rɔnrɔnɛ'ar]
to moo (vi)	**mugir** (vi)	[mu'hir]
to bellow (bull)	**bramar** (vi)	[bra'mar]
to growl (vi)	**rugir** (vi)	[ru'hir]
howl (n)	**aullido** (m)	[au'jɪdɔ]
to howl (vi)	**aullar** (vi)	[au'jar]
to whine (vi)	**gañir** (vi)	[ga'ɲɪr]
to bleat (sheep)	**balar** (vi)	[ba'ʎar]
to oink, to grunt (pig)	**gruñir** (vi)	[gru'ɲɪr]
to squeal (vi)	**chillar** (vi)	[ʧi'jar]
to croak (vi)	**croar** (vi)	[krɔ'ar]
to buzz (insect)	**zumbar** (vi)	[θum'bar]
to stridulate (vi)	**chirriar** (vi)	[ʧir'rjar]

215. Young animals

cub	cría (f)	['krija]
kitten	gatito (m)	[ga'titɔ]
baby mouse	ratoncillo (m)	[ratɔn'ʧijo]
pup, puppy	cachorro (m)	[ka'ʧɔrrɔ]
leveret	cría (f) de liebre	['krija dɛ 'ʎjebrɛ]
baby rabbit	conejito (m)	[kɔnɛ'hitɔ]
wolf cub	lobato (m)	[lɔ'βatɔ]
fox cub	cría (f) de zorro	['krija dɛ 'θɔrrɔ]
bear cub	osito (m)	[ɔ'sitɔ]
lion cub	cachorro (m) de león	[ka'ʧɔrrɔ dɛ le'ɔn]
tiger cub	cachorro (m) de tigre	[ka'ʧɔrrɔ dɛ 'tigrɛ]
elephant calf	elefantino (m)	[ɛlefan'tinɔ]
piglet	cerdito (m)	[θær'ditɔ]
calf (young cow, bull)	ternero (m)	[tɛr'nɛrɔ]
kid (young goat)	cabrito (m)	[kab'ritɔ]
lamb	cordero (m)	[kɔr'dɛrɔ]
fawn (young deer)	cervato (m)	[θær'vatɔ]
young camel	cría (f) de camello	['krija dɛ ka'mejo]
baby snake	serpezuela (f)	[sɛrpɛθu'ɛʎa]
baby frog	ranita (f)	[ra'nita]
nestling	pajarillo (m)	[paha'rijo]
chick (of chicken)	pollo (m)	['pɔjo]
duckling	patito (m)	[pa'titɔ]

216. Birds

bird	pájaro (m)	['paharɔ]
pigeon	paloma (f)	[pa'lɔma]
sparrow	gorrión (m)	[gɔrri'jon]
tit	paro (m)	['parɔ]
magpie	cotorra (f)	[kɔ'tɔrra]
raven	cuervo (m)	[ku'ɛrvɔ]
crow	corneja (f)	[kɔr'nɛha]
jackdaw	chova (f)	['ʧɔβa]
rook	grajo (m)	['grahɔ]
duck	pato (m)	['patɔ]
goose	ganso (m)	['gansɔ]
pheasant	faisán (m)	[faj'san]
eagle	águila (f)	['agiʎa]
hawk	azor (m)	[a'θɔr]

falcon	halcón (m)	[aʎ'kɔn]
vulture	buitre (m)	[bu'itrɛ]
condor (Andean ~)	cóndor (m)	['kɔndɔr]
swan	cisne (m)	['θisnɛ]
crane	grulla (f)	['gruja]
stork	cigüeña (f)	[θigy'ɛɲa]
parrot	loro (m), papagayo (m)	['lɔrɔ], [papa'gajo]
hummingbird	colibrí (m)	[kɔlib'ri]
peacock	pavo (m) real	['paβɔ rɛ'aʎ]
ostrich	avestruz (m)	[avɛst'ruθ]
heron	garza (f)	['garθa]
flamingo	flamenco (m)	[fʎa'mɛŋkɔ]
pelican	pelícano (m)	[pɛ'likanɔ]
nightingale	ruiseñor (m)	[ruisɛ'ɲɔr]
swallow	golondrina (f)	[gɔlɔnd'rina]
thrush	tordo (m)	['tɔrdɔ]
song thrush	zorzal (m)	[ðɔr'ðaʎ]
blackbird	mirlo (m)	['mirlɔ]
swift	vencejo (m)	[bɛn'θæhɔ]
lark	alondra (f)	[a'lɔndra]
quail	codorniz (f)	[kɔ'dɔrniθ]
woodpecker	pico (m)	['pikɔ]
cuckoo	cuco (m)	['kukɔ]
owl	lechuza (f)	[le'ʧuθa]
eagle owl	búho (m)	['buɔ]
wood grouse	urogallo (m)	[urɔ'gajo]
black grouse	gallo lira (m)	['gajo 'lira]
partridge	perdiz (f)	[pɛr'diθ]
starling	estornino (m)	[ɛstɔr'ninɔ]
canary	canario (m)	[ka'nariɔ]
hazel grouse	ortega (f)	[ɔr'tɛga]
chaffinch	pinzón (m)	[pin'θɔn]
bullfinch	camachuelo (m)	[kamaʧu'ɛlɜ]
seagull	gaviota (f)	[ga'vʲɔta]
albatross	albatros (m)	[aʎ'batrɔs]
penguin	pingüino (m)	[piŋu'inɔ]

217. Birds. Singing and sounds

to sing (vi)	cantar (vi)	[kan'tar]
to call (animal, bird)	gritar (vi)	[gri'tar]

to crow (rooster)	cantar (vi)	[kan'tar]
cock-a-doodle-doo	quiquiriquí (m)	[kikiri'ki]
to cluck (hen)	cloquear (vi)	[klɔke'ar]
to caw (vi)	graznar (vi)	[graθ'nar]
to quack (duck)	hacer cua cua	[a'θær ku'a ku'a]
to cheep (vi)	piar (vi)	[pjar]
to chirp, to twitter	gorjear (vi)	[gɔrhɛ'ar]

218. Fish. Marine animals

bream	brema (f)	['brɛma]
carp	carpa (f)	['karpa]
perch	perca (f)	['pɛrka]
catfish	siluro (m)	[si'lurɔ]
pike	lucio (m)	['luθiɔ]
salmon	salmón (m)	[saʎ'mɔn]
sturgeon	esturión (m)	[ɛsturi'ɔn]
herring	arenque (m)	[a'rɛŋke]
Atlantic salmon	salmón (m) del Atlántico	[saʎ'mɔn dɛʎ at'lantikɔ]
mackerel	caballa (f)	[ka'βaja]
flatfish	lenguado (m)	[leŋu'adɔ]
zander, pike perch	lucioperca (m)	[luθiɔ'pɛrka]
cod	bacalao (m)	[baka'ʎaɔ]
tuna	atún (m)	[a'tun]
trout	trucha (f)	['trutʃa]
eel	anguila (f)	[a'ɲiʎa]
electric ray	tembladera (f)	[tɛmbʎa'dɛra]
moray eel	morena (f)	[mɔ'rɛna]
piranha	piraña (f)	[pi'raɲja]
shark	tiburón (m)	[tibu'rɔn]
dolphin	delfín (m)	[dɛʎ'fin]
whale	ballena (f)	[ba'jena]
crab	centolla (f)	[θæn'tɔja]
jellyfish	medusa (f)	[mɛ'dusa]
octopus	pulpo (m)	['puʎpɔ]
starfish	estrella (f) de mar	[ɛst'rɛja dɛ mar]
sea urchin	erizo (m) de mar	[ɛ'riθɔ dɛ mar]
seahorse	caballito (m) de mar	[kaba'jitɔ dɛ mar]
oyster	ostra (f)	['ɔstra]
shrimp	camarón (m)	[kama'rɔn]
lobster	bogavante (m)	[bɔga'βantɛ]
spiny lobster	langosta (f)	[ʎa'ŋɔsta]

219. Amphibians. Reptiles

| snake | serpiente (f) | [sɛr'pjentɛ] |
| venomous (snake) | venenoso (adj) | [bɛnɛ'nɔsɔ] |

viper	víbora (f)	['biβɔra]
cobra	cobra (f)	['kɔbra]
python	pitón (m)	[pi'tɔn]
boa	boa (f)	['bɔa]

grass snake	culebra (f)	[ku'lɛbra]
rattle snake	serpiente (m) de cascabel	[sɛr'pjentɛ dɛ kaska'βəʎ]
anaconda	anaconda (f)	[ana'kɔnda]

lizard	lagarto (f)	[ʎa'gartɔ]
iguana	iguana (f)	[igu'ana]
monitor lizard	varano (m)	[ba'ranɔ]
salamander	salamandra (f)	[saʎa'mandra]
chameleon	camaleón (m)	[kamale'ɔn]
scorpion	escorpión (m)	[ɛskɔrpi'ɔn]

turtle	tortuga (f)	[tɔr'tuga]
frog	rana (f)	['rana]
toad	sapo (m)	['sapɔ]
crocodile	cocodrilo (m)	[kɔkɔd'rilɔ]

220. Insects

insect, bug	insecto (m)	[in'sɛktɔ]
butterfly	mariposa (f)	[mari'pɔsa]
ant	hormiga (f)	[ɔr'miga]
fly	mosca (f)	['mɔska]
mosquito	mosquito (m)	[mɔs'kitɔ]
beetle	escarabajo (m)	[ɛskara'βahɔ]

wasp	avispa (f)	[a'βɪspa]
bee	abeja (f)	[a'βəha]
bumblebee	abejorro (m)	[abɛ'hɔrrɔ]
gadfly	moscardón (m)	[mɔskar'dɔn]

| spider | araña (f) | [a'raɲa] |
| spider's web | telaraña (f) | [tɛʎa'raɲa] |

dragonfly	libélula (f)	[li'βəluʎa]
grasshopper	saltamontes (m)	[saʎta'mɔntɛs]
moth (night butterfly)	mariposa (f) nocturna	[mari'pɔsa nɔk'tyrna]
cockroach	cucaracha (f)	[kuka'ratʃa]
tick	garrapata (f)	[garra'pata]

| flea | **pulga** (f) | ['pulga] |
| midge | **mosca** (f) **pequeña** | ['mɔska pɛ'kɛɲia] |

locust	**langosta** (f)	[ʎa'ŋɔsta]
snail	**caracol** (m)	[kara'kɔʎ]
cricket	**grillo** (m)	['grijo]
lightning bug	**luciérnaga** (f)	[lu'sjernaga]
ladybug	**mariquita** (f)	[mari'kita]

leech	**sanguijuela** (f)	[saɲihu'ɛʎa]
caterpillar	**oruga** (f)	[ɔ'ruga]
earthworm	**gusano** (m)	[gu'sanɔ]
larva	**larva** (f)	['ʎarva]

221. Animals. Body parts

beak	**pico** (m)	['pikɔ]
wings	**alas** (f pl)	['aʎas]
foot (of bird)	**pata** (f)	['pata]
feathering	**plumaje** (m)	[ply'mahɛ]
feather	**pluma** (f)	['plyma]
crest	**penacho** (m)	[pɛ'natʃɔ]

gill	**branquias** (f pl)	['braŋkias]
spawn	**huevas** (f pl)	[u'əβas]
larva	**larva** (f)	['ʎarva]
fin	**aleta** (f)	[a'leta]
scales (of fish, reptile)	**escamas** (f pl)	[ɛs'kamas]

fang (canine)	**colmillo** (m)	[kɔʎ'mijo]
paw (e.g., cat's ~)	**garra** (f), **pata** (f)	['garra], ['pata]
muzzle (snout)	**hocico** (m)	[ɔ'sikɔ]
mouth (of cat, dog)	**boca** (f)	['bɔka]
tail	**cola** (f)	['kɔʎa]
whiskers	**bigotes** (m pl)	[bi'gɔtɛs]

hoof	**casco** (m)	['kaskɔ]
horn	**cuerno** (m)	[ku'ɛrnɔ]
carapace	**caparazón** (m)	[kapara'θɔn]
shell (of mollusk)	**concha** (f)	['kɔntʃa]
eggshell	**cáscara** (f)	['kaskara]
animal's hair (pelage)	**pelo** (m)	['pɛlɔ]
pelt (hide)	**piel** (f)	[pjeʎ]

222. Actions of animals

| to fly (vi) | **volar** (vi) | [bɔ'ʎar] |
| to make circles | **dar vueltas** | [dar bu'ɛltas] |

| to fly away | echar a volar | [ɛ'tʃar a bɔ'ʎar] |
| to flap (~ the wings) | batir las alas | [ba'tir las 'alas] |

to peck (vi)	picotear (vt)	[pikɔtɛ'ar]
to sit on eggs	empollar (vt)	[ɛmpɔ'jar]
to hatch out (vi)	salir del cascarón	[sa'lir dɛʎ kaska'rɔn]
to build the nest	hacer el nido	[a'θær ɛʎ 'nidɔ]

to slither, to crawl	reptar (vi)	[rep'tar]
to sting, to bite (insect)	picar (vt)	[pi'kar]
to bite (ab. animal)	morder (vt)	[mɔr'dɛr]

to sniff (vt)	olfatear (vt)	[ɔfʎatɛ'ar]
to bark (vi)	ladrar (vi)	[ʎad'rar]
to hiss (snake)	sisear (vi)	[sise'ar]
to scare (vt)	asustar (vt)	[asus'tar]
to attack (vt)	atacar (vt)	[ata'kar]

to gnaw (bone, etc.)	roer (vt)	[rɔ'ɛr]
to scratch (with claws)	arañar (vt)	[ara'njar]
to hide (vi)	esconderse (vr)	[ɛskɔn'dɛrsɛ]

to play (kittens, etc.)	jugar (vi)	[hu'gar]
to hunt (vi, vt)	cazar (vi, vt)	[ka'θar]
to hibernate (vi)	hibernar (vi)	[ibɛr'nar]
to become extinct	extinguirse (vr)	[ɛksti'ŋirsɛ]

223. Animals. Habitats

| habitat | hábitat (m) | ['aβitat] |
| migration | migración (f) | [migra'θjon] |

mountain	montaña (f)	[mɔn'taɲa]
reef	arrecife (m)	[arrɛ'θifɛ]
cliff	roca (f)	['rɔka]

forest	bosque (m)	['bɔske]
jungle	jungla (f)	['huŋʎa]
savanna	sabana (f)	[sa'βana]
tundra	tundra (f)	['tundra]

steppe	estepa (f)	[ɛs'tɛpa]
desert	desierto (m)	[dɛ'sjertɔ]
oasis	oasis (m)	[ɔ'asis]

sea	mar (m)	[mar]
lake	lago (m)	['ʎagɔ]
ocean	océano (m)	[ɔ'θæanɔ]
swamp	pantano (m)	[pan'tanɔ]
freshwater (adj)	de agua dulce (adj)	[dɛ 'agua 'duʎθæ]

pond	estanque (m)	[ɛs'taŋke]
river	río (m)	['rio]
den	cubil (m)	[ku'βiʎ]
nest	nido (m)	['nidɔ]
hollow (in a tree)	agujero (m)	[agu'hɛrɔ]
burrow (animal hole)	madriguera (f)	[madri'gɛra]
anthill	hormiguero (m)	[ɔrmi'gɛrɔ]

224. Animal care

zoo	zoo (m)	['θɔ:]
nature preserve	reserva (f) natural	[re'serva natu'raʎ]
breeder, breed club	club (m) de criadores	[klub dɛ kria'dɔrɛs]
open-air cage	jaula (f) al aire libre	['hauʎa aʎ 'airɛ 'librɛ]
cage	jaula (f)	['hauʎa]
kennel	perrera (f)	[pɛr'rɛra]
dovecot	palomar (m)	[palɔ'mar]
aquarium	acuario (m)	[aku'ariɔ]
dolphinarium	delfinario (m)	[dɛʎfi'nariɔ]
to breed (animals)	criar (vt)	[kri'ar]
brood, litter	crías (f pl)	['krias]
to tame (vt)	domesticar (vt)	[dɔmɛsti'kar]
feed (fodder, etc.)	pienso (m), comida (f)	['pjensɔ], [kɔ'mida]
to feed (vt)	dar de comer	[dar dɛ kɔ'mɛr]
to train (animals)	adiestrar (vt)	[adjest'rar]
pet store	tienda (f) de animales	['tɪenda dɛ ani'malɛs]
muzzle (for dog)	bozal (m) de perro	[bɔ'θal dɛ 'pɛrrɔ]
collar	collar (m)	[kɔ'jar]
name (of animal)	nombre (m)	['nɔmbrɛ]
pedigree (of dog)	pedigrí (m)	[pɛdig'ri]

225. Animals. Miscellaneous

pack (wolves)	manada (f)	[ma'nada]
flock (birds)	bandada (f)	[ban'dada]
shoal (fish)	banco (m) de peces	['baŋkɔ dɛ 'pɛθæθ]
herd of horses	caballada (f)	[kaba'jada]
male (n)	macho (m)	['matʃɔ]
female	hembra (f)	['ɛmbra]
hungry (adj)	hambriento (adj)	[amb'rjentɔ]
wild (adj)	salvaje (adj)	[saʎ'vahɛ]
dangerous (adj)	peligroso (adj)	[pɛlig'rɔsɔ]

226. Horses

| horse | caballo (m) | [ka'βajo] |
| breed (race) | raza (f) | ['raθa] |

| foal, colt | potro (m) | ['potrɔ] |
| mare | yegua (f) | ['jegua] |

mustang	caballo mustang (m)	[ka'βajo mus'tan]
pony	poni (m)	['pɔni]
draft horse	caballo (m) de tiro	[ka'βajo dɛ 'tirɔ]

| mane | crin (f) | [krin] |
| tail | cola (f) | ['kɔʎa] |

hoof	casco (m)	['kaskɔ]
horseshoe	herradura (f)	[ɛrra'dura]
to shoe (vt)	herrar (vt)	[ɛr'rar]
blacksmith	herrero (m)	[ɛr'rɛrɔ]

saddle	silla (f)	['sija]
stirrup	estribo (m)	[ɛst'riβɔ]
bridle	bridón (m)	[bri'dɔn]
reins	riendas (f pl)	['rjendas]
whip (for riding)	fusta (f)	['fusta]

rider	jinete (m)	[hi'nɛtɛ]
to break in (horse)	desbravar (vt)	[dɛsbra'βar]
to saddle (vt)	ensillar (vt)	[ɛnsi'jar]
to mount a horse	montar al caballo	[mɔn'tar aʎ ka'βajo]

gallop	galope (m)	[ga'lɔpɛ]
to gallop (vi)	ir al galope	[ir aʎ ga'lɔpe]
trot (n)	trote (m)	['trɔtɛ]
at a trot (adv)	al trote (adv)	[aʎ 'trɔtɛ]

| racehorse | caballo (m) de carreras | [ka'βajo dɛ kar'rɛras] |
| horse racing | carreras (f pl) | [kar'rɛras] |

stable	caballeriza (f)	[kabaje'riθa]
to feed (vt)	dar de comer	[dar dɛ kɔ'mɛr]
hay	heno (m)	['ɛnɔ]
to water (animals)	dar de beber	[dar dɛ bɛ'bɛr]
to wash (horse)	limpiar (vt)	[lim'pjar]
to hobble (tether)	trabar (vt)	[tra'βar]

to graze (vi)	pastar (vi)	[pas'tar]
to neigh (vi)	relinchar (vi)	[rɛlin'ʧar]
to kick (horse)	cocear (vi)	[kɔθæ'ar]

Flora

227. Trees

tree	**árbol** (m)	['arbɔʎ]
deciduous (adj)	**foliáceo** (adj)	[foli'aθæɔ]
coniferous (adj)	**conífero** (adj)	[kɔ'nifɛrɔ]
evergreen (adj)	**de hoja perenne**	[dɛ 'ɔha pɛ'rɛŋɛ]
apple tree	**manzano** (m)	[man'θanɔ]
pear tree	**peral** (m)	[pɛ'raʎ]
sweet cherry tree	**cerezo** (m)	[θæ'rɛθɔ]
sour cherry tree	**guindo** (m)	['gindɔ]
plum tree	**ciruelo** (m)	[θiru'ɛlɔ]
birch	**abedul** (m)	[abɛ'duʎ]
oak	**roble** (m)	['rɔble]
linden tree	**tilo** (m)	['tilɔ]
aspen	**pobo** (m)	['pɔβɔ]
maple	**arce** (m)	['arsɛ]
spruce	**picea** (m)	[pi'θæa]
pine	**pino** (m)	['pinɔ]
larch	**alerce** (m)	[a'lerθæ]
fir tree	**abeto** (m)	[a'βɛtɔ]
cedar	**cedro** (m)	['θædrɔ]
poplar	**álamo** (m)	['aʎamɔ]
rowan	**serbal** (m)	[sɛr'baʎ]
willow	**sauce** (m)	['sausɛ]
alder	**aliso** (m)	[a'lisɔ]
beech	**haya** (f)	['aja]
elm	**olmo** (m)	['ɔʎmɔ]
ash (tree)	**fresno** (m)	['frɛsnɔ]
chestnut	**castaño** (m)	[kas'taɲɔ]
magnolia	**magnolia** (f)	[mag'nɔlija]
palm tree	**palmera** (f)	[paʎ'mɛra]
cypress	**ciprés** (m)	[θip'rɛs]
mangrove	**mangle** (m)	['maŋl]
baobab	**baobab** (m)	[baɔ'βab]
eucalyptus	**eucalipto** (m)	[əuka'liptɔ]
sequoia	**secoya** (f)	[sɛ'kɔja]

228. Shrubs

bush	**mata** (f)	['mata]
shrub	**arbusto** (m)	[ar'busto]
grapevine	**vid** (f)	[bid]
vineyard	**viñedo** (m)	[bi'ɲjedo]
raspberry bush	**frambueso** (m)	[frambu'ɛso]
redcurrant bush	**grosella** (f) **roja**	[gro'sɛja 'roha]
gooseberry bush	**grosellero** (m) **espinoso**	[grosɛ'jero ɛspi'noso]
acacia	**acacia** (f)	[a'kasija]
barberry	**berberís** (m)	[bɛrbɛ'ris]
jasmine	**jazmín** (m)	[haθ'min]
juniper	**enebro** (m)	[ɛ'nɛbro]
rosebush	**rosal** (m)	[ro'saʎ]
dog rose	**escaramujo** (m)	[ɛskara'muho]

229. Mushrooms

mushroom	**seta** (f)	['sɛta]
edible mushroom	**seta** (f) **comestible**	['sɛta komɛs'tible]
toadstool	**seta** (f) **venenosa**	['sɛta bɛnɛ'nosa]
cap (of mushroom)	**sombrerete** (m)	[sombrɛ'rɛtɛ]
stipe (of mushroom)	**estipe** (m)	[ɛs'tipɛ]
cep (Boletus edulis)	**boletus edulis** (m)	[bo'letus 'ɛdulis]
orange-cap boletus	**boleto** (m) **castaño**	[bo'leto kas'taɲo]
birch bolete	**boleto** (m) **áspero**	[bo'leto 'aspɛro]
chanterelle	**rebozuelo** (m)	[rɛboθu'ɛlo]
russula	**rúsula** (f)	['rusuʎa]
morel	**colmenilla** (f)	[koʎmɛ'nija]
fly agaric	**matamoscas** (m)	[mata'moskas]
death cap	**oronja** (f) **verde**	[o'ronha 'βərdɛ]

230. Fruits. Berries

apple	**manzana** (f)	[man'θana]
pear	**pera** (f)	['pɛra]
plum	**ciruela** (f)	[θiru'ɛʎa]
strawberry	**fresa** (f)	['frɛsa]
sour cherry	**guinda** (f)	['ginda]
sweet cherry	**cereza** (f)	[θæ'rɛθa]

grape	uva (f)	['uβa]
raspberry	frambuesa (f)	[frambu'ɛsa]
blackcurrant	grosella (f) negra	[grɔ'sɛja 'nɛgra]
redcurrant	grosella (f) roja	[grɔ'sɛja 'rɔha]
gooseberry	grosella (f) espinosa	[grɔ'sɛja ɛspi'nɔsa]
cranberry	arándano (m) agrio	[a'randanɔ 'agriɔ]

orange	naranja (f)	[na'ranha]
mandarin	mandarina (f)	[manda'rina]
pineapple	ananás (m)	[ana'nas]
banana	banana (f)	[ba'nana]
date	dátil (m)	['datiʎ]

lemon	limón (m)	[li'mɔn]
apricot	albaricoque (m)	[aʎbari'kɔkɛ]
peach	melocotón (m)	[mɛlɔkɔ'tɔn]
kiwi	kiwi (m)	['kiβɪ]
grapefruit	pomelo (m)	[pɔ'mɛlɔ]

berry	baya (f)	['baja]
berries	bayas (f pl)	['bajas]
cowberry	arándano (m) rojo	[a'randanɔ 'rɔhɔ]
field strawberry	fresa (f) silvestre	['frɛsa siʎ'vɛstrɛ]
bilberry	arándano (m)	[a'randanɔ]

231. Flowers. Plants

flower	flor (f)	[flɔr]
bouquet (of flowers)	ramo (m) de flores	['ramɔ dɛ 'flɔrɛs]

rose (flower)	rosa (f)	['rɔsa]
tulip	tulipán (m)	[tuli'pan]
carnation	clavel (m)	[kʎa'βəʎ]
gladiolus	gladiolo (m)	[gʎadi'ɔlɔ]

cornflower	aciano (m)	[a'sjanɔ]
bluebell	campanilla (f)	[kampa'nija]
dandelion	diente (m) de león	['djɛntɛ dɛ le'ɔn]
camomile	manzanilla (f)	[manθa'nija]

aloe	áloe (m)	['alɔɛ]
cactus	cacto (m)	['kaktɔ]
rubber plant, ficus	ficus (m)	['fikus]

lily	azucena (f)	[aθu'sɛna]
geranium	geranio (m)	[hɛ'raɲɔ]
hyacinth	jacinto (m)	[ha'sintɔ]

mimosa	mimosa (f)	[mi'mɔsa]
narcissus	narciso (m)	[nar'θisɔ]

nasturtium	capuchina (f)	[kapu'tʃina]
orchid	orquídea (f)	[ɔr'kidɛa]
peony	peonía (f)	[pɛɔ'nija]
violet	violeta (f)	[bʲɔ'lɛta]
pansy	trinitaria (f)	[trini'tarija]
forget-me-not	nomeolvides (f)	[nɔmɛɔʎ'widɛs]
daisy	margarita (f)	[marga'rita]
poppy	amapola (f)	[ama'poʎa]
hemp	cáñamo (m)	['kaɲjamɔ]
mint	menta (f)	['mɛnta]
lily of the valley	muguete (m)	[mu'gɛtɛ]
snowdrop	campanilla (f) de las nieves	[kampa'nija dɛ ʎas 'njevɛs]
nettle	ortiga (f)	[ɔr'tiga]
sorrel	acedera (f)	[asɛ'dɛra]
water lily	nenúfar (m)	[nɛ'nufar]
fern	helecho (m)	[ɛ'letʃɔ]
lichen	liquen (m)	['liken]
tropical greenhouse	invernadero (m)	[imbɛrna'dɛrɔ]
grass lawn	césped (m)	['θæspɛd]
flowerbed	macizo (m) de flores	[ma'θiθɔ dɛ 'flɔrɛs]
plant	planta (f)	['pʎanta]
grass, herb	hierba (f)	['jerba]
blade of grass	hierbecita (f)	[jerbe'θita]
leaf	hoja (f)	['ɔha]
petal	pétalo (m)	['pɛtalɔ]
stem	tallo (m)	['tajo]
tuber	tubérculo (m)	[tu'βərkulɔ]
young plant (shoot)	retoño (m)	[rɛ'tɔɲʲɔ]
thorn	espina (f)	[ɛs'pina]
to blossom (vi)	florecer (vi)	[flɔrɛ'sɛr]
to fade, to wither	marchitarse (vr)	[martʃi'tarsɛ]
smell (odor)	olor (m)	[ɔ'lɔr]
to cut (flowers)	cortar (vt)	[kɔr'tar]
to pick (a flower)	coger (vt)	[kɔ'hɛr]

232. Cereals, grains

grain	grano (m)	['granɔ]
cereal crops	cereales (m pl)	[θærɛ'ales]
ear (of barley, etc.)	espiga (f)	[ɛs'piga]

wheat	trigo (m)	['trigɔ]
rye	centeno (m)	[θæn'tɛnɔ]
oats	avena (f)	[a'βena]
millet	mijo (m)	['mihɔ]
barley	cebada (f)	[θæ'bada]

corn	maíz (m)	[ma'iθ]
rice	arroz (m)	[ar'rɔθ]
buckwheat	alforfón (m)	[aʎfɔr'fɔn]

pea plant	guisante (m)	[gi'santɛ]
kidney bean	fréjol (m)	['frɛhɔʎ]
soy	soya (f)	['sɔja]
lentil	lenteja (f)	[len'tɛha]
beans (pulse crops)	habas (f pl)	['aβas]

233. Vegetables. Greens

| vegetables | legumbres (f pl) | [le'gumbrɛs] |
| greens | verduras (f pl) | [bɛr'duras] |

tomato	tomate (m)	[tɔ'matɛ]
cucumber	pepino (m)	[pɛ'pinɔ]
carrot	zanahoria (f)	[θana'ɔrija]
potato	patata (f)	[pa'tata]
onion	cebolla (f)	[θæ'bɔja]
garlic	ajo (m)	['ahɔ]

cabbage	col (f)	[kɔʎ]
cauliflower	coliflor (f)	[kɔlif'lɔr]
Brussels sprouts	col (f) de Bruselas	[kɔʎ dɛ bry'sɛlas]
broccoli	brócoli (m)	['brɔkɔli]

beetroot	remolacha (f)	[rɛmɔ'ʎatʃa]
eggplant	berenjena (f)	[bɛrɛn'hɛna]
zucchini	calabacín (m)	[kaʎaba'θin]
pumpkin	calabaza (f)	[kaʎa'βaθa]
turnip	nabo (m)	['naβɔ]

parsley	perejil (m)	[pɛrɛ'hiʎ]
dill	eneldo (m)	[ɛ'nɛʎdɔ]
lettuce	lechuga (f)	[le'tʃuga]
celery	apio (m)	['apiɔ]
asparagus	espárrago (m)	[ɛs'parragɔ]
spinach	espinaca (f)	[ɛspi'naka]

pea	guisante (m)	[gi'santɛ]
beans	habas (f pl)	['aβas]
corn (maize)	maíz (m)	[ma'iθ]
kidney bean	fréjol (m)	['frɛhɔʎ]

pepper	**pimentón** (m)	[pimen'tɔn]
radish	**rábano** (m)	['raβanɔ]
artichoke	**alcachofa** (f)	[aʎka'ʧɔfa]

REGIONAL GEOGRAPHY

Countries. Nationalities

234. Western Europe

Europe	Europa (f)	[əu'rɔpa]
European Union	Unión (f) Europea	[u'ɲiɔn əurɔ'pɛa]
European (n)	europeo (m)	[əurɔ'pɛɔ]
European (adj)	europeo (adj)	[əurɔ'pɛɔ]
Austria	Austria (f)	[a'ustrija]
Austrian (masc.)	austriaco (m)	[aust'riakɔ]
Austrian (fem.)	austriaca (f)	[aust'riaka]
Austrian (adj)	austriaco (adj)	[aust'riakɔ]
Great Britain	Gran Bretaña (f)	[gran brɛ'taɲa]
England	Inglaterra (f)	[iŋʎa'tɛrra]
British (masc.)	inglés (m)	[iŋ'les]
British (fem.)	inglesa (f)	[iŋ'lesa]
English, British (adj)	inglés (adj)	[iŋ'les]
Belgium	Bélgica (f)	['bɛʎhika]
Belgian (masc.)	belga (m)	['bɛʎga]
Belgian (fem.)	belga (f)	['bɛʎga]
Belgian (adj)	belga (adj)	['bɛʎga]
Germany	Alemania (f)	[ale'manija]
German (masc.)	alemán (m)	[ale'man]
German (fem.)	alemana (f)	[ale'mana]
German (adj)	alemán (adj)	[ale'man]
Netherlands	Países Bajos (m pl)	[pa'isɛs 'bahɔs]
Holland	Holanda (f)	[ɔ'ʎanda]
Dutchman	holandés (m)	[ɔʎan'dɛs]
Dutchwoman	holandesa (f)	[ɔʎan'dɛsa]
Dutch (adj)	holandés (adj)	[ɔʎan'dɛs]
Greece	Grecia (f)	['grɛsija]
Greek (masc.)	griego (m)	[gri'egɔ]
Greek (fem.)	griega (f)	[gri'ega]
Greek (adj)	griego (adj)	[gri'egɔ]
Denmark	Dinamarca (f)	[dina'marka]
Dane (masc.)	danés (m)	[da'nɛs]

| Dane (fem.) | danesa (f) | [da'nɛsa] |
| Danish (adj) | danés (adj) | [da'nɛs] |

Ireland	Irlanda (f)	[ir'ʎanda]
Irishman	irlandés (m)	[irʎan'dɛs]
Irishwoman	irlandesa (f)	[irʎan'dɛsa]
Irish (adj)	irlandés (adj)	[irʎan'dɛs]

Iceland	Islandia (f)	[is'ʎandija]
Icelander (masc.)	islandés (m)	[isʎan'dɛs]
Icelander (fem.)	islandesa (f)	[isʎan'dɛsa]
Icelandic (adj)	islandés (adj)	[isʎan'dɛs]

Spain	España (f)	[ɛs'paɲja]
Spaniard (masc.)	español (m)	[ɛspa'ɲʲɔl]
Spaniard (fem.)	española (f)	[ɛspa'ɲʲɔʎa]
Spanish (adj)	español (adj)	[ɛspa'ɲʲɔl]

Italy	Italia (f)	[i'taʎja]
Italian (masc.)	italiano (m)	[ita'ʎjanɔ]
Italian (fem.)	italiana (f)	[ita'ʎjana]
Italian (adj)	italiano (adj)	[ita'ʎjanɔ]

Cyprus	Chipre (m)	['ʧiprɛ]
Cypriot (masc.)	chipriota (m)	[ʧipri'ɔta]
Cypriot (fem.)	chipriota (f)	[ʧipri'ɔta]
Cypriot (adj)	chipriota (adj)	[ʧipri'ɔta]

Malta	Malta (f)	['maʎta]
Maltese (masc.)	maltés (m)	[maʎ'tɛs]
Maltese (fem.)	maltesa (f)	[maʎ'tɛsa]
Maltese (adj)	maltés (adj)	[maʎ'tɛs]

Norway	Noruega (f)	[nɔru'ɛga]
Norwegian (masc.)	noruego (m)	[nɔru'ɛgɔ]
Norwegian (fem.)	noruega (f)	[nɔru'ɛga]
Norwegian (adj)	noruego (adj)	[nɔru'ɛgɔ]

Portugal	Portugal (f)	[pɔrtu'gaʎ]
Portuguese (masc.)	portugués (m)	[pɔrtu'gɛs]
Portuguese (fem.)	portuguesa (f)	[pɔrtu'gɛsa]
Portuguese (adj)	portugués (adj)	[pɔrtu'gɛs]

Finland	Finlandia (f)	[fin'ʎandija]
Finn (masc.)	finlandés (m)	[finʎan'dɛs]
Finn (fem.)	finlandesa (f)	[finʎan'dɛsa]
Finnish (adj)	finlandés (adj)	[finʎan'dɛs]

France	Francia (f)	['fransija]
Frenchman	francés (m)	[fran'sɛs]
Frenchwoman	francesa (f)	[fran'sɛsa]
French (adj)	francés (adj)	[fran'sɛs]

Sweden	Suecia (f)	[su'ɛsija]
Swede (masc.)	sueco (m)	[su'ɛkɔ]
Swede (fem.)	sueca (f)	[su'ɛka]
Swedish (adj)	sueco (adj)	[su'ɛkɔ]

Switzerland	Suiza (f)	[su'isa]
Swiss (masc.)	suizo (m)	[su'isɔ]
Swiss (fem.)	suiza (f)	[su'isa]
Swiss (adj)	suizo (adj)	[su'isɔ]

Scotland	Escocia (f)	[ɛs'kɔsija]
Scottish (masc.)	escocés (m)	[ɛskɔ'sɛs]
Scottish (fem.)	escocesa (f)	[ɛskɔ'sɛsa]
Scottish (adj)	escocés (adj)	[ɛskɔ'sɛs]

Vatican	Vaticano (m)	[bati'kanɔ]
Liechtenstein	Liechtenstein (m)	[lehtɛns'tɛjn]
Luxembourg	Luxemburgo (m)	[lyksɛm'burgɔ]
Monaco	Mónaco (m)	['mɔnakɔ]

235. Central and Eastern Europe

Albania	Albania (f)	[aʎ'banija]
Albanian (masc.)	albanés (m)	[aʎba'nɛs]
Albanian (fem.)	albanesa (f)	[aʎba'nɛsa]
Albanian (adj)	albanés (adj)	[aʎba'nɛs]

Bulgaria	Bulgaria (f)	[bul'garija]
Bulgarian (masc.)	búlgaro (m)	['bulgarɔ]
Bulgarian (fem.)	búlgara (f)	['bulgara]
Bulgarian (adj)	búlgaro (adj)	['bulgarɔ]

Hungary	Hungría (f)	[uŋ'rija]
Hungarian (masc.)	húngaro (m)	['uŋarɔ]
Hungarian (fem.)	húngara (f)	['uŋara]
Hungarian (adj)	húngaro (adj)	['uŋarɔ]

Latvia	Letonia (f)	[le'tɔnija]
Latvian (masc.)	letón (m)	[le'tɔn]
Latvian (fem.)	letona (f)	[le'tɔna]
Latvian (adj)	letón (adj)	[le'tɔn]

Lithuania	Lituania (f)	[litu'anija]
Lithuanian (masc.)	lituano (m)	[litu'anɔ]
Lithuanian (fem.)	lituana (f)	[litu'ana]
Lithuanian (adj)	lituano (adj)	[litu'anɔ]

Poland	Polonia (f)	[pɔ'lɔnija]
Pole (masc.)	polaco (m)	[pɔ'ʎakɔ]
Pole (fem.)	polaca (f)	[pɔ'ʎaka]

Polish (adj)	polaco (adj)	[pɔ'ʎakɔ]
Romania	Rumania (f)	[ru'manija]
Romanian (masc.)	rumano (m)	[ru'manɔ]
Romanian (fem.)	rumana (f)	[ru'mana]
Romanian (adj)	rumano (adj)	[ru'manɔ]

Serbia	Serbia (f)	['sɛrbija]
Serbian (masc.)	serbio (m)	['sɛrbiɔ]
Serbian (fem.)	serbia (f)	['sɛrbija]
Serbian (adj)	serbio (adj)	['sɛrbiɔ]

Slovakia	Eslovaquia (f)	[ɛslɔ'βakija]
Slovak (masc.)	eslovaco (m)	[ɛslɔ'βakɔ]
Slovak (fem.)	eslovaca (f)	[ɛslɔ'βaka]
Slovak (adj)	eslovaco (adj)	[ɛslɔ'βakɔ]

Croatia	Croacia (f)	[krɔ'asija]
Croatian (masc.)	croata (m)	[krɔ'ata]
Croatian (fem.)	croata (f)	[krɔ'ata]
Croatian (adj)	croata (adj)	[krɔ'ata]

Czech Republic	Chequia (f)	['tʃekija]
Czech (masc.)	checo (m)	['tʃekɔ]
Czech (fem.)	checa (f)	['tʃeka]
Czech (adj)	checo (adj)	['tʃekɔ]

Estonia	Estonia (f)	[ɛs'tɔɲja]
Estonian (masc.)	estonio (m)	[ɛs'tɔɲʲɔ]
Estonian (fem.)	estonia (f)	[ɛs'tɔɲja]
Estonian (adj)	estonio (adj)	[ɛs'tɔɲʲɔ]

Bosnia-Herzegovina	Bosnia y Herzegovina	['bɔsnija i ɛrθæhɔ'βina]
Macedonia	Macedonia	[masɛ'dɔnija]
Slovenia	Eslovenia	[ɛslɔ'βənija]
Montenegro	Montenegro (m)	[mɔntɛ'nɛgrɔ]

236. Former USSR countries

Azerbaijan	Azerbaidzhán (m)	[aθærbaj'dʒan]
Azerbaijani (masc.)	azerbaidzhano (m)	[aθærbaj'dʒanɔ]
Azerbaijani (fem.)	azerbaidzhana (f)	[aθærbaj'dʒana]
Azerbaijani (adj)	azerbaidzhano (adj)	[aθærbaj'dʒanɔ]

Armenia	Armenia (f)	[ar'mɛɲja]
Armenian (masc.)	armenio (m)	[ar'mɛɲʲɔ]
Armenian (fem.)	armenia (f)	[ar'mɛɲja]
Armenian (adj)	armenio (adj)	[ar'mɛɲʲɔ]

| Belarus | Bielorrusia (f) | [bjelɔr'rusja] |
| Belarusian (masc.) | bielorruso (m) | [bjelɔr'rusɔ] |

| Belarusian (fem.) | bielorrusa (f) | [bjelɔr'rusa] |
| Belarusian (adj) | bielorruso (adj) | [bjelɔr'rusɔ] |

Georgia	Georgia (f)	[hɛ'ɔrhija]
Georgian (masc.)	georgiano (m)	[hɛɔrhi'anɔ]
Georgian (fem.)	georgiana (f)	[hɛɔrhi'ana]
Georgian (adj)	georgiano (adj)	[hɛɔrhi'anɔ]
Kazakhstan	Kazajstán (m)	[kaθahs'tan]
Kazakh (masc.)	kazajo (m)	[ka'θahɔ]
Kazakh (fem.)	kazaja (f)	[ka'θaha]
Kazakh (adj)	kazajo (adj)	[ka'θahɔ]

Kirghizia	Kirguizistán (m)	[kirgiθis'tan]
Kirghiz (masc.)	kirguís (m)	[kir'gis]
Kirghiz (fem.)	kirguisa (f)	[kir'gisa]
Kirghiz (adj)	kirguís (adj)	[kir'gis]

Moldavia	Moldavia (f)	[mɔʎ'daβija]
Moldavian (masc.)	moldavo (m)	[mɔʎ'daβɔ]
Moldavian (fem.)	moldava (f)	[mɔʎ'daβa]
Moldavian (adj)	moldavo (adj)	[mɔʎ'daβɔ]
Russia	Rusia (f)	['rusija]
Russian (masc.)	ruso (m)	['rusɔ]
Russian (fem.)	rusa (f)	['rusa]
Russian (adj)	ruso (adj)	['rusɔ]

Tajikistan	Tadzhikistán (m)	[tadʒikis'tan]
Tajik (masc.)	tadzhik (m)	[ta'dʒik]
Tajik (fem.)	tadzhika (f)	[ta'dʒika]
Tajik (adj)	tadzhik (adj)	[ta'dʒik]

Turkmenistan	Turkmenia (f)	[turk'mɛnija]
Turkmen (masc.)	turkmeno (m)	[turk'mɛnɔ]
Turkmen (fem.)	turkmena (f)	[turk'mɛna]
Turkmenian (adj)	turkmeno (adj)	[turk'mɛnɔ]

Uzbekistan	Uzbekistán (m)	[uθbɛkis'tan]
Uzbek (masc.)	uzbeko (m)	[uθ'bɛkɔ]
Uzbek (fem.)	uzbeka (f)	[uθ'bɛka]
Uzbek (adj)	uzbeko (adj)	[uθ'bɛkɔ]

Ukraine	Ucrania (f)	[uk'raɲja]
Ukrainian (masc.)	ucraniano (m)	[ukra'ɲjanɔ]
Ukrainian (fem.)	ucraniana (f)	[ukra'ɲjana]
Ukrainian (adj)	ucraniano (adj)	[ukra'ɲjanɔ]

237. Asia

| Asia | Asia (f) | ['asija] |
| Asian (adj) | asiático (adj) | [a'sjatikɔ] |

Vietnam	Vietnam (m)	[vjet'nam]
Vietnamese (masc.)	vietnamita (m)	[vjetna'mita]
Vietnamese (fem.)	vietnamita (f)	[vjetna'mita]
Vietnamese (adj)	vietnamita (adj)	[vjetna'mita]
India	India (f)	['indija]
Indian (masc.)	indio (m)	['indiɔ]
Indian (fem.)	india (f)	['indija]
Indian (adj)	indio (adj)	['indiɔ]
Israel	Israel (m)	[isra'ɛʎ]
Israeli (masc.)	israelí (m)	[israɛ'li]
Israeli (fem.)	israelí (f)	[israɛ'li]
Israeli (adj)	israelí (adj)	[israɛ'li]
Jew (n)	hebreo (m)	[ɛb'rɛɔ]
Jewess (n)	hebrea (f)	[ɛb'rɛa]
Jewish (adj)	hebreo (adj)	[ɛb'rɛɔ]
China	China (f)	['ʧina]
Chinese (masc.)	chino (m)	['ʧinɔ]
Chinese (fem.)	china (f)	['ʧina]
Chinese (adj)	chino (adj)	['ʧinɔ]
Korean (masc.)	coreano (m)	[kɔrɛ'anɔ]
Korean (fem.)	coreana (f)	[kɔrɛ'ana]
Korean (adj)	coreano (adj)	[kɔrɛ'anɔ]
Lebanon	Líbano (m)	['liβanɔ]
Lebanese (masc.)	libanés (m)	[liba'nɛs]
Lebanese (fem.)	libanesa (f)	[liba'nɛsa]
Lebanese (adj)	libanés (adj)	[liba'nɛs]
Mongolia	Mongolia (f)	[mɔ'ŋɔʎja]
Mongolian (masc.)	mongol (m)	[mɔ'ŋɔl]
Mongolian (fem.)	mongola (f)	[mɔ'ŋɔʎa]
Mongolian (adj)	mongol (adj)	[mɔ'ŋɔl]
Malaysia	Malasia (f)	[ma'ʎasija]
Malaysian (masc.)	malayo (m)	[ma'ʎajo]
Malaysian (fem.)	malaya (f)	[ma'ʎaja]
Malaysian (adj)	malayo (adj)	[ma'ʎajo]
Pakistan	Pakistán (m)	[pakis'tan]
Pakistani (masc.)	pakistaní (m)	[pakista'ni]
Pakistani (fem.)	pakistaní (f)	[pakista'ni]
Pakistani (adj)	pakistaní (adj)	[pakista'ni]
Saudi Arabia	Arabia (f) Saudita	[a'raβija sau'dita]
Arab (masc.)	árabe (m)	['arabɛ]
Arab (fem.)	árabe (f)	['arabɛ]
Arabian (adj)	árabe (adj)	['arabɛ]

Thailand	Tailandia (f)	[taj'ʎandija]
Thai (masc.)	tailandés (m)	[tajʎan'dɛs]
Thai (fem.)	tailandesa (f)	[tajʎan'dɛsa]
Thai (adj)	tailandés (adj)	[tajʎan'dɛs]
Taiwan	Taiwán (m)	[taj'van]
Taiwanese (masc.)	taiwanés (m)	[tajva'nɛs]
Taiwanese (fem.)	taiwanesa (f)	[tajva'nɛsa]
Taiwanese (adj)	taiwanés (adj)	[tajva'nɛs]
Turkey	Turquía (f)	[tur'kija]
Turk (masc.)	turco (m)	['turkɔ]
Turk (fem.)	turca (f)	['turka]
Turkish (adj)	turco (adj)	['turkɔ]
Japan	Japón (m)	[ha'pɔn]
Japanese (masc.)	japonés (m)	[hapɔ'nɛs]
Japanese (fem.)	japonesa (f)	[hapɔ'nɛsa]
Japanese (adj)	japonés (adj)	[hapɔ'nɛs]
Afghanistan	Afganistán (m)	[afganis'tan]
Bangladesh	Bangladesh (m)	[baŋʎa'dɛʃ]
Indonesia	Indonesia (f)	[indɔ'nɛsija]
Jordan	Jordania (f)	[hɔr'danija]
Iraq	Irak (m)	[i'rak]
Iran	Irán (m)	[i'ran]
Cambodia	Camboya (f)	[kam'bɔja]
Kuwait	Kuwait (m)	[ku'βajt]
Laos	Laos (m)	[ʎa'ɔs]
Myanmar	Myanmar (m)	[mjan'mar]
Nepal	Nepal (m)	[nɛ'paʎ]
United Arab Emirates	Emiratos (m pl) Árabes Unidos	[ɛmi'ratɛs 'arabɛs u'nidɔs]
Syria	Siria (f)	['sirija]
Palestine	Palestina (f)	[pales'tina]
South Korea	Corea (f) del Sur	['kɔrɛa dɛʎ sur]
North Korea	Corea (f) del Norte	[kɔ'rɛa dɛʎ 'nɔrtɛ]

238. North America

United States of America	Estados Unidos de América (m pl)	[ɛs'tadɔs u'nidɔs dɛ a'mɛrika]
American (masc.)	americano (m)	[amɛri'kanɔ]
American (fem.)	americana (f)	[amɛri'kana]
American (adj)	americano (adj)	[amɛri'kanɔ]
Canada	Canadá (f)	[kana'da]
Canadian (masc.)	canadiense (m)	[kana'djensɛ]

| Canadian (fem.) | canadiense (f) | [kana'djensɛ] |
| Canadian (adj) | canadiense (adj) | [kana'djensɛ] |

Mexico	Méjico (m)	['mɛhikɔ]
Mexican (masc.)	mejicano (m)	[mɛhi'kanɔ]
Mexican (fem.)	mejicana (f)	[mɛhi'kana]
Mexican (adj)	mejicano (adj)	[mɛhi'kanɔ]

239. Central and South America

Argentina	Argentina (f)	[arhɛn'tina]
Argentinian (masc.)	argentino (m)	[arhɛn'tinɔ]
Argentinian (fem.)	argentina (f)	[arhɛn'tina]
Argentinian (adj)	argentino (adj)	[arhɛn'tinɔ]

Brazil	Brasil (f)	[bra'siʎ]
Brazilian (masc.)	brasileño (m)	[brasi'leɲɔ]
Brazilian (fem.)	brasileña (f)	[brasi'leɲja]
Brazilian (adj)	brasileño (adj)	[brasi'leɲɔ]

Colombia	Colombia (f)	[kɔ'lɔmbija]
Colombian (masc.)	colombiano (m)	[kɔlɔmbi'anɔ]
Colombian (fem.)	colombiana (f)	[kɔlɔmbi'ana]
Colombian (adj)	colombiano (adj)	[kɔlɔmbi'anɔ]

Cuba	Cuba (f)	['kuβa]
Cuban (masc.)	cubano (m)	[ku'βanɔ]
Cuban (fem.)	cubana (f)	[ku'βana]
Cuban (adj)	cubano (adj)	[ku'βanɔ]

Chile	Chile (m)	['ʧile]
Chilean (masc.)	chileno (m)	[ʧi'lenɔ]
Chilean (fem.)	chilena (f)	[ʧi'lena]
Chilean (adj)	chileno (adj)	[ʧi'lenɔ]

| Bolivia | Bolivia (f) | [bɔ'liβɪja] |
| Venezuela | Venezuela (f) | [bɛnɛsu'ɛʎa] |

| Paraguay | Paraguay (m) | [paragu'aj] |
| Peru | Perú (m) | [pɛ'ru] |

Suriname	Surinam (m)	[suri'nam]
Uruguay	Uruguay (m)	[urugu'aj]
Ecuador	Ecuador (m)	[ɛkua'dɔr]

The Bahamas	Islas (f pl) Bahamas	['isʎas ba'amas]
Haiti	Haití (m)	[ai'ti]
Dominican Republic	República (f) Dominicana	[rɛ'publika dɔmini'kana]
Panama	Panamá (f)	[pana'ma]
Jamaica	Jamaica (f)	[ha'majka]

240. Africa

Egypt	**Egipto** (m)	[ε'hiptɔ]
Egyptian (masc.)	**egipcio** (m)	[ε'hipsiɔ]
Egyptian (fem.)	**egipcia** (f)	[ε'hipsija]
Egyptian (adj)	**egipcio** (adj)	[ε'hipsiɔ]
Morocco	**Marruecos** (m)	[marru'εkɔs]
Moroccan (masc.)	**marroquí** (m)	[marrɔ'ki]
Moroccan (fem.)	**marroquí** (f)	[marrɔ'ki]
Moroccan (adj)	**marroquí** (adj)	[marrɔ'ki]
Tunisia	**Túnez** (m)	['tunεθ]
Tunisian (masc.)	**tunecino** (m)	[tunε'sinɔ]
Tunisian (fem.)	**tunecina** (f)	[tunε'sina]
Tunisian (adj)	**tunecino** (adj)	[tunε'sinɔ]
Ghana	**Ghana** (f)	['gana]
Zanzibar	**Zanzíbar** (m)	[θanθi'βar]
Kenya	**Kenia** (f)	['kenija]
Libya	**Libia** (f)	['liβɪja]
Madagascar	**Madagascar** (m)	[madagas'kar]
Namibia	**Namibia** (f)	[na'miβɪja]
Senegal	**Senegal**	[sεnε'gaʎ]
Tanzania	**Tanzania** (f)	[tan'θaɲja]
South Africa	**República** (f) **Sudafricana**	[rε'publika sudafri'kana]
African (masc.)	**africano** (m)	[afri'kanɔ]
African (fem.)	**africana** (f)	[afri'kana]
African (adj)	**africano** (adj)	[afri'kanɔ]

241. Australia. Oceania

Australia	**Australia** (f)	[aust'ralija]
Australian (masc.)	**australiano** (m)	[austra'ʎjanɔ]
Australian (fem.)	**australiana** (f)	[austra'ʎjana]
Australian (adj)	**australiano** (adj)	[austra'ʎjanɔ]
New Zealand	**Nueva Zelanda** (f)	[nu'εβa θæ'ʎanda]
New Zealander (masc.)	**neocelandés** (m)	[nεɔsεʎan'dεs]
New Zealander (fem.)	**neocelandesa** (f)	[nεɔsεʎan'dεsa]
New Zealand (as adj)	**neocelandés** (adj)	[nεɔsεʎan'dεs]
Tasmania	**Tasmania** (f)	[tas'manija]
French Polynesia	**Polinesia** (f) **Francesa**	[pɔli'nεsija fran'sεsa]

242. Cities

Amsterdam	Ámsterdam	['amstɛrdam]
Ankara	Ankara	[a'ŋkara]
Athens	Atenas	[a'tɛnas]
Baghdad	Bagdad	[bag'dad]
Bangkok	Bangkok	[ba'ŋkɔk]
Barcelona	Barcelona	[barsɛ'lɔna]
Beijing	Pekín	[pɛ'kin]
Beirut	Beirut	[bɛj'rut]
Berlin	Berlín	[bɛr'lin]
Bombay, Mumbai	Bombay	[bɔm'baj]
Bonn	Bonn	[bɔn]
Bordeaux	Burdeos	[bur'dɛɔs]
Bratislava	Bratislava	[bratis'ʎaβa]
Brussels	Bruselas	[bru'sɛʎas]
Bucharest	Bucarest	[buka'rest]
Budapest	Budapest	[buda'pɛst]
Cairo	El Cairo	[ɛʎ 'kajrɔ]
Calcutta	Calcuta	[kaʎ'kuta]
Chicago	Chicago	[ʧi'kagɔ]
Copenhagen	Copenhague	[kɔpɛ'nage]
Dar-es-Salaam	Dar-es-Salam	[darɛssa'ʎam]
Delhi	Delhi	['dɛli]
Dubai	Dubai	[du'βaj]
Dublin	Dublín	[dub'lin]
Düsseldorf	Dusseldorf	[dussɛʎ'dɔrf]
Florence	Florencia	[flɔ'rɛnsija]
Frankfurt	Fráncfort del Meno	['fraŋkfɔrt dɛʎ 'mɛnɔ]
Geneva	Ginebra	[hi'nɛbra]
The Hague	la Haya	[ʎa 'aja]
Hamburg	Hamburgo	['amburgɔ]
Hanoi	Hanói	[a'nɔi]
Havana	La Habana	[ʎa a'βana]
Helsinki	Helsinki	['ɛʎsiŋki]
Hiroshima	Hiroshima	[irɔ'sima]
Hong Kong	Hong-Kong (m)	[ɔ'ŋkɔn]
Istanbul	Estambul	[ɛstam'buʎ]
Jerusalem	Jerusalén	[hɛrusa'lɛn]
Kiev	Kiev	['kiɛv]
Kuala Lumpur	Kuala Lumpur	[ku'aʎa lum'pur]
Lisbon	Lisboa	['lisbɔa]
London	Londres	['lɔndrɛs]
Los Angeles	Los Ángeles	[lɔs 'anhɛles]

Lyons	Lyon	[li'ɔn]
Madrid	Madrid	[mad'rid]
Marseille	Marsella	[mar'sɛja]
Mexico City	Méjico	['mɛhikɔ]
Miami	Miami	[mi'ami]
Montreal	Montreal	[mɔntrɛ'aʎ]
Moscow	Moscú	[mɔs'ku]
Munich	Munich	['munih]
Nairobi	Nairobi	[naj'rɔβɪ]
Naples	Nápoles	['napɔles]
New York	Nueva York	[nu'ɛβa 'jork]
Nice	Niza	['niθa]
Oslo	Oslo	['ɔslɔ]
Ottawa	Ottawa	[ɔt'taβa]
Paris	París	[pa'ris]
Prague	Praga	['praga]
Rio de Janeiro	Río de Janeiro	['riɔ dɛ ha'nɛjrɔ]
Rome	Roma	['rɔma]
Saint Petersburg	San Petersburgo	[san pɛtɛrs'burgɔ]
Seoul	Seúl	[sɛ'ul]
Shanghai	Shanghái	[ʃan'haj]
Singapore	Singapur	[siɲa'pur]
Stockholm	Estocolmo	[ɛstɔ'kɔʎmɔ]
Sydney	Sydney	[sid'nɛj]
Taipei	Taipei	[taj'pɛj]
Tokyo	Tokio	['tɔkiɔ]
Toronto	Toronto	[tɔ'rɔntɔ]
Venice	Venecia	[bɛ'nɛsija]
Vienna	Viena	['bjena]
Warsaw	Varsovia	[bar'sɔβɪja]
Washington	Washington	['vaʃintɔn]

243. Politics. Government. Part 1

politics	política (f)	[pɔ'litika]
political (adj)	político (adj)	[pɔ'litikɔ]
politician	político (m)	[pɔ'litikɔ]
state (country)	Estado (m)	[ɛs'tadɔ]
citizen	ciudadano (m)	[θjuda'danɔ]
citizenship	ciudadanía (f)	[θjudada'nija]
national emblem	escudo (m) nacional	[ɛs'kudɔ naθɪo'naʎ]
national anthem	himno (m) nacional	['imnɔ naθɪo'naʎ]
government	gobierno (m)	[gɔ'bjernɔ]

head of state	jefe (m) de estado	[ˈhɛfɛ dɛ ɛsˈtadɔ]
parliament	parlamento (m)	[parʎaˈmɛntɔ]
party	partido (m)	[parˈtidɔ]
capitalism	capitalismo (m)	[kapitaˈlismɔ]
capitalist (adj)	capitalista (adj)	[kapitaˈlista]
socialism	socialismo (m)	[sɔθjaˈlismɔ]
socialist (adj)	socialista (adj)	[sɔθjaˈlista]
communism	comunismo (m)	[kɔmuˈnismɔ]
communist (adj)	comunista (adj)	[kɔmuˈnista]
communist (n)	comunista (m)	[kɔmuˈnista]
democracy	democracia (f)	[dɛmɔkˈrasija]
democrat	demócrata (m)	[dɛˈmɔkrata]
democratic (adj)	democrático (adj)	[dɛmɔkˈratikɔ]
Democratic party	partido (m) democrático	[parˈtidɔ dɛmɔkˈratikɔ]
liberal (n)	liberal (m)	[libɛˈraʎ]
liberal (adj)	liberal (adj)	[libɛˈraʎ]
conservative (n)	conservador (m)	[kɔnsɛrvaˈdɔr]
conservative (adj)	conservador (adj)	[kɔnsɛrvaˈdɔr]
republic (n)	república (f)	[rɛˈpublika]
republican (n)	republicano (m)	[rɛpubliˈkanɔ]
Republican party	partido (m) republicano	[parˈtidɔ rɛpubliˈkanɔ]
poll, elections	elecciones (f pl)	[ɛlekˈθjonɛs]
to elect (vt)	elegir (vi)	[ɛleˈhir]
elector, voter	elector (m)	[ɛlekˈtɔr]
election campaign	campaña (f) electoral	[kamˈpaɲja ɛlektɔˈraʎ]
voting (n)	votación (f)	[vɔtaˈθʲon]
to vote (vi)	votar (vi)	[vɔˈtar]
suffrage, right to vote	derecho (m) a voto	[dɛˈrɛʧɔ a ˈβɔtɔ]
candidate	candidato (m)	[kandiˈdatɔ]
to be a candidate	presentar su candidatura	[prɛsɛnˈtar su kandidaˈtura]
campaign	campaña (f)	[kamˈpaɲja]
opposition (as adj)	de oposición (adj)	[dɛ ɔpɔsiˈθʲon]
opposition (n)	oposición (f)	[ɔpɔsiˈθʲon]
visit	visita (f)	[biˈsita]
official visit	visita (f) oficial	[biˈsita ɔfiˈsjaʎ]
international (adj)	internacional (adj)	[intɛrnaθʲoˈnaʎ]
negotiations	negociaciones (f pl)	[nɛgɔθjaˈsʲonɛs]
to negotiate (vi)	negociar (vi)	[nɛgɔˈθjar]

244. Politics. Government. Part 2

society	sociedad (f)	[soθje'dad]
constitution	constitución (f)	[konstitu'θion]
power (political control)	poder (m)	[po'dɛr]
corruption	corrupción (f)	[korrup'θion]

| law (justice) | ley (f) | [lej] |
| legal (legitimate) | legal (adj) | [le'gaʎ] |

| justice (fairness) | justicia (f) | [hus'tiθija] |
| just (fair) | justo (adj) | ['husto] |

committee	comité (m)	[komi'tɛ]
bill (draft law)	proyecto (m) de ley	[pro'jekto dɛ 'lej]
budget	presupuesto (m)	[prɛsupu'ɛsto]
policy	política (f)	[po'litika]
reform	reforma (f)	[rɛ'forma]
radical (adj)	radical (adj)	[radi'kaʎ]

power (strength, force)	potencia (f)	[po'tɛnsija]
powerful (adj)	poderoso (adj)	[pode'roso]
supporter	partidario (m)	[parti'dario]
influence	influencia (f)	[influ'ɛnsija]

regime (e.g., military ~)	régimen (m)	['rɛhimɛn]
conflict	conflicto (m)	[konf'likto]
conspiracy (plot)	complot (m)	[komp'lot]
provocation	provocación (f)	[provoka'θion]

to overthrow (regime, etc.)	derrocar (vt)	[dɛrro'kar]
overthrow (of government)	derrocamiento (m)	[dɛrroka'mjento]
revolution	revolución (f)	[rɛvolu'θion]

| coup d'état | golpe (m) de estado | ['golpe dɛ ɛs'tado] |
| military coup | golpe (m) militar | ['golpe mili'tar] |

crisis	crisis (m)	['krisis]
economic recession	recesión (f) económica	[rɛsɛ'θion ɛko'nomika]
demonstrator (protester)	manifestante (m)	[manifɛs'tantɛ]
demonstration	manifestación (f)	[manifɛsta'θion]
martial law	ley (m) marcial	['lej mar'sjaʎ]
military base	base (f) militar	['basɛ mili'tar]

| stability | estabilidad (f) | [ɛstabili'dad] |
| stable (adj) | estable (adj) | [ɛs'table] |

exploitation	explotación (f)	[ɛksplota'θion]
to exploit (workers)	explotar (vt)	[ɛksplo'tar]
racism	racismo (m)	[ra'sismo]
racist	racista (m)	[ra'sista]

| fascism | fascismo (m) | [fa'θismɔ] |
| fascist | fascista (m) | [fa'θista] |

245. Countries. Miscellaneous

foreigner	extranjero (m)	[ɛkstran'hɛrɔ]
foreign (adj)	extranjero (adj)	[ɛkstran'hɛrɔ]
abroad (adv)	en el extranjero	[ɛn ɛʎ ɛstran'hɛrɔ]

emigrant	emigrante (m)	[ɛmig'rantɛ]
emigration	emigración (f)	[ɛmigra'sɔn]
to emigrate (vi)	emigrar (vi)	[ɛmig'rar]

the West	Oeste (m)	[ɔ'əstɛ]
the East	Este (m)	['ɛstɛ]
the Far East	Extremo Oriente (m)	[ɛst'rɛmɔ ɔ'rjentɛ]

| civilization | civilización (f) | [θiwiliθa'sɔn] |
| humanity (mankind) | humanidad (f) | [umani'dad] |

world (earth)	mundo (m)	['mundɔ]
peace	paz (f)	[paθ]
worldwide (adj)	mundial (adj)	[mun'djaʎ]

homeland	patria (f)	['patrija]
people (population)	pueblo (m)	[pu'ɛblɔ]
population	población (f)	[pobʎa'θɔn]
people (a lot of ~)	gente (f)	['hɛntɛ]

| nation (people) | nación (f) | [na'θɔn] |
| generation | generación (f) | [hɛnɛra'θɔn] |

territory (area)	territorio (m)	[tɛrri'tɔrjɔ]
region	región (m)	[rɛ'hɔn]
state (part of a country)	estado (m)	[ɛs'tadɔ]

tradition	tradición (f)	[tradi'θɔn]
custom (tradition)	costumbre (f)	[kɔs'tumbrɛ]
ecology	ecología (f)	[ɛkɔlɔ'hija]

Indian (Native American)	indio (m)	['indiɔ]
Gipsy (masc.)	gitano (m)	[hi'tanɔ]
Gipsy (fem.)	gitana (f)	[hi'tana]
Gipsy (adj)	gitano (adj)	[hi'tanɔ]

empire	imperio (m)	[im'pɛriɔ]
colony	colonia (f)	[kɔ'lɔnija]
slavery	esclavitud (f)	[ɛskʎawi'tud]
invasion	invasión (f)	[inva'sɔn]
famine	hambruna (f)	[amb'runa]

246. Major religious groups. Confessions

religion	religión (f)	[rɛli'fʲɔn]
religious (adj)	religioso (adj)	[rɛli'fʲɔsɔ]
faith, belief	creencia (f)	[kre'ɛnsija]
to believe (in God)	creer (vi)	[kre'ɛr]
believer	creyente (m)	[krɛ'jentɛ]
atheism	ateísmo (m)	[atɛ'ismɔ]
atheist	ateo (m)	[a'tɛɔ]
Christianity	cristianismo (m)	[kristja'nismɔ]
Christian (n)	cristiano (m)	[kris'tjanɔ]
Christian (adj)	cristiano (adj)	[kris'tjanɔ]
Catholicism	catolicismo (m)	[katɔli'sismɔ]
Catholic (n)	católico (m)	[ka'tɔlikɔ]
Catholic (adj)	católico (adj)	[ka'tɔlikɔ]
Protestantism	protestantismo (m)	[prɔtɛstan'tismɔ]
Protestant Church	Iglesia (f) Protestante	[ig'lesija prɔtɛs'tantɛ]
Protestant	protestante (m)	[prɔtɛs'tantɛ]
Orthodoxy	Ortodoxia (f)	[ɔrtɔ'dɔksja]
Orthodox Church	Iglesia (f) Ortodoxa	[ig'lesija ɔrtɔ'dɔksa]
Orthodox	ortodoxo (m)	[ɔrtɔ'dɔksɔ]
Presbyterianism	Presbiterianismo (m)	[prɛsbitɛrja'nismɔ]
Presbyterian Church	Iglesia (f) Presbiteriana	[ig'lesija prɛsbitɛ'rjana]
Presbyterian (n)	presbiteriano (m)	[prɛsbitɛ'rjanɔ]
Lutheranism	Iglesia (f) Luterana	[ig'lesija lutɛ'rana]
Lutheran (n)	luterano (m)	[lytɛ'ranɔ]
Baptist Church	Iglesia (f) Bautista	[ig'lesija bau'tista]
Baptist (n)	bautista (m)	[bau'tista]
Anglican Church	Iglesia (f) Anglicana	[ig'lesija aŋli'kana]
Anglican (n)	anglicano (m)	[aŋli'kanɔ]
Mormonism	mormonismo (m)	[mɔrmɔ'nismɔ]
Mormon (n)	mormón (m)	[mɔr'mɔn]
Judaism	judaísmo (m)	[huda'ismɔ]
Jew (n)	judío (m)	[hu'diɔ]
Buddhism	Budismo (m)	[bu'dismɔ]
Buddhist (n)	budista (m)	[bu'dista]
Hinduism	Hinduismo (m)	[indu'ismɔ]
Hindu (n)	hinduista (m)	[indu'ista]

Islam	**Islam** (m)	[is'ʎam]
Muslim (n)	**musulmán** (m)	[musuʎ'man]
Muslim (adj)	**musulmán** (adj)	[musuʎ'man]
Shiah Islam	**chiísmo** (m)	[tʃi'ismɔ]
Shiite (n)	**chií** (m), **chiita** (m)	[tʃi'i], [tʃi'ita]
Sunni Islam	**sunismo** (m)	[su'nismɔ]
Sunnite (n)	**suní** (m, f)	[su'ni]

247. Religions. Priests

priest	**sacerdote** (m)	[saθær'dɔtɛ]
the Pope	**Papa** (m)	['papa]
monk, friar	**monje** (m)	['mɔnhɛ]
nun	**monja** (f)	['mɔnha]
pastor	**pastor** (m)	[pas'tɔr]
abbot	**abad** (m)	[a'βad]
vicar (parish priest)	**vicario** (m)	[bi'kariɔ]
bishop	**obispo** (m)	[ɔ'βispɔ]
cardinal	**cardenal** (m)	[kardɛ'naʎ]
preacher	**predicador** (m)	[predika'dɔr]
preaching	**prédica** (f)	['predika]
parishioners	**parroquianos** (m pl)	[parrɔki'anɔs]
believer	**creyente** (m)	[krɛ'jentɛ]
atheist	**ateo** (m)	[a'tɛɔ]

248. Faith. Christianity. Islam

Adam	**Adán**	[a'dan]
Eve	**Eva**	['ɛβa]
God	**Dios** (m)	[dɨɔs]
the Lord	**Señor** (m)	[sɛ'ɲɨɔr]
the Almighty	**el Todopoderoso**	[ɛʎ tɔdɔpɔdɛ'rɔsɔ]
sin	**pecado** (m)	[pɛ'kadɔ]
to sin (vi)	**pecar** (vi)	[pɛ'kar]
sinner (masc.)	**pecador** (m)	[pɛka'dɔr]
sinner (fem.)	**pecadora** (f)	[pɛka'dɔra]
hell	**infierno** (m)	[in'fjernɔ]
paradise	**paraíso** (m)	[para'isɔ]
Jesus	**Jesús** (m)	[hɛ'sus]
Jesus Christ	**Jesucristo** (m)	[hɛsuk'ristɔ]

the Holy Spirit	Espíritu (m) Santo	[ɛs'piritu 'santɔ]
the Savior	el Salvador	[ɛʎ saʎva'dɔr]
the Virgin Mary	la Virgen María	[ʎa 'βirhɛn ma'rija]
the Devil	diablo (m)	['djablɔ]
devil's (adj)	diabólico (adj)	[dja'bɔlikɔ]
Satan	Satán (m)	[sa'tan]
satanic (adj)	satánico (adj)	[sa'tanikɔ]
angel	ángel (m)	['anhɛʎ]
guardian angel	ángel (m) custodio	['anhɛʎ kus'tɔdiɔ]
angelic (adj)	angelical (adj)	[anhɛli'kaʎ]
apostle	apóstol (m)	[a'pɔstɔʎ]
archangel	arcángel (m)	[ar'kanheʎ]
the Antichrist	anticristo (m)	[antik'ristɔ]
Church	Iglesia (f)	[ig'lesija]
Bible	Biblia (f)	['biblija]
biblical (adj)	bíblico (adj)	['biblikɔ]
Old Testament	Antiguo Testamento (m)	[an'tiguɔ tɛsta'mɛntɔ]
New Testament	Nuevo Testamento (m)	[nu'ɛβɔ tɛsta'mɛntɔ]
Gospel	Evangelio (m)	[ɛvan'hɛliɔ]
Holy Scripture	Sagrada Escritura (f)	[sag'rada ɛskri'tura]
heaven	cielo (m)	['sjelɔ]
Commandment	mandamiento (m)	[manda'mjentɔ]
prophet	profeta (m)	[prɔ'fɛta]
prophecy	profecía (f)	[prɔfɛ'sija]
Allah	Alá	[a'la]
Mohammed	Mahoma	['maɔma]
the Koran	Corán (m)	[kɔ'ran]
mosque	mezquita (f)	[mɛθ'kita]
mullah	mulá (m), mullah (m)	[mu'ʎa]
prayer	oración (f)	[ɔra'θ'ɔn]
to pray (vi, vt)	orar, rezar (vi)	[ɔ'rar], [re'θar]
pilgrimage	peregrinación (f)	[pɛrɛgrina'sɔn]
pilgrim	peregrino (m)	[pɛrɛg'rinɔ]
Mecca	La Meca	[ʎa 'mɛka]
church	iglesia (f)	[ig'lesija]
temple	templo (m)	['tɛmplɔ]
cathedral	catedral (f)	[katɛd'raʎ]
Gothic (adj)	gótico (adj)	['gɔtikɔ]
synagogue	sinagoga (f)	[sina'gɔga]
mosque	mezquita (f)	[mɛθ'kita]
chapel	capilla (f)	[ka'pija]
abbey	abadía (f)	[aba'dija]

convent	**convento** (m)	[kɔn'vɛntɔ]
monastery	**monasterio** (m)	[mɔnas'tɛriɔ]
bell (in church)	**campana** (f)	[kam'pana]
bell tower	**campanario** (m)	[kampa'nariɔ]
to ring (ab. bells)	**sonar** (vi)	[sɔ'nar]
cross	**cruz** (f)	[kruθ]
cupola (roof)	**cúpula** (f)	['kupuʎa]
icon	**icono** (m)	[i'kɔnɔ]
soul	**alma** (f)	['aʎma]
fate (destiny)	**destino** (m)	[dɛs'tinɔ]
evil (n)	**maldad** (f)	['maʎdad]
good (n)	**bien** (m)	[bjen]
vampire	**vampiro** (m)	[bam'pirɔ]
witch (sorceress)	**bruja** (f)	['bruha]
demon	**demonio** (m)	[dɛ'mɔnʲɔ]
devil	**diablo** (m)	['djablɔ]
spirit	**espíritu** (m)	[ɛs'piritu]
redemption (giving us ~)	**redención** (f)	[rɛdɛn'sʲɔn]
to redeem (vt)	**redimir** (vt)	[rɛdi'mir]
church service, mass	**culto** (m), **misa** (f)	['kuʎtɔ], ['misa]
to say mass	**decir misa**	[dɛ'sir 'misa]
confession	**confesión** (f)	[kɔnfɛ'sʲɔn]
to confess (vi)	**confesarse** (vr)	[kɔnfɛ'sarsɛ]
saint (n)	**santo** (m)	['santɔ]
sacred (holy)	**sagrado** (adj)	[sag'radɔ]
holy water	**agua** (f) **santa**	['agua 'santa]
ritual (n)	**rito** (m)	['ritɔ]
ritual (adj)	**ritual** (adj)	[ritu'aʎ]
sacrifice	**sacrificio** (m)	[sakri'fisʲɔ]
superstition	**superstición** (f)	[supɛrsti'θʲɔn]
superstitious (adj)	**supersticioso** (adj)	[supɛrsti'sʲɔsɔ]
afterlife	**vida** (f) **de ultratumba**	['bida dɛ uʎtra'tumba]
eternal life	**vida** (f) **eterna**	['bida ɛ'tɛrna]

MISCELLANEOUS

249. Various useful words

background (green ~)	**fondo** (m)	['fɔndɔ]
balance (of situation)	**balance** (m)	[ba'ʎansɛ]
barrier (obstacle)	**barrera** (f)	[bar'rɛra]
base (basis)	**base** (f)	['basɛ]
beginning	**principio** (m)	[prin'sipiɔ]
category	**categoría** (f)	[katɛgɔ'rija]
cause (reason)	**causa** (f)	['kausa]
choice	**elección** (f)	[ɛlek'θiɔn]
coincidence	**coincidencia** (f)	[kɔinsi'dɛnsija]
comfortable (~ chair)	**confortable** (adj)	[kɔnfɔr'table]
comparison	**comparación** (f)	[kɔmpara'siɔn]
compensation	**compensación** (f)	[kɔmpɛnsa'siɔn]
degree (extent, amount)	**grado** (m)	['gradɔ]
development	**desarrollo** (m)	[dɛsa'rɔjɔ]
difference	**diferencia** (f)	[difɛ'rɛnsija]
effect (e.g., of drugs)	**efecto** (m)	[ɛ'fɛktɔ]
effort (exertion)	**esfuerzo** (m)	[ɛsfu'ɛrθɔ]
element	**elemento** (m)	[ɛle'mɛntɔ]
end (finish)	**fin** (m)	[fin]
example (illustration)	**ejemplo** (m)	[ɛ'hɛmplɔ]
fact	**hecho** (m)	['ɛʧɔ]
frequent (adj)	**frecuente** (adj)	[frɛku'ɛntɛ]
growth (development)	**crecimiento** (m)	[krɛsi'mjentɔ]
help	**ayuda** (f)	[a'juda]
ideal	**ideal** (m)	[idɛ'aʎ]
kind (sort, type)	**tipo** (m)	['tipɔ]
labyrinth	**laberinto** (m)	[ʎabɛ'rintɔ]
mistake, error	**error** (m)	[ɛr'rɔr]
moment	**momento** (m)	[mɔ'mɛntɔ]
object (thing)	**objeto** (m)	[ɔb'hɛtɔ]
obstacle	**obstáculo** (m)	[ɔbs'takulɔ]
original (original copy)	**original** (m)	[ɔrihi'naʎ]
part (~ of sth)	**parte** (f)	['partɛ]
particle, small part	**partícula** (f)	[par'tikula]
pause (break)	**pausa** (f)	['pausa]

position	posición (f)	[pɔsi'θiɔn]
principle	principio (m)	[prin'sipiɔ]
problem	problema (m)	[prɔb'lema]

process	proceso (m)	[prɔ'sɛsɔ]
progress	progreso (m)	[prɔg'rɛsɔ]
property (quality)	propiedad (f)	[prɔpje'dad]
reaction	reacción (f)	[rɛak'siɔn]
risk	riesgo (m)	['rjesgɔ]

secret	secreto (m)	[sɛk'rɛtɔ]
section (sector)	sección (f)	[sɛk'θiɔn]
series	serie (f)	['sɛriɛ]
shape (outer form)	forma (f)	['fɔrma]
situation	situación (f)	[situa'θiɔn]

solution	solución (f)	[sɔlu'siɔn]
standard (adj)	estándar (adj)	[ɛs'tandar]
standard (level of quality)	estándar (m)	[ɛs'tandar]
stop (pause)	alto (m)	['aʎtɔ]
style	estilo (m)	[ɛs'tilɔ]
system	sistema (m)	[sis'tɛma]

table (chart)	tabla (f)	['tabʎa]
tempo, rate	tempo (m)	['tɛmpɔ]
term (word, expression)	término (m)	['tɛrminɔ]
thing (object, item)	cosa (f)	['kɔsa]
truth	verdad (f)	[bɛr'dad]
turn (please wait your ~)	turno (m)	['turnɔ]
type (sort, kind)	tipo (m)	['tipɔ]

urgent (adj)	urgente (adj)	[ur'hɛntɛ]
urgently (adv)	urgentemente	[urhɛntɛ'mɛntɛ]
utility (usefulness)	utilidad (f)	[utili'dad]

variant (alternative)	variante (f)	[ba'rjantɛ]
way (means, method)	modo (m)	['mɔdɔ]
zone	zona (f)	['θɔna]

250. Modifiers. Adjectives. Part 1

additional (adj)	adicional (adj)	[adiθiɔ'naʎ]
ancient (~ civilization)	antiguo (adj)	[an'tiguɔ]
artificial (adj)	artificial (adj)	[artifi'θjaʎ]
back, rear (adj)	de atrás (adj)	[dɛ at'ras]
bad (adj)	malo (adj)	['malɔ]

beautiful (~ palace)	hermoso (adj)	[ɛr'mɔsɔ]
beautiful (person)	bello (adj)	['bɛjɔ]
big (in size)	grande (adj)	['grandɛ]

bitter (taste)	amargo (adj)	[a'margɔ]
blind (sightless)	ciego (adj)	['sjegɔ]
calm, quiet (adj)	calmo (adj)	['kaʎmɔ]
careless (negligent)	negligente (adj)	[nɛgli'hɛntɛ]
caring (~ father)	cariñoso (adj)	[kari'ɲiɔsɔ]
central (adj)	central (adj)	[θænt'raʎ]

cheap (adj)	barato (adj)	[ba'ratɔ]
cheerful (adj)	alegre (adj)	[a'legrɛ]
children's (adj)	infantil (adj)	[infan'tiʎ]
civil (~ law)	civil (adj)	[θi'βiʎ]

clandestine (secret)	clandestino (adj)	[kʎandɛs'tinɔ]
clean (free from dirt)	limpio (adj)	['limpiɔ]
clear (explanation, etc.)	claro (adj)	['kʎarɔ]
clever (smart)	inteligente (adj)	[intɛli'hɛntɛ]
close (near in space)	próximo (adj)	['prɔksimɔ]

closed (adj)	cerrado (adj)	[θær'radɔ]
cloudless (sky)	sin nubes (adj)	[sin 'nuβəs]
cold (drink, weather)	frío (adj)	['friɔ]
compatible (adj)	compatible (adj)	[kɔmpa'tible]

contented (adj)	contento (adj)	[kɔn'tɛntɔ]
continuous (adj)	continuo (adj)	[kɔn'tinuɔ]
continuous (incessant)	continuo (adj)	[kɔn'tinuɔ]
convenient (adj)	conveniente (adj)	[kɔnvɛ'njentɛ]
cool (weather)	fresco (adj)	['frɛskɔ]

dangerous (adj)	peligroso (adj)	[pɛlig'rɔsɔ]
dark (room)	oscuro (adj)	[ɔs'kurɔ]
dead (not alive)	muerto (adj)	[mu'ɛrtɔ]
dense (fog, smoke)	denso (adj)	['dɛnsɔ]

difficult (decision)	difícil (adj)	[di'fiθiʎ]
difficult (problem, task)	difícil (adj)	[di'fiθiʎ]
dim, faint (light)	tenue (adj)	['tɛnuɛ]
dirty (not clean)	sucio (adj)	['susiɔ]

distant (faraway)	distante (adj)	[dis'tantɛ]
distant (in space)	lejano (adj)	[le'hanɔ]
dry (clothes, etc.)	seco (adj)	['sɛkɔ]
easy (not difficult)	fácil (adj)	['faθiʎ]

empty (glass, room)	vacío (adj)	[ba'siɔ]
exact (amount)	exacto (adj)	[ɛk'saktɔ]
excellent (adj)	excelente (adj)	[ɛkθe'lentɛ]
excessive (adj)	excesivo (adj)	[ɛssɛ'siβɔ]
expensive (adj)	caro (adj)	['karɔ]

| exterior (adj) | exterior (adj) | [ɛkstɛ'rɔr] |
| fast (quick) | rápido (adj) | ['rapidɔ] |

fatty (food)	**graso** (adj)	['grasɔ]
fertile (land, soil)	**fértil** (adj)	['fɛrtiʎ]
flat (~ panel display)	**plano** (adj)	['pʎanɔ]
even (e.g., ~ surface)	**plano** (adj)	['pʎanɔ]
foreign (adj)	**extranjero** (adj)	[ɛkstran'hɛrɔ]
fragile (china, glass)	**frágil** (adj)	['frahiʎ]
free (at no cost)	**gratis** (adj)	['gratis]
free (unrestricted)	**libre** (adj)	['librɛ]
fresh (~ water)	**dulce** (adj)	['duʎθæ]
fresh (e.g., ~ bread)	**fresco** (adj)	['frɛskɔ]
frozen (food)	**congelado** (adj)	[kɔnhɛ'ʎadɔ]
full (completely filled)	**lleno** (adj)	['jenɔ]
good (book, etc.)	**bueno** (adj)	[bu'ɛnɔ]
good (kindhearted)	**bueno** (adj)	[bu'ɛnɔ]
grateful (adj)	**agradecido** (adj)	[agradɛ'sidɔ]
happy (adj)	**feliz** (adj)	[fɛ'liθ]
hard (not soft)	**duro** (adj)	['durɔ]
heavy (in weight)	**pesado** (adj)	[pɛ'sadɔ]
hostile (adj)	**hostil** (adj)	[ɔs'tiʎ]
hot (adj)	**caliente** (adj)	[ka'ʎjentɛ]
huge (adj)	**enorme** (adj)	[ɛ'nɔrmɛ]
humid (adj)	**húmedo** (adj)	['umɛdɔ]
hungry (adj)	**hambriento** (adj)	[amb'rjentɔ]
ill (sick, unwell)	**enfermo** (adj)	[ɛn'fɛrmɔ]
immobile (adj)	**inmóvil** (adj)	[in'mɔβiʎ]
important (adj)	**importante** (adj)	[impɔr'tantɛ]
impossible (adj)	**imposible** (adj)	[impɔ'sible]
incomprehensible	**indescifrable** (adj)	[indɛθif'rable]
indispensable (adj)	**imprescindible** (adj)	[impreθin'dible]
inexperienced (adj)	**sin experiencia** (adj)	[sin ɛkspe'rjensja]
insignificant (adj)	**insignificante** (adj)	[insignifi'kantɛ]
interior (adj)	**interior** (adj)	[intɛ'rɔr]
joint (~ decision)	**conjunto** (adj)	[kɔn'huntɔ]
last (e.g., ~ week)	**último** (adj)	['uʎtimɔ]
last (final)	**último** (adj)	['uʎtimɔ]
left (e.g., ~ side)	**izquierdo** (adj)	[iθ'kjerdɔ]
legal (legitimate)	**legal** (adj)	[le'gaʎ]
light (in weight)	**ligero** (adj)	[li'hɛrɔ]
light (pale color)	**claro** (adj)	['kʎarɔ]
limited (adj)	**limitado** (adj)	[limi'tadɔ]
liquid (fluid)	**líquido** (adj)	['likidɔ]
long (e.g., ~ way)	**largo** (adj)	['ʎargɔ]
loud (voice, etc.)	**fuerte** (adj)	[fu'ɛrtɛ]
low (voice)	**bajo** (adj)	['bahɔ]

251. Modifiers. Adjectives. Part 2

main (principal)	principal (adj)	[prinsi'paʎ]
matt (paint)	mate (adj)	['matɛ]
meticulous (job)	meticuloso (adj)	[metiku'lɔsɔ]
mysterious (adj)	misterioso (adj)	[mistɛri'ɔsɔ]
narrow (street, etc.)	estrecho (adj)	[ɛst'rɛtʃɔ]

native (of country)	natal (adj)	[na'taʎ]
nearby (adj)	mas próximo	[mas 'prɔksimɔ]
near-sighted (adj)	miope (adj)	[mi'ɔpɛ]
necessary (adj)	necesario (adj)	[nɛθæ'sariɔ]

negative (~ response)	negativo (adj)	[nɛga'tiβɔ]
neighboring (adj)	vecino (adj)	[bɛ'θinɔ]
nervous (adj)	nervioso (adj)	[nɛr'vʲɔsɔ]
new (adj)	nuevo (adj)	[nu'ɛβɔ]
next (e.g., ~ week)	siguiente (adj)	[si'gjentɛ]

nice (kind)	simpático, amable (adj)	[sim'patikɔ], [a'mable]
nice (voice)	agradable (adj)	[agra'dable]
normal (adj)	normal (adj)	[nɔr'maʎ]
not big (adj)	no muy grande (adj)	[nɔ muj 'grandɛ]

unclear (adj)	poco claro (adj)	['pɔkɔ 'kʎarɔ]
not difficult (adj)	no difícil (adj)	[nɔ di'fisiʎ]
obligatory (adj)	obligatorio (adj)	[ɔbliga'tɔriɔ]
old (house)	viejo (adj)	['bjehɔ]
open (adj)	abierto (adj)	[a'bjertɔ]

opposite (adj)	opuesto (adj)	[ɔpu'ɛstɔ]
ordinary (usual)	ordinario (adj)	[ɔrdi'nariɔ]
original (unusual)	original (adj)	[ɔrihi'naʎ]
past (recent)	pasado (adj)	[pa'sadɔ]

permanent (adj)	permanente (adj)	[pɛrma'nɛntɛ]
polite (adj)	cortés (adj)	[kɔr'tɛs]
poor (not rich)	pobre (adj)	['pɔbrɛ]
possible (adj)	posible (adj)	[pɔ'sible]

destitute (extremely poor)	pobrísimo (adj)	[pɔb'risimɔ]
present (current)	presente (adj)	[prɛ'sɛntɛ]
previous (adj)	precedente (adj)	[prɛθæ'dɛntɛ]
principal (main)	principal (adj)	[prinsi'paʎ]

private (~ jet)	privado (adj)	[pri'βadɔ]
probable (adj)	probable (adj)	[prɔ'βable]
public (open to all)	público (adj)	['publikɔ]
punctual (person)	puntual (adj)	[puntu'aʎ]
quiet (tranquil)	tranquilo (adj)	[tra'ŋkilɔ]
rare (adj)	raro (adj)	['rarɔ]

raw (uncooked)	crudo (adj)	['krudɔ]
right (not left)	derecho (adj)	[dɛ'rɛtʃɔ]
right, correct (adj)	correcto (adj)	[kɔr'rɛktɔ]

ripe (fruit)	maduro (adj)	[ma'durɔ]
risky (adj)	arriesgado (adj)	[arrjes'gadɔ]
sad (~ look)	triste (adj)	['tristɛ]
sad (depressing)	triste (adj)	['tristɛ]
safe (not dangerous)	seguro (adj)	[sɛ'gurɔ]

salty (food)	salado (adj)	[sa'ʎadɔ]
satisfied (customer)	satisfecho (adj)	[satis'fɛtʃɔ]
second hand (adj)	de segunda mano	[dɛ sɛ'gunda 'manɔ]
shallow (water)	poco profundo (adj)	['pɔkɔ prɔ'fundɔ]

sharp (blade, etc.)	agudo (adj)	[a'gudɔ]
short (in length)	corto (adj)	['kɔrtɔ]
short, short-lived (adj)	de corta duración (adj)	[dɛ 'kɔrta dura'θʲon]
significant (notable)	considerable (adj)	[kɔnsidɛ'rable]
similar (adj)	similar (adj)	[simi'ʎar]

simple (easy)	simple (adj)	['simple]
skinny	demasiado magro	[dɛmasi'jadɔ 'magrɔ]
thin (person)	delgado (adj)	[dɛʎ'gadɔ]
small (in size)	pequeño (adj)	[pɛ'kɛɲʲɔ]

smooth (surface)	liso (adj)	['lisɔ]
soft (to touch)	blando (adj)	['bʎandɔ]
solid (~ wall)	sólido (adj)	['sɔlidɔ]
somber, gloomy (adj)	sombrío (adj)	[sɔmb'riɔ]
sour (flavor, taste)	agrio (adj)	['agriɔ]

spacious (house, etc.)	amplio (adj)	['ampliɔ]
special (adj)	especial (adj)	[ɛspɛ'θjaʎ]
straight (line, road)	recto (adj)	['rɛktɔ]
strong (person)	fuerte (adj)	[fu'ɛrtɛ]

stupid (foolish)	tonto (adj)	['tɔntɔ]
sunny (day)	soleado (adj)	[sɔle'adɔ]
superb, perfect (adj)	perfecto (adj)	[per'fɛktɔ]
swarthy (adj)	moreno (adj)	[mɔ'rɛnɔ]
sweet (sugary)	azucarado, dulce (adj)	[aθuka'radɔ], ['duʎθæ]

tan (adj)	bronceado (adj)	[brɔnθæ'adɔ]
tasty (adj)	sabroso (adj)	[sab'rɔsɔ]
tender (affectionate)	cariñoso (adj)	[kari'ɲʲɔsɔ]
the highest (adj)	el más alto	[ɛʎ 'mas 'aʎtɔ]

the most important	el más importante	[ɛʎ 'mas impɔr'tantɛ]
the nearest	el más próximo	[ɛʎ 'mas 'prɔksimɔ]
the same, equal (adj)	igual, idéntico (adj)	[igu'aʎ], [i'dɛntikɔ]
thick (e.g., ~ fog)	espeso (adj)	[ɛs'pɛsɔ]

thick (wall, slice)	**grueso** (adj)	[gru'εsɔ]
tight (~ shoes)	**apretado** (adj)	[apre'tadɔ]
tired (exhausted)	**cansado** (adj)	[kan'sadɔ]
tiring (adj)	**fatigoso** (adj)	[fati'gɔsɔ]
transparent (adj)	**transparente** (adj)	[transpa'rεntɛ]
unique (exceptional)	**único** (adj)	['unikɔ]
warm (moderately hot)	**templado** (adj)	[tεmp'ladɔ]
wet (e.g., ~ clothes)	**mojado** (adj)	[mɔ'hadɔ]
whole (entire, complete)	**entero** (adj)	[εn'tɛrɔ]
wide (e.g., ~ road)	**ancho** (adj)	['anʧɔ]
young (adj)	**joven** (adj)	['hɔβən]

MAIN 500 VERBS

252. Verbs A-C

to accompany (vt)	**acompañar** (vt)	[akɔmpa'ɲjar]
to accuse (vt)	**acusar** (vt)	[aku'sar]
to acknowledge (admit)	**reconocer, admitir**	[rɛkɔnɔ'sɛr], [admi'tir]
to act (take action)	**actuar** (vi)	[aktu'ar]
to add (supplement)	**añadir** (vt)	[aɲja'dir]
to address (speak to)	**dirigirse** (vr)	[diri'hirsɛ]
to admire (vi)	**admirar** (vt)	[admi'rar]
to advertise (vt)	**publicitar** (vt)	[publiθi'tar]
to advise (vt)	**aconsejar** (vt)	[akɔnsɛ'har]
to affirm (insist)	**afirmar** (vt)	[afir'mar]
to agree (say yes)	**estar de acuerdo**	[ɛs'tar dɛ aku'ɛrdɔ]
to allow (sb to do sth)	**permitir** (vt)	[pɛrmi'tir]
to allude (vi)	**aludir** (vi)	[aly'dir]
to amputate (vt)	**amputar** (vt)	[ampu'tar]
to answer (vi, vt)	**responder** (vi, vt)	[rɛspɔn'dɛr]
to apologize (vi)	**disculparse** (vr)	[diskuʎ'parsɛ]
to appear (come into view)	**aparecer**	[aparɛ'sɛr]
to applaud (vi, vt)	**aplaudir** (vi, vt)	[apʎau'dir]
to appoint (assign)	**nombrar** (vt)	[nɔmb'rar]
to approach (come closer)	**acercarse** (vr)	[asɛr'karsɛ]
to arrive (ab. train)	**llegar** (vi)	[je'gar]
to ask (~ sb to do sth)	**pedir** (vt)	[pɛ'dir]
to aspire to ...	**aspirar a ...**	[aspi'rar a]
to assist (help)	**asistir** (vt)	[asis'tir]
to attack (mil.)	**atacar** (vt)	[ata'kar]
to attain (objectives)	**lograr** (vt)	[lɔg'rar]
to revenge (vt)	**vengar** (vt)	[bɛ'ɲar]
to avoid (danger, task)	**evitar** (vt)	[ɛwi'tar]
to award (give medal to)	**condecorar** (vt)	[kɔndɛkɔ'rar]
to battle (vi)	**combatir** (vi)	[kɔmba'tir]
to be (~ a teacher)	**ser** (vi)	[sɛr]
to be (~ on a diet)	**estar** (vi)	[ɛs'tar]
to be (~ on the table)	**estar** (vi)	[ɛs'tar]
to be afraid	**tener miedo de ...**	[tɛ'nɛr 'mjedɔ dɛ]

to be angry (with …)	enfadarse con …	[ɛnfa'darsɛ kɔn]
to be at war	estar en guerra	[ɛs'tar ɛn 'gɛrra]
to be based (on …)	estar basado en …	[ɛstar ba'sadɔ ɛn]
to be bored	aburrirse (vr)	[abur'rirsɛ]
to be convinced	convencerse (vr)	[kɔmbɛn'sɛrsɛ]
to be enough	ser suficiente	[sɛr sufi'sjentɛ]
to be envious	envidiar (vt)	[ɛmbi'djar]
to be indignant	indignarse (vr)	[indig'narsɛ]
to be interested in …	interesarse por …	[intɛrɛ'sarsɛ pɔr]
to be lying down	estar acostado	[ɛs'tar akɔs'tadɔ]
to be needed	ser necesario	[sɛr nɛθæ'sarjɔ]
to be perplexed	estar perplejo	[ɛs'tar pɛrp'lehɔ]
to be preserved	estar conservado	[ɛs'tar kɔnsɛr'vadɔ]
to be required	ser indispensable	[sɛr indispɛn'sable]
to be surprised	sorprenderse (vr)	[sɔrprɛn'dɛrsɛ]
to be worried	inquietarse (vr)	[inkje'tarsɛ]
to beat (dog, person)	pegar (vt)	[pɛ'gar]
to become (e.g., ~ old)	hacerse (vr)	[a'sɛrsɛ]
to become pensive	reflexionar (vi)	[rɛfleksjɔ'nar]
to behave (vi)	comportarse (vr)	[kɔmpɔr'tarsɛ]
to believe (think)	creer (vt)	[kre'ɛr]
to belong to …	pertenecer a …	[pɛrtɛnɛ'sɛr a]
to berth (moor)	amarrar (vt)	[amar'rar]
to blind (other drivers)	cegar (vt)	[θæ'gar]
to blow (wind)	soplar (vi)	[sɔp'ʎar]
to blush (vi)	enrojecer (vi)	[ɛnrɔhɛ'sɛr]
to boast (vi)	alabarse (vr)	[aʎa'βarsɛ]
to borrow (money)	prestar (vt)	[prɛs'tar]
to break (branch, toy, etc.)	romper (vt)	[rɔm'pɛr]
to breathe (vi)	respirar (vi)	[rɛspi'rar]
to bring (sth)	traer (vt)	[tra'ɛr]
to burn (paper, logs)	quemar (vt)	[ke'mar]
to buy (purchase)	comprar (vt)	[kɔmp'rar]
to call (for help)	llamar (vt)	[ja'mar]
to calm down (vt)	calmar (vt)	[kaʎ'mar]
can (v aux)	poder (v aux)	[pɔ'dɛr]
to cancel (call off)	anular (vt)	[anu'ʎar]
to cast off	desamarrar (vt)	[dɛsamar'rar]
to catch (e.g., ~ a ball)	coger (vt)	[kɔ'hɛr]
to catch sight (of …)	avistar (vt)	[awis'tar]
to cause …	ser causa de …	[sɛr 'kausa dɛ]
to change (~ one's opinion)	cambiar	[kam'bjar]
to change (exchange)	cambiar (vt)	[kam'bjar]
to charm (vt)	fascinar (vt)	[faθi'nar]

to choose (select)	**escoger** (vt)	[ɛskɔ'hɛr]
to chop off (with an ax)	**hachear** (vt)	[atʃe'ar]
to clean (from dirt)	**limpiar** (vt)	[lim'pjar]
to clean (shoes, etc.)	**limpiar** (vt)	[lim'pjar]
to clean (tidy)	**hacer la limpieza**	[a'θær ʎa lim'pjeθa]
to close (vt)	**cerrar** (vt)	[θær'rar]
to comb one's hair	**peinarse** (vr)	[pɛj'narsɛ]
to come down (the stairs)	**descender** (vi)	[dɛθæn'dɛr]
to come in (enter)	**entrar** (vi)	[ɛnt'rar]
to come out (book)	**salir** (vt)	[sa'lir]
to compare (vt)	**comparar** (vt)	[kɔmpa'rar]
to compensate (vt)	**compensar** (vt)	[kɔmpɛn'sar]
to compete (vi)	**competir** (vi)	[kɔmpɛ'tir]
to compile (~ a list)	**compilar** (vt)	[kɔmpi'ʎar]
to complain (vi, vt)	**quejarse** (vr)	[kɛ'harsɛ]
to complicate (vt)	**complicar** (vt)	[kɔmpli'kar]
to compose (music, etc.)	**componer** (vt)	[kɔmpɔ'nɛr]
to compromise (reputation)	**comprometer** (vt)	[kɔmprɔmɛ'tɛr]
to concentrate (vi)	**concentrarse** (vr)	[kɔnsɛnt'rarsɛ]
to confess (criminal)	**confesar** (vt)	[kɔnfɛ'sar]
to confuse (mix up)	**confundir** (vt)	[kɔnfun'dir]
to congratulate (vt)	**felicitar** (vt)	[fɛliθi'tar]
to consult (doctor, expert)	**consultar a ...**	[kɔnsuʎ'tar a]
to continue (~ to do sth)	**continuar** (vt)	[kɔntinu'ar]
to control (vt)	**controlar** (vt)	[kɔntrɔ'ʎar]
to convince (vt)	**convencer** (vt)	[kɔmbɛn'sɛr]
to cooperate (vi)	**colaborar** (vi)	[kɔʎabɔ'rar]
to coordinate (vt)	**coordinar** (vt)	[kɔːrdi'nar]
to correct (an error)	**corregir** (vt)	[kɔrrɛ'hir]
to cost (vt)	**costar** (vt)	[kɔs'tar]
to count (money, etc.)	**contar** (vt)	[kɔn'tar]
to count on ...	**contar con ...**	[kɔn'tar kɔn]
to crack (ceiling, wall)	**rajarse** (vr)	[ra'harsɛ]
to create (vt)	**crear** (vt)	[kre'ar]
to cry (weep)	**llorar** (vi)	[jo'rar]
to cut off (with a knife)	**cortar** (vt)	[kɔr'tar]

253. Verbs D-G

to dare (~ to do sth)	**osar** (vi)	[ɔ'sar]
to date from ...	**datar de ...**	[da'tar dɛ]
to deceive (vi, vt)	**engañar** (vi, vt)	[ɛŋa'ɲjar]

to decide (~ to do sth)	**decidir** (vt)	[dɛsi'dir]
to decorate (tree, street)	**decorar** (vt)	[dɛkɔ'rar]
to dedicate (book, etc.)	**dedicar** (vt)	[dɛdi'kar]
to defend (a country, etc.)	**defender** (vt)	[dɛfɛn'dɛr]
to defend oneself	**defenderse** (vr)	[dɛfɛn'dɛrsɛ]
to demand (request firmly)	**exigir** (vt)	[ɛksi'hir]
to denounce (vt)	**denunciar** (vt)	[dɛnun'sjar]
to deny (vt)	**negar** (vt)	[nɛ'gar]
to depend on ...	**depender de ...**	[dɛpɛn'dɛr dɛ]
to deprive (vt)	**privar** (vt)	[pri'βar]
to deserve (vt)	**merecer** (vt)	[mɛrɛ'sɛr]
to design (machine, etc.)	**proyectar** (vt)	[prɔjek'tar]
to desire (want, wish)	**desear** (vt)	[dɛsɛ'ar]
to despise (vt)	**despreciar** (vt)	[dɛsprɛ'θjar]
to destroy (documents, etc.)	**destruir** (vt)	[dɛstru'ir]
to differ (from sth)	**diferenciarse** (vr)	[difɛrɛn'sjarsɛ]
to dig (tunnel, etc.)	**cavar** (vt)	[ka'βar]
to direct (point the way)	**encaminar** (vt)	[ɛŋkami'nar]
to disappear (vi)	**desaparecer** (vi)	[dɛsaparɛ'θær]
to discover (new land, etc.)	**descubrir** (vt)	[dɛskub'rir]
to discuss (vt)	**discutir** (vt)	[disku'tir]
to distribute (leaflets, etc.)	**difundir** (vt)	[difun'dir]
to disturb (vt)	**molestar** (vt)	[mɔles'tar]
to dive (vi)	**bucear** (vi)	[buθæ'ar]
to divide (math)	**dividir** (vt)	[diwi'dir]
to do (vt)	**hacer** (vt)	[a'θær]
to do the laundry	**lavar la ropa**	[ʎa'βar ʎa 'rɔpa]
to double (increase)	**doblar** (vt)	[dɔb'ʎar]
to doubt (have doubts)	**dudar** (vt)	[du'dar]
to draw a conclusion	**hacer una conclusión**	[a'sɛr 'una kɔŋkly'sʲon]
to dream (daydream)	**soñar** (vi)	[sɔ'njar]
to dream (in sleep)	**soñar** (vi)	[sɔ'njar]
to drink (vi, vt)	**beber** (vi, vt)	[bɛ'bɛr]
to drive a car	**conducir el coche**	[kɔndu'θir ɛʎ 'kɔtʃe]
to drive away (scare away)	**expulsar** (vt)	[ɛkspuʎ'sar]
to drop (let fall)	**dejar caer**	[dɛ'har ka'ɛr]
to drown (ab. person)	**ahogarse** (vr)	[aɔ'garsɛ]
to dry (clothes, hair)	**secar** (vt)	[sɛ'kar]
to eat (vi, vt)	**comer** (vi, vt)	[kɔ'mɛr]
to eavesdrop (vi)	**escuchar a hurtadillas**	[ɛsku'tʃar a urta'dijas]
to emit (give out - odor, etc.)	**despedir** (vt)	[dɛspɛ'dir]
to enter (on the list)	**inscribir** (vt)	[inskri'βir]

to entertain (amuse)	entretener (vt)	[ɛntrɛtɛ'nɛr]
to equip (fit out)	equipar (vt)	[ɛki'par]
to examine (proposal)	examinar (vt)	[ɛksami'nar]
to exchange (sth)	intercambiar (vt)	[intɛrkam'bʲar]
to exclude, to expel	excluir (vt)	[ɛksklu'ir]
to excuse (forgive)	disculpar (vt)	[diskuʎ'par]
to exist (vi)	existir (vi)	[ɛksis'tir]
to expect (anticipate)	esperar (vt)	[ɛspɛ'rar]
to expect (foresee)	prever (vt)	[prɛ'vɛr]
to explain (vt)	explicar (vt)	[ɛkspli'kar]
to express (vt)	expresar (vt)	[ɛksprɛ'sar]
to extinguish (a fire)	sofocar (vt)	[sɔfɔ'kar]
to fall in love (with …)	enamorarse de …	[ɛnamɔ'rarsɛ dɛ]
to feed (provide food)	alimentar (vt)	[alimɛn'tar]
to fight (against the enemy)	luchar (vi)	[lu'ʧar]
to fight (vi)	pelear (vi)	[pele'ar]
to fill (glass, bottle)	llenar (vt)	[je'nar]
to find (~ lost items)	encontrar (vt)	[ɛŋkɔnt'rar]
to finish (vt)	terminar (vt)	[tɛrmi'nar]
to fish (angle)	pescar (vi)	[pɛs'kar]
to fit (ab. dress, etc.)	quedar (vi)	[ke'dar]
to flatter (vt)	adular (vt)	[adu'ʎar]
to fly (bird, plane)	volar (vi)	[bɔ'ʎar]
to follow … (come after)	seguir …	[sɛ'gir]
to forbid (vt)	prohibir (vt)	[prɔi'βir]
to force (compel)	forzar (vt)	[fɔr'θar]
to forget (vi, vt)	olvidar (vt)	[ɔʎbi'dar]
to forgive (pardon)	perdonar (vt)	[pɛrdɔ'nar]
to form (constitute)	formar (vt)	[fɔr'mar]
to get dirty (vi)	ensuciarse (vr)	[ɛnsu'θjarsɛ]
to get infected (with …)	contagiarse de …	[kɔnta'ʰjarsɛ dɛ]
to get irritated	irritarse (vr)	[irri'tarsɛ]
to get married	casarse (vr)	[ka'sarsɛ]
to get rid of …	librarse de …	[lib'rarsɛ dɛ]
to get tired	estar cansado	[ɛs'tar kan'sadɔ]
to get up (arise from bed)	levantarse (vr)	[levan'tarsɛ]
to give a bath	bañar (vt)	[ba'ɲʲar]
to give a hug, to hug (vt)	abrazar (vt)	[abra'θar]
to give in (yield to)	ceder (vi, vt)	[θæ'dɛr]
to go (by car, etc.)	ir (vi)	[ir]
to go (on foot)	ir (vi)	[ir]
to go for a swim	bañarse (vr)	[ba'ɲjarsɛ]

| to go out (for dinner, etc.) | salir (vi) | [sa'lir] |
| to go to bed | irse a la cama | ['irsɛ a ʎa 'kama] |

to greet (vt)	saludar (vt)	[saly'dar]
to grow (plants)	cultivar (vt)	[kuʎti'βar]
to guarantee (vt)	garantizar (vt)	[garanti'θar]
to guess right	adivinar (vt)	[adiwi'nar]

254. Verbs H-M

to hand out (distribute)	distribuir (vt)	[distribu'ir]
to hang (curtains, etc.)	colgar (vt)	[koʎ'gar]
to have (vt)	tener (vt)	[tɛ'nɛr]
to have a try	intentar (vt)	[intɛn'tar]
to have breakfast	desayunar (vi)	[dɛsaju'nar]

to have dinner	cenar (vi)	[θæ'nar]
to have fun	divertirse (vr)	[divɛr'tirsɛ]
to have lunch	almorzar (vi)	[aʎmɔr'θar]
to head (group, etc.)	encabezar (vt)	[ɛŋkabɛ'θar]

to hear (vt)	oír (vt)	[ɔ'ir]
to heat (vt)	calentar (vt)	[kalen'tar]
to help (vt)	ayudar (vt)	[aju'dar]
to hide (vt)	esconder (vt)	[ɛskɔn'dɛr]
to hire (e.g., ~ a boat)	alquilar (vt)	[aʎki'ʎar]

to hire (staff)	contratar (vt)	[kɔntra'tar]
to hope (vi, vt)	esperar (vi)	[ɛspɛ'rar]
to hunt (for food, sport)	cazar (vi, vt)	[ka'θar]
to hurry (sb)	apresurar (vt)	[aprɛsu'rar]

to hurry (vi)	darse prisa	['darsɛ 'prisa]
to imagine (to picture)	imaginarse (vr)	[imahi'narsɛ]
to imitate (vt)	imitar (vt)	[imi'tar]
to implore (vt)	suplicar (vt)	[supli'kar]
to import (vt)	importar (vt)	[impɔr'tar]

to increase (vi)	aumentarse (vr)	[aumɛn'tarsɛ]
to increase (vt)	aumentar (vt)	[aumɛn'tar]
to infect (vt)	contagiar (vt)	[kɔnta'hjar]
to influence (vt)	influir (vt)	[influ'ir]

to inform (~ sb about ...)	comunicar (vt)	[kɔmuni'kar]
to inform (vt)	informar (vt)	[infɔr'mar]
to inherit (vt)	heredar (vt)	[ɛrɛ'dar]
to inquire (about ...)	informarse (vr)	[infɔr'marsɛ]
to insist (vi, vt)	insistir (vi)	[insis'tir]
to inspire (vt)	inspirar (vt)	[inspi'rar]
to instruct (teach)	instruir (vt)	[instru'ir]

to insult (offend)	insultar (vt)	[insuʎˈtar]
to interest (vt)	interesar (vt)	[intɛrɛˈsar]
to intervene (vi)	intervenir (vi)	[intɛrvɛˈnir]
to introduce (present)	presentar (vt)	[prɛsɛnˈtar]
to invent (machine, etc.)	inventar (vt)	[inbɛnˈtar]
to invite (vt)	invitar (vt)	[inbiˈtar]
to iron (laundry)	planchar (vi, vt)	[pʎanˈʧar]
to irritate (annoy)	irritar (vt)	[irriˈtar]
to isolate (vt)	aislar (vt)	[aisˈʎar]
to join (political party, etc.)	unirse (vr)	[uˈnirsɛ]
to joke (be kidding)	bromear (vi)	[brɔmɛˈar]
to keep (old letters, etc.)	guardar (vt)	[guarˈdar]
to keep silent	callarse (vr)	[kaˈjarsɛ]
to kill (vt)	matar (vt)	[maˈtar]
to knock (at the door)	golpear (vt)	[gɔʎpɛˈar]
to know (sb)	conocer (vt)	[kɔnɔˈθæer]
to know (sth)	saber (vt)	[saˈβɘr]
to laugh (vi)	reírse (vr)	[rɛˈirsɛ]
to launch (start up)	lanzar (vt)	[ʎanˈθar]
to leave (~ for Mexico)	partir (vi)	[parˈtir]
to leave (spouse)	abandonar (vt)	[abandɔˈnar]
to leave behind (forget)	olvidar (vt)	[ɔʎbiˈdar]
to liberate (city, etc.)	liberar (vt)	[libɛˈrar]
to lie (tell untruth)	mentir (vi)	[mɛnˈtir]
to light (campfire, etc.)	encender (vt)	[ɛnθænˈdɛr]
to light up (illuminate)	alumbrar (vt)	[alumbˈrar]
to love (e.g., ~ dancing)	gustar (vi)	[gusˈtar]
to like (I like ...)	gustar (vi)	[gusˈtar]
to limit (vt)	limitar (vt)	[limiˈtar]
to listen (vi)	escuchar (vt)	[ɛskuˈʧar]
to live (~ in France)	habitar (vi, vt)	[abiˈtar]
to live (exist)	vivir (vi)	[wiˈβɪr]
to load (gun)	cargar (vt)	[karˈgar]
to load (vehicle, etc.)	cargar (vt)	[karˈgar]
to look (I'm just ~ing)	mirar (vi, vt)	[miˈrar]
to look for ... (search)	buscar (vt)	[busˈkar]
to look like (resemble)	parecerse (vr)	[parɛˈsɛrse]
to lose (umbrella, etc.)	perder (vt)	[pɛrˈdɛr]
to love (sb)	querer (vt)	[kɛˈrɛr]
to lower (blind, head)	bajar (vt)	[baˈhar]
to make (~ dinner)	preparar (vt)	[prɛpaˈrar]
to make a mistake	equivocarse (vr)	[ɛkivɔˈkarsɛ]
to make angry	enfadar (vt)	[ɛnfaˈdar]

to make copies	hacer copias	[a'sɛr 'kɔpijas]
to make easier	facilitar (vt)	[faθili'tar]
to make the acquaintance	hacer conocimiento	[a'θær kɔnɔθi'mjentɔ]
to make use (of …)	usar (vt)	[u'sar]

to manage, to run	dirigir (vt)	[diri'hir]
to mark (make a mark)	marcar (vt)	[mar'kar]
to mean (signify)	significar (vt)	[signifi'kar]
to memorize (vt)	memorizar (vt)	[memɔri'θar]
to mention (talk about)	mencionar (vt)	[mɛnθiꞌo'nar]

to miss (school, etc.)	faltar a …	[faʎ'tar a]
to mix (combine, blend)	mezclar (vt)	[mɛθk'ʎar]
to mock (make fun of)	burlarse (vr)	[bur'ʎarsɛ]
to move (to shift)	mover (vt)	[mɔ'βər]
to multiply (math)	multiplicar (vt)	[muʎtipli'kar]
must (v aux)	deber (v aux)	[dɛ'bɛr]

255. Verbs N-S

to name, to call (vt)	llamar (vt)	[ja'mar]
to negotiate (vi)	negociar (vi)	[nɛgɔ'θjar]
to note (write down)	anotar (vt)	[anɔ'tar]
to notice (see)	notar (vt)	[nɔ'tar]

to obey (vi, vt)	obedecer (vi, vt)	[ɔbɛdɛ'θær]
to object (vi, vt)	objetar (vt)	[ɔbhɛ'tar]
to observe (see)	observar (vt)	[ɔbsɛr'var]
to offend (vt)	ofender (vt)	[ɔfɛn'dɛr]
to omit (word, phrase)	omitir (vt)	[ɔmi'tir]

to open (vt)	abrir (vt)	[ab'rir]
to order (in restaurant)	pedir (vt)	[pɛ'dir]
to order (mil.)	ordenar (vt)	[ɔrdɛ'nar]
to organize (concert, party)	organizar (vt)	[ɔrgani'θar]

to overestimate (vt)	sobreestimar (vt)	[sɔbrɛːsti'mar]
to own (possess)	poseer (vt)	[pɔsɛ'ɛr]
to participate (vi)	participar (vi)	[partisi'par]
to pass (go beyond)	pasar (vt)	[pa'sar]
to pay (vi, vt)	pagar (vi, vt)	[pa'gar]

to peep, spy on	mirar a hurtadillas	[mi'rar a urta'dijas]
to penetrate (vt)	penetrar (vt)	[pɛnɛt'rar]
to permit (vt)	permitir (vt)	[pɛrmi'tir]
to pick (flowers)	coger (vt)	[kɔ'hɛr]

to place (put, set)	poner, colocar (vt)	[pɔ'nɛr], [kɔlɔ'kar]
to plan (~ to do sth)	planear (vt)	[pʎanɛ'ar]
to play (actor)	interpretar (vt)	[intɛrprɛ'tar]

to play (children)	**jugar** (vi)	[hu'gar]
to point (~ the way)	**mostrar** (vt)	[mɔst'rar]
to pour (liquid)	**verter** (vt)	[ber'tɛr]
to pray (vi, vt)	**orar** (vi)	[ɔ'rar]
to predominate (vi)	**predominar** (vi)	[prɛdɔmi'nar]
to prefer (vt)	**preferir** (vt)	[prɛfɛ'rir]
to prepare (~ a plan)	**preparar** (vt)	[prɛpa'rar]
to present (sb to sb)	**presentar** (vt)	[prɛsɛn'tar]
to preserve (peace, life)	**mantener** (vt)	[mantɛ'nɛr]
to progress (move forward)	**avanzarse** (vr)	[avan'θarsɛ]
to promise (vt)	**prometer** (vt)	[prɔmɛ'tɛr]
to pronounce (vt)	**pronunciar** (vt)	[prɔnun'θjar]
to propose (vt)	**proponer** (vt)	[prɔpɔ'nɛr]
to protect (e.g., ~ nature)	**proteger** (vt)	[prɔtɛ'hɛr]
to protest (vi)	**protestar** (vi, vt)	[prɔtɛs'tar]
to prove (vt)	**probar** (vt)	[prɔ'βar]
to provoke (vt)	**provocar** (vt)	[prɔvɔ'kar]
to pull (~ the rope)	**tirar** (vt)	[ti'rar]
to punish (vt)	**castigar** (vt)	[kasti'gar]
to push (~ the door)	**empujar** (vt)	[ɛmpu'har]
to put away (vt)	**quitar** (vt)	[ki'tar]
to put in (insert)	**insertar** (vt)	[inser'tar]
to put in order	**poner en orden**	[pɔ'nɛr ɛn 'ɔrdɛn]
to put, to place	**poner** (vt)	[pɔ'nɛr]
to quote (cite)	**citar** (vt)	[θi'tar]
to reach (arrive at)	**llegar a ...**	[je'gar a]
to read (vi, vt)	**leer** (vi, vt)	[le'ɛr]
to realize (a dream)	**realizar** (vt)	[rɛali'θar]
to recall (~ one's name)	**recordarse** (vr)	[rɛkɔr'darsɛ]
to recognize (identify sb)	**reconocer** (vt)	[rɛkɔnɔ'sɛr]
to recommend (vt)	**recomendar** (vt)	[rɛkɔmɛn'dar]
to recover (~ from flu)	**recuperarse** (vr)	[rɛkupe'rarsɛ]
to redo (do again)	**rehacer** (vt)	[rɛa'θær]
to reduce (speed, etc.)	**disminuir** (vt)	[disminu'ir]
to refuse (~ sb)	**negar** (vt)	[nɛ'gar]
to regret (be sorry)	**arrepentirse** (vr)	[arrɛpɛn'tirsɛ]
to reinforce (vt)	**fortalecer** (vt)	[fɔrtale'θær]
to remember (vt)	**recordar** (vt)	[rɛkɔr'dar]
to remind of ...	**recordar** (vt)	[rɛkɔr'dar]
to remove (~ a stain)	**quitar** (vt)	[ki'tar]
to remove (~ an obstacle)	**eliminar** (vt)	[ɛlimi'nar]
to rent (sth from sb)	**alquilar** (vt)	[aʎki'ʎar]

to repair (mend)	**reparar** (vt)	[rɛpaˈrar]
to repeat (say again)	**repetir** (vt)	[rɛpɛˈtir]
to report (make a report)	**presentar un informe**	[prɛθenˈtar un inˈformɛ]
to reproach (vt)	**reprochar** (vt)	[rɛprɔˈtʃar]
to reserve, to book	**reservar** (vt)	[rɛsɛrˈvar]
to restrain (hold back)	**retener** (vt)	[rɛtɛˈnɛr]
to return (come back)	**regresar** (vi)	[rɛgrɛˈsar]
to risk, to take a risk	**arriesgar** (vt)	[arrjesˈgar]
to rub off (erase)	**borrar** (vt)	[bɔrˈrar]
to run (move fast)	**correr** (vi)	[kɔrˈrɛr]
to satisfy (please)	**satisfacer** (vt)	[satisfaˈsɛr]
to save (rescue)	**salvar** (vt)	[saʎˈvar]
to say (~ thank you)	**decir** (vt)	[dɛˈθir]
to scold (vt)	**regañar** (vt)	[rɛgaˈɲjar]
to scratch (with claws)	**arañar** (vt)	[araˈɲjar]
to select (to pick)	**seleccionar** (vt)	[selɛkθʲɔˈnar]
to sell (goods)	**vender** (vt)	[benˈdɛr]
to send (a letter)	**enviar** (vt)	[ɛmbiˈjar]
to send back (vt)	**devolver** (vt)	[dɛvɔʎˈvɛr]
to sense (danger)	**sentir** (vt)	[sɛnˈtir]
to sentence (vt)	**sentenciar** (vt)	[sɛntɛnˈsjar]
to serve (in restaurant)	**servir** (vt)	[sɛrˈwir]
to settle (a conflict)	**resolver** (vt)	[rɛsɔʎˈvɛr]
to shake (vt)	**sacudir** (vt)	[sakuˈdir]
to shave (vi)	**afeitarse** (vr)	[afɛjˈtarsɛ]
to shine (gleam)	**brillar** (vi)	[briˈjar]
to shiver (with cold)	**temblar** (vi)	[tɛmbˈʎar]
to shoot (vi)	**tirar** (vi)	[tiˈrar]
to shout (vi)	**gritar** (vi)	[griˈtar]
to show (to display)	**mostrar** (vt)	[mɔstˈrar]
to shudder (vi)	**estremecerse** (vr)	[ɛstrɛmeˈsɛrsɛ]
to sigh (vi)	**suspirar** (vi)	[suspiˈrar]
to sign (document)	**firmar** (vt)	[firˈmar]
to signify (mean)	**significar** (vt)	[signifiˈkar]
to simplify (vt)	**simplificar** (vt)	[simplifiˈkar]
to sin (vi)	**pecar** (vi)	[pɛˈkar]
to sit (be sitting)	**estar sentado**	[ɛsˈtar sɛnˈtadɔ]
to sit down (vi)	**sentarse** (vr)	[sɛnˈtarsɛ]
to smash (~ a bug)	**aplastar** (vt)	[apʎasˈtar]
to smell (scent)	**oler** (vi)	[ɔˈler]
to smell (sniff at)	**oler** (vt)	[ɔˈler]
to smile (vi)	**sonreír** (vi)	[sɔnrɛˈir]
to snap (vi, ab. rope)	**romperse** (vr)	[rɔmˈpɛrsɛ]

to solve (problem)	resolver (vt)	[rɛsɔʎ'vɛr]
to sow (seed, crop)	sembrar (vi, vt)	[sɛmb'rar]
to spill (liquid)	derramar (vt)	[dɛrra'mar]
to spill out (flour, etc.)	desparramarse (vr)	[dɛsparra'marsɛ]
to spit (vi)	escupir (vi)	[ɛsku'pir]
to stand (toothache, cold)	soportar (vt)	[sopor'tar]
to start (begin)	comenzar (vt)	[komɛn'θar]
to steal (money, etc.)	robar (vt)	[rɔ'βar]
to stop (please ~ calling me)	cesar (vt)	[θæ'sar]
to stop (for pause, etc.)	pararse (vr)	[pa'rarsɛ]
to stop talking	dejar de hablar	[dɛ'har dɛ ab'lar]
to stroke (caress)	acariciar (vt)	[akari'sjar]
to study (vt)	estudiar (vt)	[ɛstu'djar]
to suffer (feel pain)	sufrir (vi)	[suf'rir]
to support (cause, idea)	apoyar (vt)	[apɔ'jar]
to suppose (assume)	suponer (vt)	[supɔ'nɛr]
to surface (ab. submarine)	emerger (vi)	[ɛmɛr'hɛr]
to surprise (amaze)	sorprender (vt)	[sorprɛn'dɛr]
to suspect (vt)	sospechar (vt)	[sɔspɛ'ʧar]
to swim (vi)	nadar (vi)	[na'dar]
to turn on (computer, etc.)	encender (vt)	[ɛnθæn'dɛr]

256. Verbs T-W

to take (get hold of)	tomar (vt)	[tɔ'mar]
to take a bath	darse un baño	['darsɛ un 'baɲɔ]
to take a rest	descansar (vi)	[dɛskan'sar]
to take aim (at ...)	apuntar a ...	[apun'tar a]
to take away	llevar (vt)	[je'βar]
to take off (airplane)	despegar (vi)	[dɛspɛ'gar]
to take off (remove)	quitar (vt)	[ki'tar]
to take pictures	fotografiar (vt)	[fotɔgra'fjar]
to talk to ...	hablar con ...	[ab'ʎar kɔn]
to teach (give lessons)	enseñar (vi, vt)	[ɛnsɛ'ɲjar]
to tear off (vt)	arrancar (vt)	[arra'ŋkar]
to tell (story, joke)	contar (vt)	[kɔn'tar]
to thank (vt)	agradecer (vt)	[agradɛ'sɛr]
to think (believe)	pensar (vi, vt)	[pɛn'sar]
to think (vi, vt)	pensar (vi, vt)	[pɛn'sar]
to threaten (vt)	amenazar (vt)	[amɛna'θar]
to throw (stone)	tirar (vt)	[ti'rar]

to tie to ...	**atar a ...**	[a'tar a]
to tie up (prisoner)	**atar** (vt)	[a'tar]
to tire (make tired)	**cansar** (vt)	[kan'sar]
to touch (one's arm, etc.)	**tocar** (vt)	[to'kar]
to tower (over ...)	**elevarse** (vr)	[ɛle'βarsɛ]
to train (animals)	**adiestrar** (vt)	[adjest'rar]
to train (sb)	**entrenar** (vt)	[ɛntrɛ'nar]
to train (vi)	**entrenarse** (vr)	[ɛntrɛ'narsɛ]
to transform (vt)	**transformar** (vt)	[transfɔr'mar]
to translate (vt)	**traducir** (vt)	[tradu'θir]
to treat (patient, illness)	**curar** (vt)	[ku'rar]
to trust (vt)	**confiar** (vt)	[kɔn'fjar]
to try (attempt)	**tratar de ...**	[tra'tar dɛ]
to turn (~ to the left)	**girar** (vi)	[hi'rar]
to turn away (vi)	**volverse de espaldas**	[bɔʎ'vɛrsɛ dɛ ɛs'paʎdas]
to turn off (the light)	**apagar** (vt)	[apa'gar]
to turn over (stone, etc.)	**volver** (vt)	[bɔʎ'vɛr]
to underestimate (vt)	**subestimar** (vt)	[subɛsti'mar]
to underline (vt)	**subrayar** (vt)	[subra'jar]
to understand (vt)	**comprender** (vt)	[kɔmprɛn'dɛr]
to undertake (vt)	**emprender** (vt)	[ɛmprɛn'dɛr]
to unite (vt)	**unir** (vt)	[u'nir]
to untie (vt)	**desatar** (vt)	[dɛsa'tar]
to use (phrase, word)	**emplear** (vt)	[ɛmple'ar]
to vaccinate (vt)	**vacunar** (vt)	[baku'nar]
to vote (vi)	**votar** (vi)	[vɔ'tar]
to wait (vt)	**esperar** (vt)	[ɛspɛ'rar]
to wake (sb)	**despertar** (vt)	[dɛspɛr'tar]
to want (wish, desire)	**querer** (vt)	[ke'rɛr]
to warn (of the danger)	**advertir** (vt)	[advɛr'tir]
to wash (clean)	**lavar** (vt)	[ʎa'βar]
to water (plants)	**regar** (vt)	[rɛ'gar]
to wave (the hand)	**agitar la mano**	[ahi'tar ʎa 'manɔ]
to weigh (have weight)	**pesar** (vt)	[pɛ'sar]
to work (vi)	**trabajar** (vi)	[traba'har]
to worry (make anxious)	**inquietar** (vt)	[inkje'tar]
to worry (vi)	**preocuparse** (vr)	[prɛɔku'parθæ]
to wrap (parcel, etc.)	**empaquetar** (vt)	[ɛmpakɛ'tar]
to wrestle (sport)	**luchar** (vi)	[lu'ʧar]
to write (vt)	**escribir** (vt)	[ɛskri'βɪr]
to write down	**tomar nota**	[tɔ'mar 'nɔta]

38999905R00150

Made in the USA
San Bernardino, CA
16 September 2016